Connectionism and Psychology:
A Psychological Perspective on New Connectionist Research

PHILIP T. QUINLAN

Department of Psychology, University of York

 HARVESTER
WHEATSHEAF

New York   London   Toronto   Sydney   Tokyo   Singapore

First published 1991 by
Harvester Wheatsheaf,
66 Wood Lane End, Hemel Hempstead,
Hertfordshire, HP2 4RG
A division of
Simon & Schuster International Group

Typeset in 10/12 pt Times Roman
by Witwell Ltd, Southport.

Printed and bound in Great Britain by
Cambridge University Press.

British Library Cataloguing in Publication Data

Quinlan, Philip T.
  Connectionism and psychology: A psychological
  perspective on new connectionist research.
  I. Title
  153
  ISBN 0-7450-0834-8
  ISBN 0-7450-0835-6 pbk

---

1 2 3 4 5   95 94 93 92 91

Contents

Preface

In 1987 I wrote a paper (Quinlan, 1987) in order to critically review the collected articles on parallel models of human associative memory edited by Hinton and Anderson (Hinton & Anderson, 1981). It was my attempt to unravel the points of psychological significance in this work and to present them in an easily digestible form. My feeling at the time was that that book contained the seeds of a radically different way of thinking about cognitive and perceptual processes: a way quite unlike anything I had been taught about. The problem was that the book was difficult to read, and to understand, and, therefore, quite possibly off-putting to someone like myself who has had little formal training in mathematics and had little interest in neurophysiology.

For me, at least, cognition was the study of mental processes in which the only conceivable way of portraying internal states and processes was in terms of an arrows and boxes diagram. I had been schooled into thinking about human cognition solely within the traditional (henceforth, classical) information processing framework. Clearly demarcated component processes were easily understood in terms set out by simple flow diagrams. Moreover, the framework was pleasingly consistent: taken together with additive factors logic, it gave licence to a complete methodology for studying human perceptual and cognitive processes. Indeed, given its popularity, it became acceptable to argue that cognition and perception could be studied with little regard for the brain. Indeed, brain-talk was deemed quite irrelevant to the task at hand. In retrospect, the naiveté of the approach is all somewhat depressing.

Perhaps it was the simplicity of the classical framework that seduced cognitive psychologists into thinking that there could be no serious alternative. Such a trenchant view remains in some quarters, for there is still great resistance to even contemplating that cognition can be understood outside of the traditional framework. Whatever the reasons, flow-diagram psychology was still thriving at the beginning of the 1980s just prior to the revolutionary revival of connectionism. True there had been some dissenters: Neisser, having been partially responsible for the growth in popularity of classical cognitive psychology, published his forceful critique of the discipline (Neisser, 1976) and McClelland published a careful and seemingly damning account of why additive factors might not be appropriate in all cases (McClelland, 1979). Nevertheless, complete areas of human information processing, like cognitive neuropsychology, were being accounted for in terms of component processes and clearly defined processing subsystems.

Even though psychology has always been riven with rival factions, there is now a major debate raging over the fundamental nature of cognition. Historically the central debate has been over whether the study of internal, intervening events is necessary to understanding human behaviour. Radical behaviourists thought not. In contrast, cognitivists had arrived at some consensus over the sorts of accounts of mental life that were acceptable. Such a consensus, however, has been threatened by the advent of new connectionism. Now because of the rapid development of new connectionism, radically opposing ideas about how best to construe mental processes exist. Academic psychologists have either acquiesced and are busily engaged in connectionist research, they remain loyal to their traditional roots, or they are simply uninterested in the enterprise. Nevertheless, whatever else is the case, it is simply no longer feasible to try to maintain that there is only one way of thinking about human intellectual functioning. At the very least, new connectionism promises a serious and radical alternative to the classical framework. Part of the rationale of this book is to try to shed some light on what the nature of this alternative really is.

As with my previous paper on connectionism, similar reasons exist for why I am writing this text. New connectionism has spawned a vast and ever-growing literature. For certain, much will have occurred between the date of writing this preface and the final date of publication. The field is growing so rapidly that in order to keep up one has to ask for preprints rather than reprints of journal articles. Other problems have also emerged. In developing at such a rate, the field has tended to fractionate in order to accommodate the many disciplines that neural network research now impinges on. This is also witnessed by the variety of new journals now being published. A rather unfortunate aspect is that whereas many of the new journals deal with the mathematical and engineering aspects, few are concerned with issues psychological in nature. Some workers are unashamedly uncaring of the psychological consequences of their results, and they are happy not to bother with trying to open up to a wider audience. As a consequence, whilst psychology is in danger of being ignored, much of what is going on in new connectionism is relevant to psychology.

Now, as before, this is my attempt to throw light on some of the frantic activity. To be fair, it is difficult for me to decide as to how much of a mathematician/ computer scientist/neurophysiologist one has to be in order to enter the realms of new connectionism. From my own example the answer is perhaps not much. It is undeniably true, though, that in order to make a substantial contribution to the field, being something of some of the above helps. It is also undeniably true that psychologists cannot easily continue their endeavours without some grasp of the basic issues underlying new connectionism (even if this is only to forestall any possible feelings of being left out). In particular, it would be most unfortunate to try to be taken seriously as a cognitive neuropsychologist without having some understanding of the lesioning work that has been undertaken with artificial neural networks. One of the most striking things about such networks is their impressive face validity regarding neural plausibility.

Originally when I was approached to write this book circumstances dictated that it was not feasible for me to take on such a commitment and I had to decline. However, early on in 1988 I was invited by José Morais of the Laboratoire de Psychologie expérimentale, Université Libre de Bruxelle, to give a series of lectures on connectionism under the auspices of the National Incentive Program for Fundamental Research in Artificial Intelligence. Having received and accepted this invitation I was then approached, coincidentally, by Robert Bolick to again contemplate writing an introductory text on connectionism. This time circumstances appeared ideal so I readily agreed: the research for the lectures formed the research for the book. Indeed, it would be remiss of me not to thank the following for providing funding and other forms of support during the gestation period of this book.

Firstly, I thank the National Incentive Program for Fundamental Research in Artificial Intelligence in Belgium for financing my Brussels lectures. I have also been in receipt of funding from the SERC and MRC of Great Britain whilst engaged on the work for the book. It concerns me greatly to see these important institutions being starved of funds and it would be negligent of me not to acknowledge how vital a role they play in supporting academic life in the UK. I also received a small Travel Award from the Society of the Study of Artificial Intelligence and Simulation of Behaviour.

Whilst in Belgium I had many fruitful exchanges with members of the Laboratoire de Psychologie expérimentale including Alain Content, Paul Bertelson, Daniel Holender and Ronald Peereman. I am particularly indebted to Ronald for his friendship and company during my visit to Belgium. Marco Sareans of the Institut de Phonétique, Université Libre de Bruxelle, helped a great deal in introducing me to many of the references on the little-known aspects of back-propagation.

Many people have been very kind in forwarding copies of documents that still remain unpublished or would have proved difficult, if not impossible, for me to obtain. Others simply alerted me to work I was unaware of. In particular I thank Martyn Barrett, Marlene Behrmann, Derek Besner, Gordon Brown, Nick Chater, Alain Content, Shimon Edelman, Brok Glenn, Geoff Hinton, Glyn Humphreys, Andrew Jeavons, Ralph Linsker, Jay McClelland, Ennio Mingolla, Mike Mozer, David Plaut, Marco Sareans, John Shawe-Taylor, Alex Waibel, Stephen Walker, Rob Ward and Robert West.

Several people have helped in reading and commenting on various drafts. These include Nick Chater, Charles Hulme, Mike O'Leary, Sean Mullarkey, Liz Valentine, Nick Wade, Steve Walker, John Wilding and, in particular, Richard Wilton. It would also be remiss of me not to thank the many people who have set me straight on a number of issues. These include John Shawe-Taylor, David Plaut, Max Coltheart, John Taylor and, again, Richard Wilton. I have also benefited from presenting talks to the Cognitive Neuropsychology group at Birkbeck College and to the Intelligent Systems group at Brunel University.

Most of the writing and research for the book was completed whilst I was employed at the University of London: first at Birkbeck College, and, then at Royal Holloway and Bedford New College.

In closing I sketch what follows in the rest of the book. (I write now having completed the text.) My suspicion is that there will be a tendency to pick up the book, glance at Chapter 1 then skip to the final chapter and read that. This, I feel, will only foster a rather jaundiced view of connectionism. Chapter 1 includes a highly personal view of the early history of connectionism. Chapter 6 sets out what I consider to be the substantive limitations of the approach.

Together Chapters 1 and 2 provide an in-depth introduction to the fundamental ideas that underpin neural network research. Unless you are already familiar with the field, the material in the later chapters will be quite opaque, in places, if you do not read the first two chapters. I should also stress that I have included formulae where necessary. After each formula I have provided a complete description of the constituent symbols and terms. It is simply impossible to attain a proper understanding of what a neural net is doing in the absence of understanding some of the basic mathematics. Advanced knowledge of mathematics is not, however, a prerequisite for understanding the main points in the book. Indeed, I suspect that it is quite possible to skip most of the formulae and still arrive at a general feel for how a particular network operates.

The middle chapters of the book, Chapters 3, 4, and 5, deal, respectively, with connectionist models of vision, language processing and certain higher-order aspects of cognition. The aim in writing these chapters has been to describe several of the best neural net applications that speak to psychology. Much of this material is expository in nature although some critical comment is included where appropriate. It might appear, from considering the criticisms, that the sole objective has been to demolish the whole approach. This is a mistaken view. The guiding principle has been to see how well each model stands up to scrutiny when treated as being just another embodiment of a psychological theory.

Acknowledgements

The author would like to thank the following for permission to reproduce the figures cited below:

Figure 1.4. (From 'Perceptrons: An Introduction to Computational Geometry' by M. Minsky and S. Papert, 1988, p. 28. Copyright © 1969 by The MIT Press. Adapted with permission).

Figure 1.5. (From 'Explorations in Parallel Distributed Processing: A Handbook of Models, Programs, and Exercises' by J. L. McClelland and D. E. Rumelhart, 1988, p. 124. Copyright © by The MIT Press. Adapted with permission.)

Figure 1.6. (From 'What Connectionist Models Learn: Learning and Representation in Connectionist Networks' by S. J. Hanson and D. J. Burr, 1990, *Behavioral and Brain Sciences, 13*, p. 478. Copyright © 1990 by Cambridge University Press. Adapted with permission.)

Figure 1.7. (From 'Perceptrons: An Introduction to Computational Geometry' by M. Minsky and S. Papert, 1988, p. 10. Copyright © 1969 by The MIT Press. Adapted with permission.)

Figure 1.8. (From 'Perceptrons: An Introduction to Computational Geometry' by M. Minsky and S. Papert, 1988, p. 5. Copyright © 1969 by The MIT Press. Adapted with permission.)

Figure 1.9. (From 'Perceptrons: An Introduction to Computational Geometry' by M. Minsky and S. Papert, 1988, p. 13. Copyright © 1969 by The MIT Press. Adapted with permission.)

Figure 1.10. (From 'Perceptrons: An Introduction to Computational Geometry' by M. Minsky and S. Papert, 1988, p. 141. Copyright © 1969 by The MIT Press. Reprinted with permission.)

Figure 1.12. (From 'Perceptrons: An Introduction to Computational Geometry' by M. Minsky and S. Papert, 1988, p. 23. Copyright © 1969 by The MIT Press. Reprinted with permission.)

Figure 2.1. (From 'A Model of Visual Shape Recognition' by P. M. Milner, 1974, *Psychological Review, 81*, p. 527. Copyright © 1974 by the American Psychological Association. Adapted with permission.)

Figure 2.5. (From 'Explorations in Parallel Distributed Processing: A Handbook of Models, Programs, and Exercises' by J. L. McClelland and D. E. Rumelhart, 1988, p. 90. Copyright © by The MIT Press. Adapted with permission.)

Figure 2.8. (From 'An Introduction to Neural Computing' by I. Aleksander and H. Morton, 1990, p. 135. Copyright © 1990 by Chapman and Hall. Adapted with permission.)

Figure 2.11. (From 'A Distributed Connectionist Production System' by D. S. Touretzky & G. E. Hinton, 1988, *Cognitive Science, 12*, p. 445. Copyright © 1988 by the Ablex Publishing Corporation. Adapted with permission.)

Figure 3.1. (From 'Vision' by D. Marr, 1982, p. 113. Copyright © 1982 by W. H. Freeman and Company. Adapted with permission.)

Figure 3.2. (From 'Vision' by D. Marr, 1982, p. 123. Copyright © 1982 by W. H. Freeman and Company. Adapted with permission.)

Figure 3.4. (From 'Competitive Learning: From Interactive Activation to Adaptive Resonance' by S. Grossberg, 1987, *Cognitive Science, 11*, p. 49. Copyright © 1987 by the Ablex Publishing Corporation. Adapted with permission.)

Figure 3.5. (From 'Separating Figure from Ground' by P. K. Kienker, T. J. Sejnowski, G. E. Hinton and L. E. Schumacher, 1986, *Perception, 15*, p. 201. Copyright © 1986 by Pion Limited. Adapted with permission.)

Figure 3.6. (From 'Separating Figure from Ground' by P. K. Kienker, T. J. Sejnowski, G. E. Hinton and L. E. Schumacher, 1986, *Perception, 15*, p. 203. Copyright © by Pion Limited. Adapted with permission.)

Figure 3.7. (Figure 2a is from 'Subjective Contours' by G. Kanizsa, 1976, *Scientific American, 234*, p. 51. Copyright © 1976 by Scientific American, Inc. Adapted with permission. Figure 2b is from 'Neural Dynamics of Form Perception: Boundary Completion, Illusory Figures, and Neon Color Spreading' by S. Grossberg and E. Mingolla, 1985, *Psychological Review, 92*, p. 177. Copyright © 1985 by the American Psychological Association. Adapted with permission.)

Figure 3.8. (From 'Neural Dynamics of Form Perception: Boundary Completion, Illusory Figures, and Neon Color Spreading' by S. Grossberg and E. Mingolla, 1985, *Psychological Review, 92*, p. 191. Copyright © 1985 by the American Psychological Association. Adapted with permission.)

Figure 3.9. (From 'Neural Dynamics of Form Perception: Boundary Completion, Illusory Figures, and Neon Color Spreading' by S. Grossberg and E. Mingolla, 1985, *Psychological Review, 92*, p. 187. Copyright © 1985 by the American Psychological Association. Adapted with permission.)

Figure 3.10. (From 'A Parallel Computation that Assigns Canonical Object-Based Frames of Reference' by G. E. Hinton, 1981. In *Proceedings of the Seventh International Joint Conference on Artificial Intelligence*, Los Altos, CA: International Joint Conferences on Artificial Intelligence, p. 684. Copyright © 1981 by Morgan Kaufman. Adapted with permission. Copies of this and other International Joint Conferences on Artificial Intelligence Proceedings are available from Morgan Kaufman Publishers, 2929 Campus Drive, Dan Mateo, California 94403.)

Figure 3.15. (From 'A Network that Learns to Recognise Three-Dimensional Objects' by T. Poggio and S. Edelman, 1990, *Nature, 343*, p. 263. Copyright © 1990 by Macmillan Magazines Ltd. Adapted with permission.)

Figure 4.1. (From 'Building Blocks for Speech' by A. Waibel and J. Hampshire, 1989, *BYTE, August*, p. 236. Copyright © 1989 McGraw-Hill Inc. Adapted with permission.)

Figure 4.2. (From 'Building Blocks for Speech' by A. Waibel and J. Hampshire, 1989, *BYTE, August*, p. 236. Copyright © 1989 McGraw-Hill Inc. Adapted with permission.)

Figure 4.3. (From 'Building Blocks for Speech' by A. Waibel and J. Hampshire, 1989, *BYTE, August*, p. 236. Copyright © 1989 McGraw-Hill Inc. Adapted with permision.)

Figure 4.4. (From 'The TRACE model of Speech Perception' by J. L. McClelland and J. L. Elman, 1986, *Cognitive Psychology, 1986, 18*, pp. 1–86. Copyright © 1986 by Academic Press, Inc. Adapted with permission.)

Figure 4.5. (From 'The TRACE model of Speech Perception' by J. L. McClelland and J. L. Elman, 1986, *Cognitive Psychology, 1986, 18*, pp. 1–86. Copyright © 1986 by Academic Press, Inc. Adapted with permission.)

Figure 4.6. (From 'Mapping Part-Whole Hierarchies into Connectionist Networks' by G. E. Hinton, 1990, *Artificial Intelligence, 46*, p. 64. Copyright © 1990 by Elsevier Science Publishers B. V. (North Holland). Adapted with permission.)

Figure 4.7. (From 'An Interactive Activation Model of Context Effects in Letter Perception: Part 1. An Account of Basic Findings' by J. L. McClelland and D. E. Rumelhart, 1981, *Psychological Review, 88*, p. 330. Copyright © 1918 by the American Psychological Association. Reprinted with permission.)

Figure. 4.8. (From 'Putting Knowledge in its Place: A Scheme for Programming Parallel Processing Structures on the Fly' J. L. McClelland, 1985, *Cognitive Science, 9*, p. 122 and p. 124. Copyright © 1985 by the Ablex Publishing Corporation. Adapted with permission.)

Figure 4.9. (From 'Cognitive Neuropsychology and Language: The State of the Art' by M. S. Seidenberg, 1988, *Cognitive Neuropsychology, 5*, p. 404. Copyright © 1988 by Lawrence Erlbaum Associates. Adapted with permission.)

Figure 4.10. (From 'A Distributed, Developmental Model of Word Recognition and Naming' by M. S. Seidenberg and J. L. McClelland, 1989, *Psychological Review, 96*, p. 524. Copyright © 1989 by the American Psychological Association. Adapted with permission.)

Figure 4.11. (From 'A Distributed, Developmental Model of Word Recognition and Naming' by M. S. Seidenberg and J. L. McClelland, 1989, *Psychological Review, 96*, p.

535. Copyright © 1989 by the American Psychological Association. Adapted with permission.)

Figure 5.1. (From 'Distributed Representations' by G. E. Hinton, J. L. McClelland and D. E. Rumelhart, 1986, in D. E. Rumelhart, J. L. McClelland and the PDP Research Group, *Parallel Distributed Processing: Explorations in the Microstructure of Cognition. Volume 1: Foundations*, p. 98. Copyright © 1986 by the MIT Press. Adapted with permission.)

Figure 5.3. (From 'Lesioning an Attractor Network: Investigations of Acquired Dyslexia' by G. E. Hinton and T. Shallice, 1991, *Psychological Review, 98*, p. 80. Copyright © 1991 by the American Psychological Association. Adapted with permission.)

Figure 5.5. (From 'Distributed Representations' by G. E. Hinton, J. L. McClelland and D. E. Rumelhart, 1986, in D. E. Rumelhart, J. L. McClelland and the PDP Research Group, *Parallel Distributed Processing: Explorations in the Microstructure of Cognition. Volume 1: Foundations*, p. 83. Copyright © 1986 by The MIT Press. Adapted with permission.)

Figure 5.6. (From 'Implementing Semantic Networks in Parallel Hardware by G. E. Hinton, 1981, in G. E. Hinton and J. A. Anderson (Eds.), Parallel Models of Associative Memory, p. 171. Copyright © 1981 by Lawrence Erlbaum Associates. Adapted with permission.)

Figure 5.7. (From 'Distributed Representations' by G. E. Hinton, J. L. McClelland and D. E. Rumelhart, 1986, in D. E. Rumelhart, J. L. McClelland and the PDP Research Group, *Parallel Distributed Processing: Explorations in the Microstructure of Cognition. Volume 1: Foundations*, p. 107. Copyright © 1986 by The MIT Press. Adapted with permission.)

Figure 6.1. (From 'Some Criticisms of Connectionist Models of Human Performance' by D. W. Massaro, 1988, *Journal of Memory and Language, 27*, p. 220. Copyright © 1988 by Academic Press, Inc. Adapted with permission.)

Figure 6.2. (From 'Some Criticisms of Connectionist Models of Human Performance' by D. W. Massaro, 1988, *Journal of Memory and Language, 27*, p. 227. Copyright © 1988 by Academic Press, Inc. Adapted with permission.)

Figure 6.3. (From 'Some Criticisms of Connectionist Models of Human Performance' by D. W. Massaro, 1988, *Journal of Memory and Language, 27*, p. 230. Copyright © 1988 by Academic Press, Inc. Adapted with permission.)

Figure 6.4. (From 'How to Build a Connectionist Idiot (Savant)' by D. Norris, 1990, *Cognition, 35*, p. 284. Copyright © 1990 by Elsevier Science Publishers B. V. (North Holland). Adapted with permission.)

Figure 6.5. (From 'Evaluating an Adaptive Network Model of Human Learning' by M. A. Gluck and G. H. Bower, 1988, *Journal of Memory and Language, 27*, p. 169. Copyright © 1988 by Academic Press, Inc. Adapted with permission.)

Figure 6.6. (From 'Perceptrons: An Introduction to Computational Geometry' by M. Minsky and S. Papert, 1988, pp. 252-3. Copyright © 1988 by The MIT Press. Adapted with permission.)

Chapter 1

Connectionism: An historical perspective

Since the phenomenal growth in interest in neural network research began in the early 1980s, several papers have been published that provide historical perspectives on the approach (Barrow, 1989; Papert, 1988; Valentine, 1989; Walker, 1990). This is hardly surprising given the dramatic course of events that took place as the discipline developed. By the mid-1960s neural network research (henceforth, connectionism) was thriving. However, following the publication of Minsky and Papert's (1969) careful analysis of one class of network models, interest in the research waned considerably. The 1980s have witnessed a connectionist renaissance.

Some general definitions are in order before continuing. Initially, the term 'connectionism' will be given the rather neutral definition of any work concerning the behaviour of systems comprising interconnected sets of simple processing units. New connectionism is defined as all such work carried out since the beginning of the 1980s. Old connectionism is, correspondingly, all such work up to and including the publication of Minsky and Papert's perceptrons book (1969). These definitions will be clarified as the discussion proceeds.

This first chapter starts out by tracing two main strands in connectionist history. Firstly, a brief sketch of some basic ideas concerning associationism will be included. This leads naturally on to a consideration of the work of Hebb (1949) and his theory of neurological development. The second strand to be traced concerns ideas about formal neurons as put forward by McCulloch and Pitts (1943/1965). These latter ideas are more typically discussed as being seminal and as forming the foundations of connectionism. Nevertheless, the influence of Hebb's work is still felt today and it would be inappropriate not to consider it along-side the work of McCulloch and Pitts. Towards the end of the chapter a

1

brief sketch of the early history of perceptron research is included. Rosenblatt's work (1962) will be mentioned in passing, but the work of Minsky and Papert will be considered in some detail. There remains a considerable amount of controversy over what Minsky and Papert showed and what exactly their contribution to the field has been. Indeed the typical perception of their work is that they only drew negative conclusions about the capabilities of perceptrons. This is a misunderstanding and, as a consequence, their conclusions about perceptrons need to be carefully examined.

Apart from providing context for the forthcoming material, this initial discussion of history is important for other reasons. It has recently been claimed that there is little of substance that is new in the recent research (Fodor & Pylyshyn, 1988). To appreciate fully this accusation, history has to be carefully examined. It would therefore be remiss in a book such as this not to attempt some such analysis of history.

Early connectionism and the associationistic tradition

In many accounts of the history of psychology, the discussion typically begins by attributing some responsibility to either Plato or Aristotle. This is also true with connectionism. The very roots of the enterprise can be found in Aristotle's writings on the formation of associations (Anderson & Bower, 1973; Valentine, 1989). This is not to argue that connectionism can be reduced to associationism. This important issue will be considered in detail later; all that is being stated is that connectionism and associationism share many fundamental characteristics.

Anderson and Bower (1973) in their synopsis of the history of associationism stipulate that there are two fundamental ways in which associations are formed. These are, respectively, successive associations and synchronous associations. Both implicate the putative and well-worn principle of learning based upon contiguity. A successive association forms between two sequential events through their temporal contiguity. A simultaneous association forms between two concurrent events through their spatial contiguity. The argument continued that whereas successive associations control the sequencing of thoughts, synchronous associations are the means by which simultaneously occurring simple ideas are combined into more complex thoughts. According to Anderson and Bower these basic notions can be traced back to the writings of Aristotle. The general principles of learning came to form the foundations of associationistic psychology. Indeed the notions of successive and synchronous associations are so firmly entrenched in the traditional learning literature that many have been seduced into believing that they form the basis of all aspects of psychological life. For instance, James (1890/1983) in *The Principles of Psychology* (see Walker, 1990) discusses an account of neuropsychological functioning based essentially on these two forms of associations. The quote is that, 'When two elementary brain-processes have been active together or in immediate succession, one of them, on recurring, tends to propagate its excitement into the other' (p. 534). Clearly both successive and sequential associations are being written about here. Moreover, this statement is about attempting to understand brain functioning in terms of elementary events, spreading activation, and, excitation: three notions that continuously recur in the connectionist literature. In essence, James (1890/1983) was attempting to marry ideas from associationism with ideas about neural processes. Such an attempt contrasts strikingly with the later radical behaviourists (e.g. Watson, as discussed by Hilgard and Bower, 1966), who were only concerned with trying to explain observable behaviour in terms of observable events.

Other fundamental properties of connectionism can be found in *The Principles of Psychology* when James writes about 'the amount of activity of any given point in the brain being the sum of the other tendencies of all other points to discharge into it' (*op. cit.*). These tendencies in turn are assumed to be proportionate to: (a) the number of previous times that both points have been co-active previously, (b) their corresponding intensities, and (c) the absence of any rival point into which the excitation might be diverted. Such ideas about summing activation, the importance of the frequency of co-occurrence of two events and of the possibility of rival events, recur repeatedly in the connectionist literature. It should be stressed, however, that the later behaviourist notions of reward and of stimulus–response contingencies remained undiscussed. This is of interest because although there are clear similarities between some connectionist learning procedures and early behaviourist learning principles, there are also glaring disparities. For example, a direct comparison can be made between James' ideas and Thorndike's law of effect. For whereas contiguity of activation is sufficient to form neural associations in James' framework, Thorndike's law of effect states that the strengthening or weakening of an association (between a stimulus and a response) comes about as a result of its consequences: satisfying associations become strengthened whereas annoying associations are weakened (see Hilgard & Bower, 1966). Nevertheless, a glaring difference between James' associationism and later behaviourism remains. The early learning theorists were primarily concerned with observable stimulus–response events; in contrast the early connectionists are distinctive in their attempts to marry psychology with neurology. Indeed it seems that the early connectionists were almost reductionist in their approach. They typically justified their statements about psychological processes with reference to neurology.

After James, the next significant connectionist to attempt to provide a consistent account of associationistic principles and brain functioning is Hebb. In his seminal book, entitled *The Organisation of Behavior* (1949), Hebb set out other fundamentals of connectionism. Again the aim was to provide a theory of brain functioning that in turn explained psychological processes. Of the comprehensive list of topics that Hebb covered in his book, it is his ideas about neurological development that form the basis of the connectionist approach. For Hebb there was a direct isomorphism between the growth of actual neural networks (i.e. well-defined sets of interconnected neurons), on the one hand, and memory and perception, on the other. Moreover, central to his account are the principles of simultaneous and sequential associations: both play different roles in explaining how putative neural networks or (as he preferred) 'cell assemblies' develop. Nevertheless, it is the repeated stimulation of cells that is fundamental so the account is again one based upon principles of the frequency of co-occurrence of events. What makes Hebb's account special is the serious attempt to put forward a neurophysiologically plausible account of psychological processes by taking into consideration the then received ideas about the structure and functions of nerve cells.

Hebb's major concerns were with trying to account for memory in terms of structural and metabolic changes at cell–cell junctions. Typically, nowadays, the only cell–cell junction discussed is the synapse. A synapse exists when one of the processes emanating from one cell comes into contact with part of another cell. For Hebb, though, synaptic knobs were paramount. Hebb quotes the work of Lorente de Nó (1938) as showing the existence of synaptic knobs and describes these as not necessarily being terminal structures but as being more typically the irregular thickening in the unmyelinated part of the axon near its ending. Put simply, the synaptic knobs were seen to be the points of contact between parts of the axon of one cell and the body of another. It was growth in and of the synaptic knobs together with some form of metabolic change, that Hebb saw as being the fundamental neurophysiological processes underlying memory. Although the particular ideas about synaptic knobs are no longer discussed, the influence of Hebb's general idea about memory and learning being inexorably tied up with synaptic changes is still very influential (Changeaux & Dehaene, 1989; McNaughton & Nadel, 1990; Stanton & Sejnowski, 1989).

Hebb described two ways in which neuronal changes are governed respectively by simultaneous and sequential associations. The central idea was that if two cells are repeatedly simultaneously active, then, over time, activity in one will cause activity in the other. This can happen when the two cells share contact with a third cell as is the case with simultaneous associations forming. Alternatively, one cell can map directly onto another and through mutual activity the pre-synaptic cell can come to cause activity in the post-synaptic cell. This would be the case with successive associations. Both forms of associations have tended to become conflated into the general Hebb rule. This states that when two adjacent neurons are repeatedly active then contingent metabolic changes lead to a lowered synaptic resistance between the two cells. This in turn increases the probability that activity in one cell will cause activity in the other. As Anderson and Hinton (1981) remark, the Hebb rule predicts that cells will tend to become correlated in their responses. Varieties of the Hebb rule abound in the current connectionist literature.

Most retrospective accounts of connectionism tend to leave the discussion of Hebb at that, but this fails to do justice to the depth of his analysis concerning neurological development and the mapping between psychology and neurology. Firstly, it is important to look at the reasons why his account is as it is. Hebb wanted to put forward plausible ideas about the growth of neural networks in order to explain perceptual development and hence adult perceptual abilities: an objective which fits well with empiricist doctrine. In addition to the discussion of how inter-cell associations are formed, Hebb's general aim was to put forward an account of how whole networks of associations are formed. Although not quite a theory based on the notion of the infant mind being a tabula rasa, Hebb's is one in which a structured brain is seen to develop through exposure to a structured world.

It is straightforward to see how whole chains of associations and hierarchies of associations could be built up over time by the recursive application of the general principles of Hebbian learning. Two simultaneously active cells map onto a third, causing it to become co-active with a fourth. In turn the third and fourth cells map onto a fifth whose behaviour eventually comes to represent a whole pattern of associations. This is an account of the structural development of neural networks, but perhaps of more importance are Hebb's ideas concerning the functional role of these cell assemblies. To understand this, the notions of reverberatory action and phase sequences must be introduced.

Firstly consider the notion of reverberatory action. Hebb was concerned that the transient activity exhibited by cells would be of too brief a duration to allow for the necessary structural synaptic changes to take place. Consequently, he postulated that some form of prolongation of activity was necessary and introduced the ideas about reverberatory activation. On the assumption that associations may well lead to cyclical sets of connections, Hebb argued that activity could reverberate and hence prolong the co-activity of pairs of pre- and post-synaptic cells. By allowing for such chains of activation, long-term structural changes could then occur.

To understand the notion of a phase sequence it is important to digress into Hebb's concerns about perception. Hebb developed a theory of perception where there was a direct mapping between salient perceptual features and neural structures. In this account certain primitive cell assemblies act as feature detectors to pick up information specifying lines and angles. Moreover, whole cell assemblies were seen to develop at higher levels. These higher-level assemblies captured both feature and eye-movement parameters. By this account hierarchies of feature detectors were combined together in ways given by co-activity of the underlying assemblies and by the associated sequences of eye movements.

Within the theory, the initial assumption was that all visual inputs are decomposed into primitive elements (e.g. lines and angles) through the operation of innate perceptual analysers: the analysers are activated whenever the eyes fixate the feature in question. Simple cell assemblies are built up around the stimulation of these kinds of perceptual analysers. In turn, complex assemblies are formed when the simple assemblies become associated through repeated sequential fixations of the corresponding features. Figural information is therefore conveyed by the spatial disposition of the features provided by relative eye-movement information. Consequently it is the temporal relationship of activity in the various sub-assemblies, known as a phase sequence, that gives rise to neural networks that act to detect 'superordinate perceptions' (Hebb, 1949, p. 98). This was the neural account of figural perception.

A strong claim made by Hebb was that at the outset the brain consists of random wiring between neurons. As will become clear this assumption has been made repeatedly by connectionists when they discuss ideas about developing brains. However, for Hebb this posed something of a problem for his explanation of perception. His account demanded that one network, or cell assembly, develop for each discernible percept, yet the theory only allowed for the modification of already existing connections. The implication, therefore, was that all necessary connections must be already hardwired. All the theory allowed for was existing connections to be modified through exposure to the world. Hebb was concerned about the plausibility of this claim but was encouraged by the immense number of interconnections in the cortex. Hence the assumption about random wiring was justified on the grounds of the plethora of connections.

Before moving on from the discussion of Hebb's contribution, it is important to note further points he made about neural growth. These are that changes in the neural system can be viewed both as fractionation and recruitment of certain neural connections. Fractionation corresponds to the state of affairs where previously synchronous cells cease to synchronize. Here the connection between the two cells would cease to be operational if they no longer continued to be co-active. Recruitment corresponds to that state affairs where two previously asynchronously firing cells now operate synchronously. This is not the formation of completely novel connections but the functional recruitment of existing connections. Some new connectionist systems embody both fractionation and recruitment because neural changes are modelled by the strengthening and weakening of already established connections. However, fractionation, defined as the complete loss of connections, and, recruitment, defined as the growth of new connections, have not been studied extensively. Some researchers very recently have considered the possibilities of cutting out whole connections when they cease to be of any functional importance (see Kindermann & Linden, 1988; Mozer & Smolensky, 1989). The generation of completely new connections has also been recently discussed, but only in a very ad hoc way (see Ratcliff, 1990). A fuller discussion of these ideas is included in Chapter 2.

In summary, it remains true that many ideas fundamental to connectionism were set out by Hebb. At a very general level, his commitment to trying to account for psychological processes given certain neurophysiological constraints has endured. At a very specific level, Hebbian learning, as conveyed by the Hebb rule, continues to be applied even in the most recent systems (see Linsker, 1986a,

1986b, 1986c; Hopfield 1982, 1984). Nevertheless, the framework is not without its problems and limitations.

Something that was rather odd about Hebb's commitment to neurological processes was that he limited his discussion to neural growth predicated on excitation. He simply ignored inhibition. The account only invoked the notion of mutual co-activity or excitation and although inhibition is mentioned in passing, Hebb did not fully integrate it in his theory. The reasons for this are unclear although it may well have been something to do with parsimony. Hebb may have considered his theory to be parsimonious because only one process (excitation), was invoked to explain learning. The problem of introducing a second process (inhibition) is that this implies complex interactions. There seems to have been no obvious and parsimonious way of integrating inhibitory processes with excitatory processes (cf. Milner, 1957, p. 243). Hebb proceeded by assuming that neurological development could be accounted for solely in terms of excitation. Inhibition when dealt with at all was considered to be either a lack of excitation or was equated with neuronal refractoriness.

A second point concerns modern neurophysiology and criticisms of Hebb's original ideas. As Alkon (1989) has recently argued, Hebb's account is predicated upon the idea that the whole of the pre-synaptic and post-synaptic cells must be active for learning to occur. This hypothesis does not seem to be consistent with recent evidence. It seems that what may be of more importance is the spread of electrical and possibly chemical signals from different post-synaptic sites on the same cell regardless of the state of the post-synaptic cell itself. It appears that it is localized electrochemical changes that are important rather than global cell–cell states (Alkon, 1989).

Regardless of these neurophysiological considerations, perhaps the main reason why the original Hebbian model was discarded was that it failed to pass a test of sufficiency when embodied in a computer program. Here the critical study was carried out by Rochester, Holland, Haibt and Duda (1956/1988). In a series of simulations Rochester *et al.* initially examined an artificial neural net composed of simple processing units and their interconnections. Units received input from 10 input connections and each unit had an additional 10 output connections. The aim was to attempt to simulate the growth of cell assemblies in line with the basic tenets of Hebb's theory. In this model units were divided into sensory units and 'hidden' units. Sensory units received input from the external world. Hidden units received no such inputs, but were connected to the sensory units and to other hidden units.

With each unit certain parameters had to be stored in order to get the simulation started. Initially, the parameters were the name of each unit, how long it had been since the unit fired, how 'tired' the unit was, the name of the efferent unit that it fired and also the magnitude of its input into the efferent unit. Units could take on either of two states, i.e. ON (rendered numerically as 1) or OFF (rendered numerically as 0). A string of 0s and 1s was also recorded for each unit as a representation of its firing history. The program operated by simulating time in discrete time steps. At each time step units could either fire or be in some state of recovery from firing. The program was able to examine each unit's firing history, for it was these representations that revealed repeated patterns of reverberation across sets of units. Mutually synchronous firing patterns were then used by the program to systematically increment the tendency for one unit to fire another in accordance with the Hebb learning rule. When presented with input, the units fired accordingly. The program iteratively updated the states of the units and invoked the Hebb learning procedure to make the necessary cell–cell adjustments.

The instructive demonstration was that, with the above minimum assumptions built into the model, no cell assembly structures were formed. It was only when additional characteristics were added that such structures began to emerge. The most important additional characteristics were: (a) a distance bias such that 'near' units were allowed to fire more readily than more distantly connected units, and, (b) inhibitory as well as excitatory connections. When such features were added, cell assembles did form around the stimulated neurons.

Both of the additional features introduced into the simulations by Rochester *et al.* arose from a consideration of the work by Milner, one of Hebb's followers. Milner (1957) developed Hebb's theory by introducing inhibition in a principled way. One of the impressive aspects of this account, apart from its elegance, is its consistency with current neurophysiological evidence (see Crick & Asanuma, 1986). For Milner, the primary form of neural activity was excitation carried by cells with long axons. According to this view, the long axon cells innervate similar long axon cells as well as other cells with smaller axons. The small axon cells are inhibitory cells that act as a break on the spreading excitation propagated by the large axon cells. More specifically, each small axon cell shares fewer inhibitory connections with its own long axon afferent cell than it does with other cells. This ensures that as long as the excitatory cell continues to fire it inhibits its neighbours more than it inhibits itself. (This follows from the assumption that a given small axon cell shares fewer inhibitory connections with its afferent cell than it does with other efferent cells.) Moreover, because the inhibitory connections are limited to those cells in the immediate locale, excitation is well dispersed throughout the cortex. Milner continued to incorporate the standard Hebbian learning principles in his model, but he embellished the ideas with certain assumptions about neural inhibition. The ideas about inhibition came from contemporary neurophysiology.

It is unfortunate that most of the early development of the Hebbian learning principles has been ignored by new connectionism. At the very least the early studies showed that little is gained by assuming that connectivity and propagation of activity are random. Both the evidence from the simulation work and from neurophysiology showed that degrees of systematicity are warranted. This early work suggested that neural structures do not develop in the presence of random wiring or the random propagation of activity. Moreover, Milner happily adopted the assumption that there may well be more than one sort of neuron. Something that new connectionism has tended to ignore is that qualitatively different neurons may well be defined according to their contrasting functional roles. Indeed, as Crick and Asanuma (1986) have recently documented, there is some evidence that there are excitatory neurons that are quite different from inhibitory neurons. Consequently, if the neurophysiological data are to play a serious role in the development of connectionist models, it seems rather odd to build neural networks comprising just one sort of neural unit. All of this tends to suggest that the mapping from connectionist models to real neural nets remains problematic.

Formal neurons and their logical characteristics

Having traced the early development of Hebbian learning and cell assemblies, there is another strand of history to follow and this concerns the work of McCulloch. This work was carried out quite independently of Hebb's, though, now with the benefit of hindsight, it can be seen to be related. Indeed the rationale for McCulloch's work differs in many important ways from that just discussed. Whereas before the concern was with psychology mapping onto neurology here the emphasis is different. It was agreed that psychological functioning is intimately bound up with brain functioning, yet for McCulloch the crucial link was between neurology and computational theory. The fundamental aim was to develop an account of intellectual functioning based on ideas about the logical nature of the operating characteristics of neurons. The development of neural structures was not of primary concern in this work. Of main interest was how primitive logical operations might be carried out by neurons, and how complex logical processes might be carried out by networks of neurons.

For McCulloch (1961/1965) the breakthrough came in positing the 'psychon' or 'least kind of psychic event' (p. 8). His main concern in positing the 'psychon' was to try to show how propositional logic might be captured at the neural level. The first step was to show how the behaviour of a digital system might be understood as signalling the truth or falsity of certain primitive propositions. So for McCulloch, a psychon was characterized by the following four properties: (1) it was to be so simple that it either happened or it did not; (2) it happened only if its bound cause happened – in this way it implied its temporal antecedent; (3) it proposed subsequent psychons; and (4) subsequent psychons in turn could be compounded to produce the equivalents of more complicated propositions. In other words, assumptions were being made about an atomic system in which the atoms (psychons) stood for primitive logical operations. It is useful to consider how the firing of a single neuron with one input line captures a proposition. Consider material implication; the 'only if' of logic. The consequent obtains 'only if' the conditions for the antecedent are met. The antecedent condition is that the input line is firing at a rate over and above a certain critical rate. (Other logical primitives are considered below in discussing neurons with two inputs.) By

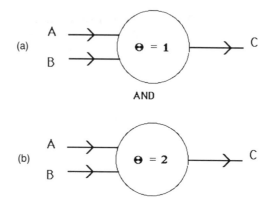

Figure 1.1. In (a) the threshold, θ, is set at 1. If the sum of the inputs over A and B equals or exceeds this value the unit comes ON and 'fires' by sending a signal along C. Either A, B, or both A and B can be ON and fire C. In (b) the threshold has been raised to 2. Now the only condition that fires C is that both A and B must be ON.

extension, the interactions amongst these atomic elements stood for complex thoughts. In this way McCulloch's ideas are very much in the spirit of characterizing the science of the mind as mental chemistry.

McCulloch's main objective was to explain how primitive digital events gave rise to complex thought. To meet this aim McCulloch and Pitts (1943/1965) started by defining a formal neuron around certain currently agreed properties of actual neurons. The formal neuron put forward by McCulloch and Pitts was defined according to the following properties: (1) the activity of a neuron is all or nothing; (2) a fixed number of synapses must be excited within a certain critical period in order to excite the neuron; (3) the only significant delay is synaptic delay; (4) the activity of any inhibitory synapse absolutely prevents excitation of the neuron at that time; and (5) the structure of the interconnections amongst neurons does not change. As can be seen, within this framework synapses could either be excitatory or inhibitory and in addition to all the above properties the eventual formal neuron was attributed a threshold. Although thresholds were allowed to vary, from (5) above, the actual structure of connections was not allowed to change. It will become clear that these two assumptions are central to most research within modern connectionism. By attributing thresholds to the neurons and by introducing the property of all-or-nothing activity, the elements of this system could either be in an ON state or an OFF state. Consequently, the proposed digital system was dealing with a binary, or two-valued, logic. The McCulloch and Pitts neuron has come to be known as a binary threshold logic unit and examples of these kinds of neurons are shown in Figure 1.1.

Although there is some correspondence between two-valued Boolean algebra and the McCulloch and Pitts system, in the latter system some importance was attached to the temporal operating characteristics of neural networks. McCulloch and Pitts attempted to honour the then known temporal constraints of neural processing in order to put forward a neurologically plausible account of thought. As a consequence the theory addressed the neural properties of: (a) the refractory period, i.e. a neuron having fired needs a certain amount of time to recover independently of its inputs; (b) latent addition, where a neuron sums (i.e., adds) its inputs before firing; and (c) synaptic delay – there is some delay between receiving input and producing output. (Synaptic delay is in addition to the pauses caused by refractoriness and latent addition.)

Overall McCulloch and Pitts were strongly committed to trying to understand how a logical system could be modelled by a real neural network. Indeed, they set out a formal argument about how the operating characteristics of interconnected neurons might capture propositional logic. Central to this enterprise was the consideration of circuits made up of neuronal units with only two inputs and a modifiable threshold. An initial aim though was to see the degree to which these particular binary threshold logic units could compute the truth value of each of the 16 logical functions of two propositions. It is this particular issue that forms a cornerstone to the development of connectionism.

McCulloch and Pitts were particularly concerned with the fact that there are only 16 possible logical functions of two propositions. They went to examine this in terms of the functional characteristics of the kinds of binary threshold logic unit just described. Such a unit receives just two inputs and each of the inputs can be either ON or OFF. As a consequence, there are only four distinct pairs of input cases. Consider the inputs A and B. The four basic cases are: (i) only A ON, (ii) only B ON, (iii) A ON and B ON, and, (iv) A OFF and B OFF. A processing unit can now take these inputs and compute an output. In this sense the unit is said to compute its output as a function of its input. The function is the mapping between the states of the two input lines (i.e. A and B) and the output state of the processing unit. Any such function describes those input cases that switch the unit ON and those that switch it OFF. The two extreme cases are where, (i) the unit never fires across the four input cases – McCulloch (1950/1965) terms this function 'contradiction'; and (ii) where the unit always fires across the four input cases – McCulloch (1950/1965) terms this function 'tautology'. Mapping out all possible input–output contingencies gives rise to a total of 16 different functions. These are shown in Figure 1.2.

Figure 1.2 is most easily explained by working through the details. Figure 1.2 shows the notational system (developed by Minsky and Selfridge; see McCulloch, 1961/1965) that McCulloch used to convey these ideas. A dot can appear between any of the four arms of an 'X'. Each 'X' stands for a different function: it specifies the different conditions under which a processing unit comes ON. A dot on the left signifies that only A is ON; a dot on the right signifies that only B is ON; a dot above signifies that both A and B are ON; and, a dot below signifies that A and B

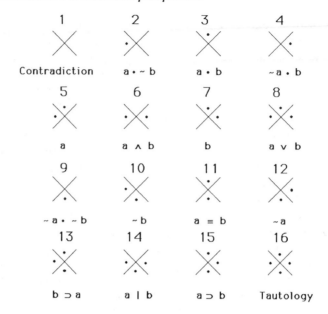

Figure 1.2. The 16 different sets of input cases that may fire a McCulloch and Pitts neuron. In each case a particular set of the four possible conditions that fire the unit are specified. The complete set of four possible conditions are (i) A being ON, (ii) B being ON, (iii) both A and B being ON, and, (iv) neither A or B being ON. A dot in any particular arm of the 'X' specifies which of the conditions fires the unit. The 16 cases respectively map onto the logical functions: (1) Contradiction, (2) Only A, (3) A and B, (4) Only B, (5) A, (6) EXOR, (7) B, (8) Inclusive-OR, (9) Neither A or B, (10) Not B, (11) Identity (i.e. Negative EXOR), (12) Not A, (13) B implies A, (14) Not both A and B, (15) A implies B, and (16) Tautology.

are both OFF. So a dot on the left of a cross signifies that the unit only comes ON when its A input line is ON.

Given this formalism, the state of an input line signals the truth of a single proposition. The truth values of two propositions in turn corresponds to the ON/ OFF states of the two (A/B) input lines. There are two ways of construing the overall system conveyed in Figure 1.2. Firstly, it is possible to think of 16 different processing units each dedicated to one individual function. The second way of thinking about the system is to construe it as setting out different cases of the same unit. Here the idea is that the same unit might capture the different functions given a changeable threshold. By allowing the unit's threshold to shift (see Figure 1.1), the thought was that the same unit might be able to compute the whole range of 16 functions. (On this latter point, McCulloch (1961/1965), in following von Neumann, was particularly interested in the problem of how neural nets could operate consistently if all the thresholds on all the constituent units were allowed to shift. The assumption was that an analogous state of affairs happens with the human central nervous system, (henceforth, CNS), in conditions ranging from coma to convulsion. By this view, coma occurs when thresholds are so high that few units fire: convulsion occurs when thresholds are so low that many units fire.) McCulloch and Pitts revealed, however, that a binary threshold logic unit, as defined above, can only deal with 14 of the basic 16 functions of two propositions (see Figure 1.2). The two functions it is incapable of dealing with are the Exclusive-OR (henceforth EXOR) and its negation. This crucial conclusion requires further examination.

Firstly, it is important to deal with the difference between the two sorts of logical OR because this distinction is typically not made explicit in normal usage. The two sorts of logical OR are known, respectively, as the Inclusive-OR and EXOR. For instance, when the truth of two propositions (i.e. proposition A and proposition B) is being considered the Inclusive-OR is true when both A and B are true, when A alone is true or when B alone is true. Otherwise the Inclusive-OR is false. In contrast, EXOR is true when A alone is true or when B alone is true. Otherwise EXOR is false. In terms of the two binary inputs to a McCulloch and Pitts neuron it is easiest to think of the two sorts of logical OR in terms of the input–output contingencies of the ON/OFF states of two input lines and the ON/OFF state of the unit itself. The standard binary notation is to use a one to signify ON (or true) and a 0 to signify OFF (or false).

For Inclusive OR the input–output contingencies are:

Input A to unit c	Input B to unit c	Output from unit c
1	1	1
0	1	1
1	0	1
0	0	0

In contrast, the input-output contingencies for EXOR are:

Input A to unit c	Input B to unit c	Output from unit c
1	1	0
0	1	1
1	0	1
0	0	0

It is common to refer to EXOR as 'A or else B'. Its negation is given by the following input–output contingencies:

Input A to unit c	Input B to unit c	Output from unit c
1	1	1
0	1	0
1	0	0
0	0	1

The negation of EXOR is known as the logical identity. It is in turn commonly known as 'both or else neither': as McCulloch noted, the 'if and only if' of logic.

To reiterate, a major insight of working with units with only two inputs was that it was only possible to account for 14 of the 16 possible logical functions: EXOR and its negation remained unaccounted for. To understand the significance of this point fully, it is necessary to turn to Minsky and Papert (1969).

Minsky and Papert and the EXOR problem

Although Minsky and Papert dealt at length with the formal limitations of simple neural networks, they also discussed the formal limitations of the McCulloch and Pitts neuron (as defined above). Points here to remember are: (1) that each unit has only two inputs, (2) that each unit has a threshold, (3) that each unit sums it inputs, and (4) that a unit comes ON only if the sum of the activity on the input lines equals or exceeds its threshold. Without complicating matters too much, it is also possible to consider that the contribution of each input line (to the eventual firing of the unit) can vary. By this assumption it is possible to attribute a weight (or coefficient) to each input line.

It is now possible to offer a formal definition of a binary threshold logic unit with two binary inputs. Let the unit be known as Unit c. The two input lines are labelled respectively A and B. Line A connects unit a with unit c: Line B connects unit b with unit c. It is now possible to define the conditions under which unit c will turn OFF and turn ON. All of the above properties reduce to the following expression:

$$w_A.a + w_B.b > = \theta_c \begin{cases} -1 - \text{the unit comes ON,} \\ 0 \ - \text{otherwise OFF} \end{cases} \tag{1.1}$$

w_A signifies the weight on connection line A.
w_B signifies the weight on connection line B.
a signifies the state of unit a. This can either be ON (i.e. 1) or OFF (i.e. 0).
b signifies the state of unit b.
θ_c signifies the threshold of unit c.

Expression (1.1) shows that what unit c is doing is adding up the product of each respective weight on a connection line with the corresponding state of the connected input unit. In detail, the weight on input line to A is multiplied by the state of the afferent unit a (the $w_A.a$ term in Equation (1.1)), the weight on input line B multiplied by the state of the afferent unit b (the $w_B.b$ term in Equation (1.1)), these two products are then added together and this total is compared against the figure specified by unit c's threshold (i.e. θ_c). Remember that the system under consideration only deals with binary threshold logic units so units a and b can themselves only be in one of two states; respectively, 1 for ON and 0 for OFF.

Several straightforward yet important mathematical properties can now be discussed. When characterized in this manner the processing unit is carrying out a *linear* function. This characteristic is defined properly in Chapter 2, here it suffices to note that if the outputs from the unit were plotted against its summed inputs the resulting graph would show a straight *line*. Expression (1. 1) essentially defines this straight line function. Using a standard x–y depiction of such a straight line certain characteristics are typically of primary concern. These are where the line cuts the x and y axes; (respectively, the x- and y-intercepts), and the gradient of the line. It turns out that the analogy between the processing characteristics of a binary threshold logic unit and the geometry of two-dimensional (2-D) graphs is very revealing. It is quite appropriate to characterize a processing unit by a straight line on a 2-D graph. Roughly speaking, the threshold of the unit specifies the y-intercept of this straight line and the weights on two input lines collectively specify the gradient of this line. Changing the threshold changes the y-intercept of the line. Changing the weights alters the gradient of the line. Figure 1.3 shows an example of just one such graphical representation of one binary threshold logic unit. On the graph the four marked points of interest correspond to the four possible states of the two input units a and b. Both units being OFF corresponds to the point (0,0), both ON corresponds to (1,1) and the two cases where only one is ON are (0,1) and (1,0), respectively. Essentially what the straight line is doing is dividing the 2-D surface of the graph into two parts. On one side of the line are the conditions under which the processing unit will come ON. On the other side of the line are the conditions under which the unit will turn OFF. Figure 1.3 shows the case where the unit comes ON whenever both afferent units a and b are ON. For all other three cases it turns OFF. This unit is signalling a logical AND because it only comes ON when both units a and b are ON.

Given this general framework, it is possible to consider the effects of changing the values of the weights and threshold and by considering only those cases that divide up the input–output contingencies in ways distinct from one another. By applying this technique it soon becomes apparent that there are only seven such critical straight lines, and these are shown in Figure 1.4. Figure 1.4 shows that the 7 lines account for only 14 of the 16 possible functions. This proves that a binary threshold logic unit, as defined, can only capture 14 of the 16 basic propositions. In other words, 7 basic propositions and their negations are accounted for. Figure 1.5 shows why it is impossible to achieve the correct input–output contingencies for either EXOR or its negation simply by drawing a straight line in the manner

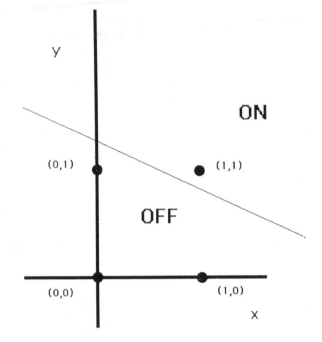

Figure 1.3. The figure shows a 2-D graph that represents the contingencies under which a particular unit will come ON. The unit receives inputs
along two lines, x and y, respectively. The four points on the graph
represent the four pairwise combinations of the possible states of the two
lines: (1,1) signifies both lines ON, (0,0) signifies both lines OFF, (1,0)
signifies x ON and y OFF, and (0,1) signifies y ON and x OFF. The straight
line cuts the plane of the graph into two parts. With the case shown
there is only one condition above the line which specifies when the unit
should come ON. It is the condition (1,1). All other conditions fall below
the line. When these conditions obtain the unit remains OFF. It can be
seen therefore that this figure describes a unit that signals a logical AND.
The unit only comes ON when x AND y are ON together.

described above. More technically, this shows that EXOR and its negation are
not linearly separable problems.

Given the finding that EXOR and its negation cannot be realized by formal
neurons with two inputs and modifiable threshold, McCulloch went on to argue
that these two functions could be realized by nets of these neurons given the
presence of various interconnections. McCulloch (1961) states that these logical
functions could be realized if the outputs of one unit gated (or vetoed) the outputs
of another. In other words, the activity of one unit should inhibit the activity of
another so as to stop the afferent unit from reaching threshold. Hanson and Burr

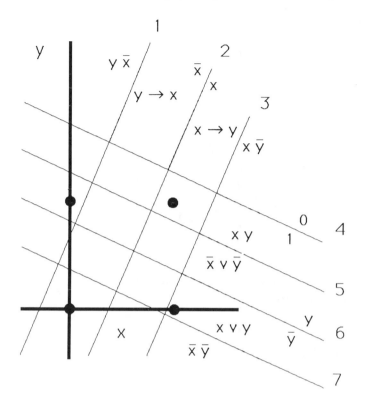

Figure 1.4 This figure is similar in kind to Figure 1.3. In this case seven lines are shown. These are the only possible lines that divide the space into 14 distinct halves. These seven lines specify 14 different input–output contingencies. The contingencies are paired. This is because, for each pair, one serves as the negation of the other. For instance, *x* and its negation, i.e., NOT *x* (see line 2) specify completely the reverse mappings.

Consider another example, this time with line 4. The line divides up the space where in one half the unit is always ON (labelled 1), and in the other half the unit is always OFF (labelled 0). When the unit is always ON this signals the logical function TAUTOLOGY, when the unit is always OFF this signals CONTRADICTION.

Line 1. $y\,\bar{x}$ *signifies ONLY y.* $y \rightarrow x$ signifies *y* IMPLIES *x*.
Line 2. $\bar{x}$ *signifies NOT x.* *x* signifies *x*.
Line 3. $x \rightarrow y$ signifies *x* IMPLIES *y*. $x\,\bar{y}$ *signifies ONLY x*.
Line 4. 0 signifies CONTRADICTION. 1 signifies TAUTOLOGY.
Line 5. *x y* signifies *x* AND *y*. $\bar{x} \vee \bar{y}$ *signifies NEITHER x OR y.*
Line 6. *y* signifies *y*. $\bar{y}$ *signifies NOT y.*
Line 7. *x* ∨ *y* signifies *x* OR *y*. $\bar{x}\,\bar{y}$ *signifies NOT BOTH x AND y.*
(From Minsky and Papert, 1988, adapted with permission, *see* p. xiv.)

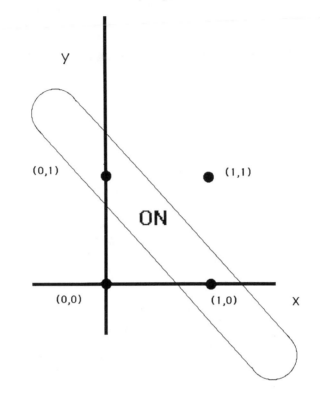

Figure 1.5. Diagrammatic representation of the input–output contingencies that specify EXOR. Clearly no straight line can be drawn to divide the
space up in an appropriate manner. The unit must ONLY come ON when
just one input line is ON. There are two such conditions and both fall
within the area shown. (From McClelland and Rumelhart, 1988, adapted
with permission, *see* p. xiv.).

(1990) provide an example of a net for computing EXOR (see Figure 1.6). They
claim that the kind of solution shown is one that McCulloch and Pitts may have
had in mind when discussing the limitations of binary threshold logic units.

The failure of binary threshold logic units to deal with the full 16 basic
propositions is of critical interest with respect to the later development of new
connectionism. Moreover, it can be used to argue that EXOR and its negation are
not primitive functions at the level of the implementation. In the system envisaged
by McCulloch, these functions have to broken down into constituent functions,
which, in turn, must be dealt with by other units. The implication is that EXOR
and its negation are not realized at the neural level as primitives. At the
neurological level other primitive units must be combined to give the correct
input–output contingencies for EXOR and its negation.

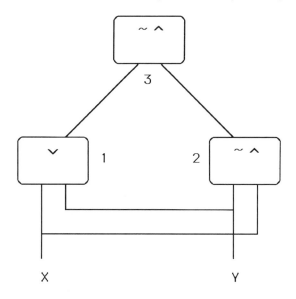

Figure 1.6. A solution to the EXOR problem suggested by Hanson and Burr (1990) as being something 'McCulloch and Pitts may have had in mind'. The net comprises two input units (1 and 2) and a single output unit (3). Units 2 and 3 are known as NOR gates: they only come ON if both input lines are OFF. When $x = 0$ and $y = 1$ then units 1 and 2 turns OFF, hence unit 3 turns ON. When $x = 1$ and $y = 1$ then unit 2 comes ON and 1 turns OFF, hence unit 3 turns OFF. When $x = 1$ and $y = 0$ then units 1 and 2 turn OFF, hence unit 3 turns ON. When $x = 0$ and $y = 0$ then unit 1 turns OFF and unit 2 turns ON hence unit 3 turns OFF. Overall this means that unit 3 is signalling an EXOR over the x and y input lines. (From Hanson and Burr, 1990, adapted with permission, *see* p. xiv.)

Early neural nets and pattern recognition: perceptrons

The early papers describing the McCulloch and Pitts neuron influenced a number of researchers to begin serious work on the formal and operational characteristics of abstract neural networks (see Rosenblatt, 1958, for a brief review). In retrospect the culmination of this work centred on the perceptron research group headed by Frank Rosenblatt. There is much to discuss about this work, but the main thrust can be summarized in a few general statements.

Essentially attempts were made to build a device, comprising formal neurons, capable of learning to recognize (i.e. discriminate) classes of visual patterns. Such devices were named perceptrons. The work itself was based on a number of fundamental assumptions about perception and memory. Following Corcoran's example (1971), it is easiest to discuss the work initially in terms of perception: learning will be dealt with later.

The overall aim was to produce a device capable of assigning a number of different input patterns to their respective categories. Given this, the model of perceptual processing realised by a perceptron can be directly contrasted with template-matching accounts (see Pinker, 1984). In template-matching accounts it is assumed that successful pattern recognition is achieved by matching an input pattern with a stored internal replica. Template matching rests on assumptions about the storage of patterns and the later stages of searching the store and matching the input to its stored internal replica. In contrast, the perceptron account of recognition is radically different and is set out in terms of a number of assumptions about abstract neural mechanisms. In perceptron accounts, the CNS is regarded as a giant switching mechanism in which information is retained via the connections between the intervening neurons. Stated in this way the spirit of this account is very much in the early learning theorists' tradition of assuming that the only important internal events are covert stimulus–response sequences (Hilgard & Bower, 1966). There is no processes of matching or search in this account; information flows through the system via pathways selected by reinforcement. Similar stimuli are processed via similar pathways from the input side of the system to the response, or, motor, side of the system. Consequently, there is a direct mapping from stimuli to their respective responses. Insofar as similar stimuli take similar pathways, then similar stimuli will evoke similar responses. There is no separate process of recognition or identification according to this account (cf. Rosenblatt, 1958).

Although these ideas in the abstract sound somewhat mystical, Rosenblatt began work by attempting to embody them in a working device known as a perceptron. It should be stressed that many variants of the perceptron were tried and tested. So it easiest therefore to begin by considering an elementary perceptron, as defined by Rosenblatt (1962). An elementary perceptron is any perceptron that possesses one layer of sensory or S-units, one layer of association or A-units and just one response or R-unit. S-units receive input directly from the environment; indeed it is normally assumed that the mosaic of S-units corresponds to the perceptron's retina. The R-unit interfaces with the environment at the other end of system and emits an identifiable response. The A-units simply intervene between the S- and R-units. In the elementary perceptron under consideration, all the A-units connect to the R-unit. Another important aspect of this system is that the A- and R-units all possess a threshold and all compute a weighted sum of their inputs. Each connection in the net had a coefficient or a weight associated with it. In other words, activity from a unit was weighted according to which connection it was spreading along. More formally the units computed the following weighted sum of their inputs:

$$S_j = \Sigma w_{ij} \cdot x_i \qquad\qquad (1.2)$$

S_j is the weighted sum of inputs to the *j*th unit.
x_i is the state of the *i*th input unit.
w_{ij} is the weight on the connection between *i*th and *j*th units.
The Σ symbol simply means sum. In its full form a range is specified. So here the full form would be:

$$S_j = \sum_{i=1}^{n} w_{ij} \cdot x_i \qquad (1.3)$$

This shows that each product of a weight and state is computed for every *i*th connection. If there are n connections then the cases 1 to *n* are considered. These products are then summed to give the total input.

Expression (1.2) is an extension to the ideas set out above about the operating characteristics of binary threshold logic units. In the perceptron though, units could receive many more than two input lines. Moreover, the A- and the R-units possessed different operating characteristics. For the A-units the output contingencies were such that the unit came ON if the weighted sum of its inputs was greater than or equal to its threshold, otherwise it remained OFF. In contrast, thresholds on the R-units were fixed at zero and these units produced an output of +1 if the sum of its inputs was positive (i.e. greater than the threshold), it produced an output of –1 if the sum of its input was less than 0. If the sum of the inputs equalled 0 the R-unit was said to be in an indeterminate state. As Barrow (1989) notes, the R-units are computing a three-valued logic.

A major point is that whereas the weights on the connections between the S-units and the A-units were fixed, the weights between the A-units and the R-units could vary. Consequently, the elementary perceptron, as defined, is also known as a simple perceptron with one layer of modifiable weights. It is just this sort of perceptron Minsky and Papert (1969) went on to study in great detail in their seminal work. Something that is rarely acknowledged nowadays is that Rosenblatt's group studied, amongst other things, perceptrons with interconnections within layers, perceptrons with bi-directional connections between layers and perceptrons with multiple layers of units. It is unfortunately true that in the rush to embrace new connectionism, these aspects of Rosenblatt's work seem to have been largely ignored. Nevertheless, it is generally agreed that a major contribution Rosenblatt made to the field of neural networks is the proof of a particular learning theorem known as the perceptron convergence theorem. In order to understand the proof, it is necessary to first understand how a perceptron learns.

Consider the simplest case where the machine must learn to respond differently to two patterns: for instance, the letters 'A ' and 'B'. Assume the R-unit must signal +1 for 'A' and –1 for 'B'. A pattern is then presented on the retina, activity is propagated through the net via the connections to the S-units and from the S-units to the R-unit. The output of the R-unit is compared against the correct classification response and if there is a mismatch changes are made to the system.

The most well known variant of making changes is described below. However, if the output is correct, no changes are made to the system: learning only takes place in the presence of mistakes. If there is any mismatch between the actual and the desired response, then there are two general principles for correcting these errors.

Case 1 is where an 'A' is present and the R unit fails to respond correctly with a +1. Here the weights on the active connections (between the S- and R-units) need to be increased and the thresholds of the active S-units need to be lowered. (Changes are only made to those units and connections responsible for the error.) The consequence of these actions is that they increase the probability of the R-unit being correct if the 'A' were to be immediately re-presented. Case 2 is where a 'B' is presented and the R-unit fails to respond correctly with a −1. Here the relevant weights need to be decreased and the relevant thresholds need to be increased. These actions are intended to limit the possibility that the R-unit will fire inappropriately the next time a 'B' is presented. The general point is that the machine learns by comparing its actual output with the desired output, and the contingent error-correcting procedure changes the weights and the thresholds in principled ways. The discrepancy between the actual output and the desired output is known as the error signal. The general principles operate so as to stop the net from committing the same immediate error again. Now the principles can vary and Rosenblatt considered a number of different ways of making changes and of distributing the error signal across the weights. (Remember learning corresponds to adapting weights on connections.) In a typical case, changes were made in some proportion to the error signal. For instance, the same small amount of alteration could be applied to all active connections on all trials. Alternatively, the size of the alterations could vary across each trial. Here the idea was to allow the changes to be of such a size so as to ensure that the current instance was classified properly.

This kind of learning might be criticized on the grounds that changes in the system only occur when errors are made and that no reward is forthcoming for correct responses. However, although it is possible to criticize this theory of learning on psychological grounds, there was a reason for only making changes contingent on errors. The elegance of the procedure is that there is a clear end-point to learning. Given that nothing happens when the machine correctly classifies a pattern, if the machine correctly classifies all patterns, no more changes are necessary. If no more changes accrue, the perceptron will have reached a stable state: it classifies all patterns correctly. If correct responses were rewarded and contingent changes were being made continuously then there is no natural end-point to learning.

A concern with the perceptron learning procedure was that it was unclear whether the machine could learn anything. Expressed more technically, it was not obvious that the machine could learn the values of the coefficients (i.e. weights and thresholds) that satisfied the constraints set out by a given learning problem. On a priori grounds, it seemed possible that the machine might never reach a stable state because the coefficients might be updated constantly. The presentation of one pattern might lead to changes in one direction, the next pattern might lead to a completely compensatory set of changes in the opposite direction. Therefore the changes in the coefficients might oscillate and never stabilize.

In addressing this issue Rosenblatt proved the perceptron convergence theorem. This states that if a set of coefficients exist that satisfies the constraints of a particular classification problem, then given sufficient experience of the input cases, a perceptron will learn the coefficients. However, the crucial point was that the input patterns must fall into linear separable categories. As long as sets of input patterns conform to the principle of linearly separability then there exists a simple perceptron that will be able to learn to discriminate between them. There is an exact analogy to be drawn here with the lines shown in Figures 1.3–1.4. Remember the lines demarcate distinctions between the set of input patterns that turn the formal neuron ON and that set of input patterns that turn the neuron OFF. The crucial point was that of the four patterns considered, only certain linearly separable groupings were possible. The linear separable cases are those where the two categories can be divided up according to a straight line in the manner described above. If the condition of linear separability does not hold, then for the simple perceptron the classification scheme is unlearnable. A more formal definition of linear separability is given in Chapter 2.

An early simulated version of a simple perceptron known as the Mark 1 perceptron comprised: a retina of 400 photocells arranged into a 20 × 20 array; one layer of A-units and 5 binary response units (Block, 1962). The aim of one experiment was to train this network to discriminate the 26 letters of the alphabet when the letters were normalized for position, size and orientation. The perceptron was able to learn this discrimination after only 15 presentations of each letter (i.e. 390 presentations in total). Rosenblatt also reports various experiments carried out on simple perceptrons that demonstrate their abilities on a number of pattern recognition and discrimination tasks. Principally the aim of these experiments was to examine things like whether ordering of the presentation of instances, or the relative frequency of presentation of instances affected the ability to learn to discriminate various classes of geometric stimuli.

To digress slightly, it is interesting to consider an argument of Block's (1970) about some of Rosenblatt's assumptions about the random wiring of the connections in a simple perceptron. Rosenblatt introduced the assumption of randomized connections on the grounds that if a perceptron with random connections can learn a given classification scheme then so can one with carefully specified connections. The 'worst case' or 'minimal constraint' condition is associated with a perceptron with random wiring. The possible folly of this approach (i.e. starting out with a perceptron with random wiring) is that it is never clear whether it is the architecture or the learning procedure that is at fault when the device fails. Indeed, to assume that known biological constraints imply that the initial wiring is random seems contrary to all of the evidence.

Irrespective of the early successes of perceptron research, interest in this kind of science almost evaporated after the publication of Minsky and Papert's (1969) detailed mathematical analysis of simple perceptrons. Consideration of Minsky and Papert's book forms the basis for discussion in the next section.

Perceptrons: Minsky and Papert's analysis

Following the excitement generated by Rosenblatt's research, Minsky and Papert (1969) wrote a careful analysis of what were in principle the capabilities of simple perceptrons. The simple perceptron, for Minsky and Papert, comprised a set of input or retinal units, a set of A-units, and a set of R-units. There is only one layer of modifiable weights in this system and these are on the connections between the A- and R-units. The main aim of the perceptrons book was to consider carefully what type of discriminations such simple perceptrons were capable of in principle and in practice. For Minsky and Papert the principles were provided by logic and by mathematics yet much of what they write about concerns the psychological plausibility of these devices. Some of these points were couched in terms of the biological and time constraints placed on the development of human brains. For although certain learning theorems regarding the capabilities of perceptrons were found to be mathematically tractable, the underlying assumptions seemed to belie neurological plausibility. For instance, even though the proof of the perceptron convergence theorem states that a perceptron will find the coefficients that exist to solve a problem, there are no guarantees that the device will succeed in a reasonable amount of time (cf. Arbib, 1987, p. 69).

There is no denying the fact that Minsky and Papert's book is a crucial text in the development of the field of connectionism, yet, rather paradoxically, even though the book is much quoted, it appears not to have been widely read. A possible reasons for this is that the book is difficult for anyone who is not a trained mathematician. Indeed, even those conversant with mathematics and perceptron research (Arbib, 1987; Block, 1970) admit that the book is difficult. As a consequence, only a very general treatment of some of the material is included here. The aim is to try to put across those aspects that are of direct psychological significance.

It is perhaps useful to set out initially some general statements about formal definitions used by Minsky and Papert. Consider the simple perceptron shown in Figure 1.7.

The A-units take as inputs outputs from the S-units. The A-units then propagate outputs to the R-units. More formally the outputs of the A-units can be considered as simple inputs known as predicates ($\varphi_1 \ldots \varphi_n$) that are either true (i.e. they equal 1) or false (i.e. they equal 0). In the example shown, a simple predicate signals the presence or absence of some primitive visual feature on the retina. In computer science the smallest point of light on a visual display is known as a pixel. Hence the simplest predicates would signal whether an individual pixel was ON or OFF. In a perceptron, the values of these predicates can be combined

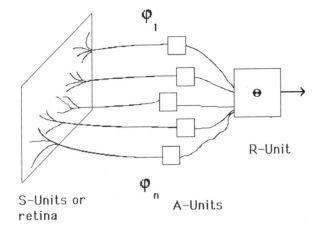

S–Units or
retina

A–Units

Figure 1.7. Schematic representation of a simple perceptron (based on Minsky and Papert, 1969, Figure 0.2). The perceptron comprises a retina to which a set of A-units are connected. The A-units are designated by the φs. In this figure each A-unit samples three retinal points. There is a single R-unit that computes the sum of its inputs (from the A-units) and compares this sum to its threshold, θ. If the sum is greater than its threshold the unit fires. (From Minsky and Papert, 1998, adapted with permission, *see* p. xiv.)

in particular ways by applying a function that takes these values and computes an output. As before, the term 'function' refers to a method for mapping a set of inputs on to a set of outputs.

It is true that there are an indefinite number of functions that could be used, but in perceptrons the R-units simply take a weighted sum of the products of the states of afferent A-units and the weights on the corresponding connections. The value of this function (or the output of the R-unit) can itself be considered to be a complex predicate (ψ) that is either true or false. Remember the perceptron was primarily considered to be a pattern-recognition device, consequently many of the complex predicates discussed by Minsky and Papert concern geometry. The general aim was to consider the kinds of distinctions that the perceptron could make between classes of input patterns presented on the retina. Initially, the retina was characterized as a 2-D plane of S-units. The S-units could be ON or OFF to the extent that ON signalled the presence and OFF signalled the absence of part of the input pattern. Patterns of 0s and 1s therefore characterized the input and, in Minsky and Papert's notation, the character 'X' denoted a given pattern.

Rather surprisingly, though, in order to discuss some geometrical transformations the retina was taken to be a torus. The retina was redefined in this manner in order to derive proofs about continuous pattern transformations. Minsky and Papert were interested in the sorts of pattern transformations that simple perceptrons could deal with. For a pattern-recognition device to be useful in any general sense, it should be able to operate in respect of certain pattern transformations. This is because, overwhelmingly, in the real world the identity of a stimulus remains constant over certain transformations such as rigid translations and rotations. For example, the letter 'F' remains the same pattern regardless of whether it is shifted up/down, left/right, i.e. translated; or, whether it is rotated. Given the ecological importance of these facts the aim was to offer formal proofs of the sorts of transformations that a perceptron could in principle deal with.

The general point was that a simple perceptron should be able to take instances of input patterns and assign them to the correct category. In turn the correct category assignment is externally defined by a teacher who is supplying the feedback during training. For example, the perceptron in learning the complex predicate 'the input depicts a circle' should be able to signal true, whenever the input pattern X corresponds to a circle, otherwise it should signal false. In Minsky and Papert's notation the output contingencies are given by:

$$\psi_{circle}(X) = \begin{cases} 1 \text{ if X is a circle} \\ 0 \text{ otherwise} \end{cases} \tag{1.4}$$

Ideally this predicate (i.e. the $\psi_{circle}(X)$) should signal 1 whenever a circle is presented irrespective of its size, position and 'orientation'.

Although such problems are easily identifiable with those facing the human visual system, Minsky and Papert deal with a number of other complex predicates that are perhaps not so obviously associated. Of the figural predicates they deal with, three were: (a) connectivity – whether the input pattern depicts a connected figure; (b) convexity – whether the input pattern depicts a convex figure; and, (c) (for want of a better term) solidity – whether a figure contains one or more holes. Whereas all these predicates concern the geometrical aspects of figures, connectivity and solidity are also topological features: a connected figure remains connected irrespective of any form of continuous distortion such as knotting and stretching. Certain kinds of stretching can render a convex line straight.

It is difficult to be clear about how to classify other predicates that Minsky and Papert discuss. For example, they discuss the EXOR, parity, and, 'symmetry along a line' predicates. Taking the latter first, 'symmetry along a line' seems very much a kind of perceptual predicate. With this predicate the device must be able to distinguish whether an input pattern is symmetrical with respect to a certain point. From the human psychology literature it is clear that symmetry is an extremely important perceptual characteristic (see Barlow & Reeves, 1979).

EXOR has been considered in some detail above. An alternative way of thinking about it is that the device, in learning EXOR, learns to signal when the retina is completely covered (1,1) or empty (0,0) versus when only a subset of the points are covered as is the case with (0,1) and (1,0). Minsky and Papert discuss only this interpretation of EXOR, yet there are other reasons why it is of psychological import. Two examples will be described. The first was pointed out to me by Content (personal communication) and concerns a selective attention task designed by Garner (1974). The task is known as condensation. Consider four stimuli composed of the different combinations of two featural values on two dimensions. The stimuli can be referred to as: pattern 1 – $D_1F_1D_2F_1$ (i.e. dimension 1/feature 1 plus dimension 2/feature 1); pattern 2 – $D_1F_2D_2F_2$; pattern 3 – $D_1F_1D_2F_2$; and, pattern 4 – $D_1F_2D_2F_1$. There is an exact correspondence between this set of patterns and the inputs that define the EXOR problem. The four patterns map on to 00, 11, 01 and 10, respectively. Moreover, as with EXOR, in the condensation task the patterns 00 and 11 are mapped onto one response and 01 and 10 are mapped onto another. In being able to do this form of classification task, humans are solving an EXOR problem.

The second example of a psychological EXOR problem relates to something known as the negative patterning task (Kehoe, 1988). With this task, an animal in a learning experiment is presented with random series of three kinds of trials. These trials are where: (i) one conditioned stimulus (CSA) precedes the unconditioned stimulus (US), (ii) a second conditioned stimulus is used (CSB), and, (iii) the compound of CSA and CSB is presented. The animal solves this problem by responding in the presence of either CSA or CSB alone, and, by not responding to the compound. This is again an example of solving an EXOR problem.

Parity is a little more difficult to consider, even though EXOR is special case of parity. Parity distinguishes between patterns comprising an odd and an even number of components. Minsky and Papert deal with the cases where an odd and an even number of points on the retina are illuminated. EXOR is a parity problem because when the device correctly outputs a 1 this signals the presence of one and only one input being ON. From a psychological point of view, there seems little sense why the visual system should be sensitive to this kind of parity. There must be other reasons as to why this kind of predicate is viewed as being important. This issue will be dealt with at length below. It turns out, however, that the argument is not so much a defence of the psychological necessity of the brain having to solve parity problems, but more a claim about the impractical solution arrived at by a perceptron.

Having considered the types of problems that Minsky and Papert devised for perceptrons, it is now appropriate to look at how they actually examined these devices. A primary aim of the work was to look at the sorts of predicates that simple perceptrons could in principle learn given various critical assumptions about wiring. Two sorts of simple perceptrons were considered: namely, diameter-limited and order-limited perceptrons. Figure 1.8a shows a diameter-limited perceptron. Figure 1.8b shows an order-limited perceptron. In both sorts of perceptrons the limitations on wiring apply to the connections between the A-units and the retina.

Minsky and Papert divided the general problem of pattern recognition into two stages. At the first stage the idea was to let the computation proceed by allowing

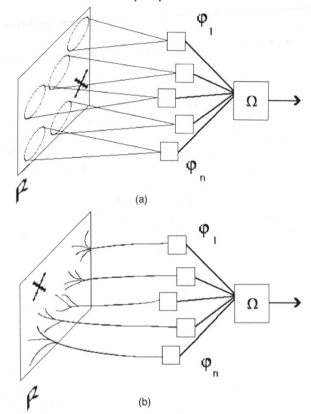

(a)

(b)

Figure 1.8. (a) A schematic representation of a diameter-limited perceptron. (b) A schematic representation of an order-limited perceptron.
(From Minsky and Papert, 1988, adapted with permission, *see* p. xiv.)

many 'primitive' visual features to be analysed in parallel. At the second stage the
results of the feature analysis were combined and some decision was arrived at
about the nature of the pattern presented on the retina. The overall desire was to
have an account in which complex pattern characteristics are decomposed and
analysed by primitive feature detectors (the φ predicates in Figure 1.8). Minsky
and Papert argued that if no restrictions are placed on the types of predicates that
are allowed, then the problem of pattern recognition becomes trivial. For
instance, one predicate could simply be allowed to compute the desired pattern
characteristic (like 'symmetry-along-a-line'). However, such a manoeuvre avoids
the problem of explaining how such a pattern characteristic is actually
recognized. Therefore Minsky and Papert argued that the A-unit (the predicates)
should be restricted in some sense and they chose to analyse the restrictions
imposed by diameter- and order-limitations. In the main they discussed order-
limited perceptrons, but initially some properties of diameter-limited perceptrons
were of interest.

Diameter-limited perceptrons

With diameter-limited perceptrons the receptive field of a given A-unit is defined with respect to a central point on the retina. The diameter of the receptive field is defined relative to this centre point. Wiring between the retina and a given A-unit was limited to the S-units within the circle described. Although diameter-limited perceptrons are of subsidiary interest in the perceptrons book an interesting aside is that Rosenblatt discusses one case where the distribution of connections in a diameter-limited perceptron is Gaussian. That is, the number of connections are most densely packed at the centre of the receptive field and the number of connections decreases according to a normal distribution with increases in distance from the centre. The identical assumption about wiring has recently been used by Linsker (1986a, 1986b, 1986c) in his model of the developing visual system (see Chapter 3). For ease of exposition, this kind of wiring will be referred to as Gaussian wiring.

The main result that Minsky and Papert reported about diameter-limited perceptrons was that such devices cannot deal with the predicate 'connectivity' (see Figure 1.9). The proof of this result is worth repeating here. Firstly, consider the four figures X_{00}, X_{01}, X_{10} and X_{11} shown in Figure 1.9. The problem is for the perceptron to be able to distinguish the unconnected patterns X_{00} and X_{11} from the connected patterns X_{01} and X_{01}. The receptive fields of three groups of A-units are shown. Group 1 units sample only the left-hand side of the retina, group 2 units only the middle of the retina and group 3 units only the right-hand side of the retina. These sets of A-units link up to a single R-unit which is computing the weighted sum of these units according to the following condition:

$$\left[\underset{\text{group 1}}{\Sigma \alpha_\varphi \varphi(X)} + \underset{\text{group 2}}{\Sigma \alpha_\varphi \varphi(X)} + \underset{\text{group 3}}{\Sigma \alpha_\varphi \varphi(X)} - \theta \right] > 0 \qquad (1.5)$$

Although the expression (1.5) may look horrendous, it is reasonably straightforward. The three main terms in the expression each correspond to the sums of inputs for each group of A-units. The R-unit adds these values up and compares this total with its threshold value as specified by θ. If the total is greater than the threshold then the difference between its input and its threshold is positive (i.e. greater than 0), hence the unit comes ON. In this case the input is a connected pattern. If this difference is not positive then the R-unit should not fire for now the input is not a connected pattern. Minsky and Papert showed that a diameter-limited perceptron cannot learn to distinguish connected from unconnected patterns. A sketch of their proof is now included. This proof requires that the R-unit only comes ON if an unconnected pattern is presented.

When X_{00} is presented the R-unit should remain OFF. When X_{10} is presented it should come ON. The only group of units affected across this pattern change is group 1. That is, the only group of units that can distinguish between the two patterns is group 1. The critical feature difference between the two patterns occurs

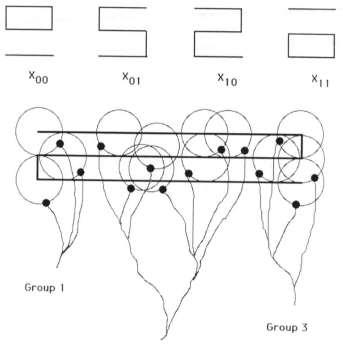

Figure 1.9. Connectivity and a limitation of diameter-limited perceptrons. This perceptron has three A-units each with their corresponding group of input lines. The three groups are, respectively, labelled group 1, group 2 and group 3. Each input line samples from a circular receptive field of retinal points. X_{00} and X_{11} are not connected figures. X_{01} and X_{10} are connected figures. The figure helps demonstrate how a diameter-limited perceptron cannot learn to distinguish connected from the unconnected figures. See text for a full explanation. (From Minsky and Papert, 1988, adapted with permission, *see* p. xiv.)

in the receptive field of the group 1 units. Consequently, the outputs from group 1 should increase in order to make the overall weighted sum at the R-unit greater than the threshold. Functionally, the group 1 units should respond more vigorously in the presence of a vertical line at the bottom left of the figure (as it appears in X_{10}) than when such a line is absent (as in X_{00}). A similar argument holds in making the change from X_{00} to X_{01}. Here the outputs from group 2 are the only ones that should increase. Again the group 2 units should respond more vigorously in the presence of a vertical line at the bottom right of the figure (as it appears in X_{01}) than when such a line is absent (as is the case in X_{00}). Having made these changes the net responds correctly and vigorously to the connected figures (X_{01} and X_{10}). It also behaves correctly in not responding to the unconnected figure X_{00}. However, in making the changes necessary to deal with these three patterns the perceptron will respond very vigorously when presented with the unconnected figure X_{11}. This is clearly wrong because that pattern is not a connected figure. The general conclusion therefore is that the diameter-limited perceptron cannot learn to distinguish connected from unconnected figures.

Having shown this proof, Minsky and Papert stressed two points. Firstly, that the proof has nothing to do with either learning or probability theory. All it concerns is relating pattern geometry to the algebra of weighted predicates. Secondly, they stretch a biological moral concerning visual processing in animals. Even though there are real cells that do possess diameter-limited receptive fields, something more than 'neurosynaptic "summation" (Minsky & Papert, 1969, p. 14) is needed for the animal to discern connectedness. As Minsky has stated, it is impossible to distinguish connected from unconnected patterns by simply 'adding up the evidence', because all the information about the relations between the parts of the figures is lost (Minsky, 1987, p. 202).

Order-limited perceptrons

In contrast to diameter-limited perceptrons, order-limited perceptrons are simply those in which the number of connections between S-units and A-units is limited. The number of connections to each A-unit can vary from 1 to the nth order of the perceptron. So with an order-2 perceptron the maximum number of connections to any A-unit is 2. The order of a perceptron is given by the maximum number of connections to any one unit in the system. The overall concern with limitations on wiring was paramount for Minsky and Papert. It was central to their analyses of whether solutions found for perceptrons with 'toy' examples on small problems would generalise to the larger problems that the human brain has to deal with. Part of the exercise was to examine whether a perceptron of finite order could solve a particular problem. Clearly, if the order of a perceptron scales with the size of the problem, say, by increasing with the number of patterns or by increasing with the size of the retina, then the eventual system can break the bounds of neurological credibility. Such a case would be where the order of a perceptron is greater than the known number of connections in the brain.

A critical point, which has been mainly ignored in the new connectionist literature, is that some of the conclusions arrived by Minsky and Papert critically depend on assumptions about order. In summary, what they showed was the following. Firstly, consider the geometric predicates. Minsky and Papert showed that convexity is of limited order, in fact it is an order-3 predicate. As long as A-units are wired up to S-units that are collinear then each A-unit needs only three connections (see Figure 1.10).

Block (1970) objects somewhat to this demonstration because although Minsky and Papert showed that convexity is of limited order, the solution requires

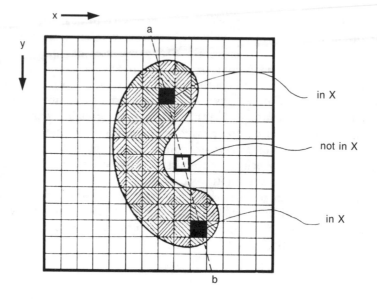

Figure 1.10. An example of how an order-limited perceptron can discern convex figures. Each of its A-units must connect to three retinal points that align. Furthermore, whereas the middle point must not coincide with part of the figure, the outer two points must coincide with parts of the figure (in the manner shown). See text for further details. (From Minksy and Papert, 1969, reprinted with permission, *see* p. xiv.)

essentially an infinite number of A-units. Hence he claims that convexity should really be considered to be of infinite order (p. 518).

In addition, Minsky and Papert showed that connectedness is not of finite order. At least one A-unit must be wired to a proportion of the number of S-units. Therefore connectedness is said to 'scale' with the size of the retina. A similar result obtains with the parity predicate (see below). EXOR was also shown to be an order-2 predicate, a result that should be discussed alongside McCulloch's earlier finding. McCulloch reported that a McCulloch and Pitts neuron with only two input lines could not compute EXOR. In comparison, Minsky and Papert showed that EXOR is an order-2 problem. What this means is that a simple perceptron with only two S-units must possess more than one A-unit. At least one of the A-units must be wired to both S-units for the device to be capable of learning and hence computing EXOR (and its negation). The remaining 14 Boolean predicates are of order 1.

The problem with EXOR can be explained more formally. Assume that the two retinal S-units are x and y respectively and that the weights on their connections to the A-unit are α and β. θ stands for the A-unit's threshold. For the EXOR predicate to be true the following inequality must be satisfied:

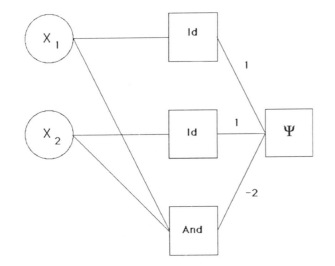

Figure 1.11. Example of a simple perceptron that can compute EXOR (based on Fogelman Soulie, 1988). There are two input points, X_1 and X_2. Three A-units sample these two points in the manner shown. The top two units are each connected to a different retinal point. These units come ON whenever their corresponding input line is ON. The third A-unit computes an AND of the two input points. This unit only comes ON when both X_1 and X_2 are ON. Weights on the connections between the A-units and the R-unit are as shown. Simple hand calculations reveal that the R-unit does indeed signal an EXOR of X_1 and X_2.

$$\alpha x + \beta y > \theta \tag{1.6}$$

For this inequality to be satisfied the following conditions on the coefficients must in turn be satisfied. The conditions are:

(i) $\psi_{EXOR}(1,0) = 1 \Rightarrow 1.\ \alpha + 0.\ \beta > \theta \Rightarrow \alpha > \theta$
(ii) $\psi_{EXOR}(0,1) = 1 \Rightarrow 0.\ \alpha + 1.\ \beta > \theta \Rightarrow \beta > \theta$
(iii) $\psi_{EXOR}(1,1) = 0 \Rightarrow 1.\alpha + 1.\beta < \theta \Rightarrow \alpha + \beta < \theta$
(iv) $\psi_{EXOR}(0,0) = 0 \Rightarrow 0 < \theta$

As McClelland and Rumelhart (1988) state, it is not possible to have both α and β greater than θ in cases (i) and (ii) and at the same time have their sum less than θ in case (iii). In other words, it is impossible to satisfy the four conditions on the coefficients with the simple perceptron described. This shows that EXOR is not a linearly separable problem. The same result applies to the negation of EXOR.

It remains true that the result with EXOR has been widely misconstrued, however. It is easy to demonstrate that a simple perceptron can compute EXOR given the right sort of wiring. Figure 1.11, taken from Fogelman Soulie (1988), shows such a perceptron.

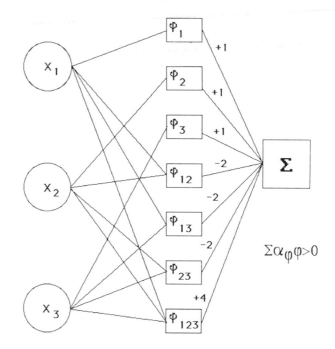

Figure 1.12. An example of a simple perceptron that solves the parity predicate. The wiring and the weights are critically important. (From Minsky and Papert, 1969, reprinted with permission, *see* p. xiv.)

As a consequence, it is simply wrong to assert, as Johnson-Laird (1987, p, 184) has done, that no simple perceptron can compute the EXOR function or that EXOR can only be computed with a perceptron with more than one layer of modifiable weights. Further points concerning EXOR will be considered below.

Concerning the general predicate parity, Minsky and Papert proved that the order of parity scales with the size of the retina. In other words, at least one of the A-units must be wired up to all of the S-units. Figure 1.12 shows an example of such a scheme.

Given the plethora of real neural connections this result might not be construed as worrying. What is worrying, however, is that the size of the coefficients grows exponentially with respect to the size of the retina. The real concern is that if the weights on the connections are to make any neurological sense, then the corresponding numerical quantities must be relatively manageable in biological terms. Immensely large numbers such as those demanded by the solution to the parity problem make no biological sense whatsoever.

The perceptron account of parity is also attacked by Minsky and Papert on other grounds. They note that the information capacity needed just to store the coefficients is equivalent to that needed to store the actual training patterns themselves. In other words, the device might be better off storing direct replicas of the input patterns in some form of localist representation rather than attempting to build distributed representations across a set of interconnected units.

Perceptrons as computational devices

In closing it is perhaps useful to consider why so much has been made of predicates like EXOR and parity. There has been no explicit discussion of these issues in the connectionist literature. It has never really been spelt out why these predicates might be useful in terms of brain functioning. Some ideas concerning the geometric nature of some of the predicates have already been covered. Here other considerations will be dealt with.

It seems that the only consistent account of why the set of predicates discussed by Minsky and Papert might be important is on the grounds that the brain computes similar functions to those computed by a digital computer. Following the work of McCulloch, the aim seems to have been to show how perceptrons are not capable of constituting a universal computing machine. At the very least what Minsky and Papert showed was that a universal computing machine cannot be built from a single layer of neurons of finite order. Nevertheless, some of the predicates studied by Minsky and Papert are fundamental to binary arithmetic. So, for example, the EXOR function corresponds to addition modulo 2 (see Arbib, 1989). Indeed the EXOR function occurs in the instruction set of some computers in order to do subtraction. By masking a binary number with an equivalent number of 1s, the end result is the complement of the number (EXOR is a limited case of parity checking: the predicate distinguishes between only 1 input line being ON and the cases where neither or both are ON). The complement of a number is important in this system because subtraction reduces to adding a complement. Subtraction in a sense reduces to addition and it is far easier to form a complement of a number than to design special purpose facilities to do subtraction.

It is more difficult to be clear about the general status of the parity predicate. Parity checking is used in information transmission systems as a rough test of whether the transmitted and received signals are of the same size. It is perhaps stretching the imagination too much to assume that the brain uses parity checking either for a similar purpose or indeed at all. Parity checking can be used in other binary arithmetic applications although Minsky and Papert only argued about the heuristic value of the result with the parity predicate (p. 240). They claimed that working with the predicate revealed a firm result about the computational limitations of simple perceptrons that generalized to other situations.

It seems therefore that interest in some of the predicates studied by Minsky and Papert is justified in terms of binary arithmetic. For example, consider another predicate Minsky and Papert discussed, namely, 'translation-along-a-line'. It is true that translation-along-a-line has a geometric application: due to separation of the eyes in the head the image in the left retina is a translation of the image in the right retina. In solving binocular correspondence, i.e. the problem of matching up the two images, the brain must somehow be solving the translation problem. Nevertheless, translation-along-a-line predicate has an application in conventional computers when they do binary arithmetic. Translation-along-a-line is useful for keeping track of the contents of a shift register. Any number in binary arithmetic is represented as a set of 0s and 1s and in a conventional computer each number is rendered into a fixed number of 0s and 1s, say eight digits. In order to do some form of arithmetic operations a shift register is used. At appropriate stages in the computation a number (i.e. a string of 0s and 1s) is transferred into the shift register. The register takes one pattern of eight digits. For example, multiplication (by 2) corresponds to shifting bits to the left (e.g. 1×2 is rendered into binary as $00000001 \rightarrow 00000010$), division (by 2) corresponds to shifting bits to the right. Translation-along-a-line could be usefully employed to detect the overflow conditions on these shifting operations. For example, the pattern 10010111 when multiplied by 2 no longer gives a result that conforms to translation along a line: the register overflows because there are only enough places to hold eight digits. A violation of the translation therefore signals that the register has overflowed.

In summary, most of the predicates studied by Minsky and Papert are important owing to their significance in terms of pattern recognition. The argument is that if the perceptron is to be taken as a model of human pattern recognition then it should be able to deal with those patterns that humans deal with. However, a different set of issues in the book relate to perceptrons as computational devices. Here the subtext seems to be that if perceptrons are to be taken as computational devices then they should be able to account for the primitive binary arithmetic operations that any computational device must be able to deal with. From a psychological point of view, the underlying assumption is that the results with predicates relevant to doing binary arithmetic are only of interest if the brain is construed as being a binary computer. By implication, if perceptrons can do binary arithmetic and if the brain is construed as a binary computer then perceptrons may be taken as a model of the brain. Of course, if this line of reasoning is not accepted, then some of the demonstrations of the limitations of perceptrons are completely irrelevant to psychological theory.

Coda

This brief sketch of the early history of connectionism has concluded with a discussion of Minsky and Papert's demonstrations of the limitations and capabilities of one kind of perceptron. Immediately, following the publication of these results, the general academic community readily accepted the conclusions about the limitations, interpreted them to be true of all perceptrons and, no longer took any serious interest in the research. For over the next ten years, and barring a few exceptional cases, researchers ceased to carry out neural network research. However, since the the turn of the 1980s, attitudes have changed dramatically and connectionism has recently been been hailed as a paradigm shift for psychology (Schneider, 1987).

The connectionist renaissance has no doubt arisen because of a number different factors. Nevertheless, the major impetus concerns the development of techniques that overcome some of the limitations of simple perceptrons. In particular much excitement surrounds new learning algorithms. It is to these that the discussion now turns.

Chapter 2

Memory and learning in neural networks

Following the publication of the perceptrons book, interest in neural networks quickly dissipated and for over the next ten years, only a handful of individuals (e.g., J. A. Anderson, Grossberg and Kohonen) continued to show any serious interest in these devices. The information-processing framework was in its ascendency and cognitive psychology flourished as a discipline centred on the flow-diagram conceptions of internal representations and processes. Work in mainstream cognitive psychology typically dwelt on a limited aspect of adult performance and in the rush to posit the next boxes-and-arrows 'model' of this or that aspect of cognition (cf. Newell, 1973), many simply ignored problems about how the putative systems might have developed. It is perhaps not so surprising therefore that research into neural networks only began to be taken seriously again when interesting results were published about learning. It became difficult to ignore systems capable of modelling aspects of adult cognition when they also provided an account of how such abilities might have developed.

Most of the remaining chapters of this book will deal with examples of recent connectionist models that primarily deal with adult human cognition. Some of these models use the principles of learning developed during the early 1980s. However, with these models learning is treated as something of an aside and the main interest is with simulating mature adult performance. It is in this chapter that a sample of new connectionist learning procedures are discussed in detail. An aim is to describe how new connectionism has addressed the limitations of perceptrons and to show how some of the new connectionist learning procedures are said to overcome some of these limitations.

Parallel distributed processing and representation in neural networks

It is quite striking that from meagre beginnings in the early 1980s, there is now a vast and growing literature on a plethora of connectionist systems and learning procedures. It is simply impossible to address each of them here. As a consequence, all that will be attempted will be a review of those instances that are either of major influence, are oft-quoted in the psychological literature or are both. However, before considering the details of the learning procedures, it is important first to consider some very general characteristics of new connectionist models. Many follow on naturally from the early perceptron research, so some of the text is simply an embellishment of some of the material presented in Chapter 1.

All connectionist models comprise independent processing units (like binary threshold logic units) that are interconnected. These interconnections have associated weights. Weights may be fixed or they may vary. They may be of a positive value and hence define an excitatory connection; they may be of a negative value and hence define an inhibitory connection; or they may have a value of zero. A weight equal to zero signals that the connection is not used. The units and their connections define a network. Given certain constraints within the network it is sometimes possible to define layers of units. Typically there is an input layer of units – these units receive input directly from the environment; there is an output layer of units – these units provide output from the network; and, finally, there may well be one or more layers of hidden units – these units neither receive direct input from, nor produce output directly to, the environment.

Layers are either defined topologically or with respect to the types of connections in the network. For instance, the units within a layer may either have no interconnections or possess only inhibitory connections. Meanwhile both excitatory and inhibitory connections may exist between layers. In the simplest multiple layered systems, the units within a layer are not interconnected.

The pattern of activity across a layer of units refers to the instantaneous states of the units in a given layer. Given that the units can be in one of a possible number of states, at any given time, then different representations correspond to the different patterns of activity across the same set of units. In this sense the same set of units can specify a number of different representations.

Distributed representation is typically contrasted with localist representation. In localist schemes one unit, and only one, specifies a unique representation. As Hanson and Burr (1990, p. 477) note, 'In the simplest kind of local representation, inputs are mapped consistently onto the correct category.' One unit encodes that category. The archetypal localist representation is conveyed by the grandmother detector discussed widely in the literature on the neurophysiological instantiation of certain theories of pattern recognition (e.g. Barlow, 1972). Indeed it is only at the level of instantiating a representation in hardware that the localist/distributed distinction makes any sense. A given instance may well be treated within the abstract representational system as being localist even though it is captured by a pattern of activity across a particular and unique set of units.

Traditional artificial intelligence (AI) has only dealt with localist representation schemes and in so far as these have proved effective, it is pertinent to consider what if any are the merits of distributed processing and representation. Typically, the case for distributed systems is built around points about (a) neural plausibility, and (b) formal advantages to do with the temporal processing characteristics of these systems. For instance, Winograd and Cowan (1963) considered the overall reliability of information-processing systems comprising many interconnected unreliable components. This work is very much in the spirit of the earlier work carried out Von Neumann and McCulloch (see McCulloch, 1965). Here the issues focused on how systems comprising many unreliable units, such as real neurons, could perform reliably overall. Von Neumann and McCulloch were primarily concerned with systems in which the units computed outputs on a probabilistic basis. Winograd and Cowan, however, went further and showed that such systems, in using distributed representations, would be more reliable than one based on localist representations. This point demonstrates properties of distributed systems that Block (1962) examined in his paper on a simulated perceptron.

Block's (1962) main interests were with: (1) resistance to noise, and (2) graceful degradation. Concerning resistance to noise, Block considered a perceptron taught to discriminate the character 'X' from the character 'E'. Here the learning was assessed (a) when visual noise was added to the characters by randomly switching on an additional 30% of inappropriate input units, and (b) when the actual feedback by the teacher was incorrect 30% of the time. In both cases, although performance was impaired relative to the 'noise-free' situation, the device did learn to discriminate the characters. This ability to deal with noisy inputs is referred to as 'resistance to noise'.

Graceful degradation refers to the breakdown in the ability of distributed systems to keep functioning effectively when some of the components (i.e. connections and/or units) are damaged (cf. Winograd & Cowan, 1963). Block systematically removed units from a test network and showed that the decline in discriminatory performance was gradual rather than sudden and that it varied directly with the amount of damage to the system. It is generally accepted that these properties are quite unlike traditional AI systems that are based on serial sequential processing and localist representations. For as Rumelhart and McClelland (1986a) note, removal of any part of this kind of system is very likely to have catastrophic consequences: the system will simply crash.

Having dealt with neurophysiological considerations it is now possible to consider arguments regarding the temporal characteristics of neural nets. Consideration of the temporal characteristics of parallel processing systems has occupied a number of researchers who remain outside the new connectionist framework (see Anderson, 1976, 1979; Hayes-Roth, 1979; Townsend, 1972). This is even though many points they make are of relevance to new connectionist models. Of the many important points they make, all that needs mention here is that certain models of the parallel search of a store of information are able to retrieve desired material in very few computational steps. For instance, Fahlman has shown that with a parallel search of a semantic net, time to access a given node can be proportional to the depth of the node in the network (see Fahlman, 1979, 1981, for a comprehensive discussion of this point). In contrast, it is typically the case that serial search procedures scale with the size of the store to be searched and the amount of information to be found. It is this contrast between serial and parallel processing that is sometimes used to argue for the psychological credibility of parallel distributed processing systems.

Indeed, it is generally accepted today that collectively the properties of resistance to damage, graceful degradation and the favourable timing characteristics provide parallel distributed processing (PDP) systems with neurological and psychological plausibility.

Distributed representation as coarse coding

In 1974 Milner made several observations about the fidelity of information coding in the visual system that in many ways pre-date ideas about distributed representation and coarse coding put forward in the new connectionist literature. Discussion of Milner's ideas follows shortly. Some general points about coarse coding will be made initially.

As Hinton (1984) notes, a coarse coding scheme refers to a distributed system in which 'each (input) feature activates many different units and each unit is activated by many different units' (p. 11). In contrast, in some distributed schemes, each of the units signals the presence/absence of a single input feature: each unit only encodes a particular feature. Hence it is quite possible to have distributed systems that do not use coarse coding. By way of example consider three systems for encoding the letter 'L'. In first, the coarse coding scheme, each of the constituent features of the letter (e.g. the horizontal and vertical bars and their angle of incidence) will activate many encoding units. It is the pattern of activity across these units that stands for the representation of the letter. Moreover, it may well prove difficult to say what exactly a particular unit is encoding because many features activate it to varying degrees. In contrast, in the non-coarse coding distributed scheme, although the letter will be encoded by many units, each of the units is only activated by one particular input feature. For instance, in this scheme one unit encodes the horizontal bar, one encodes the vertical bar and one encodes the angle. Nevertheless, it is again the pattern of activity across these units that stands for the representation of the letter. Finally, in a localist scheme a single 'L' detector is activated when the corresponding input letter is presented. Each kind of scheme has its advantages and disadvantages and, indeed, many models in the literature use both localist and coarse coding units. Nevertheless, the central issue

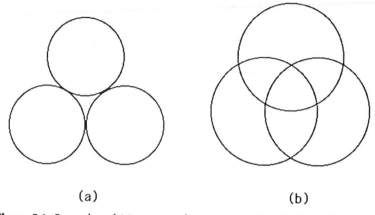

(a)   (b)

Figure 2.1. Examples of (a) non-overlapping receptive fields, and, (b) overlapping receptive fields (From Milner, 1974, adapted with permission, *see* p. xv.)

in discussing the different schemes relates to the minimum number of units needed to maintain accurate encoding of input. An early discussion of this issue was provided by Milner (1974).

Milner (1974) takes the example of retinal acuity and uses this to make many important points about coarse coding schemes in general. He considers a system in which a pair of cells map onto a third cell and this cell operates by forming an AND gate of the two inputs (see Chapter 1). The two input cells possess separate and non-overlapping receptive fields and the third cell only comes ON if both input lines are active. Milner considers the case where the input cells respond to the presence of the end-points of lines. As a consequence, each AND cell in the system detects the distance between the end-points of lines on the retina. AND cells were therefore termed 'distance cells'. Such an hypothetical system could account for how the human visual system is configured to detect straight lines. However, a problem with such a system is that it would appear to need an inordinate number of distance cells: one for each possible line. Clearly therefore, this is not a plausible account of how the human line-detection system works, if distance cells are to be equated with real neurons. A different method of encoding must therefore be used and according to Milner the acuity of the visual system is based on a system using input cells with overlapping, not non-overlapping, receptive fields.

In considering a system of input cells with overlapping fields, Milner had the important insight that 'the greater the overlap of fields, the fewer cells it takes to provide a given acuity' (1974, p. 527). This is easily demonstrated by contrasting two schemes where, respectively, the fields are non-overlapping and overlapping (see Figure 2.1).

In this example the same absolute area of the retina is covered in both cases. However, although the receptive fields of the three cells are larger in the overlapping than the non-overlapping case, the acuity is greater in the overlapping than the non-overlapping case. Whereas in the non-overlapping case there are three discriminable areas (the three circles), in the overlapping case there are seven discriminable areas given by the separate circles and their intersections. Acuity, in these schemes, is given by how far a target point has to move across the retina in order to receive a different encoding. The acuity of the system is given by how far the point has to move in order to fall into another discriminable area. From Figure 2.1 it can be seen that in the non-overlapping case (where the diameter of the fields is 1°), a point must move through 1° on average to accrue a different coding. In the non-overlapping case a target point has to move through a small fraction of a degree in order to accrue a different encoding. Therefore acuity is higher in the overlapping than in the non-overlapping case. This is even though the overall receptive field size is 20% greater in the overlapping case than in the non-overlapping case.

Milner draws several important conclusions. For instance, he points out that a system comprising units with overlapping receptive fields needs comparably fewer units than does one with units possessing non-overlapping fields. However, the benefits that accrue in positing fewer (overlapping) units may well be offset by the complexity in encoding gained by the system. In the non-overlapping case the position of a point on the retina can be read off from a single unit. With the overlapping case the position of a point must be decoded from the pattern of activity over several units. Different positions will give rise to different patterns of activity over the units. It is because of this that the overlapping case can be considered to be an example of a coarse coding scheme.

Most of Milner's conclusions about coarse coding schemes are reiterated in the chapter by Hinton, McClelland and Rumelhart (1986) in the first of the PDP volumes (McClelland, Rumelhart and the PDP Research Group, 1986; henceforth PDP/1). Hinton *et al.*, however, do note that problems arise with the overlapping scheme if more than one feature (or point of light in Milner's scheme) is simultaneously present in the same receptive field. Here the system will not be able to resolve the presence of the two features. The general conclusion therefore is that coarse coding can be very accurate but will only be effective in certain cases. Such cases are where isolated single features occur and where many features are positioned sparsely over the input units. These limitations emphasize Milner's original concerns about the problems of decoding distributed representations.

Introduction to the formal properties of PDP systems

Having discussed some of the general characteristics of PDP systems, it is now important to now consider their detailed characteristics. Following the spirit of Rosenblatt's (1962) book, Rumelhart, Hinton and McClelland (1986) begin their

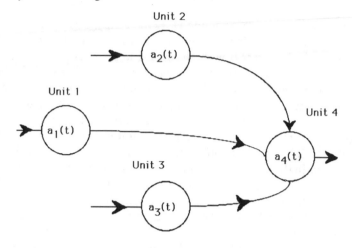

Activation of Unit 4 at time t

$$= \sum_i w_{ij} \cdot a_i(t)$$

$$= w_{14} \cdot a_1(t) + w_{24} \cdot a_2(t) + w_{34} \cdot a_3(t)$$

here i indexes Units 1 – 3, j refers to Unit 4

Figure 2.2. Schematic representation of a set of processing units. Each unit in this example computes a state of activation. At time *t* this is represented as $a_i(t)$ – the state of activation of unit a at time *t*. Unit 4 takes as input signals from units 1, 2 and 3 and computes its new state by summing these signals. Each input signal is considered in turn. Each signal is computed as the product of the weight on the input line and the state of the propagating unit (i.e. unit 1, 2 or 3). The rule of activation is therefore the sum of these products.

Having computed $a_i(t)$ this state of activation is passed through an output function. In this (simplest case) the state of activation is compared with the unit's threshold. If the state is greater than or equal to the threshold the unit fires. The unit is therefore a binary threshold unit: its output is a non-linear function of its input.

description of PDP systems by characterizing them by eight properties. These are: (i) a set of processing units; (ii) a state of activation; (iii) a pattern of connectivity; (iv) an output function; (v) a propagation rule; (vi) an activation rule; (vii) a learning rule; and (viii) an environment. Some of these properties have been discussed at length already; others still need clarification. Figure 2.2 helps illuminate some of these distinctions.

Despite the seeming clarity of these distinctions, some of the divisions are subtle and apply in only certain cases. However, every neural net is characterized by a set of units and the interconnections between the units (i.e. the pattern of connectivity). Also with every case an environment of inputs is specified. In addition, the vast majority of current neural network research concerns learning. Some of the many learning rules that exist will be discussed in detail in the rest of the chapter. Of initial concern though are the differences between the remaining properties of neural nets.

Firstly, consider the state of activation. The binary threshold logic units discussed in Chapter 1 can take on one of two states. They can either be ON or OFF. Such units are known as discrete units. Their states can be characterized by whole (or integer) numbers such as 0 and 1. Other units are known as continuous units. The states of these units are realized by fractional (or real) numbers. These units can potentially take on an infinite number of states. Both discrete and continuous units, however, compute their states from their inputs (and in some cases a unit's current state can be derived in part from its immediately prior state). This is where the rule of activation comes in. Again, one such rule was given in Chapter 1 where the state of a unit was given by the sum of the products of the weights on the connections to active units and the states of the active units. In this case the state of activation of a unit is given by this sum and the rule of activation is a rule of addition. It turns out that several other activation rules can be used and some of these will be discussed in detail later on.

As for the output function, there are cases where the output from a unit may be different from its state. For example, the state of a unit is entered into a function which in turn produces the unit's total output. This function is known as the output function. In other cases, the state of the unit is equivalent to its output.

Finally, consider the rule of propagation. Here what is being defined is the manner in which the outputs from units are combined with the weights on the relevant interconnections. The best way to think about the rule of propagation is to consider it as being the specification of what is happening to activation as it passes along the interconnections between units. So far only one rule of propagation has been discussed. This is where connections multiply their weights with the outputs from units. However, more complicated cases are possible. Special conditions obtain where some units veto, or gate, the activation spreading along the connections between other units. Mathematically, this obtains when activation from one unit is multiplied by activation from another. If either value is 0 then the contingent result is 0. Hence activation from one unit is seen to gate activation from another. Units that operate under these constraints are known as sigma-pi units (Rumelhart *et al.*, 1986) and have been used in a number of different new connectionist systems. Some relevant examples will be discussed later.

Preliminary comments about units and their interconnections

The main form of learning that has been studied in connectionist research has been learning based on some form of external feedback. Here the learning algorithm is characterized by an error-correcting procedure that alters the coefficients (i.e. the weights on the connections and the thresholds belonging to the units) in the network. From Chapter 1 it will be remembered that in applying the original perceptron learning theorem to networks with threshold logic units, both the weights and thresholds (i.e. the coefficients) were changed. When the weights were increased, the thresholds were decreased and vice versa.

Weights and thresholds

In real neural systems it is important to distinguish weights from thresholds: synapses clearly vary in their importance and cells clearly vary in their inertia to respond. However, in simulated nets sometimes it is expedient to treat the thresholds as being equivalent to weights. Here the idea is to treat each threshold as being equivalent to a negative weight on a single connection to another (abstract) unit that is continuously active. This is illustrated in Figure 2.3 as adapted from Hinton (1989b).

Such special weights as these are known as a unit's bias. The elegance of this system is that the same learning procedure treats the acquisition of appropriate weight and threshold values as a uniform process. The system does not therefore distinguish learning weights from learning thresholds and, at the very least, it simplifies the mathematical analysis of the system.

Linear versus non-linear units

Initially and for expository convenience, it is useful to consider a simple case where units do not possess thresholds. Moreover, irrespective of the finer distinction between the activation rule and the output function, it is simplest to consider a very basic system in which the units are modelled by a single input–output function. Here the output of the units is in some form of monotonic relationship to the input. For linear units this relationship is a straight line, as discussed at length in Chapter 1. For non-linear units there is some form of more complicated function relating input to output. Examples of both sorts of units are given in Figure 2.4.

Here the term 'function' merely means the mathematical description of the manner in which outputs are computed from inputs. More formally, Jordan (1986) defines a linear function according to the two equations:

$$f(cx) = cf(x) \tag{2.1}$$

$$f(x_1 + x_2) = f(x_1) + f(x_2) \tag{2.2}$$

Any function is linear if these two equations hold. Equation (2.1) means that whatever input x is multiplied by a constant c then the output will be in a

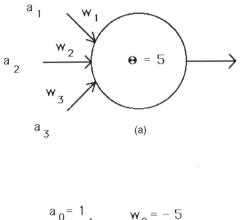

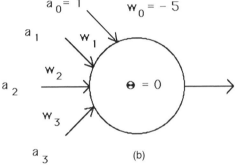

Figure 2.3. The two units shown are functionally equivalent. The (a) unit possesses three input lines and a threshold. This unit can be modelled exactly with unit (b). (b) has one more input line than (a). The extra line is always active with a value of 1. Its initial weight is −5. With (b) the ultimate value of the weight (i.e. the threshold) can be learnt in the same manner as all of weights in the system. Therefore there is a uniform manner in which all coefficients in the net can be acquired (taken from Hinton, 1989b).

corresponding proportion to c. Equation (2.2) implies that if the outputs for x_1 and x_2 are noted when x_1 and x_2 are presented separately then the sum of these two quantities will equal the total output when x_1 and x_2 are presented together. Non-linear systems violate either or both of these conditions.

There is much debate about whether it is best to deal with networks comprising only linear units, only non-linear units or a mixture of both (Anderson & Silverstein, 1978; Grossberg, 1978; Sejnowski, 1981). These considerations impinge on whether the simulated net comprises only linear units, non-linear units or both. In many ways, however, this debate is misguided from a neurological point of view. For instance, Marrocco (1986) describes the X and Y

(a)

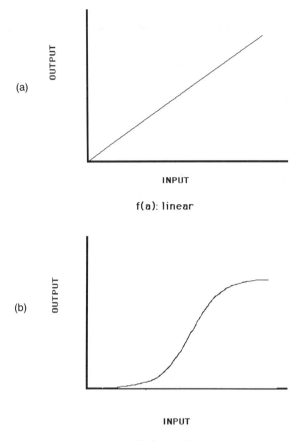

f(a): linear

(b)

INPUT

f(a): non-linear

Figure 2.4. (a) an example of a linear input–output function. (b) An example of a non-linear input–output function. In (b) the S-shaped or sigmoid function is explained more fully in the text later.

retinal ganglion cells as being, respectively, linear and non-linear summators of light intensity changes. Anderson and Silverstein (1978) make the allied point that cells typically respond linearly for only part of their overall response profile (see also Hopfield, 1982). Clearly therefore the neurophysiology is more subtle than some connectionists would have us believe.

Two further points are in order. The primary point is that real subtext of the debate about linearity/non-linearity of the processing units is about mathematics. For whereas the mathematics of linear systems are well understood and can be applied universally, each non-linear model demands a separate and difficult individual analysis (Jordan, 1986; Sejnowski, 1981). The subsidiary yet important point is that there are clear operational reasons why the simulated system is composed of linear or non-linear units. If the simulated network is to have more than one layer of modifiable weights then it is only sensible to deal with non-linear units. For as Rumelhart *et al.* (1986) state, if linear units are to be used then if something can be computed from two or more steps in one model, that same thing can be computed from a single step in another linear model with a different connectivity matrix (see PDP/1, p. 62, for an illustrative example). Consequently, with linear units there is never any need for more than one layer of modifiable weights, for these will be redundant with respect to some other model. Moreover, nothing is gained by allowing feedback in a network comprising linear units, for the same reasons. Nearly all of the advances of new connectionism are attributable to networks comprising multiple layers of non-linear units. In order to appreciate this work fully, it is first best to consider other limitations of simple one-layered systems.

Pattern associators

The vast majority of new connectionist systems have been primarily concerned in equating memorial changes with changes in the weights on the connections between processing units. There has been little work on the growth of new connections or the atrophy of connections that are no longer functionally useful (though see Mozer & Smolensky, 1989, and Kindermann & Linden, 1988, for recent counterexamples). It is therefore best to consider how weight changes might be construed as memorial changes and how a network can be said to **store** information in its connections. The easiest way to deal with these points is by considering the simplest networks known as pattern associators.

Pattern associators are perhaps the simplest associative memories because they comprise an input layer of units, an output layer of units, and one layer of modifiable connections between these two sets of units. There are no hidden layers in these systems. Typically the aim is to take a set of input patterns and train a network to associate each input pattern with a given output pattern. Procedurally there is a clear demarcation between a presentation, or training, phase and a testing phase. During training each pattern is presented in turn and weights on the modifiable connections are changed according to some learning rule. If the device is working properly at test, then when a given input pattern is presented its corresponding output pattern should accrue at the output layer. In so far as the only changes that are allowed in the system are weight changes then memorial changes are equated with weight changes. Learning in these systems reduces to adaptive changes in the weights. A given input pattern is 'recognized' when it is presented to the net and the net manages to reproduce the correct output pattern. Moreover, in so far as the correct output pattern is generated correctly at test, it seems that it must somehow be stored in the network. Yet, unlike traditional cognitive psychological accounts of memory, the net does not possess internal replicas of the output patterns. All that the net stores are values that correspond to weights on links. In this sense the type of storage of information in a PDP system is quite unlike anything that is envisaged in the type of 'localist' representational schemes typically discussed in mainstream cognitive psychology. In the PDP system what are stored are values that, when entered into some form of input–output function, reproduce the appropriate state on another set of units. Therefore it is slightly misleading to state that the net stores the actual output patterns in the weights: this is not strictly true. The type of memory exhibited by PDP models is essentially reconstructive. Memories are reconstructed by transforming patterns of activity as a function of the weights on the net's connections. All of this in turn implicates the notion of content addressable memory.

Content addressable memory

To computer scientists the notion of content-addressable memory is quite unmysterious and straightforward. To psychologists, however, this is something of an unnatural concept. It is easiest to begin by considering the example of lexical access.

Since Treisman (1960) introduced the idea of an internal store of information about single words, the idea of a mental lexicon is now widely regarded as a well-established fact. Prior to the rejuvenation of connectionism, the generally received opinion was that the lexicon comprised something akin to a card index system where each card carried the lexical information about a given word in the language. The recognition of a given word was therefore explained in terms of searching this card system in a serial fashion (see Forster, 1976) until the appropriate card was accessed. Although many variants of this simple kind of scheme have been proposed, the central ideas of localist representation and serial search abound. This is despite the fact that radically different schemes for searching and accessing information can be envisaged. Indeed many of these form the basis of a substantial literature in computer science. Perhaps the most radical of all, from the cognitive psychologist's point of view, is that of content-addressable memory.

Within computer science 'hashing' is a reasonably straightforward way of storing and accessing information in a content addressable format. By way of a simple example; suppose that a given target string of characters acts as input to the system and that an address is computed from the content of its constituent letters; e.g. the address of the string CAT might be 03/01/20 (where each two-digit number corresponds to a letter's ordinal position in the alphabet). The system only needs to go directly to that address and retrieve the information stored at that address. (For a more psychological approach to hashing see

Andreae, 1977, who considers how it might be used in simulating the acquisition of a knowledge base.)

One of the important properties of content-addressable memory is that there is a very strict mapping between the input and how and where it is stored. Essentially, the content of the inputs determines their storage. In stark contrast, in traditional AI systems, and indeed, in many programming applications, the mapping between input and storage is loose and seems almost arbitrary. PDP systems utilize content-addressable memory in a way that is different from both hashing systems and more traditional AI systems.

For example, with a pattern associator, upon the presentation of a given input, i.e. when an input pattern is clamped onto the input units, the net retrieves information from the connections between the input and output units. The content of the constituent values of the states of the input units plus the values of the weights on the connections determine what information is recalled. In this respect the content of the input determines what is recalled. However, regardless of the elegance of this approach, there are reasons to doubt that it provides a full account of human memory. At the very least it ignores the major issue of how the input makes contact with the net in the first place. The mapping of input patterns onto the net is carried out by the programmer. Therefore many fundamental problems concerning encoding of input are simply side-stepped. Such problems as these are hotly debated in the literature on human memory research (see Schacter, 1988). Moreover, they cannot be ignored if an adequate account of human performance is to be provided.

Learning in pattern associators

Two main sorts of learning rules have been used in training pattern associators: namely the Hebb rule and the Delta rule. Each will be considered briefly in turn below. For a far more detailed treatment see McClelland and Rumelhart (1988; henceforth PDP/3).

The Hebb rule

Figure 2.5 shows, in schematic form, a simple pattern associator. The units on the input layer will be indexed by the subscript i the units on the output layer by the subscript j and a given weight on the connection between the ith and jth units is known as w_{ij}. In the net shown there are eight input units and eight output units. Given this, a particular input pattern can be construed as a list of eight numbers. Each of these numbers corresponds to the state or activation level of a given input unit. In the simplest case a unit is either ON (i.e. its state is 1) or it is OFF (i.e. its state is 0). An input pattern to this particular net would therefore be an ordered list of eight numbers. Formalized in this way an input to the net is construed as

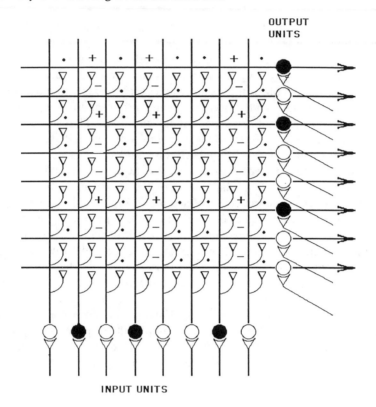

Figure 2.5. Pattern associator comprising eight input units and eight output units. Every input unit is connected to every output unit. All connections are weighted. A '+' signifies an excitatory link and a '–' signifies an inhibitory link. (From McClelland and Rumelhart, 1988, adapted with permission, *see* p. xv.)

being a vector. A set of inputs constitute a set of vectors. Each input vector is paired with a corresponding output vector and in the autoassociative mode each input vector is paired with itself. Each input pattern forms the corresponding output pattern. In the autoassociative mode, the aim is to get the net to reproduce the input pattern over the output units. Each input vector is presented to the net in turn and the weights on the corresponding connections are changed according to Hebbian learning rule. The change in the weight, δw_{ij}, is given by:

$$\delta w_{ij} = \varepsilon.a_i.a_j \tag{2.3}$$

a_i is the state of the input unit i.

a_j is the state of the output unit j.
ε is a constant of proportionality known as the learning rate.

In words, the rule says that the change in weights for any given input pattern is given by multiplying the learning rate by the state of the input unit and the state of the corresponding output unit. Two things are made transparent by this rule. Firstly, that there will be no change in the weight if either or both of the units are OFF. Both units must be ON for the weights to change. The rule is correlational in nature because changes only accrue on connections between co-active units. All that the weight changes are sensitive to are the pairwise correlations between states of input–output units. Secondly, the size of the weight change is scaled by the size of the learning rate: bigger changes go with larger learning rates. An additional point relates to the kind of learning that is being carried out here.

Essentially, connectionist learning regimes can be classified as either supervised learning, unsupervised learning or reinforcement learning (Klimasauskas, 1988). Taking the latter first, reinforcement learning occurs when an external teacher indicates only whether the output is right or wrong for each presentation. An example of reinforcement learning is that provided by the perceptron. Supervised learning is where an external teacher provides a more sophisticated form of feedback: typically by providing the net with a complete specification of the desired output whenever the net produces an output. Unsupervised learning occurs when the net learns in the absence of any form of externally provided feedback. There is a weak sense in which the pattern associator learns under supervision because the states of the output units must be known in order to change weights. For example, in the autoassociative case the net must be provided with the same pattern over the input and output units at the same time. However, there are cases of unsupervised Hebbian learning. With these cases, the net learns simply by producing its own output patterns. Target or desired output patterns are not provided by an external teacher. (A detailed description of one example of unsupervised Hebbian learning set out by Linsker is included in the next chapter.)

Given that patterns of activity in the pattern associator can be construed as vectors, then the formal capabilities of the device can be fleshed out in terms of vector algebra. What this means is that the weight changes are described by algebraic manipulations of the input and output vectors. Using vector algebra, the sizes of the weights are represented in something known as a weight matrix (or connectivity matrix) and algebra dictates just how many and what kinds of associations a given network can learn. Indeed there is no obvious way to model anything but simple weight changes in this system because the sizes of the vectors and the corresponding connectivity matrix are fixed from the outset. Although it is a simple matter to model the absence of a connection between two units in this scheme (by allowing weights to reduce to 0), it is not at all as easy to show how new connections might develop. The structure of the connectivity matrix is immutable. In this sense pattern associators appear not to provide an ideal tool to model recruitment and fractionation of units (see Chapter 1).

Nevertheless, a few brief points suffice. Firstly, the behaviour of this device is highly constrained by the similarity relations that exist across the set of input patterns. The optimal conditions are where the input patterns define an orthogonal set and each has length 1. Given these conditions following training the net will be able to reproduce each input pattern perfectly. The point about the input vectors being orthogonal essentially means that they are not correlated with (i.e. they are unrelated to) one another. (For psychologists, it is perhaps best to think of 'orthogonal vectors' as having a direct counterpart in the sets of coefficients needed for orthogonal contrast techniques applied to analysis of variance; see e.g. Keppel, 1973, Chapter 7). The point about vectors being of length 1 reduces to one about normalizing the set of vectors so each has a similar salience for the system. The behaviour of a pattern associator can be swamped by a minority of the set of vectors if the vectors are not normalized.

Overall, it is unfortunately true that the real importance of these statements can only readily be grasped with some understanding of vector algebra. Detailed summaries of vector algebra can be found elsewhere (see e.g. Jordan, 1986). However, some feeling for the capabilities of pattern associators can be attained by experimenting with the McClelland and Rumelhart simulations provided with PDP/3. The general point remains though, that given orthonormality of the input patterns, the pattern associator learns perfectly.

Training a pattern associator is straightforward. Each pattern is presented in turn and the weights are adjusted according to Equation (2.3). When all the patterns have been presented and all the weights have been adjusted, one training epoch has been completed. Following just one training epoch, with the ideal orthonormalized training set, the presentation of any input pattern will produce the correct output pattern on the output units. Moreover, interesting conditions arise if the device is tested with a new pattern similar to one, and only one, of the input patterns. Here the corresponding output pattern will be most similar to the original learnt pattern's output. The device produces a response to a new stimulus on the basis of how similar the new pattern is to another previously experienced one. In this way the device can be said to generalize because it assigns equivalent or nearly equivalent responses to a family of similar stimuli. As can be imagined, because the device's responses reveal correlations between input patterns, it gives a response of 0 when a test pattern is presented that is orthogonal to, or uncorrelated with any member of the original set. A vector orthogonal with all members of the input set shares a correlation of 0 with them. Indeed, because the device recalls patterns on the basis of their similarity to previously learned instances, then this sort of content-addressable memory is quite unlike hashing. For as Hinton (1981a) notes, even small differences in an input string to a hashing procedure will access quite different addresses to those intended. The more forgiving nature of the pattern associator's memory is taken as being in favour of its psychological credibility. By producing similar outputs to similar inputs the device is said to exhibit a form of generalization.

McClelland and Rumelhart (1988) provide a reasonably comprehensive account of pattern associators that use Hebbian learning. As they note, a major limitation of the Hebbian learning rule is that learning is only sensitive to correlations between co-active units and this is not sufficient to ensure that the network will learn necessary associations between whole patterns of activity (see McClelland & Rumelhart, 1988, pp. 85–6). This is construed as an important limitation because in many cases successful learning demands more than changing weights in proportion to the correlated activity between pairs of units.

The delta rule

To overcome some of the limitations of Hebbian learning it was realized that the learning procedure might proceed by using the difference between corresponding pairs of output patterns and desired output patterns to adjust weights. The delta rule, or Widrow–Hoff rule (1960), operates by comparing complete output patterns with complete target patterns. The size of the difference between the actual and target outputs is then used as an index for changing the weights. As with the Hebb rule, McClelland and Rumelhart (1988) have also provided a fairly comprehensive account of learning by the delta rule in pattern associators. Therefore only some fairly general points will be made here.

Firstly, it is important to note that in using the delta rule, a pattern associator can be trained on sets of vectors that are not orthogonal. However, as McClelland and Rumelhart (1988) note, when the input patterns do form an orthogonal set, the delta rule behaves in a similar fashion to the Hebb rule. The delta rule is not without its own limitations, however. In order for the the rule to be effective, the input patterns must be linearly independent of each other (Jordan, 1986, covers this point in detail). All this means essentially is that for a set of vectors to be linearly independent, no one vector can be a weighted average of the others. Again this property is a property of vector algebra and can only readily be grasped by studying vector algebra.

Formally the weight change dictated by the delta rule is defined as :

$$\Delta w_{ij} = \varepsilon (t_j - a_j)\, a_i \tag{2.4}$$

t_j is the activity on the jth output component of the target pattern.
a_j is the activity on the jth output unit.
a_i is the activity on the ith input unit.
ε is the learning rate.

As can be seen, the delta rule only works when the target or desired pattern of activity is somehow available or is provided by a teacher. In order to calculate the error term, i.e. $(t_j - a_j)$, the target pattern must be accessible. In this respect it is proper to treat the delta rule as an instance of supervised learning. Over a whole set of input patterns the rule operates by reducing the mean squared difference between the corresponding output–target pattern pairings. For those cases where there is some discrepancy between actual and target outputs the weight change is proportional to the size of this error or discrepancy and to the state of activation of the input unit (McClelland & Rumelhart, 1988). When the output pattern matches the target pattern, there is no error; $(t_j - a_j)$ equals 0 and no changes are made. Consequently, in the ideal case learning ceases when the device produces the correct outputs for all the target patterns: across all instances $(t_j - a_j)$ will equal 0. In reality this ideal condition is hardly ever met so some tolerance has to be set on the minimum acceptable error over the whole set of patterns. The delta rule therefore is typically referred to as least-mean-square (LMS) rule. The aim is to minimize the overall least-mean-squares difference between the actual and target patterns.

Whether in principle such a framework is either physiologically or psychologically plausible is a matter of much concern (see Lynch, Granger, Larson & Baudry, 1989, for an optimistic appraisal, and Grossberg, 1988, for a more pessimistic view). Nevertheless, there is still much interest in this rule. Part of the reason for this is that a special case of the delta rule is formally equivalent to the Rescorla–Wagner (1972) rule for behavioural change during classical conditioning (see Gluck & Bower, 1988; Lynch *et al*., 1989; Sutton & Barto, 1981; Walker, 1990). The Rescorla–Wagner rule (1972) has in turn provided a reasonable account of certain phenomena in the animal learning literature (though see some detailed criticism by Gluck & Bower, 1988; and Pearce & Hall, 1980). Residual interest with the rule comes about because it seems to work reasonably well with other more powerful learning devices than pattern associators. Nevertheless, the formal constraint of linear independence of the input patterns is severely limiting. A typical ploy therefore is to try to fix up the inputs beforehand so that they do form a linearly independent set. Alternatives to this are: (a) to use a different learning rule, (b) to introduce hidden units, or (c) to do both of these. Much of the excitement generated by new connectionism has stemmed from studies involving 'new' learning procedures with networks possessing multiple layers of modifiable weights.

Back-propagation

Although now it is generally agreed that the perceptrons book (Minsky & Papert, 1969) signalled the demise of research into neural networks, there has been much misunderstanding of what Minsky and Papert actually showed. It is difficult not to speculate that many were unaware of the distinction between simple perceptrons and perceptrons with multiple-layers of modifiable weights (i.e. multi-layered perceptrons). Yet both Rosenblatt (1962) and Block (1970) were clear that many interesting and, possibly, the most interesting problems should be addressed with multi-layered perceptrons. Minsky and Papert, however, discuss these devices almost in passing (1969, Chapter 13, in the section on Gamba perceptrons), and they were reasonably pessimistic about the fruitfulness of such research. The general issue of whether all perceptrons suffer from the same crippling limitations as simple perceptrons will be dealt with in detail later. The current point of interest is that most of excitement generated by new connectionism stems from the work with networks comprising multiple layers of modifiable weights. Despite Minsky and Papert's seemingly damning appraisal of multi- layered perceptrons, most of new connectionism deals with these sorts of devices. To be fair though, some of this work is not entirely novel given the similar earlier work carried out by Rosenblatt (1962) and Block (1970).

In spite of the early work with multi-layered perceptrons, there remained a fundamental problem relating to learning. This was that whenever an error accrued on the output layer there was no way of knowing which of the many weights in the net was responsible for the error (Anderson & Hinton, 1981, p. 14). This is more generally known as the credit assignment problem (Minsky, 1987). The major hurdle facing researchers now was to arrive at a principled means for deciding which of the connections was to blame for the error and to consequently change weights on these connections in an appropriate manner. In general the problem has been addressed by developing procedures that iteratively consider each layer in turn from the output layer backwards to the input layer and to make compensatory adjustments to the weights along the way. Hence the label 'back-propagation'. The idea has been to derive a measure of error across the output units and then to propagate this error measure backwards through the net making necessary weight changes at each (hidden) layer of units. Before continuing though, it is important to dispel two possible misconceptions at this point. Firstly, as Valentine (1989) notes, the whole idea of back-propagating error signals through multi-layered networks was put forward by Rosenblatt (1962, Section 13.3). Secondly, it is also a mistake to believe that the something 'new' in 'new connectionism' is the derivation of an effective means for back-propagating an error signal through a multiple-layered network (Rumelhart *et al.*, 1986). Such techniques have been well understood for number of years in the branch of mathematics known as optimization theory (see Walsh, 1975, for a number of different solutions to this general class of problems, and also Werbos, 1988). Nevertheless, given the excitement generated by the back-propagation algorithm, it is only reasonable to discuss it in some detail.

Preliminary remarks

There is simply no point in having a multi-layered network comprising linear units because such a net can be modelled by a single layered net comprising more complex units (see above). Consequently, multi-layered networks must comprise non-linear units. The problem is that the capabilities and formal properties of such networks are poorly understood (Jordan, 1986). Therefore in the absence of any firm principles, it is unclear whether work on learning in such nets would be fruitful. In order to forestall any such misgivings therefore, Rumelhart *et al.* (1986) go to some lengths to offer a formal proof of the behaviour of multi-layered nets given a certain kind of learning algorithm. They begin by showing that the sort of learning algorithm (the back-propagation algorithm) they derive is simply another method of doing learning by gradient descent. The argument is that, in so far as gradient descent is well-understood then, by implication, the behaviour of the back-propagation algorithm is amenable to analysis. It is therefore important to grasp what learning by gradient descent is.

Gradient descent

Perhaps the easiest way of thinking about learning by gradient descent is by thinking of its converse; learning by gradient ascent (cf. Minsky & Selfridge, 1961). Consider the situation of being on a hillside in total darkness with no map, compass or means of illumination. It is also reasonably important that you reach the top of the hill. On the understanding that you can only operate on the basis of local information, by testing the gradient in the immediate vicinity, the claim is that the most effective means of reaching the top of the hill is by judging the direction of the steepest gradient and by moving in that direction. This strategy is bound to work if the gradient of the hill is monotonically increasing: if the gradient rises smoothly towards the summit. For clarity, this will be known as a 'good' hill (after Minsky & Papert, 1969). The major limitation of this strategy is that it is guaranteed to work only for good hills. For if you know nothing about the overall surface of the hill and if the gradient does not rise smoothly then you will be unable to tell if you have reached the summit. This is because, by operating with this rule, you will halt at the first place where the gradient falls off in all directions. On a 'good' hill this condition specifies the summit: on other hills you will halt at the top of the first hillock. This specific problem is known, more generally, as the problem of getting stuck at a local maximum. The gradient ascent procedure is unable to avoid the problem of sticking at local maxima. The moral is that gradient ascent works, but it only works in certain contexts.

   With gradient descent all you need imagine is the reverse scenario where you are walking down a hill rather than up it. It should be clear though that similar 'getting stuck' problems occur. Here the problems are known as getting stuck in local minima. There is simply no way of knowing if you have reached the bottom of the hill (the global minimum) if the hill has any local minima. Consequently, the procedure halts when it falls into a minimum. Such a minimum however, may not correspond to the bottom of the valley. By analogy, and in terms of neural nets, getting to the bottom of the hill corresponds to arriving at the best solution to a particular learning problem – a point to be returned to below.

   To reiterate: because learning by gradient descent is a well understood procedure, Rumelhart *et al.* begin by showing that their particular learning procedure can be understood as being a technique of learning by gradient descent. Gradient descent is well understood, therefore any learning algorithm that does learning by gradient descent must be understandable.

The formal reason why it easier to deal with gradient descent rather than ascent is covered below. Initially it is important to clarify how learning can be characterized in these terms.

Learning as gradient descent

For simplicity just consider a network with one layer of input units, two hidden layers of units and one set of output units (see Figure 2.6).

This net has to learn a given set of pairings of input–output patterns and each input pattern is presented to the net in turn. After each pattern is presented an error term is computed. As with the pattern associator, one training epoch is defined as one complete cycle of presenting all the patterns. The weights can be changed after each presentation of an instance or these individual error terms can be summed and then this global error term can be used to change the weights after each epoch.

The only changes taking place during learning are weight changes. Learning therefore corresponds to changing the weights in ways that will allow the net to approximate to the perfect solution for a given set of input–output pairings. In terms of gradient descent, Rumelhart *et al.* (1986) characterize a given net as defining a particular multidimensional space where the dimensionality of the space is given by the number of coefficients in the network. This is typically known as 'weight space'. Two kinds of parameters fix positions in this space: (i) the values of the coefficients (i.e. the weights on connections and the thresholds on the units), and (ii) the overall, or global, error. The global error is defined as the total error, summed over all input–output pairings, that remains after n training epochs. Figure 2.7 shows a very simplified sketch of such a space.

The horizontal axes correspond to two coefficients and different values on these axes correspond to different values of the corresponding x and z weights. The vertical axis corresponds to the error dimension. For any given x and z pairing there is a corresponding y value or error score. The general idea therefore is to arrive at an effective means of carrying out gradient descent in this weight space.

Rumelhart *et al.* begin by stating the generalized delta rule for changing weights following the presentation of a given pattern p:

$$\Delta_p w_{ij} = (t_{pj} - o_{pj}).i_{pi} \qquad (2.5)$$

The j's and i's index, respectively, units in adjacent upper and lower layers.
t_{pj} refers to the jth component of the desired target pattern.
o_{pj} refers to the corresponding jth component of the actual output pattern.
i_{pi} refers to the ith component of the input pattern.

Error for output units:

$\delta_{pj} = (t_{pj} - o_{pj}) . o_{pj} . (1 - o_{pj})$

p indexes a particular pattern

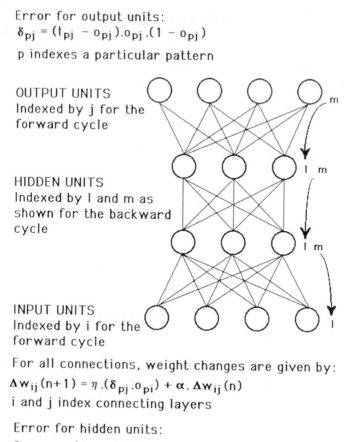

OUTPUT UNITS
Indexed by j for the
forward cycle

HIDDEN UNITS
Indexed by l and m as
shown for the backward
cycle

INPUT UNITS
Indexed by i for the
forward cycle

For all connections, weight changes are given by:

$\Delta w_{ij}(n+1) = \eta . (\delta_{pj} . o_{pi}) + \alpha . \Delta w_{ij}(n)$

i and j index connecting layers

Error for hidden units:

$\delta_{pl} = o_{pl} . (1 - o_{pl}) . \sum_m \delta_{pm} . w_{lm}$

l and m index connecting layers

Figure 2.6. Schematic representation of a multi-layered net. Error terms for the various layers are shown as is the general form of the method for changing weights. All symbols and terms are explained in the text.

Rumelhart *et al.* use this form of the delta rule to define error as a measure of the mean squared difference between the actual output and the target output. So:

$$E_p = \frac{1}{2} \sum_j (t_{pj} - o_{pj})^2 \qquad (2.6)$$

E_p is the error for pattern *p*.

Error

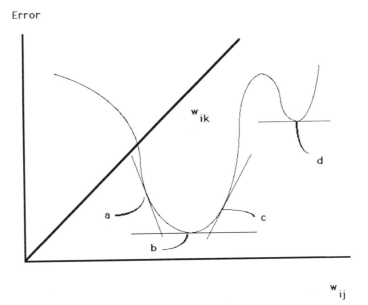

$$w_{ik}$$

a

b

c

d

$$w_{ij}$$

Figure 2.7. A simplified version of weight space. Only two weights are considered; w_{ij} and w_{ik}. Values of w_{ij} are mapped out along the x axis. Values of w_{ik} are mapped out along the z axis. Error values are mapped out along the y axis. The figure show a 2-D section of the error surface. Point b corresponds to a global minimum; it is the deepest valley in the space. Point d corresponds to a local minimum. Points a and c illustrate crudely why the negative of the differential of the error with respect to the weights is important.

Consider the points in the vicinity of b. The slope at c is positive so this implies that the weight is too large, it therefore has to be decreased. The slope at point a, however, is negative. This implies that the weight is too small and needs to be increased (based loosely on PDP/3, Chapter 5, Figure 5).

The Σ means that each *j*th output unit must be taken into account because the error is summed over each output unit. In other words, the error corresponds to the sum of the differences between the actual state of each output unit and the target or desired state as specified in the target pattern. It can be seen that the quantity

$$\frac{(t_{pj} - o_{pj})^2}{2} \tag{2.7}$$

is the mean squared difference between actual and desired states. Half the difference between the target and actual output is the mean difference. The ½ is a constant and is included for completeness. Sometimes it is cited (Rumelhart *et al.*, 1986) and sometimes not (McClelland & Rumelhart, 1988). Global error, (i.e. *E*, the total error over all patterns) is the sum of the separate E_p's.

What Rumelhart *et al.* go on to show is that there is an effective means of minimizing this global error. This corresponds to gradient descent in weight space. To carry out gradient descent in this space it is necessary to discover the gradient at each point in the space. One way of doing this is to take the derivative of the error (*E*) with respect to the weights. The differential of the error with respect to the weights gives the gradient of the surface at the current location in weight space. The reason for taking the negative of this differential is explained in Figure 2.7 (taken from McClelland & Rumelhart, 1988). The overall point is that the procedure is attempting to minimize the error score on the assumption that zero error corresponds to a good solution. As low errors correspond to points further down a given surface the aim is to travel down the surface in search of a minimum. A global error score of 0 would correspond to a global minimum in the weight space; in the language of geography this would correspond to the deepest valley in the space. Such a location corresponds to the net responding perfectly in all cases. Figure 2.7 also shows the local minima problem. Essentially the error-correcting procedure halts whenever the gradient in weight space is zero. As the gradient is zero at every minimum in that space, the procedure can get stuck in a local minimum.

So far all that has been established is a relationship between error scores and weight changes. However, difficulties remain for nets with hidden units: the credit-assignment problem looms large. There is no obvious way of relating weight changes on connections to and from the hidden units to the measure of error computed on the output units. There is no way of knowing which weights in the net are responsible for the errors in the output pattern produced by the net. In order to address this problem Rumelhart *et al.* consider processing units of a very special type.

From above it was argued that it is not sensible to deal with multi-layered nets comprising of linear units. Hence the introduction of non-linear units of the type shown in Figure 2.8. Figure 2.8 shows the plot of the function relating the unit's state of activation to its output level. The output of this unit is a non-linear (logistic) function of its activation level and is defined as:

$$y_j = \frac{1}{1 + e^{-x_j}} \qquad (2.8)$$

The state of activation of this unit (i.e. x_j) is in turn given by the product of the weights on the connections to all active efferent units:

$$x_j = \sum_i y_i . w_{ij} \qquad (2.9)$$

x_j is the total input to unit *j*.

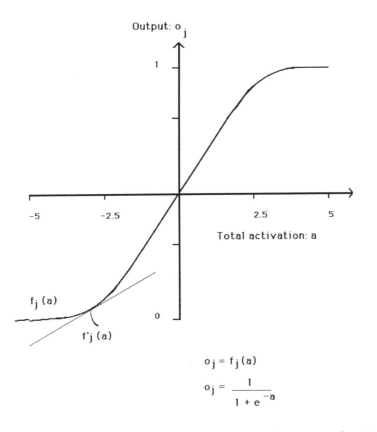

Figure 2.8. A sigmoid input–output function. The total activation of unit *j* is computed and entered into the sigmoid function, f_j (a), to give o_p, the output from the unit. The derivative f'_j (a) of the function gives the gradient of the function. (From Aleksander & Morton, 1990, adapted with permission, *see* p. xv.).

y_i is the state of the *i*th unit.

w_{ij} is the weight on the connection between the *i*th and *j*th units.

From Equation (2.9) it can be seen that there is a relationship between weights on connections to and activation of units. Clearly therefore, weight changes will alter the state of activation of a given unit. In turn, changes in the state of activation of the unit will alter its output. Indirectly therefore there is a relationship between weight changes to a hidden unit and its output. Ultimately, what is desired is being able to see how the rate of change of any weight in the net affects the rate of change of the error on the output units. This in turn breaks down to seeing what effect the rate of change an input to any unit is going to have on its output. The rate of change of the output given its input is given by the

Output

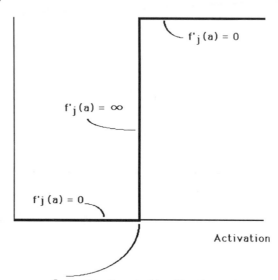

$f'_j(a) = 0$

$f'_j(a) = \infty$

$f'_j(a) = 0$

Activation

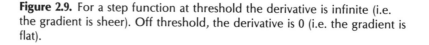

θ_j : unit's threshold activation value

Figure 2.9. For a step function at threshold the derivative is infinite (i.e. the gradient is sheer). Off threshold, the derivative is 0 (i.e. the gradient is flat).

derivative of its input–output function. Therefore, the derivative of the input–output function is important. It is for this reason that the choice of the particular input-output function is critical. In this regard Minsky and Papert (1988) make an interesting point. They note that it is not possible to apply this kind of analysis to networks comprising threshold units. This is because the derivative of the corresponding step function is either 0 (where the function is flat) and infinity where the function is vertical (see Figure 2.9). The importance of the logistic function is that, unlike the step function associated with binary threshold logic units, it has a manageable derivative. Moreover, as Mozer (1987) has shown, it can also be made to approximate to a step function, if necessary. In other words, the continuous units can be made to simulate the approximate behaviour of discrete elements.

The problems to be solved now are to arrive at the means for deciding how to compute errors for (a) the output units, and (b) the hidden units. Remember the overall problem is to arrive at a means for determining how to change any weight on any connection in the network. What is required is a means for changing the weights on connections to and from hidden units on the basis of information local to each hidden unit.

Rumelhart *et al.* did indeed derive such a method, which forms the basis of the back-propagation algorithm. The full proof of the back-propagation method is given in Rumelhart *et al.* (1986) and there is little point in duplicating it here (alternative treatments are provided by le Cun, 1988a; Plaut & Hinton, 1987; and Plaut, Nowlan & Hinton, 1986). A few general statements are worthwhile though. Rumelhart *et al.* show that the error for the output units is:

$$\delta_{pj} = (t_{pj} - o_{pj}).o_{pj}.(1 - o_{pj}) \tag{2.10}$$

δ_{pj} is the error for output unit *j* for pattern *p*.
t_{pj} is the target output for unit *j* for pattern *p*.
o_{pj} is the actual output for unit *j* for pattern *p*.

For hidden units Rumelhart *et al.* show that the error is given by:

$$\delta_{pl} = o_{pl}.(1 - o_{pl}). \sum_{m} \delta_{pm}.w_{lm} \tag{2.11}$$

(Here hidden units in layer *l* feed into the next layer of units in layer *m*.)
δ_{pl} is the error term for the hidden unit *l* for pattern *p*.
o_{pl} is the output of the hidden unit *l* for pattern *p*.
The term $\sum_{m} \delta_{pm}.w_{lm}$ is the sum of the product of the weights to all units in the next higher level and their respective error terms. This equation only includes terms that can be computed by each hidden unit on information that is available locally.

Having arrived at these error terms for output and hidden units it is now possible to put into effect the weight changes. The weight change on the connection between the penultimate hidden layer and the output units is given by:

$$\Delta w_{ij}(n + 1) = \eta.(\delta_{pj}o_{pi}) + \alpha.\Delta w_{ji}(n) \tag{2.12}$$

$\Delta w_{ij}(n + 1)$ is the weight change at time *n* + 1 on the connection between the *i*th hidden unit and the *j*th output unit.
η is known as the learning rate.
δ_{pj} is the error of the *j*th output unit.
o_{pi} is the state of the *i*th hidden unit.
α is known as the momentum term.
$\Delta w_{ji}(n)$ is the previous weight change at time *n*.
Exactly the same form of equation applies in determining the error on hidden layers where the *i* and *j* subscripts respectively index the hidden unit in question and the units to which it is connected in the immediate lower layer. This method stipulates a means of doing gradient descent by changing any weight in the net in a principled manner.

The algorithm for back-propagation can be further understood as the iteration of the following steps. Firstly, an input pattern is presented to the net and the activation of each layer in the net is computed in turn. This is known as forward propagation. The eventual output on the output layer is then compared against the desired output and the error signal is computed via Equation (2.10). This error signal is used initially to compute the new weights on the connections to the penultimate hidden units. The weight changes calculated via Equation (2.12) are applied to the existing weights to give new weights. These new weights are needed to compute the error signal over the hidden units: they are the w_{lm} in Equation (2.11). This is the start of the backward pass. Having computed the error over the hidden units the new weights can be determined for the next lower level of connections. This backward pass is continued until the input units are reached. Two final observations are worth making before considering the sorts of problems that the back-propagation algorithm was originally tested on.

Firstly, as it stands, the procedure is entirely deterministic. This means that if two units within a layer share the same connections and weights then they must accrue the same changes: one is redundant with respect to the other. To minimize the probability of this happening the weights are initially randomized when the network is set up.

The second point concerns the momentum term in Equation (2.12). This term was introduced in part because the weights can change very rapidly. This means that the system can oscillate in weight space as it converges on a solution. The consequence is that the system can take an inordinate amount of time to converge (Kindermann & Linden, 1988; Plaut & Hinton, 1987; Rumelhart *et al.*, 1986). In Equation (2.12) previous weight changes, scaled by a momentum term, are used to modify current weight changes. This means that the system will tend to maintain its direction of descent over successive iterations. Without this added feature, the system is likely to oscillate between the sides of a ravine in weight space: with the momentum term added the system tends to move in the direction of the floor of the ravine. Additional advantages may also accrue if the momentum terms is itself systematically altered over the learning trials (see Plaut *et al.*, 1986, although they set out no principled means for doing this). Further extensions to the standard algorithm are discussed below.

Applications of the back-propagation algorithm

One of the initial problems that Rumelhart *et al.* (1986) address with the back-propagation algorithm is the EXOR problem. They demonstrate a number of ways in which the back-propagation algorithm solves EXOR given certain network architectures. Two such networks are shown in Figure 2.10.

The general point, however, is that both networks comprise hidden units. Nevertheless, as was argued in Chapter 1, a simple perceptron (without hidden units) can also solve the EXOR problem as long as the appropriate wirings exist. Net a shown in Figure 2.10 uses a rather contrived wiring system; in contrast Net b uses full connectivity between all adjacent layers. As one of the many claims of

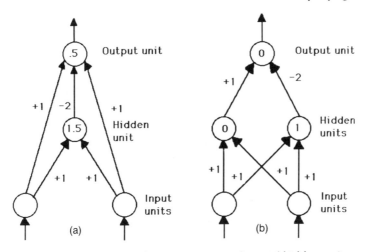

Figure 2.10. Two networks each comprising one layer of hidden units, capable of solving EXOR. (a) is taken from PDP/1, (b) is discussed by Touretzky & Pomerleau (1989).

new connectionism is that hidden units discover interesting and unpredictable internal representations (see the later discussion of the work by Lehky & Sejnowski, 1988, in Chapter 3), it seems appropriate to consider the sorts of representations that the hidden units do discover in solving the EXOR problem. On least two occasions, the characteristics of the hidden units in Net b have been dealt with in the literature (Hanson and Burr, 1990; Touretzky and Pomerleau, 1989; Winograd & Cowan, 1963). Indeed, Hanson and Burr even suggest that the solution was considered by McCulloch and Pitts (1943/1965). The solution the net hits upon is to have one hidden unit compute an inclusive OR; it comes on for (0,1), (1,0) or (1,1) and the other computes an AND; it only comes on for (1,1). However, whereas the first unit shares a positive connection with the output unit, the second shares a negative connection with the output unit. Consequently, only hidden unit 1 fires for both (1,0) and (0,1). Neither of the units fire when (0,0) is presented. Both units fire when (1,1) is presented, but the negative effect of unit 2 stops the output unit from firing. Clearly, therefore this network learns to solve the EXOR problem.

Apart from the EXOR problem, Rumelhart *et al.* (1986) deal with a number of others that Minsky and Papert addressed in their original perceptrons book. The intention seems to have been to show that regardless of the limitations of simple perceptrons, multi-layered nets with the back-propagation learning algorithm do not exhibit the same shortcomings. For example, Rumelhart *et al.* demonstrate how such nets can learn to solve the problems of parity and symmetry and something known as the T-C problem. Parity and symmetry were discussed in detail in Chapter 1. The T-C problem is a different kind of problem in so far as it is purely a geometric problem.

The general idea here is show how a net can learn to discriminate a capital T from a capital C, independently of any within-the-plane rotation or translation of the two letters. In order to solve this problem, Rumelhart *et al.* introduce a reasonably complicated network comprising a set of input units, that formed a 2-D planar retina; one layer of hidden units, that coarse-code the retinal information; and a single output unit. The hidden units shared overlapping receptive fields with their neighbouring hidden units (hence the coarse coding). In addition, Rumelhart *et al.* constrained the system so that every unit learnt the same pattern of weights. This ensured that the units all learnt the same kind of receptive field, and, hence, translation invariance was achieved. A rather cynical view though is that the net had so many built-in constraints on units and wiring that it could do nothing other than achieve translation invariance. Regardless of the system's ability to solve this problem, Rumelhart *et al.* dwell on the fact that the hidden units do acquire, over several different attempts, many interesting and counter-intuitive kinds of effective receptive fields. The full force of this kind of demonstration is dealt with in the next chapter.

Extensions to the standard back-propagation algorithm

Although it is typically stated that there are two general procedures for changing weights in back-propagation, Kindermann & Linden (1988) discuss three. The first is where the weights are changed for every input–output pairing. This is known as periodical learning: each pattern is presented in turn to the net and its corresponding error is back-propagated a fixed number of trials. The problem with this method is that it is computationally expensive; moreover, the method does not strictly conform to the proof of the algorithm (Rumelhart *et al.* 1986, p. 324). However, as Plaut & Hinton (1987) note, an advantage is that the individual error derivatives do not need to be stored. The subtle variation on this theme is to do something called sequential learning where each pattern is presented in turn and its error is back-propagated until that pattern is learnt. The disadvantage with this method is that it leads to oscillations in weight space (Kindermann & Linden, 1988).

The third procedure is to run something known as back-propagation in batch (Hush & Salas, 1988; Kindermann & Linden, 1988; Plaut & Hinton, 1987). Here the error signal is summed over all input–output pairings and then this grand error score is back-propagated after each training epoch. The advantage of this method is that it is a more effective means of gradient descent (the system does not oscillate in weight space); moreover, it is easier to monitor the global error term with respect to a set of weights (Plaut & Hinton, 1987). The disadvantage with this method is that there are situations where it does not work because positive and negative errors cancel each other out (Kindermann & Linden, 1988).

Other modifications to the standard procedure concern η, the learning rate. This is also known as the step size because, in a sense, this constant determines how large the step down the gradient should be. By taking the second derivative of the error with respect of the weight this gives an index of how quickly the gradient is changing at each given position in weight space. The insight here is that a useful heuristic is to take large step sizes when the gradient itself is changing slowing (as would be the case in a long ravine in weight space) and to take small step sizes when the gradient is changing quickly (Parker, 1987; Watrous, 1987). Unpredictable results are likely if large steps are taken when the gradient itself is changing rapidly. Regardless of the possible advantages of this system (i.e. that it might converge quickly on a particular solution), Plaut and Hinton (1987) note that the algorithm is complex and can be difficult to implement. Moreover, as Shawe-Taylor (personal communication) has noted, the method is particularly suspect and it only moderately increases convergence speeds when the system is in the vicinity of a minimum.

Another idea put forward, as an improvement over the standard 1986 version of the back-propagation algorithm, is to alter, systematically, η, the learning rate, and α, the momentum term in concert (see Chan & Fallside, 1987). Here η and α are changed across epochs because the momentum term was originally introduced to partially counteract the effect of having η, the learning rate parameter. Large values of η force the system to oscillate across the floor of ravines in weight space. The momentum term acted to dampen these oscillations down. In examining the reciprocal nature of the η and α terms, Chan and Fallside arrived at a means of altering α in direct proportion to η. Under these circumstances the system shows significant improvements in performance over the standard algorithm.

More recently, Jacobs (1988) has offered four heuristics for improving the rate of convergence of the procedure. The general ideas here are that the procedure ought to be more dynamic to the extent that other learning rate terms ought to be introduced and that these should change over time. Other ideas relate to the system being sensitive to the sign of the derivative. If over several epochs the sign of the derivative is the same then the error surface continues to slope in the same direction for some significant distance. Consequently, large steps are advisable (i.e. η should be increased). Alternatively, if the sign of the derivative changes over successive epochs then η should be decreased to avoid oscillations. Jacobs reports a number of simulations involving these heuristics that all show improved convergence rates over the standard algorithm.

Finally, Solla, Levin and Fleisher (1988) have experimented with computing alternative error terms and carrying out gradient descent with respect to these errors. They report improved convergence times when a particular logarithmic error is computed.

Drawbacks and limitations of back-propagation

From the above it should be clear that the major drawback of the standard back-propagation algorithm is its slow rate of convergence. As Jacobs (1988) notes, many researchers find its rate of convergence prohibitively slow in many practical situations. Irrespective of these complaints though, other problems remain. For instance, although there is an intense amount of research into back-propagation, it is still true that the dynamic properties of the method are poorly understood (Kindermann & Linden, 1988). It is difficult, if not impossible, to predict what the effects of changing the training set, or the number of hidden units, are likely to be. For example, as Kindermann & Linden (1988) argue, if extra instances are added to the training set, the nature of weight space may alter radically. For what was previously a minimum may no longer be, and moreover, there is no way of knowing how far the nearest minimum is from the previous one. Indeed, it may well turn out that a better strategy is to re-train the net from scratch with the new expanded set of instances.

There are other reasons why the dynamic aspects of the procedure are poorly understood. For instance, it is never obvious why the net failed to generalize for a given instance. This point ties in with the allied point that, with complex networks, it may be quite unfeasible to attempt to interpret how the net is solving a given problem. In other words, the hidden units may become sensitive to extremely subtle and complex regularities in the input–output pairings that are difficult or impracticable to decipher.

Also although there have been some reasonably successful attempts at speeding up the learning procedure (Becker & le Cun, 1988; Plaut & Hinton, 1987; Plaut *et al.*, 1986; Shawe-Taylor & Cohen, 1990), it remains true that the standard back-propagation algorithm can take an inordinate amount of time to converge to a reasonable solution. Part of the reason for this is that, for every epoch, errors from each unit in an upper layer have to communicated to every unit in the connected lower layer. Part of the problem has to do with the system tending to oscillate in weight space. Other problems arise with the nature of the weight space itself. With reasonably large input vectors the weight space becomes unfeasibly complex.

A further extension to the standard algorithm has recently been put forward by Shawe-Taylor and Cohen (1990). They were particularly concerned with a problem that the system can quite easily stray off into weight space away from the global minimum. The standard procedure essentially minimizes the average error over a set of input–output pairings. It can do this by operating correctly for the majority of pairings at the expense of erring on the minority. In other words, the procedure can perform optimally for some of the pairings but in doing so it may continually fail to perform correctly for the others. Having experimented with many simulations using the technique, it turns out that this pattern of performance recurs with startling regularity. Moreover, this is clearly a pathological aspect to the procedure that has no obvious psychological counterpart. Moreover, if the net does happen upon this state of affairs then it can never recover. Shawe-Taylor and Cohen derived a method for ensuring that a network never commits such an irretrievable mistake. The method used is to calculate changes to the weights in such a way that individual performance errors never increase. By doing this the system can never be side-tracked into an inappropriate part of weight space. As with the many variants of the back-propagation algorithm, performance with this method is impressive with small-scale nets, because very large improvements in convergence speeds can be obtained. Nevertheless, the computational costs of using the method are extremely demanding and the algorithm falls well outside of the realms of neurological plausibility.

In conclusion, the major problem with the standard back-propagation algorithm and all variants thereof is that they fail to avoid the problem of getting stuck at a local minimum. There are no guarantees that the system will not converge to a solution that corresponds to a local minimum. Rumelhart *et al.* deal with problem by stating that this hardly ever occurs with most of the real simulations they consider. However, this is clearly no solution to the problem. One attempt at a solution to the problem of avoiding local minima comes from a quite different net architecture. This will be considered in detail next.

Probabilistic update of units

Independently of the work carried out by Rumelhart and co-workers, part of the impetus for new connectionism stems from the influence of John Hopfield. Hopfield, in the late 1970s, helped advise on the formation of the Center of Biological Information Processing at MIT. It is reputed that, in the process of considering this proposal, he became interested in the idea of neural networks (see Guiver & Klimasauskas, 1988). It is also clear that Hopfield's research tended to give neural networks a more general academic credibility. His early work on neural networks was published in the highly regarded *Proceedings of the National Academy of Sciences* (Hopfield, 1982, 1984); additionally, his reputation as an eminent physicist gave further credence to neural network research (see Hinton & Anderson, 1989).

Hopfield nets

Hopfield's original framework is based on the idea that memory states can be construed as being analogous to the stable states of a dynamic physical system. The behaviour of such systems can be understood in terms of the local interactions of many simple elements. Here the analogy is with things like the stable conditions in magnetic systems and fluid flow systems (Hopfield, 1982, p. 2554). Such systems may have many stable states and it is therefore possible to equate different memories with these different states. The overall aim was to simulate these systems with neural nets. A fairly comprehensive and approachable account of Hopfield nets has recently been provided by Aleksander and Morton (1990). Rather than repeat the details of their account it is more appropriate here to make some general statements about the functional characteristics of these devices.

Initial interest with these devices was with their memory capabilities. The general concern was with how it was possible to store sets of patterns in these nets. With this scheme a given pattern was defined as a vector of 0's and 1's. Each element in the vector corresponded to a unit in the net and the value of the element signified the state of the unit. The general approach was to present each pattern to the net in turn, with the intention that the net would settle into a different attractor for each pattern. The process of settling into an attractor is discussed in detail below. Having stored a set of patterns in the net, remembering corresponded to the net settling down into a previous stable state when a pattern was re-presented at test. An interesting feature of these systems is that if at test a pattern is presented that partially resembles a previously learned pattern then the system will tend to settle into the attractor that corresponds to the original pattern. Indeed, if the test pattern only specifies part of the original pattern then the system will also tend to settle into the appropriate attractor (Hopfield, Feinstein & Palmer, 1983). In this way the system models pattern completion, or alternatively, cued recall. This is again another means of operationalizing content-addressable memory: the content of the input determines what is recalled.

In the original neural network simulation of these ideas Hopfield used McCulloch and Pitts ON/OFF neurons with something known as random asynchronous up-dates. This terminology is explained below. Here the units propagated either +1 for ON and 0 for OFF. The corresponding threshold was set at 0. Within a given net every unit had inputs directly from the environment and inputs from other units. Units did not feedback on directly on themselves, however. An additional simplifying assumption (which can be violated – Campbell, Sherrington & Wong, 1989; Hopfield, 1982; Hopfield & Tank, 1986) is that the weights between units are symmetric (i.e. $w_{ij} = w_{ji}$). The idea of asynchronous updates is that a given unit on a random basis interrogates its inputs and decides if the sum of its input exceeds its threshold. If this condition is met then the unit will come ON. In effect, the asynchrony means that only one unit is considered at a time (this makes the mathematics and the simulations tractable – Campbell *et al.*, 1989; Hopfield & Tank, 1986). The biological justification for asynchronous updates is given in terms of 'a combination of propagation delays, jitter and noise in real neural systems' (Hopfield, 1984, p. 3088).

One of Hopfield's main results was his proof that a particular form of random asynchronous updates forced the net to always converge onto a stable state in a finite number of steps. The initial stages in the proof were to define the total energy of the system and to characterize its behaviour relative to an energy landscape. The dimensionality of the associate energy space was given by the number of units in the net. Each unit contributed to the overall energy of the system.

In a simplified case, where the thresholds on the units were set to 0, Hopfield defined the total energy of the system according to the equation:

$$E = -\frac{1}{2}\sum_i \sum_{j \neq i} w_{ij} \cdot x_i \cdot x_j \tag{2.13}$$

x_i is the state of the *i*th unit.
x_j is the state of the *j*th unit
w_{ij} is the weight between unit *i* and unit *j*.

(Multiplying by the ½ is what Aleksander and Morton (1990) call a 'nicety'. It acts to compensate for the fact that because the summation is carried out twice, every unit is considered twice. However, to compute the total energy of the system the energy due to each unit must be considered only once.) Having defined energy thus, the aim was to use this measure in a similar way as error measures are used in other gradient descent applications. So the first step was to discover the rate of change of the energy given the rate of change of any unit's state in the system. Moreover, in so far as there are only local interactions in this system, then such calculations had to be based on information that was locally available at each unit. As a consequence, differentiating the energy with respect to a unit's state gives:

$$\Delta E_i = -\Delta x_i \sum_{j \neq i} (w_{ij}.x_j) \tag{2.14}$$

ΔE_i is the change in the energy of the system associated with Δx_i, the change in state of the *i*th unit.

$\sum_{j \neq i} (w_{ij} \cdot x_j)$ is the total input to the *i*th unit.

Equation (2.15) dictates that the energy in the system either decreases or remains at a constant minimum. The argument is quite subtle, however. The important thing to remember here is that a unit (the *i*th unit) can either be ON and have value +1 or be OFF and have a value of 0. Moreover, its threshold is 0. Consider the case where the unit is OFF. If this unit is to come ON then the total input to the unit must be positive (i.e. greater than 0). Moreover, to come ON the change in state must also be positive (the change in state equals +1: the unit changes from 0 to +1). Multiplying these two positive numbers together and then taking the negative results in an overall decrease in energy.

Now consider the case where the unit is ON (i.e. has a value +1). For this unit to change state it must turn OFF and for this to occur it means that the total input to the unit must be negative (i.e. less than the threshold of 0). So the total input to the unit is negative and the change in state will be negative (i.e. the units changes from 1 to 0: a change of −1). Multiplying these negatives together gives a positive value. However the negative of this value is demanded by Equation (2.15). Here again therefore, the energy of the system decreases. If units do not change state then the energy of the system remains constant. However, the elegance of the method is that any state change results in a lowering of the energy of the system. As a consequence changes will continue until a minimum value of E is reached. Indeed, a rather counter-intuitive result is that the overall energy of the system can remain constant even though the states of individual units are changing.

In some applications of the Hopfield net the weights between units are allocated at random and remain fixed when the to-be-remembered patterns are presented to the net. There are ways of modifying weights however. One method, discussed by Hopfield (1982), is shown in Equation 2.15.

$$\delta w_{ij} = (2x_i - 1). (2x_j - 1) \tag{2.15}$$

δw_{ij} is the weight change between the ith and jth units.
By this method, weights on the interconnections between units that are in different states are reduced. Weights increase between units that are either both ON or are both OFF. A number of different procedures do exist, however, for changing the weights to force the net into a particular attractor for a particular pattern (see Aleksander & Morton, 1990; Hinton, 1987; Hopfield, 1982).

A more general observation is that the Hopfield net operationalizes something known as mutual constraint satisfaction. Consider the simple example of just two interconnected units. The states of the units are taken to be analogous to the truth/falsity of elemental propositions where ON signifies true and OFF signifies false. In turn the weight on the connection between the two units can be seen as a logical relationship between the two corresponding propositions. Typically, a negative weight signifies a negative relationship; for instance, that both propositions cannot be true at the same time. Operationally, a negative weight between two units means that one unit being ON acts to stop the other unit from being ON. On the other hand, a positive weight can signify either a conjunction or an implication. Operationally, either unit being ON acts to turn the other unit ON. In this way the weights are analogous to constraints. They act to constrain the operation of the net. In simulating psychological processes however, these constraints are taken to reflect constraints that exist between properties of the real world. The network therefore affects a means for simultaneously satisfying as many local constraints as is possible. A stable state of the network occurs when all possible constraints are satisfied at the same time.

These ideas can be further fleshed out in terms of the energy of the system. It is interesting to consider the characteristics of the energy space because it is quite different from weight space. Here the dimensionality of the space is given by the number of units in the net because each unit contributes to the overall energy level of the whole system. Indeed, scrutiny of Equation 2.13 shows that the total energy of the system is, in part, given by the weights on the connections between pairs of mutually active units. Simple hand simulations show that active units joined by positive weights contribute negative values to the computation. On the other hand, active units joined by negative weights contribute positive values to the computation. In so far as the aim is to reduce the energy in the system then negative values are more beneficial than are positive values. Indeed, what this shows is that overall higher energy levels accrue when many pairs of co-active units are joined by negative weights. Such a state of affairs occurs when many local constraints are being violated. Indeed, as Kienker, Sejnowski, Hinton & Schumacher (1986: p. 204) state, 'energy is a useful measure of how well all the constraints are being satisfied by the network'.

Initial demonstrations with Hopfield nets concerned pattern completion and cued recall. Given this, some effort was given to uncovering how many patterns can be stored in a Hopfield net of a particular size. The general consensus now is that for a net of N units it is capable of storing $0.15N$ uncorrelated patterns (Campbell, Sherrington & Wong, 1989; Hinton, 1987; Hopfield, 1982). As Campbell *et al.* (1989) note, Hopfield nets are therefore relatively inefficient storage devices. Other problems remain, however, because convergence times can be very slow and spurious memories can be formed when acquiring certain sets of patterns. A by-product of storing some patterns is that this can force the system to behave as though it has been presented with others. Moreover, the presence of these spurious attractors can swamp eventual recall (see Hopfield *et al.*, 1983). For example, consider the three patterns:

        Walter ++++---- ++-+-+-- White
        Walter ++++---- --+-+-++ Black
        Harold ++--++-- +--++--+ Grey

Each '+' and '−' in these strings corresponds to an activation level of a given unit in the net. Moreover, in this version of the net, units could take on the values of +1 or −1 (see Hopfield *et al.*, 1983). The important point with this example was that in storing these patterns a spurious memory was also created. The spurious pattern corresponded to

        Walter ++++---- +--++--+ Grey

Hopfield *et al.* (1983) state that such spurious memories are not reasonable but are 'illogical associations'. They go on to to sketch a means of ridding the net of these spurious memories by allowing 'unlearning' to take place. Briefly, the idea is to allow the system to settle into a stable state and then to decrement weights by an amount proportionate with their stable state values. This tends to reduce the salience of the spurious memories relative to the 'real' memories. The problem with all of this is that too much unlearning can rid the system of all memories and there is no principled means of carrying out the procedure.

Later work concerned mutual constraint satisfaction and the ability of a Hopfield net to solve the travelling salesman problem (Hopfield & Tank, 1986). The typical problem is to find the shortest route through a network of cities without revisiting any city. As Pelton (1988) states, this is generally accepted as being a hard optimization problem. Hopfield and Tank (1985) quote impressive solutions to this problem using a network with N^2 number of units where N equals the number of cities. In this net the units came to signify the positional order of the cities in the sequence. The links in the net came to represent the constraints that lead to that particular ordering being developed. However, when Pelton (1988) attempted a replication of this simulation, he stressed that an awful amount of tinkering had to be carried out before he could get his own network to converge on a sensible solution. He rather cryptically notes that his network appeared to be feeling its way around a wandering salesman problem.

The history of the development of Hopfield nets is of interest for other reasons, though. In the 1982 paper Hopfield discusses units with discrete activity levels (-1 or $+1$) and a deterministic decision function. In the 1984 paper Hopfield extends his ideas to discuss units with continuous activity levels. Moreover, he introduces the concept of a stochastic decision function. Here the idea is that regardless of the activity level of the unit, its output state is determined on a probabilistic basis of its activity level. It is with recourse to these sorts of units that progress has been made in attempting to avoid the problem of nets getting trapped in local minima.

Boltzmann machines

A rather general view of the learning procedures so far considered is that they are interesting models of gradient descent. However, all fall foul of the problem of getting stuck in local minima. By only allowing 'downhill moves' there are no guarantees that the device will arrive at a global minimum or optimal solution (Hinton & Sejnowski, 1986). To overcome this general limitation, the insight was that progress could be made if the device is allowed to sometimes take uphill steps. The problem, however, is to decide about a principled means for making such uphill steps. Without such principles, the behaviour of the system would be uncontrolled and unpredictable.

Something of a solution to this problem was advanced by Kirkpatrick, Gelatt and Vecchi (1983) in a procedure known as simulated annealing. Simulating annealing brings together a number of concepts that have been discussed so far so it is best to consider some preliminaries before continuing.

Functional characteristics of the units in a Boltzmann machine

Firstly, simulated annealing is discussed in the new connectionist literature with respect to a particular sort of network known as a Boltzmann machine (see Ashley, Hinton & Sejnowski, 1985; Hinton & Sejnowski, 1983b; Hinton, Sejnowski, & Ackley, 1984; Kienker *et al.*, 1986; Touretzky & Hinton, 1988). In these nets it is again possible to discriminate between input units, hidden units and output units. Using similar ideas to those set out by Hopfield it is possible to define a measure of global energy for these kinds of nets, the assumption being that high energy states correspond to poor solutions of a given mutual constraint satisfaction problem. In contrast, low-energy states correspond to good solutions. As a consequence the aim is to arrive at a principled means for minimizing this so-called 'global energy'. As Hinton *et al.* (1984) note, it is possible to do this if the right sorts of assumptions are built into the units. One such assumption is that the units turn ON probabilistically. In other words, the units take on an output value that is determined by a probability function relating a unit's total input to its eventual state. (In this respect it is legitimate to draw a distinction between the total activation of a unit and its eventual state.) The probability that unit k will come ON is given by:

$$P_k = \frac{1}{1 + e^{-\Delta E_k / T}} \tag{2.16}$$

ΔE_k is known as the energy gap and is a measure how far the unit's activity is removed from its threshold. In a Hopfield net the units turn ON whenever their energy gap is positive; i.e. whenever their inputs exceed their threshold. In contrast, with the units in a Boltzmann machine, the energy gap is used to determine the probability that the unit will come ON (as is shown in Equation (2.16)). The actual energy gap of a given unit is given more formally as:

$$\Delta E_k = \sum_j s_j . w_{jk} - \theta_k \tag{2.17}$$

s_j is the state of the jth unit.
w_{jk} is the weight on the connection between the jth and kth units.
θ_k is the threshold on the kth unit.

The term $e^{-\Delta E_k / T}$, in Equation (2.16) is essentially equivalent to the Boltzmann factor discussed by Kirkpatrick *et al.* (1983) in their paper on simulated annealing. An important variable in this expression is T, the temperature of the system. Something of a feel for what the temperature term is doing is conveyed by Figure 2.11.

Figure 2.11 shows the probability that a certain unit will come ON plotted as a function of both the unit's energy gap and the system's temperature. As might be expected, for negative energy gap values (i.e. for all cases where the unit's inputs

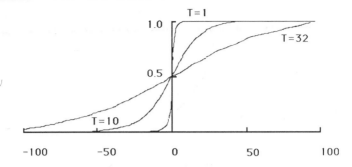

Figure 2.11. Graph showing the probability of a given unit in a Boltzmann net coming ON plotted as a function of temperature (i.e. *T*) and activation level. As can be seen, as *T* increases the probability function approximates to a step function. With small *T* values therefore, the units behave almost like binary threshold units. As *T* increases the units begin to behave almost linearly. (From Touretzky & Hinton, 1988, adapted with permission, *see* p. xv.)

are less than the threshold), the probability that the unit will turn ON is less than 0.5. However, the probability that the unit will come ON clearly varies as a function of the temperature of the system. At high temperatures the units can turn ON almost at random. At low temperatures (when T approaches 0) the behaviour of the unit approximates to a binary logic threshold unit. Therefore at low temperature values the Boltzmann machine appears to behave like a Hopfield net. As can be seen from the figure, the associated probability function for the lowest temperature value approximates to a step function.

The general point is that regardless of a unit's activity level, it changes its state with a certain probability. This probability is a function of the temperature of the system, which is a global variable, and the energy gap of the unit itself, which is a local value. Even if a unit's inputs do *not* exceed its threshold, it can come ON with a certain probability and the likelihood of this happening increases with increases in temperature. Hence at high temperature values the unit appears to behave almost randomly. Indeed for the cases where a unit does come ON when its inputs do *not* exceed the threshold, the system can move to a higher energy level. True, the general trend is for the system to move towards lower energy states; however, on occasion the system can take on higher energy values. It is by allowing the system to take on such higher energy states that, in the language of geography, it can be seen to be taking uphill steps. The promise of this approach is that these uphill steps will allow the system to avoid getting stuck in local minima. At a more metaphorical level, the way the system escapes from a local minimum is by climbing out of them.

The ultimate aim is to get the system to settle into a global minimum. However things are complicated by having the influence of temperature in the system. At any given temperature the system can settle into a stable state where the energy remains at a constant value. The states of the individual units can change but the overall energy of the system remains constant. Such a state of affairs is known as thermal equilibrium.

The idea espoused by Kirkpatrick *et al.* (1983) and Geman and Geman (1987) is to start the system off at a high temperature and to gradually lower the temperature. However, to guarantee success the system must be allowed to reach thermal equilibrium at each temperature. This sequence of reducing the temperature and of allowing the system to settle, is known as an 'annealing schedule' (Geman & Geman, 1987), hence the phrase 'simulated annealing'. Geman and Geman caution that the process is 'delicate': if the temperature is reduced too rapidly and thermal equilibrium is not attained at each stage, particularly at low temperatures, then there are no guarantees that the system will eventually settle at a global minimum.

Perhaps an easier way of thinking about this is with respect to a landscape that can be described either in gross overall terms or in the very fine details of its local features. At high temperatures the system behaves as though it is moving over the coarse features of the landscape: it does not get bogged down with the fine details. At lower temperatures the finer details of the surface matter. Essentially the annealing schedule starts off by moving the system in the general direction of the global minimum, and as the temperature cools the system begins to feel its way around where exactly the global minimum is located. Remember at all temperatures the system can move from a lower energy state to an higher state: the system can make 'uphill steps' and hence avoid the local minima problem.

However, as with many theories their true nature is only revealed when attempts are made to implement them. Hinton and Sejnowski (1986) describe an number of implementations, one of which will be discussed in depth here.

An important distinction made in relation to a Boltzmann machine is between input units that receive input directly from the environment and hidden units that do not. The Boltzmann learning procedure involves 'clamping' an input pattern or vector on the input units and letting the weights on the connections between the units be updated. As Hinton and Sejnowski (1986) note, in this way the hidden units come to represent complex hypotheses between the states of the input units. Remember it is the weights on the links in these nets that are taken to represent constraints between the units. If the units are seen to represent properties of the environment, then the weights represent relations between these properties. Moreover, given that there are many links and hidden units in the net, it is legitimate to state that the hidden units represent complex hypotheses about these sets of properties.

As with all of the research on network learning procedures described here, the primary aim in Hinton and Sejnowski's work was to arrive at a means for updating weights in a principled manner. This was necessary so that guarantees could be made about the net converging on a sensible set of weight values for a given input–output mapping. An initial step therefore was to define some measure of error or cost. Having arrived at such a measure, the next step was to show how changing weights on connections could be construed as a process of gradient descent. The details of the derivations and proofs need not be re-presented here, although some general points are worth making. Weight changes in the Boltzmann machine are given by:

$$\Delta w_{ij} = \varepsilon.(p^+_{ij} - p^-_{ij}) \tag{2.18}$$

Δw_{ij} is the size of weight change on the connection between units i and j
p^+_{ij} is the probability of finding both the ith and jth units ON at thermal equilibrium when an input is clamped on the input units.
p^-_{ij} is the probability of finding both the ith and jth units ON at thermal equilibrium when nothing is clamped on the input units.
ε is essentially a learning rate parameter.

The elegance of this method is that the weight changes can be carried out on the basis of information that is available locally at each unit. However, these changes demand that the probability distributions of the states of the units are computed in two cases: (a) when an input is clamped on the input units, and, (b) when nothing is clamped. Moreover, in both cases these computations must take place when the system has attained thermal equilibrium. Irrespective of these strictures, these conditions are never actually met in practice, and, indeed, some very rough approximations have been reported by Hinton and Sejnowski (1986).

For example, they configured a net in an attempt to solve something known as the shifter problem. The net had three sets of a total of 19 visible units and one set of 24 hidden units. Of the visible units the eight V1 units were matched with eight V2 units. There were three kinds of correspondence across the patterns on the V1 and V2 units. V1 and V2 patterns could be identical – an example of a no-shift condition. The right-shift condition was where the pattern in V1 was shifted one place to the right and this shifted pattern was provided on the V2 units. The left-shift condition was where a one shift left pattern correspondence was used. Of the three remaining visible units, one signalled the presence of a left-shift correspondence, one signalled the presence of a right-shift correspondence and one signalled the no-shift condition. The reason why this problem is of interest is because it is most obviously solved by a device that is sensitive to pairwise interactions between the states of the visible units. (The possible psychological significance of this problem has been discussed more thoroughly in Chapter 1.) In this application, the aim was to see if the hidden units could learn useful representations of such higher-order constraints. However, the actual simulation seems to have been incredibly laborious.

In summary, the simulation was initially split into two stages. In the + stage the states of the visible units were clamped and an annealing schedule was carried out. Here an iteration was defined as the number of random choices it took to update every unit in the net. The temperature was reduced according to the series of values 40, 35, 30, 25, 20, 15, 12, 10 and two iterations were carried out for each temperature value. When the temperature reached 10 the system was assumed to be in a state of thermal equilibrium. A further 10 iterations were then carried out so that the frequency with each pair of connected units were ON could be computed. This whole schedule was repeated a further 20 times with different clamped vectors. The average co-occurrence statistics over these 20 runs were noted so that the value of p^+_{ij} could be computed for every connection.

In the – stage nothing was clamped on the visible units. A similar annealing schedule and method was again employed to that just described for the + stage. This time, however, the p^-_{ij} values were computed. Together the + and – stages constitute something known as a sweep. After each sweep the weights were adjusted according to Equation 2.18. The ε value was set at 5.

Hinton and Sejnowski (1986) report that the system did indeed learn to solve the shifter problem after 9000 sweeps, but they do admit that this seems incredibly slow. The very slow convergence times severely question the psychological plausibility of the account even though Hinton and Sejnowski do suggest that the + and – phases may have psychological counterparts. The claim is that the – phase has a counterpart in the processes going on during REM (cf. Crick & Mitchison, 1983). In turn, p^+ values are assumed to be computed during the waking state. Without any evidence at hand, though, it is difficult to assess the seriousness of the proposal.

Unfortunately, this discussion of Boltzmann machines ends on rather a sour note. For although thorny problems remain in trying to validate psychological claims on the basis of arguments about parsimony, it remains true that the Boltzmann procedures constitute the most tortuous account of learning that has ever been advanced. It therefore perhaps not so surprising that no real contact has been established between psychological theory and this form of new connectionism.

Concluding comments

In this chapter a number of new connectionist learning procedures have been described in some detail. It would have been impossible to provide a thorough analysis of all such methods. As it turns out, though, many of the 'newer' methods are either extensions to old procedures or, are some form of novel amalgam of them. A rather cautionary note, perhaps, is that no major breakthroughs in research on learning have been forthcoming since the publication of the PDP books in 1986. Indeed, a rather worrying trend is the arbitrary manner in which some new learning procedures are being developed. For instance, Sharkey (1989) has recently put forward an extension to the original learning procedure developed by Hopfield. Sharkey's extension is known as a pulse-net. Here the idea is to allow a unit to switch OFF all units that it shares inhibitory connections with, when it turns ON. The worry with this mechanism is that no formal justification for the procedure is given. Moreover, the procedure only seems to work effectively if the weights in the net have been hand-tuned. Although such work might be justified on the grounds that it provides 'good' results, the arbitrary nature of the procedure militates against it being given serious consideration, especially in the absence of a formal proof of its capabilities.

The folly of such an enterprise is evident in those cases when the system fails to provide the correct results. Firstly, in the absence of a formal proof of the procedure's capabilities, then there can be no clearly defined way of knowing why the device fails. It may have well failed because of some trivial implementational detail. Alternatively, it may have failed because it is incapable of ever solving the particular target problem. The general morals drawn by Minsky and Papert in the late 1960s, about deriving the in-principle characteristics of network models, are as apposite now as they were then. For instance, without consideration of Minsky and Papert's conclusions about simple perceptrons, a considerable amount of research may well have been directed at trying to get these devices to learn to recognize patterns that they were incapable of learning. With the very complex systems being developed now, the need for in-principle statements about learning capabilities are crucially important. Without such guidelines the research can degenerate into trial-and-error tinkering.

The remaining expository chapters in the book concern several of the many new connectionist models of perceptual and cognitive mechanisms. Some of these implicate learning procedures; many do not. The aim of these chapters is to provide a range of examples of how new connectionism is contributing to current psychological theory about adult human performance.

Chapter 3

Aspects of vision

In this chapter a number of examples of new connectionist approaches to some problems of visual information processing will be described and the functional characteristics of the related models will be assessed, primarily in terms of psychological relevance. Much excitement has been generated by a number of demonstrations of how nets learn to solve previously difficult pattern recognition problems. Indeed, very interesting results have arisen because of the unpredicted and counter-intuitive hidden unit representations that the nets acquire. Particularly captivating is the fact that certain hidden units seem to correspond in fairly direct ways to the sorts of neural mechanisms that underlie primate, and possibly human, vision. Several such examples will be considered in detail here.

As a general framework for the chapter, a gross distinction is made between low- and high-level visual processes: a distinction original set out by Marr (1982). Put crudely, low-level processes typically concern the extraction of visual features such as the surface and edge characteristics of objects from images of those objects. In new connectionism, the relevant models tend to have direct implications for neural mechanisms. In contrast, and again put crudely, high-level visual processes concern things like attention and object recognition. New connectionist models of low-level and high-level vision will be considered in turn.

Low-level vision

It would be remiss in a chapter such as this not to devote some space to Marr's innovative work on low-level vision. The example chosen for discussion is his work on stereopsis. Marr espoused a view of human information processing based around principles of modularity. The basic conception was of the brain being composed of many special-purpose and functionally independent inform-ation-processing devices. On a superficial reading therefore it is easy to contrast this view with the massively parallel and distributed accounts of processing espoused by many new connectionists. However, such a contrast would be misleading because in many respects, Marr's work is a major precursor to new connectionism: witness his discussion of mutual constraint satisfaction, relaxa-tion, competitive/cooperative processes, etc. (1982). His work on stereopsis is a testament to his commitment to connectionist ideas, and as later sections reveal, he also applied connectionist principles to the higher levels of vision which concern object recognition.

Visual information processing and levels of explanation

In discussing any of Marr's work it is important to be clear about his ideas about the different 'levels of explanation' that could be applied to understanding the nature and functioning of any information processing system. Indeed, much debate continues to surround the three-tiered taxonomy of levels of explanation (Broadbent, 1985; Humphreys & Quinlan, 1986; Peacocke, 1986; Rumelhart & McClelland, 1985) and discussion of it recurs repeatedly in the new connectionist literature (e.g. see Smolensky, 1988, and commentaries). In outline the taxonomy comprises: (i) the computation level, (ii) the level of the representation plus the algorithm and, (iii) the hardware level.

In its final form (cf. the earlier Marr & Poggio, 1976, version) the computation-al level concerned the goals and logic of a given process abstracted from any implementational details. With regard to vision, and according to Marr, the computational level should specify what the purposes are subserved by visual information processing. The intention would be to arrive at a functional description independently of any regard for how actual processes might be embodied in a particular device.

The level of the representation and the algorithm was rather more concerned with technical details, and Marr uses the term 'representation' in a rather eclectic manner. For Marr, a representation comprises a primitive vocabulary of symbolic tokens and a method, or grammar, for combining these tokens in useful ways. According to this view, the symbolic tokens make explicit certain visual features present in a given image. The algorithm, on the other hand, specifies the manner in which these symbolic tokens are manipulated and transformed into other representations. For instance, at an early level of processing, the raw image is stipulated by a set of light intensity values which in turn is converted into a description comprising a set of symbolic 'place' tokens. These place tokens specify segments of oriented edges, or other salient boundaries in the image, points of

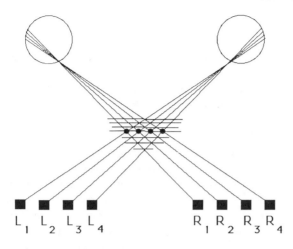

Figure 3.1. Schematic representation of the correspondence problem in vision. Four lines of sight from each of the eyes are shown. For any one line of sight there are four possible matches. The brain has to arrive at a set of consistent mappings for each line of sight. The solid points pick out the correct mappings that all fall on the same depth plane. (From Marr, 1982, adapted with permission, *see* p. xv.)

discontinuity in edge orientation, edge terminators, or, 'blobs' (i.e. doubly terminated bars). Given these symbolic tokens, an algorithm then operates to group these primitives into coherent sets, so as to give rise to a description of a particular contour in the image. It is the tokens and the grouping algorithm that constitute something known as a primal sketch representation.

Finally, and put simply, the hardware level deals with the physical instantiation of the representation and the algorithm. In human terms this level deals with neurophysiological considerations.

Stereopsis

Initially this discussion of low-level vision centres on stereopsis: the ability of the human visual system to fuse the two disparate retinal images into a single percept that specifies depth. At the computational level, Marr divided the problem of stereopsis according to the following goals: (i) select a particular surface element in one image, (ii) identify the same element in the other image, and (iii) measure the disparity between these two corresponding image points. Although these steps are seemingly straightforward, the situation is exacerbated by the 'false target problem' – there is no obviously unambiguous way to match elements in one image with corresponding elements in the other (see Figure 3.1).

Marr's primary insight in solving this problem was to introduce the idea of building in a priori constraints into the algorithm. He established two such constraints: that of uniqueness and that of continuity. The uniqueness constraint stipulates that any image element can only be assigned one disparity value; i.e. a surface element can occur at only one position in depth, relative to the viewer at any given time. The continuity constraint stipulates that surface disparity varies smoothly almost everywhere. This constraint was justified on the grounds that 'matter is cohesive' and that only a relatively small fraction of the area of an image constitute boundaries. Both of these constraints were built into Marr and Poggio's (1976) initial co-operative stereo algorithm. However, an interesting aside is that if the theory is taken as an account of human information processing, then the whole idea of building constraints into the model can be taken as an argument for a degree of nativism. It is as though the model is being innately endowed with knowledge of constraints that exist between properties of objects in the world. In this respect the network model of stereopsis, as put forward by Marr, was highly structured.

Operation of the Marr–Poggio model

Figure 3.2 shows a schematic representation of how the algorithm operated. The y and x axes correspond to the planar retinal images for the right and left eyes, respectively. For each element in the right image a short horizontal line is drawn. For each element in the left image a vertical line is drawn. These lines respectively signify the lines of sight for the two eyes for each point on the retina. Intersections of these lines of sight signify disparity values. The uniqueness constraint means that only one such intersection point can be ON for each pair of horizontal and vertical lines; each surface element can exist at only one position in depth. The continuity constraint is embodied by only allowing one disparity value to obtain for all elements in the image. In effect, all image elements in the two eyes must align at the same disparity and this was modelled by having all image elements align on the same diagonal in Figure 3.2.

The connectionist implementation of this algorithm came about by assigning one processing unit to every point of intersection in the disparity map. Inhibitory connections were set up between neighbouring units on the same line of sight; i.e. units aligning on the same horizontal line of sight were mutually inhibitory, and units aligning on the same vertical line of sight were mutually inhibitory. Excitatory connections were set up between neighbouring units on the diagonals. Here units on the same diagonals signify surface elements at the same retinal disparity. The network was initialized by setting all possible target positions for each element with 1s: they were all switched ON. All non-target positions were initialized with 0s: they remained OFF. Each unit then computed a weighted sum of the states of the units to which it was connected taking into account the inhibitory/excitatory nature of the connection strengths. This weighted sum was then compared with a threshold value and if the weighted sum exceeded the unit's

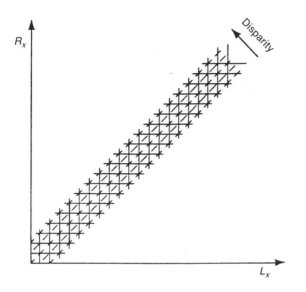

Figure 3.2. Graphical representation of the network solution to the correspondence. R_x represents axial distance across an horizontal cross-section of the right retina. L_x represents axial distance across the corresponding cross section in the left retina. Vertical lines signify position-specific lines of sight from the left eye. Horizontal lines signify the corresponding position-specific lines of sight from the right eye. Intersections signify possible depth matches. Each diagonal dotted line signifies a consistent depth match across all retinal positions.

In the simulation each intersection corresponds to a unit and units share both excitatory and inhibitory connections. Units that lie along a particular diagonal are mutually excitatory. Units that are orthogonal share inhibitory connections. (From Marr, 1982, adapted with permission, *see* p. xv.)

threshold then the unit remained ON; otherwise it was switched OFF. By iterating this process the network proved successful in fusing a range of different random-dot stereograms (Julesz, 1971) known to be fused successfully by human perceivers.

Appraisal of the Marr–Poggio model

The performance of this competitive-cooperative algorithm is perhaps not as impressive as was first thought given that it has been severely criticized (Marr, 1977, 1982; Mayhew & Frisby, 1980) and extended (Marr & Poggio, 1979). Moreover, by now, far more sophisticated fusion algorithms exist (e.g. Pollard, Mayhew & Frisby, 1985). Yet even though the details of the implementation have been widely disputed, what endures in the connectionist literature is the spirit of mutual constraint satisfaction as exemplified by the model (see e.g. Ballard, 1986). The important characteristic of the model is that, given suitable inputs, the network settles into a global stable state in which a maximum number of local constraints are satisfied. The network settles into a globally consistent solution, which corresponds to a stable set of active units, on the sole basis of local constraints instantiated as weights on connections. This ability to attain global solutions by satisfying many local constraints simultaneously is one of the fundamental properties of many new connectionist models.

The eventual debate over the sufficiency of the Marr–Poggio algorithm rested with psychological considerations about the sorts of stereograms that humans could fuse (Julesz, 1971; Mayhew & Frisby, 1976, 1985). However, aligned with these psychological considerations, Marr did also discuss neurophysiological evidence regarding the existence of certain 'disparity-detecting' neurons found in real brains (1982, p. 126). In the next example of connectionist research on visual processing hardly any neurophysiological assumptions are built into the model, yet it demonstrates a possible way in which certain well-documented neural mechanisms might develop.

New connectionism and the visual cortex

In series of papers Linsker (1986a, 1986b, 1986c) has described a model that provides a possible account of how the neural architecture of the visual cortex may actually develop. This model draws on many ideas originally espoused in the old connectionist literature (cf. Hebb, 1949; Rosenblatt, 1962) and provides a paradigm case of unsupervised Hebbian learning.

Much of the following in this section is reasonably technical but a serious attempt has been made to try to elucidate some of the functional characteristics of the model that may be of interest to psychologists. However, something that is an omission is a thorough explanation of why the model develops the particular structures it does. This is no accident, for as Hinton (1987, 1989a) has noted, Linsker does not actually discuss this issue. As a consequence, all that can be passed on is a feel for some of the properties of the model.

Description of Linsker's model

In the first paper Linsker (1986a) shows how spatial-opponent cells may develop. Consider Figure 3.3, which shows two layers of units in which there is a special connectivity between units in adjacent layers but no connectivity amongst units in the same layer. Consider the connectivity between layers L and M and assume that layer M is superimposed above layer L. Any unit in layer M, say , at position x_{ml}, y_{ml} is connected to a number of units in layer L. The point on L

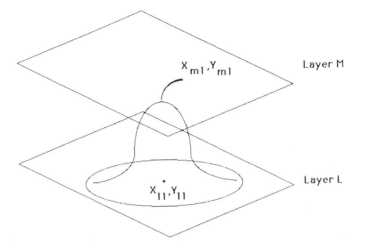

Figure 3.3. Schematic representation of Gaussian wiring used by Linsker. The density of wires between layers M and L is governed by a Gaussian as shown (see text for a fuller explanation).

corresponding to x_{m1}, y_{m1} is x_{l1}, y_{l1}. Most importantly the density of the connections between layers M and L from a central position (x_{l1}, y_{l1}) falls off in a Gaussian fashion as distance from that position increases (see Figure 3.3). For ease of exposition this kind of wiring will be referred to as Gaussian density connectivity. This kind of wiring has already been described in Chapter 1. Gaussian weight connectivity is the case where the strengths of the weights over a uniformly dense set of connections vary according to a Gaussian distribution. In Linsker's model the actual wiring between layers is random within the constraints of Gaussian connectivity. Importantly, M cells, i.e. cells in an upper layer, share overlapping receptive fields on the immediately prior layer.

The work progresses by assuming random activity over the input units in layer L. Such patterns of random activity were taken as being the actual input to the net. The algorithm considers: (a) the correlated activity between all pairs of pre-synaptic units in layer L that map on to the same unit in layer M, and (b) the correlated activity between each of the pre-synaptic units in layer L and the activity in the postsynaptic M unit. Units compute a linear combination of their inputs and the weight change on connections is of a simple Hebbian type. The weight change on connection i between layers L and M for the input π is:

$$\Delta c_i \pi = k_a + k_b \, (F^{M\pi} - F_0^M)(F_i^{L\pi} - F_0^L) \tag{3.1}$$

At a first glance this equation appears quite awesome, yet everything but the terms $F^{M\pi}$ and $F_i^{L\pi}$ are constants (and $k_b > 0$). $F^{M\pi}$ is the output activity of the post-synaptic M cell.

$F_i^{L\pi}$ is the activity of the pre-synaptic L cell.

Overall, Equation (3.1) ensures that the weight change is greater when input activity at the ith synapse is correlated with the activity of the post-synaptic cell than in all other situations.

Over many presentations it is possible to calculate the rate of change of c_i as $\dot{c}_i$:

$$\dot{c}_i = k_1 + \frac{1}{N_M}\sum_{j}^{L}(Q_{ij}^{L} + k_2)c_j \qquad (3.2)$$

k_1 and k_2 are themselves composite terms but they are fixed for each layer. N_M is the number of synapses onto the Mth cell. The i and j index connections to the same M unit. Q_{ij}^{L} is perhaps the most interesting term and is defined as being proportional to the two-point autocorrelation between pairs of connections (in this case connections i and j) from layer L to the same Mth cell. It is like an index of the covariance between the activity on pairs of links that share the same postsynaptic cell. Equation (3.2) is particularly useful because weight changes are assumed to be small for individual presentations; consequently, it is the changes over an 'ensemble' of presentations that are of interest.

A feature of Hebbian learning is that the weights can grow without limit so Linkser sets upper and lower bounds of 0 to +1 for excitatory connections and −1 to 0 for inhibitory connections. In the simulations, the system was seen to be mature when the all, or all but one, of the L→M connections had reached their limiting values (for this is a purely feedforward net: activation spread only forwards from the input units and there was no feedback from higher to lower layers).

In Linsker's first paper he considers a three-tier system of cells considered respectively as layers A, B and C. (A is the input layer or retina.) In the simulations, connections between layers A and B were allowed to mature first. Three types of B cells were seen to emerge, namely: (i) all-excitatory where all the corresponding A→B connections were excitatory, (ii) all inhibitory, and (iii) mixed excitatory–inhibitory. In the first simulations discussed, parameter values were chosen so that only all-excitatory cells were seen to develop in layer B. After the connections to layer B mature, the B→C connections were considered. Connection strengths between B and C were randomized with weights in the range of +0.5 to −0.5. They in turn matured to either +0.5 or −0.5. Remember positive weights signify excitatory connections and negative weights signify inhibitory connections. The striking thing about Linsker's model is the nature of the pattern of connectivity that develops on the B→C connections.

The critical point to consider is the assumption of Gaussian density connectivity between layers. This means that the density of connections for any cell is greater near the centre of its receptive field than it is further into the periphery.

Adjacent B cells become reasonably correlated because their receptive fields tend to overlap. This has a profound effect for the development of connections between B and C. Remember that the assumption of Gaussian density connectivity also obtains between the B and C levels as well as between the A and B levels; consequently, pairs of connections near to the centre of a C cell are more likely to correlate than are pairs of connections further into the periphery. The significance of this fact is spelt out shortly; first it is necessary to consider Equation (3.2) in more detail.

In the simulation where ON-centre-OFF-surround C cells were seen to develop, k_1 was given a positive value, and k_2 was given a negative value. The positive k_1 value ensures that all c values tend to increase. Moreover, in so far as the activity of central connections is more highly correlated than it is for peripheral connections, the contribution of the Q term to the change in a weight c_i is greater when the synapse to be modified is central than if it is peripheral. This means that central synapses saturate first to their maximum excitatory level. The contribution of the negative k_2 value is small in the case of central connections. However, with peripheral connections k_2 relative to Q is large because peripheral connections have low covariance, hence peripheral connections tend to decrease and saturate at their maximum inhibitory level.

By varying the values of k_1 and k_2, other kinds of layer C cells were seen to develop. For instance, OFF-centre-ON-surround cells developed when k_1 was given a negative value. In addition, all-excitatory and all-inhibitory cells obtained for other values of k_2.

Extending the simulation Linsker demonstrated how orientation-selective cells developed at a later layer (1986b). In this model Linsker added layers D through G, and examined the response characteristics of the cells as each layer matured. The first step here was to compute Q values for all pairs of mature C cells. Linsker found that the value of Q varied according to a Mexican-hat form. Values of Q for nearby C cells with overlapping receptive fields were positive because the activity of the C cells correlated. Q values were 0 for distantly spaced C cells whose receptive fields did not overlap. The Q values were negative for intermediately spaced C cells because the inhibitory surround of one cell overlapped with the excitatory centre of another. Consequently, the cells activities were anticorrelated. Linsker found that circular symmetric cells of the type developed at layer C also developed in layers D , E and F. However, at the higher layers, the Mexican-hat form of the Q values became sharper by having more pronounced peaks and troughs. Although Linsker provides few details, it is this Mexican-hat characteristic of the values of the autocorrelation function in concert with the procedure for changing weights that produced a systematic connectivity to the higher G layer. Essentially, an emergent property of the system was that each connection to the G layer tended to take on the characteristics of its near neighbours (either excitatory or inhibitory). Connections also tended not to take on the characteristics of other connections at mid-range distances. Similar connection types, particularly between layers F and G, tended to line up together in order to minimize neighbourhood differences and to maximize neighbourhood similarities.

Given this, only a small number of possible solutions arose. In other words, only a small number of kinds of G cells developed. Amongst these were G cells whose connectivity resembles an orientation-selective cell or 'simple' cortical cell (Hubel & Wiesel, 1962). For example, in one case the connections to a G cell exhibited a central bar of excitatory connections flanked either side by inhibitory connections. This is a kind of oriented bar detector and across the various G cells the orientation of the central band varied in an arbitrary fashion. A more complex version of a mature G cell exhibited a series of alternate excitatory/inhibitory bands arranged in parallel stripes, although in some cases the bands appeared curved rather than straight.

In the final paper Linsker (1986c) showed how the G cells tend to cluster into orientation columns when interconnections between the cells are introduced. G–G interconnections were either excitatory or inhibitory and their maturation was governed by similar principles to those for inter-layer connections. As with between-layer connections, the density of connections from one G cell to others decreased as the distance between the cells increased. Two cases were considered. In the first, discussed only briefly, G–G interconnections were either excitatory or inhibitory and the F→G connections matured first. In the second case, only excitatory G–G connections were allowed and these matured before the F→G connections. In this case neighbouring G cells influenced the development of one another. Again, because of the Hebbian procedures for changing weights on connections the general trend was for like-neighbours to cluster together. At the outset the G layer was divided into local regions and these regions were assigned arbitrary orientations on a random basis. The final choice of orientation selectivity for each grouping of G cells was arrived at after a process of simulated annealing (see Chapter 2). Here a measure of energy was derived and used with a measure of temperature that allowed for the best-fit of orientations to cell groupings. Consequently, it was the final assignment of orientations to the complete grid of cells that was governed by the process of simulated annealing.

The results of this procedure gave rise to cells of similar orientations being organized into 'band-like regions'. These in turn are strikingly similar to orientation columns found in the macaque striate cortex (Blasdel & Salama, 1986; Hubel & Wiesel, 1977). An interesting feature was that G cells displaced by an intermediate distance in a direction perpendicular to their preferred orientation had anti-correlated activities. This is a rather counter-intuitive result because the cells exhibited a kind of lateral inhibition by sharing excitatory and not inhibitory connections. There were no G–G inhibitory connections in this simulation.

Appraisal of Linsker's model

A number of points can be made in summary about Linsker's work. Firstly, it is clear that even though the system does rest on simple processes of Hebbian modification of synaptic connections, many aspects of the model were built in at the design stage. So although the A–G layers were justified on the grounds that these layers can be 'loosely identified' with real cell layers from retina to cortex, the impression is that the correspondence is perhaps more speculative than real. Moreover, it appears that a lot of effort was expended in order to arrive at the systematic groupings in the G layer. Nevertheless, none of this should detract from the very interesting contribution that the work makes to trying to understand how the very specialized neural mechanisms underlying vision may actually develop. However, as Durbin and Mitchison (1990) have recently demonstrated, there may well be a more parsimonious account of how orientation cortical maps self-organize into occular dominance columns. In their work the primary consideration is to honour constraints imposed by the developing brain trying to minimize the lengths of connections between neurons. Nevertheless, irrespective of these quibbles, it is difficult to read Linsker's paper and not come away with the impression that simulated neural networks can provide profound insights into how real brains develop and process sense-data.

Shape-from-shading

A quite different account of the spontaneous development of neural-like structures has been described by Lehky and Sejnowski (1988). They were particularly concerned with training a network to extract the magnitude and orientation of the two principal surface curvatures from images of shaded surfaces. The aim was to build a net to extract this information independently of position of the surface information impinging on the retina and independently of the direction of the light source on the surface. Such an ability is typically referred to as the extraction of shape-from-shading and is clearly a fundamental property of human visual information processing.

Architecture of the Lehky and Sejnowski model

Lehky and Sejnowski designed their net around an input layer of 122 units, a hidden layer of 27 units and an output layer of 24 units. The input units themselves were modelled on real neurons found both in the retina and lateral geniculate nuclei (henceforth, LGN). In the simulated net, these units possessed overlapping circular receptive fields that had either ON-centre/OFF surround or OFF-centre/ON-surround characteristics and there were equal numbers of both kinds of input units. The 24 output units were divided into 4 groups of 6; the 6 divisions were given by the magnitude of curvature (0° ... 150° in steps of 30°), the 4 groups were, respectively, positive-large curvature, negative-large curvature, positive-small curvature, negative-small curvature. There was also full connectivity between all input units and hidden units and between all hidden units and output units. Connection strengths were randomized at the outset. Hidden units computed the weighted sum of the weights and respective states on their connections to the input units. Their outputs were a sigmoid function of these activities (see Chapter 2).

Functional characteristics of the model

The network was trained via back-propagation with many (though exactly how many is not specified) digitized images of various illuminated curved smoothed surfaces. After 40,000 presentations of these images the correlation between the actual and desired outputs reached a plateau of 0.88. Essentially, the net acquired the ability to code the orientation and curvature of smooth surfaces independently of the direction of illumination of the surfaces. The ability of the net to generalize to novel inputs was also claimed to be good. However, the most striking thing was the nature of the hidden units and the connectivity matrix that the net finally acquired. The hidden units appeared to fall into three general kinds. Type 1 units mapped onto groups of output units signalling orientation of the principal curvature of the input surfaces. Type 2 mapped onto groups of output units primarily concerned with the convexity/concavity (the sign) of the curvature. Finally, Type 3 units mapped onto groups of output units primarily concerned with the magnitude of the principal curvature.

   Examination of the weights on the connections between the input and hidden units revealed many hidden units that resembled those found in the visual cortex. For instance, the connections to several hidden units were organized in an orientation-specific manner with parallel bands of excitatory and inhibitory weights. Other hidden units revealed circular-symmetric receptive fields. When 'probed' with bars of light these hidden units responded like 'simple' cells in the visual cortex. As Moorhead, Haig and Clement (1989) state, this supports the rather tantalizing suggestion that neurons previously assumed to be carrying out primitive feature extraction may well be playing a primary role in a system concerned with shape-from-shading operations.

Appraisal of the Lehky and Sejnowski model

The work of Lehky and Sejnowski provides yet another demonstration of the seemingly spontaneous growth of processing units that resemble actual neurons found in real brains. It is indeed true that Lehky and Sejnowski's model was highly motivated and highly constrained by neurological considerations. For example, the receptive fields of the input units were clearly motivated by biological considerations. However, Lehky and Sejnowski end their paper on a rather cautionary note for neurophysiologists. In a passage that is seemingly directed against using single-cell electrode recording techniques, they make the following point. From the example of the hidden units in their network they claim that it is simply impossible to be certain about what a given cell is doing unless there is also a reasonably complete mapping of both its receptive and projective fields. (Lehky and Sejnowski, 1988), define the connections to a given unit as its receptive field; they define the connections from the unit as its projective field.) Although this point is well taken in terms of understanding units in a connectionist net, as Moorhead *et al.* (1989) note neither the receptive nor projective fields of a real neuron are amenable to analysis by any current neurophysiological techniques.

Irrespective of the neurophysiological flavour of the work, there are several reasons why Lehky and Sejnowski's contribution is not quite as satisfying as Linsker's. For example, Linsker demonstrated the natural growth of different kinds of processing units at different levels of a reasonably well-structured system. Equally impressive is the fact that the ordering of the units arose for non-arbitrary reasons concerning both wiring and learning constraints. In contrast, in Lehky and Sejnowski's work, the circular-symmetric and orientation-sensitive units arose at the same level of the system. According to Moorhead *et al.* (1989), this does not gel with present knowledge of real neurological systems. In addition, there is also no obvious reason as to why some units acquired one kind of response characteristic whilst others acquired a quite different kind. In Linsker's model there were well-understood conditions under which a uniformity of type of unit at a given layer emerged.

Of perhaps more importance, however, is the question of the neurological implausibility of the mechanisms of back-propagation. For whereas Linsker's network was a feedforward net based around principles of Hebbian learning, Lehky and Sejnowski's used back-propagation with its feedforward and feedback components. Arguably the main dilemma for work such as that of Lehky and Sejnowski (see also Zipser & Andersen, 1988), is that many of the demonstrations of the growth of neural-like structures arise through the application of method that is allegedly biologically implausible (Hinton, 1987, 1989a). Therefore, before moving the discussion on to aspects of the higher-levels of vision, it is useful to consider some of the reasons as to why back-propagation is accused of being a biologically implausible process.

The biological implausibility of back-propagation

The most thorough criticism launched against back-propagation, that lays charges of biological implausibility, is that provided by Grossberg (1987). The detailed argument can be summarized with respect to a three-layered net comprising F1, the input layer, F2, a single layer of hidden units, and F3, the output layer (see Figure 3.4). Grossberg argues that back-propagation implicates one ascending pathway (F1, F2 and F3) and one descending pathway known as

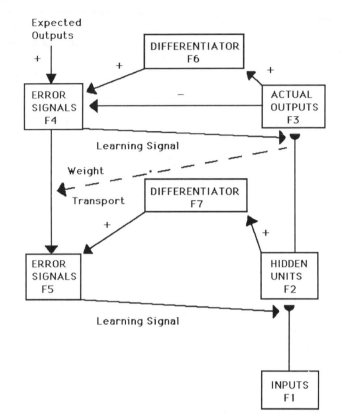

Figure 3.4. Grossberg's (1987, Figure 8) interpretation of the necessary neural hardware needed to implement back-propagation. A fuller explanation is given in the text. (From Grossberg, 1987, adapted with permission, *see* p. xv.)

F4 and F5. Figure 3.4 is an abridged version of one used by Grossberg to convey the argument. Grossberg argues that the weights computed on the feedforward cycle need to be 'transported' or somehow made available to the top-down F4–F5 pathway. It is the combination of the error signals on the F4–F5 pathway and the weights originally calculated that allows for the connection to be altered on the feedback cycle. Grossberg argues that the original weights cannot co-exist in the F2–F3 pathways and in the F4–F5 pathways. As a consequence, they have to be transported from one pathway to another. This idea of weight transportation is what Grossberg claims has no 'plausible physical interpretation' (p. 50). Moreover, the F3 and F4 layers cannot be physically identical because whereas the F3 layer must record actual outputs, the F4 layer records the output errors. Clearly, a single unit cannot do both. By a similar argument, the layer F6 and F7 is necessitated because the complexity of taking the derivative of each output.

Hinton (1987, 1989a) is also clear that real neurons cannot both propagate an error derivative backwards using a linear input–output function whilst having to propagate activity forwards using non-linear processes. He also claims that 'There is no evidence that synapses can be used in the reverse direction' (p. 15). In contrast though, recent work, on long-term synaptic potentiation (henceforth, LTP) does suggest that synaptic transmission may indeed operate in both directions, from the pre-synaptic terminal to the post-synaptic cell and vice versa (Davis, Lester, Reymann & Collingridge, 1989; Stevens, 1989). This suggests strongly that synapses do operate in both directions: although here the argument is more to do with the plausibility of Hebbian-type learning rather than back-propagation.

Irrespective of the above, Stork (1989) has provided one example of a net that seemingly honours some neurological constraints in implementing a version of back-propagation. It is difficult not to question the reasonableness of this scheme, but some credit must be given for the ingenuity of the model. The model itself comprises five different sorts of neurons and two different sorts of synapses. Stork meets some of Grossberg's objects by allowing separate ascending and descending pathways and by allowing a cluster of units and connections to deal with the problem of weight transportation. However, he is clear that there remains a problem for back-propagation and indeed other variants of learning by gradient descent. The difficulty rests with the mathematics demanding that the weight modification is governed by pre-synaptic activity and a learning signal independent of the post-synaptic activity. In contrast, it is generally regarded that real synaptic modification; i.e. LTP, is sensitive to both a pre-synaptic and a post-synaptic component (Bliss, Errington, Feasey & Lynch, 1986). Overall, these difficulties in interpreting the neurological status of new connectionist models reveal a real tension between new connectionism and neurophysiology. This tension is examined in detail in the final chapter.

Edge extraction and figure–ground segmentation

In moving between the lower and higher levels of vision it is interesting to consider certain demonstrations of the local processes governing edge extraction and the global processes governing figure–ground segmentation. Initially consideration will be given to the work of Kienker *et al.* (1986). An ancillary aspect of this work is that it provides an example of how attentional processes may be simulated in a connectionist network. A discussion of some of Grossberg's work on low-level to intermediate-level visual processing is then included.

The Kienker et al. model

The work of Kienker *et al.* fits in the tradition of applying the principles of constraint satisfaction to perceptual processing. In their model a given processing unit embodies a certain local hypothesis about a part of an object in an image. Connections between the units stand for constraints between these hypotheses. The model of figure–ground segmentation is therefore built around certain well-known and commonsense statements about real objects and their edges.

Architecture of the model

The architecture of the model is straightforward, comprising a set of edge units and a set of figure units. The edge units receive input directly from the environment and feed in information to the figure units. Attention is conceptualized as being an extra source of information fed into the figure units. In the model 400 figure units were arranged in a 20 × 20 array. It is this array that essentially defines the visual field of the net. Within the model a figure unit being ON signifies that information specifying part of a figure is present at the corresponding retinal position. Each figure unit is connected to all its immediate 8 neighbours. Topologically, however, these units form a torus rather than a plane because units at the boundaries of the area are interconnected to their opposite neighbours (cf. Minsky and Papert, 1969, Section 2.1.1). This is to ensure a uniform connectivity matrix and so avoid any possible boundary effects. Otherwise the constraints of real objects and their edges are captured in the network by special connectivity between edge units, between edge units and figure units, and between the figure units themselves.

Firstly consider the connectivity between figure units. Connection strengths between figure units are symmetrical and excitatory. This kind of wiring means that neighbouring figure units are mutually supportive; if one figure unit accrues evidence then it attempts to switch its neighbouring figure units ON. This operationalizes a kind of nearness constraint; namely, that locations close to a part of a figure are most likely to be other parts of the same figure. For connected figures this nearness constraint is only violated at edges. Constraints about edges are embodied in the connections between edge units and between edge units and figure units. Consider first the connections between edge and figure units. An example is shown in Figure 3.5. Here the set of connections between an edge unit and figure units is shown. As can be seen, the edge unit essentially inhibits the spread of activity between figure units to the extent that it shares excitatory connections with figure units on the 'figure' side of the edge; it shares inhibitory connections with those figure units falling on the 'ground' side of the edge. Again these links are symmetrical.

This figure–ground constraint is further embellished by allowing edge units to interact directly. Edge units facing each other share an inhibitory connection. The case where surfaces of two figures abut one another is disallowed in the model. The final edge constraints concerned other local hypotheses about edges. Two possible edge configurations and two impossible edge configurations are shown in Figure 3.6.

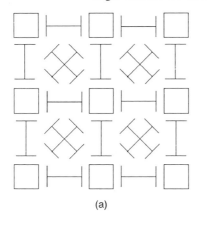

(a)

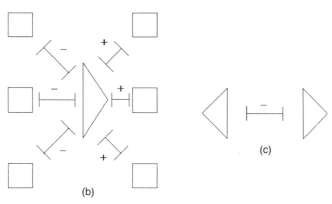

(b)

(c)

Figure 3.5. (a) shows how the centre figure unit shares mutually excitatory connections with each of its eight immediate neighbours. Similar connectivity obtains for all figure units in the net.
(b) shows how a given edge unit (signified by the triangle) connects up to the figure units. It shares inhibitory connections with those figure units on the outside of the edge (the base of the triangle); it shares excitatory connections with those figure units on inside of the edge.
(c) is an example of an inhibitory connection between adjacent and opposing edge units. (From Kienker *et al.*, 1986, adapted with permission, *see* p. xv.)

A rather jaundiced view of the model is that given the number and sophisticated nature of the wiring constraints introduced it is hardly surprising that some degree of success was shown in simulating figure–ground segmentation. However, it is the failures of the model that reveal its true limitations. Given that some of the failures appear to be quite unlike anything perceptual experience provides, the psychological plausibility of the account of figure–ground segmentation is seriously weakened.

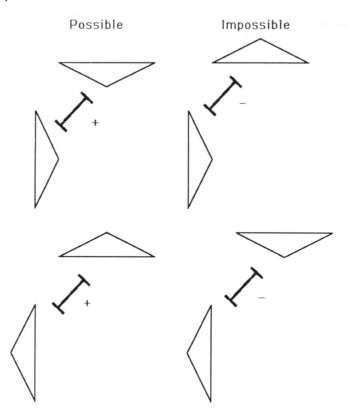

Figure 3.6. Constraints that set out possible and impossible combinations of adjacent edges of a solid figure. Each triangle represents a different edge unit. The base of each triangle represents the outer edge of the figure. Weights on connections between the edge units can be either excitatory (signified by a '+') or inhibitory (signified by a '−'). (From Kienker *et al.*, 1986, adapted with permission, *see* p. xv.)

Operation of the model

Connection weights were set by hand so the model was not one about learning; rather the task set was one of solving a fundamental perceptual problem, i.e. figure–ground segregation, by mutual local constraint satisfaction. The model itself was of the Hopfield/Boltzmann type. Each unit possesses a threshold and computes an activity level according to the weighted sum of the states of its neighbouring units added to the value of its external input. The total input to the *i*th unit is given by:

$$\Delta E_i = \sum_j w_{ij} s_j - \theta_i + \eta_i \tag{3.3}$$

ΔE_i is the total input to the ith unit (see further discussion below).

w_{ij} is the weight on the connection between the ith and the jth units.

s_j is the state of the jth unit.

θ_i is the threshold of the ith unit.

η_i is the external input to the ith unit.

For edge units the external input is information specifying line information in the figure. This input information is clamped onto the edge units. For the figure units the 'external' input is given by an attentional source. Here the η_i was given by:

$$\eta_i = A \, \exp(\tfrac{-d}{\sigma})^2 \tag{3.4}$$

This defines the net's attentional spotlight. At the presentation of an input image, the centre of the attentional spotlight was fixed somewhere on the retinal mosaic of figural units. The shape of the spotlight was circular and the level of attentional input decreased in a Gaussian manner as distance from the centre of the spotlight increased. In (3.4) the A term specifies the amplitude of the Gaussian, σ specifies the width of the Gaussian and the d specifies the distance (of the ith unit) from the centre of the spotlight. For a given run, the A and σ terms were held constant, as was the spotlight's position on the image.

Two modes of operation were considered. In the first, the gradient descent mode, the units were simple binary threshold units whose outputs were governed solely by the application of Equation (3.3). The second mode of operation was simulated annealing. In this case, the states of the units were determined by passing their current activity levels through the following sigmoid function. This function stipulated that the ith unit came ON with a probability:

$$p_i = \frac{1}{[1 + \exp\left(\frac{-\Delta E_i}{T}\right)]} \tag{3.5}$$

T is the temperature of the system.

ΔE_i is given by Equation (3.3) and is known as a unit's energy gap as defined previously in Chapter 2. It is simply the degree to which the unit's activation exceeded its threshold.

In so far as the net operated to lower the overall energy in the system (in the manner of a Boltzmann machine), large energy changes were desirable: large energy gaps contributed to large decreases in the total energy of the whole system. In functional terms, the total energy of the net was used as a measure of the degree to which the net was satisfying the set of local constraints. Low-energy states corresponded to good solutions with a state of minimum energy corresponding to the correct figure–ground segmentation of the particular input image. In contrast, high-energy states corresponded to poor solutions where many units joined by inhibitory connections were both ON. Such would be the case where two adjacent but opposing edge units were both ON. Perceptually, high-energy states corresponded to incorrect codings of aspects of the figure and the ground.

In the simulated annealing case the system started with a high temperature value and an annealing schedule was put into operation. Here a unit was chosen at random and updated according to Equations (3.3) and (3.5). In so far as the states of the units were probabilistically determined, a rather counter-intuitive aspect of the net was that units came ON in the absence of external input. True, this state of affairs diminishes as time progresses, but initially the pattern of activity over the net is a more or less random configuration of states of the units. It perhaps is an obvious point, but this initial random activity on the retina of the net makes little perceptual sense.

The net was tested with a number of different kinds of stimuli with the attentional spotlight fixed, sometimes on the figure, sometimes on the ground. For simple figures the net was reasonably successful in arriving at good solutions, although occasionally the net stuck in local minima where local inconsistencies could not be resolved. As part of an empirical exercise, comparisons between the simulated annealing and the gradient descent methods were drawn as a function of σ, the width of the attentional spotlight, and whether the spotlight was focused on or outside the figure. For both methods there was a critical band of spotlight widths that provided good proportions of correct solutions with repeated runs with the same stimuli. The general result, though, was that the band of critical widths was appreciably smaller for the gradient descent technique than for the simulated annealing method. Moreover, with the gradient descent technique the position of the spotlight had to be 'finely tuned'. Overall therefore the impression gained is that the simulated annealing technique is a far more tolerant procedure than the simple gradient descent technique. The simulated annealing technique provided successful solutions when certain amounts of noise were added to the input image, when parts of figures were missing and when the size and position of the attentional spotlight were varied.

An interesting example stimulus that the net was able to deal with was an incomplete rectangle. Here all the net was presented with was the four corner segments of a rectangle. The net correctly identified these edge segments and, in addition, affected filling in by switching ON all the appropriate figure units within the bounds of the imaginary rectangle. In this respect it is tempting to impute that the net simulated the perception of subjective contours (Kanizsa, 1979). In so far as Kienker *et al.* treat this demonstration as something of an aside, it is perhaps more appropriate to consider the more serious efforts of Grossberg and co-workers to explain a vast number of illusory perceptual phenomena. The ensuing theory developed by this group of workers is elaborate and comprehensive and only a simple sketch is included here.

Grossberg's BCS/FCS model

Three perceptual phenomena were central to the development of Grossberg's

BCS/FCS model. These are, respectively, effects uncovered by experiments by: (1) Land (1977); (2) Yarbus (1967); and Grossberg and Mingolla (1985). A brief resume of these effects is now given.

Land (1977) demonstrated a fundamental property of the human colour system when subjects viewed patterns made up of overlapping patches of colour under a variety of lighting conditions. The central result was that it was the relative contrast at the conjoining edge of two patches that determined the perceived colours of the patches. Given that edges in the patterns were sharply spatially defined, the difference in illumination across any edge was typically insignificant. Across a whole patch, though, there was likely to be a relatively large variation in illumination. Consequently, the visual system is seen to 'discount the illumination' in determining the perceived colour of the patch. In effect this means that the visual system is suppressing, or in some sense ignoring the illumination signals in determining colour. Moreover, given that illumination *per se* is an unreliable cue to colour, it is the chromatic contrasts across edges that critically determine the final percept. In the absence of any other mechanism this means that all that would be perceived is a world of coloured edges. Some other mechanism therefore is needed to supply the perception of solid coloured forms. In the BCS/FCS theory this other mechanism provides what is known as featural filling-in. The theory posits that while one mechanism deals with edges, a separate 'filling-in' mechanism deals with surfaces.

Evidence for featural filling-in comes from a perceptual demonstration documented by Yarbus (1967). The demonstration uses a stimulus that comprises a 2-D image of a circular disk divided into two halves: respectively, a black hemidisk and a white hemidisk. The complete disk is located on a red background and is presented to a subject so that it becomes stabilized on the retina. A small red dot is then moved between the centres of the two hemidisks. The dot has the same luminance as the background red. Under these conditions the overall disk disappears because the background red floods the field. The significance of this effect is explained below.

Taken together the Land and Yarbus experiments give rise to the following ideas that are central to the BCS/FCS theory. Firstly, it is argued that the visual system comprises separate systems that are sensitive to quite different perceptual properties: respectively, the two systems are, the boundary contour system (hence the BCS in BCS/FCS); and the feature contour system (the FCS in BCS/FCS). The BCS generates signals that give rise to both real and illusory perceptual boundaries. A real edge corresponds to an actual edge present in the image; an illusory edge is perceptually 'real', but it is not actually present in the image. The FCS is responsible for the filling-in witnessed in the Yarbus demonstration. In so far as the perceptual world does not comprise amorphous shapes or sets of coloured edges, the BCS and the FCS are seen to interact. For instance, colour and brightness spread because of the action of the FCS. This process of spreading can either terminate naturally, i.e. it will only occur over a certain limited area of the visual field, or it will be halted by the boundaries produced by the BCS. The

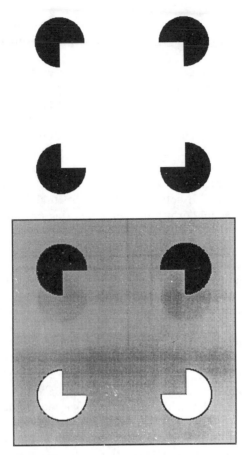

Figure 3.7. Examples of illusory exemplified by the (a) standard Kanizsa square, and, (b) a novel Kanizsa square designed by Grossberg and Mingolla (1985). (b) shows that the impression of contour survives the change in contrast across the top and bottom corners. (From Kanizsa, 1976 and Grossberg & Mingolla, 1985, adapted with permission, *see* p. xv.)

Yarbus demonstration is important in showing what happens when the BCS fails to operate appropriately. With a stabilized image the BCS fails to generate appropriate boundary signals: this system is somehow habituated and hence unable to signal the presence of boundaries. The background colour therefore floods the whole field. This occurs because of the operation of the FCS. Indeed, further support for the notion of colour spreading has been documented, in its pathological form, in a patient described by Hendricks, Holliday and Ruddock (1981). The patient experienced colour flooding when viewing red forms. A consequence was that the patient was unable to perceive the veridical shape of the stimulus because its colour spread beyond its actual boundaries.

Further properties of the BCS have been revealed by a demonstration designed by Grossberg and Mingolla (1985). After Kanizsa (1974), Grossberg and Mingolla experimented with the illusory square as shown in Figure 3.7a. Figure 3.7b shows the variant of the illusory square designed by Grossberg and Mingolla. In both examples the impression gained is of a square superimposed over four disks. In Figure 3.7a the disks, and, consequently, the corners of the square, possess the same contrast difference: namely, white square to black background. This property is violated in Figure 3.7b, where two of the disks are black and two are white. Nevertheless, regardless of this difference in contrast across the pairs of corners in Figure 3.7b, the impression of an illusory square is still compelling. Given this, Grossberg and Mingolla reasoned that the boundaries provided by the BCS must be insensitive to direction of contrast.

In order to account for illusory contours Grossberg and Mingolla invoked a process known as boundary completion. They argued that boundary completion is a quite natural consequence of normal visual processing. This is simply because the real retinal mosaic is far from being a perfect surface of photoreceptors: witness the intricate vein structure that is superimposed over the receptors and blind spot. Neither obstructs the seamless impression of the visual world. Nevertheless, given the physical presence of these occluding structures, some form of boundary completion is necessary to fill in the details of edges that are partially obscured.

The model in detail

In developing an account of the perceptual phenomena outlined above, Grossberg and Mingolla went on to set out a detailed model that honours well-documented neurophysiological properties of the visual system. Of particular interest here are their writings about the BCS. They state that the BCS comprises a set of oriented masks, or units possessing elongated receptive fields. These masks are sensitive to the orientation of an edge and to the amount of contrast across the edge: they are insensitive to the direction of contrast across the edge. The neurological flavour of the theory is given by assuming that inputs to the elongated masks are outputs from ON/OFF centre–surround units found in the LGN. The BCS is itself elaborated around units akin to the simple, complex and hypercomplex cells discussed by Hubel and Wiesel (1977). For example, within the theory, and early on in processing, pairs of simple cells are considered. In one simple cell the direction of contrast is black → white; in the other the direction of contrast is white → black. By allowing the outputs of these two cells to map onto a third 'complex' cell, this complex cell will be insensitive to the direction of contrast of the edge in the image, but it will be sensitive to the position of the edge. The outputs of these complex cells in turn feed into hypercomplex cells which are arranged in ways that honour orientation constraints.

In the BCS the oriented masks interact in a number of different ways. Masks of similar orientations that are aligned and are adjacent, mutually compete. To be

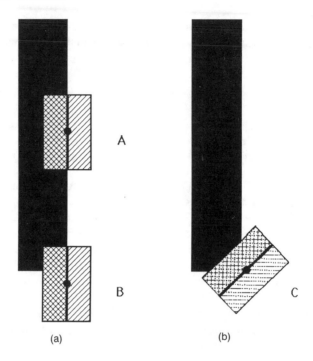

Figure 3.8. Examples of the elongated masks posited by Grossberg and Mingolla to be responsible for edge detection. In (b) masks near the end of a thin line are all weakly activated. (From Grossberg & Mingolla, 1985, adapted with permission, *see* p. xv.)

precise there is an initial stage of short-range competition between like-oriented masks. These short-range competitive processes contribute to something known as end-stopping. In the absence of competition between collinear adjacent masks the spread of activity would be otherwise unconstrained along the length of a line. As a consequence, the system would be faced with severe problems in locating the end of a line. Indeed, within the theory interesting effects occur at the ends of very thin lines. This is because, as Figure 3.8 shows, elongated receptive fields are insensitive to orientation at and near line ends and corners. For instance, as the figure shows, a number of masks are weakly activated at ends and corners. In this sense the system possesses conflicting information. This conflict is resolved at a secondary stage of processing.

The outputs of the first stage of competition feed into a next stage of competition where masks of different orientations compete at the same locations. Indeed, if a mask of one orientation becomes inhibited its perpendicular partner becomes disinhibited. The units at this stage of the system are assumed to be analogous to the hypercomplex cells documented by Hubel and Wiesel (1965) (see

Grossberg & Marshall, 1989). Outputs of the second stage of competition now feed in to a third stage in which like-oriented masks that align at a distance mutually co-operate. This is known as long-range co-operation. It is this long-range co-operation that is used to explain the perception of the illusory Kanizsa squares. A brief sketch of the processes that give rise to boundary completion along an illusory contour is included in Figure 3.9. It is best to think in terms of there being an initial feedforward of information from the complex units to the hypercomplex units (pathways marked 1 in the figure). The hypercomplex units are mutually co-operative and send feedback signals downwards to intervening complex cells (pathway 2). These in turn excite new intervening hypercomplex cells (pathways marked 3) and again there is further activation feedback (pathway 4). This particular process is known as competitive–cooperative feedback exchange or a CC loop. Remember the complex cells are mutually competitive. This competition is necessary for the marking of line terminators and in order for the CC loop to be effective the feedback activation has to overcome the natural tendency for the complex units to compete.

Appraisal of the model

It is difficult to be more precise about the model because it is fleshed out in a manner quite unlike any other connectionist research. For example, there is no easily digestible treatment of the properties of the units or their connectivity. These details can only be uncovered by a painstaking process of deciphering many equations. Moreover, the full account of the derivation of the equations is itself distributed over many papers. In so far as the psychological flavour of the model can be passed on without carrying out a very fine-grained analysis of the complete works, the above discussion suffices.

An enduring impression gained from reading some of the papers is that a precise account has been given of the details of certain aspects of low-level vision. However, the work is also important in showing how low-level processes may account for perceptual phenomena that have otherwise been given a high, almost cognitive, level of explanation. For instance, consider the framework set out by Gregory (1973, 1974). Gregory is firm that the impression of solid bounded figures arises through the generation and testing of perceptual hypotheses. This so-called active theory of processing aligns with the more traditional ideas about perception being a process of embellishing an otherwise impoverished input (cf. Gordan, 1989, Chapter 6). Indeed, Gregory (1973) even goes as far as to state that 'The brain sometimes invents objects to try to make sense of what is presented to the eye.' (p. 187). True, the BCS/FCS model does provide an explanation of embellishment of impoverished information about edges and surfaces, but the spirit of the theory is different from Gregory's. For example, embellishment is viewed as a natural property of the primitives of the visual system. According to this view, it is possible to argue that the visual system is forming and testing hypotheses about the nature of edges and surfaces in the input, but this is far

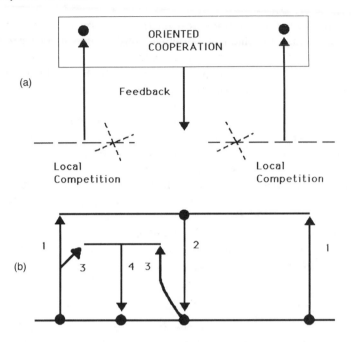

Figure 3.9. Boundary completion in a cooperative–competitive feedback exchange: the CC loop.
(a) shows a schematic representation of the general types of putative processes.
(b) depicts the actual pathways that are used to simulate activation exchanges.
Local competition occurs between different orientations at each spatial location. Aligned orientations (signified by 1s in (b)) that survive the competition can then cooperate at a distance. This cooperation produces feedback to similar orientations at intermediate points (signified by 2). The iterative nature of the process then can invoke similar filling in effects at shorter intermediate locations (see pathways 3 and 4). (From Grossberg & Mingolla, 1985, adapted with permission, *see* p. xv.)

removed from the kinds of hypothesis generation and testing set out by Gregory. Gregory is more inclined to view perceptual processing as being inherently guided by knowledge of particular objects. As it stands, the BCS/FCS model operates in the absence of such knowledge. For example, the system builds a percept of a square in the absence of any knowledge of what a square is. Nevertheless, the BCS/FCS theory does allow for later extensions to the model to take account of higher-order processes in vision and, in its current form, the theory does a good job of explaining a range of perceptual effects purely in terms of the details of interacting neurons. Such an aspiration fits well within the new connectionist framework.

Higher-level vision: object and shape recognition

As with much work in vision since 1982 the influence of Marr pervades new connectionist research. Indeed, a very general distinction that Marr made about different representations underlying object recognition is central to an influential new connectionist account of shape recognition (Hinton, 1981b, 1981c, 1981d). This model has been widely discussed in the literature (Ballard, 1986; Jolicoeur, 1985; Jolicoeur & Kosslyn, 1983; Humphreys & Quinlan, 1987; Pinker, 1984; McClelland & Rumelhart, 1986); therefore the main concern here is with those aspects of the model that are not often discussed as well as those that have been extended since it was first described. Initially though, a brief résumé of some of Marr's ideas about object recognition will be included.

Marr's account of object recognition

To provide a perspective for Marr's model, it is important to consider the general distinction Marr drew between viewpoint-dependent and viewpoint-independent representations of an object. Whenever there is a change in the relative position of angle of regard between a viewer and an object, the viewpoint-dependent representation of that object changes. The appearance of the object from a particular view is known as a viewpoint-dependent representation. A prime example of a viewpoint-dependent representation is the retinal projection of the view of an object. In contrast, a viewpoint-independent representation is known as a canonical representation because it does not change when the viewer's vantage point changes. Within Marr's framework, this kind of canonical representation specified an object's volumetric properties in an abstract propositional manner. More particularly, it specified the spatial disposition of the salient parts of an object within a co-ordinate system centred on the object itself. Being such an object-centred representation, it remained constant irrespective of the angle of regard of the observed object.

Recognition in Marr's account was the matching of a viewpoint-dependent description derived from an input image with the corresponding viewpoint-independent description as stored internally. A person's knowledge of the visual attributes of objects was said to comprise a store or 'catalogue' of such viewpoint-independent descriptions. In developing his account of recognition, Marr invoked some new connectionist processes to explain how the visual system might achieve a match between a derived and a stored description of an object. In order to appreciate this point though, it is necessary to consider some more details of the theory.

Marr was particularly interested in the recognition of biological shapes such as the shapes of animals. Here the central idea was that the shapes of the salient parts of animals, i.e. the limbs, torso and head, could be captured by a device known as a generalized cone or cylinder (see Marr, 1977, for a thorough discussion of generalized cones and cylinders). Formally, such a device specifies the volume swept out by passing a certain cross-section of a particular shape along a given axis. The cross-section is allowed to vary in size but its shape remains constant. Within the theory, knowledge of the volumetric shape of an animal corresponds to a set of connected generalized cones and cylinders. For a given object this knowledge was instantiated in something known as its three-dimensional (3-D) model representation. This was the object's viewpoint-independent description as stored in the catalogue of 3-D model representations.

In the theory the most important property of any given cone or cylinder is its major axis. According to the theory therefore, the main problem facing the visual system is to recover the set of major axes of the cones and cylinders of an object from its 2-D image. In the knowledge store the 3-D model representation of a given object comprises a corresponding propositional description of the appropriate set of interconnected cones and cylinders with special reference to their intrinsic axes. These connected axes are related by something known as an adjunct relation: basically a formal device for specifying the spatial disposition of two connected cones/cylinders relative to their point of contact. Of particular importance in the adjunct relation is the angle of incidence of the two axes of the conjoining cones/cylinders. Given the biological constraint of the range of possible angles between body parts, the adjunct relation also specifies the tolerance of the angle between the two axes, a constraint being that there is a range of angular relationships that exist between, say, limbs and torso. As with many such constraints in Marr's theory this is primarily not a constraint imposed by the nature of the visual system: it is given by the properties of real objects. Again therefore, the general point is that the visual system has evolved in order to take advantage of these sorts of facts. In this way the system is endowed with certain constraints that honour properties of the external environment. Such constraints are quite independent of the other physical (hardware) constraints that exist in the visual system.

A central problem now for the theory was to explain how to match up connected parts as specified in the input with the connected parts as specified in the 3-D model representation. Remember that the input is in viewpoint-dependent co-ordinates whereas the model representation is in object-centred co-ordinates. Given this, there is no reason to believe that the values of the parameters in the adjunct relations derived from the image will correspond directly with those specified in the adjunct relation in the model. Consequently, Marr invoked a process of relaxation to explain how such a correspondence might be achieved.

Prior to any input there will be certain angular values specified in the adjunct relations in the 3-D model representation between the salient axes. From the examples given in Marr's text (1982), each 3-D model representation appears to be naturally arranged in its prototypical disposition. Therefore, some of the time there will be a mismatch between the set of angular values derived from the image and those specified in the 3-D model. To achieve a match between the corresponding two sets of adjunct relations, one way is to incrementally change the angles in the model to try to obtain a fit with the axes in the input representation. To operationalize these ideas, Marr implemented a relaxation procedure by allowing the angle changes and the checking to be carried out iteratively. The original constraints in the model, i.e. the angles between the model's axes, are successively relaxed by increasing them over time. In its original form (see Marr & Nishihara, 1978) this application of relaxation techniques to a visual information processing problem was a precursor to the many different applications in the new connectionist literature (see Hinton & Anderson, 1981).

Before moving on though, a worthwhile digression concerns whether there is any psychological evidence for processes of relaxation. The following is perhaps nothing more than speculation but it seems that certain accounts of mental rotation can be understood as accounts based on principles of relaxation. The central result in the mental rotation literature is that documented by Shepard and Metzler (1971). In this study subjects were presented with pairs of 2-D perspective line drawings of 3-D block structures. Under reaction time conditions, subjects had to decide whether the two pictures depicted views of the same object or whether a view of one object was paired with a view of its mirror reflection.

Since the original study was first reported, there is now a vast literature on many other studies using variants of the basic paradigm (see Shepard & Cooper, 1982, for a partial review). All that it is of interest here though is a subset of the initial results. Shepard and Metzler (1971) showed that the reaction time to make an identity judgement increased with the angular difference between the two views of the object in 3-D space. As Metzler and Shepard (1974) state, the results suggest that the subjects solve the problem using some form of analogical operations on internal representations that bear a strict isomorphism with the depicted objects: hence the idea of mental rotation. Subjects are assumed to mentally rotate an internal analogue of the external object in a manner consistent with a smooth, real movement of the actual physical objects. More precisely, in solving a given problem, each state of the internal device corresponds to an intermediate orientation between the two orientations depicted in the two input stimuli. Perhaps the most profound implication of this pattern of results is that, over time, the device is seen to mimic an ordered sequence of intermediate orientations.

As with many psychological phenomena, there is an indefinite number of possible explanations of mental rotation. However, at least one of these explanations can be construed as being one based around a relaxation process. The explanation has been put forward by Hinton and Parsons (1981). Hinton and Parsons argue that the spatial disposition of the parts of an object are specified in term of an abstract structural description. Typically, whenever structural descriptions are discussed it is usually also claimed that the underlying format of the representation is propositional in nature. However, Hinton and Parsons use a hierarchical tree structure in which nodes represent object parts and arcs represent relations between parts. Attached to some of the nodes are labels specifying how parts relate to the current viewer-centred frame of reference. In this scheme, the simulation of mental rotation can be carried out by relaxing the co-ordinate values specified on these labels. In this way a structural description which is not an analogical structure can be used to mimic an analogical operation.

Hinton's (1981a) model of shape recognition

In terms of Marr's account of object recognition the central idea that has endured in the connectionist literature is that the main problem facing the visual system is to recover a viewpoint-independent representation of an object from its viewpoint-dependent description. This central assertion forms the basis of Hinton's (1981) model of shape recognition. Nevertheless, within the more recent literature the claim has been widely discussed and disputed (see e.g. Palmer, Rosch & Chase, 1981; Pentland, 1986; Perret & Harries, 1988; Rock & DiVita, 1987; Rock, Wheeler & Tudor, 1989).

Architecture of the model

Figure 3.10 shows a schematic representation of the model. At the lowest level in the network are retinal units. These units encode primitive visual features, namely, lines of different orientations as detected on the retina. The retinal units provide a featural description of the stimulus in terms of a retinal co-ordinate system. The second layer of units are known as mapping units. Each of these units encodes a frame of reference of a particular size of a particular orientation at a particular retinal location. In this account a frame of reference fixes a co-ordinate system which allows the spatial disposition of parts of a perceived shape to be described. The mapping units provide a mapping between retinally defined and object-centred featural representations. They operationalize another idea of Marr's, namely that the description of an object's shape is generated relative to a frame of reference. What the mapping units are doing is to impose a frame of reference on the retinal features so that these features can be matched up with the same features specified in object co-ordinates. (The difference between retinal and shape-based coordinate schemes is conveyed by Figure 3.11, as taken from Wiser, 1981.) In this sense the mapping units are affecting a co-ordinate transformation between features defined relative to the retina and those defined within an object-centred coordinate system. Ballard (1986), in an essentially similar account, has described the mapping units as 'transformational units' because they effect a co-ordinate transformation between the retinal units and the object-based units. Further points about the mapping units are included below.

The third layer of units are known as object-feature units. These code canonical

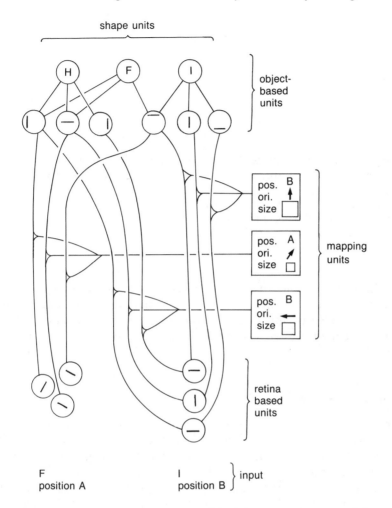

Figure 3.10. Hinton's connectionist model of shape recognition. A full description is given in the text. (From Hinton, 1981a, adapted with permission, *see* p. xvi.)

feature information abstracted away from retinal co-ordinates. For instance, a particular unit being ON might signal the presence of a vertical line to the left of the object-centred frame of reference. Collectively these object-feature units encode a distributed representation of the featural information present on the retina: the pattern of activity across the object-feature units is the parallel distributed representation.

In contrast to the distributed representation captured by the object-feature units, the final, so-called object units capture a localist representation. A different object unit is needed to represent each particular object, because each represents

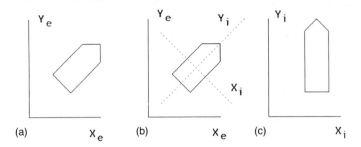

Figure 3.11. The differences between an extrinsically defined and an intrinsically defined (shape-based) co-ordinate system (based on Wiser, 1981).
(a) Description in terms of external coordinates (X_e, Y_e).
(b) Position of the intrinsic axis Y_i in the external frame.
(c) Description in terms of intrinsic coordinates (X_i, Y_i).

the canonical description of a different object. So whereas the retinal units encode the viewpoint-dependent representation of the object, the object units provide the corresponding object-centred or viewpoint-independent description. The mapping units are needed to affect the transformation between retinally and object-centred co-ordinates.

Operation of the model

The model's operation can be sketched as follows. Initially the retinal units are activated when they are stimulated by the appropriate primitive features falling on the retina. These units then activate all appropriate mapping units to which they are connected, and in turn the mapping units activate all of their superordinate object-based units. In this respect, information is passed from the bottom up. Strictly speaking, the product of the activity in each retinal unit and that in each mapping unit is sent to the appropriate object-based units. Top-down processing then occurs when the activity in the object-based units influences the behaviour of the mapping units. Again the product of each pair of mutually activated retinal and object-based units is sent to the mapping units. The important point to note here is the gated connection between the object-based units, the retinal-based units and the mapping units. As Hinton and Lang (1985) note, each pairing of an activated object-based feature and its corresponding retinal feature sends activation to the appropriate mapping unit. Consequently, it is possible to view the mapping units as an example of the sigma-pi units described in Chapter 2. They operate by gating the activity between the retinal units and the object-based units. Mapping units that remain OFF simply nullify the activity on the gated connections between inappropriate pairings of object-based and retinal feature units.

An additional constraint built into the model is the commonsense notion that for a given shape only one mapping can exist between retinal and object-based units. There can only be one object of a certain size of a certain orientation at a given position in the image. This constraint is realized by letting the mapping units compete against one another via inhibitory connections.

On a given trial, excitation is propagated through the net upwards from the retinal units and then in all directions from all units. By iteratively updating the units in the net, it will eventually settle on a consistent set of ON units, if one exists, for that input. Given a single input shape a set of retinal units will be ON, a single mapping unit will be ON, a set of object-feature units will be ON and a single object unit will be ON. This final state of the network corresponds to its interpretation of the input.

Hinton's model and the simulation of psychological phenomena

Although the model passes a test of sufficiency in being able to assign the correct object-based description to an input shape, it ought to exhibit something more if it is to be taken seriously as a psychological account of human visual processing. Research reported by Hinton and Lang (1985) provides the 'something more' in terms a set of simulations that mimic the perception of illusory conjunctions. The details of this work will now be considered.

In one of a series of experiments Treisman and Schmidt (1982) showed that under appropriate circumstances people report wrong combinations of letters and colours from an array of coloured letters. For example, presented with a red 'A' and green 'H', subjects on a significant number of trials would report seeing a green 'A' and/or a red 'H'. Such errors occurred when three coloured letters were flanked by two black digits, when the displays lasted only 100 msec and when the display was immediately replaced by a pattern mask. Subjects were instructed to report the two digits first and then report which coloured letters occurred in which positions. Under these circumstances illusory conjunctions of colours and letters were reported. Many experiments have subsequently been carried out on illusory conjunctions and there remains a hotly debated question about whether it is sensible to treat them as being the products of purely a 'perceptual' process (see for example Virzi & Egeth, 1984). Irrespective of these considerations Hinton and Lang took the phenomenon at face value and offered a perceptual account in terms of the original Hinton model. Yet, regardless of the kind of illusory conjunctions reported by Treisman and Schmidt (of colours and forms), Hinton and Lang simulated the incorrect re-combinations of parts of letters. Illusory conjunctions in this model therefore correspond to the derivation of letters not present in the input array. This kind of effect was originally implicated by Treisman and Gelade (1980) in studies of visual search.

Hinton and Lang's simulations

Hinton and Lang (1985) report a model that is structurally equivalent to the original Hinton model. It is interesting to consider some of the architectural details, though. The retina comprised a 2-D 13 × 13 array of pixels. Input to the retina fed directly into the retinal feature units. There were two sorts of retinal units for strokes (1092 in number) and for junctions of strokes (2028 in number). Junction units were in turn divided into corner units and T-junction units. In so far as junctions correspond to the end-points of line segments, all of the information conveyed by the junction units was recoverable from the stroke units. Consequently one system appears to be redundant with respect to the other. The crucial point, however, is that whereas stroke units encode the presence of primitive line segments, the junction units encode the relationships between the line segments. Information in the junction units therefore conveys which line primitives go with which and how. In this model, this information was vital to the process of correctly re-combining the line segments. As a slight digression, it is interesting to compare Hinton and Lang's model with Grossberg's BCS/FCS model. Hinton and Lang used units specifically designed to detect junctions and terminators. In Grossberg's model there are no such devices: all that sufficed were units that operated as elongated oriented masks. Junction and terminator information was directly recoverable from the pattern of activity over these units. On these grounds it seems that special-purpose junction units used in Hinton and Lang's model are not of fundamental necessity.

The object feature units were arranged into a 2-D 5 × 4 array and the same kind of stroke and junction units were used as before, although now there were only 100 stroke units and 300 junction units. Remember the model was designed around the aim of mapping many retinal features onto a single set of canonical object features. Remember also that the single set of object-feature units in turn mapped onto many different object (or letter) units. In other words, a single object-feature unit attempted to switch ON more than one letter unit. Within the model only six canonical letter units were used: one for each of 'E', 'F', 'L', 'I', 'T' and 'H'. It was primarily because of the one-to-many connections between object-feature and letter units that the model generated illusory conjunctions in the first place. For instance, whenever an 'E' was input a consequence was that the 'L' and 'F' letter units tended to come ON. This was purely because all of the object features of the 'L' and 'F' were contained in 'E'. Given this, the pattern of activity over the object-feature units was always ambiguous when more than one letter was present on the retina. With multiple-letter displays, the distributed represent-ation over the object-feature units could only be disambiguated when the total pattern of activity across the whole net was taken into account. Indeed, the primary aim of the original simulation seems to have been to try to see whether the model could correctly identify a single letter when more than one was present on the retina. By correctly perceiving one letter, in multiple-letter displays, the net was sometimes also able to concurrently assign the correct interpretation to other

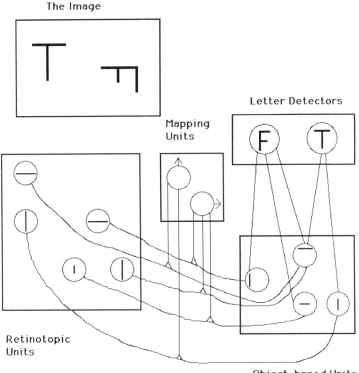

Figure 3.12. Example of how the Hinton and Lang model should process two letters at once. The model is, in principle, capable of recovering the correct mapping for each letter at the same time (based on Hinton & Lang, 1985, Figure 1.1).

members of the input array. Figure 3.12 shows the ideal state of the net when presented with two letters at once.

Between the object-feature and the retinal units were 324 mapping units. Whereas in the 1981 model the mapping units were sensitive to the size of the input letter, here they did not perform size scaling. Letters were normalized for size before they were presented to the model. The 324 units were necessary to take account of the cross-product of 9 *x*-translations, 9 *y*-translations and 4 rotations. A separate mapping unit was therefore dedicated to each possible combination of an *x* position, a *y* position and one of the four (up, right, down, left) clock-face rotations.

Whereas above it was argued that the mapping units act to gate the activity between retinal and object-feature units, in this model it is more appropriate to view the retinal units as gating the activity between the object-feature and mapping units. It is this property of the model that is central to the account of illusory conjunctions. If the retinal input is removed prior to the model settling into a stable state then the object-feature and mapping units can settle into inconsistent states. In these cases the overall pattern of activity over the whole network of units was taken to correspond to an illusory conjunction. The illusory conjunction, though, was where a letter feature was perceived either in the wrong location, in the wrong orientation, or in both. In the simulations reported the model tended to produce letter features in wrong positions. Combinations of these misplaced features could, in turn, give rise to the misperception of whole letters.

Hinton and Lang state that when the net was allowed to run to completion it never erred. However, if a random mask replaced the image prior to the net settling into a stable state then illusory conjunctions of letter features did obtain. Interestingly, if the mask occurred too soon after the onset of the input then the net configured itself into a random pattern of activity across the units. As a consequence, the mask had to follow the input after a certain critical duration for illusory conjunctions to occur: such is the case with human performance. Indeed, the model was so prone to making illusory conjunctions that the main research effort was in trying to get the model from stopping producing them.

Additional mechanisms were invoked to get the net to behave appropriately. The most important of these was competition within planes. Here the different types of units were divided into 'planes' by type; i.e. separate planes for the mapping, object-feature and letter units, respectively. The idea was to allow units within each plane to compete with one another by allowing the highly activated units to force weakly activated units to die out. Indeed, the interdependency between units within the same plane was embellished further by normalizing activation across the plane. Overall, these processes of competition and normalization further distinguished the different sorts of units from each other. This manoeuvre emphasizes a reasonably important psychological point about the functional separation of units. In the model there is a clear separation between the mechanisms dealing with shape extraction (i.e. contour), namely the retinal units, and those, namely the mapping units, dealing with the imposition of a frame of reference. This is consistent with evidence in the human experimental literature showing frame priming effects on subsequent shape-recognition performance (Humphreys & Quinlan, 1988) and evidence showing that people can rotate an abstract frame independently of letter shape (Hinton & Parsons, 1981).

Overall therefore, even though the system is highly interactive, it is also clearly modular in organization. Indeed, in one later version of the model, the modular organization increased in functional importance. Processing was controlled to the extent that each plane was allowed to arrive at a decision about which units ought to be ON before this decision was passed on to the next level of processing. So even though this model was developed within the spirit of massive parallelism, it in fact provides a serial and sequential stage account of shape processing.

In extending the work, the dynamics of the system were complicated further by introducing competition schedules that governed the amount of competition between units within the separate planes over time. Indeed, different schedules were applied to the mapping plane, the object plane and the letter plane. Given these different competition schedules, the work was mainly concerned with trying and testing out different combinations of schedules on the three planes of units. Eventually, success was achieved by hitting on a reasonable combination of schedules across the three planes. Rather oddly though, the only way to get the net to behave appropriately was to allow the system to run for some time and then to abruptly increase the competition on the letter unit plane. By allowing the competition to so increase, this forced the system to begin to make sensible choices between the partially activated letter units. However, as Zemel, Mozer and Hinton (1988) note, this is far from a satisfying solution. In terms of theory development, adding post hoc processes makes the exercise unfortunately unprincipled. Indeed, the empirical work seems to reduce to nothing more than trial and error.

General appraisal of Hinton's framework

A number of points about the general characteristics of this framework are worth making. Firstly, through the operation of the mapping units, the 1981 model affects a process of normalization whereby an input letter could be accepted at any position, size and orientation on the retina and then matched against an internal canonical representation of its shape. This is clearly an advantage over the traditional template-matching accounts of pattern recognition, which could not take into account variations in position, size and orientation (see Humphreys & Quinlan, 1987; Lindsay & Norman, 1972; Neisser, 1966; Pinker, 1984). However, in its original form the 1981 model seems to demand an indefinitely large number of mapping units to code all possible combinations of values of position, size and orientation. If this is considered an objection then it has been addressed by the claim that economies can in principle be made. Here the claim is that such large numbers of mapping units may be unnecessary if a system of coarse coding were to be adopted across the mapping units (see Chapter 2). An objection to this, though, is that coarse coding schemes are only effective when only a very limited number of possible features are simultaneously present in the input (see Chapter 2, and Zemel *et al.*, 1988, for more on this point). The model also demands an immense number of connections, for as Hinton and Lang (1985) note, N^2 gated connections are needed to map N retinal features onto N object-based feature. It is this flagrant demand for processing units that clearly questions the neurological plausibility of the scheme. However, some further interest has been directed towards the model since its inception.

For instance, according to Rumelhart and McClelland (1986a), Hinton's model can also be used to make arguments about how attentional mechanisms can be simulated in neural networks. They state that the model shows how the focusing of attention can play a role in pattern recognition through the constraint of only allowing one input pattern to be mapped onto the canonical feature units at a time. Indeed, they extend this idea to suggest that mapping units might also be set up to code translational as well as rotational mappings. They argue that the attention of the system could be moved from one object to another by merely switching ON an alternative translational mapping unit. This in turn might be construed as the movement of a spotlight of attention around the visual field.

Expectations about subsequent shapes can also be simulated in the model. For example, assume that the identity of a given shape, a letter, is known in advance. To simulate this, the letter's corresponding object and object-feature units will be turned ON prior to an input. At presentation of the letter, the appropriate retinal feature units will be turned ON. Now the only problem facing the system is to find the appropriate mapping between the set of retinal units and the corresponding set of object-feature units. Such a process will be speeded relative to the no-prior-knowledge case because in this case the system has to decide about an appropriate mapping but also possible object-feature and object units.

A final general point concerns the manner in which the model imposes a frame of reference on the input shape. Marr, in his account of object recognition, argued that the imposition of a frame of reference ought to proceed from the bottom up without recourse to any knowledge about the nature of the shapes of any objects. He went on to argue that the initial stage of processing is sensitive to those geometric characteristics of the imaged object that can be uncovered without addressing specific knowledge about the shapes of particular objects. Essentially, he examined most thoroughly a specific idea about the nature of bilateral symmetry. He also discussed other ideas about the device being sensitive to the gross elongation of the imaged object. On this account the imposition of a frame of reference is primarily determined by the recovery of either the axis of symmetry or that of an axis of elongation. Empirical evidence exists that is generally consistent with these claims (see Humphreys, 1983, 1984; Humphreys & Quinlan, 1987, 1988; Quinlan, 1988).

Irrespective of these claims, Hinton's model operates in the absence of any sort of mechanisms that might be sensitive to any aspect of shape geometry. On these grounds the account is presently wanting, although the possibility of embellishing the mapping units with some such knowledge of shape geometry is currently being considered (Plaut, personal communication).

Alternative connectionist accounts of object recognition

Dissatisfaction with the Hinton (1981a) model led to the development of further ideas about how object recognition might be explained within a connectionist framework. One alternative account that follows directly in the tradition of the Hinton model is that put forward by Zemel *et al.* (1988). Radically different accounts have more recently been set out by Poggio and Edelman (1990) and Edelman and Weinshall (1989). Initially consideration will be given to the TRAFFIC model set out by Zemel *et al.* (1988). This is because the model is predicated on the belief that object recognition is a process of going from a viewpoint-dependent representation, i.e. a 2-D retinal description of an object, to a viewpoint-independent object-centred representation. The more recent work by Edelman and co-workers takes a quite different perspective. Here the view is that object recognition is more appropriately seen as a process of matching one viewpoint-dependent representation to one of a small number of other viewpoint-dependent representations. In this framework the stored viewpoint-dependent representations each capture a description of an object from a privileged view. In this sense the Edelman account honours a quite different 'computational' explanation of object recognition to that espoused by either Marr or Hinton. A slight worry therefore is that given that either computational theory can be implemented in neural net architectures, it seems that the underlying issues about object recognition can only be settled by traditional cognitive experiments with humans.

TRAFFIC: object recognition as a process of 'transforming feature instances'

The central idea behind the TRAFFIC model (Zemel *et al.*, 1988) is that, at least for rigid objects, there is a fixed viewpoint-independent transformation that exists between an object and its features. This is simply a statement of the fact about rigidity: the spatial disposition of the parts of a rigid object is fixed relative to a frame of reference centred on the object itself. In capitalizing on this fact, it is possible to do away with the mapping units used in the previous models. Remember problems in scaling the size of the original 1981 model arose because of the explosion in growth of the number of contingent mapping units. A different mapping unit was needed for each different possible combination of values of size, orientation and position of a given feature. As in the 1981 model, the TRAFFIC model deals with features specified by four parameters; the x and y co-ordinates in 2-D Euclidian space, orientation as specified by the angle, θ, and scale as specified by the variable, s. However whereas a different mapping unit was needed for every distinct combination of these four parameters, in the TRAFFIC model only four separate units are needed. Each unit takes on a range of values of x, y, θ, and s, respectively. Collectively the four units code different combinations of parameter values. In doing away with the mapping units, the TRAFFIC model avoids the explosion in the number of required processing units when larger-scale problems are addressed.

Essentially, the model includes one layer of retinal feature units, one layer of object units and a set of connections that exist between these two layers. In replacing the mapping units, the retinal units are more properly called feature-instantiation units and the object units are more properly called object-instantiation units. The feature-instantiation units specify relationships between a frame of reference intrinsic to a particular feature and a frame of reference centred on the image. The object-instantiation units specify the relationship between an object-centred frame of reference and that of the image. The major problem now facing this system is to recover the correct mapping between the imaged object and the stored representation of that object.

Figure 3.13 illustrates differences between the different spatial relationships being discussed in this model. These differences arise primarily from Marr's ideas about the nature of representations underlying object recognition, although preliminary ideas about the framework were also expressed by Hinton and Parsons (1981). Three different sorts of frame of reference are postulated, namely: one centred on the image – an image-based frame of reference; one centred on a given feature – a feature-based frame of reference; and one centred on the object – an object-centred frame of reference. Firstly, the system recovers the discernible features of an object and fixes the spatial disposition, orientation and size of these features in terms of image co-ordinates. A co-ordinate transform is then used to specify the origin of image space relative to each feature. The idea is to transform parameter values of each feature specified in terms of the image frame of reference into the actual feature's frame of reference. As Zemel (1989) notes, a reference frame transformation is a change in co-ordinate systems combining a rotation, translation and scaling that aligns one set of axes with another (p. 11). At the level of the object representations information about the spatial disposition, orientation and size of each object feature is specified in terms of a co-ordinate system centred on the object itself. Consequently the central problem that remains is to recover the correct mapping or transformation that exists between the image frame of reference and the object-centred frame of reference. This is where the weights on the connections between the feature- and object-instantiation units play a crucial role. Each pair of feature instantiation/object instantiation units has its own set of weighted connections that are capable of dealing with the linear transformation between retinal features and object features. This point is explained below.

The method is to consider just a single feature. There are three sets of transformations that are important: (i) T_{if} – the image-to-feature transformation; (ii) T_{oi} – image-to-object transformation; and (iii) T_{of} – feature-to-object. T_{if} is directly computable from the input because it is easy to recover the spatial disposition of the feature in terms of image co-ordinates. Formally, it is given by the following transformation matrix that converts points specified relative to the reference frame of the whole image into points specified relative to the intrinsic reference of the feature:

$$T_{if} = \begin{bmatrix} s_{if} \cos\theta_{if} & -s_{if} \sin\theta_{if} & x_{if} \\ s_{if} \sin\theta_{if} & s_{if} \cos\theta_{if} & y_{if} \\ 0 & 0 & 1 \end{bmatrix} \qquad (3.6)$$

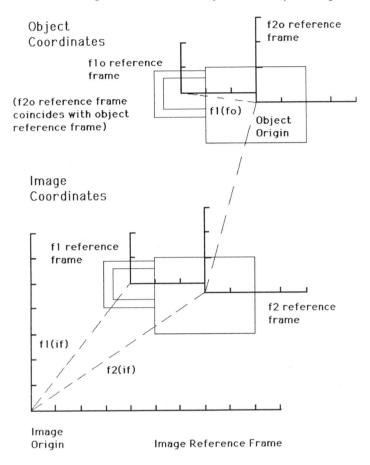

Figure 3.13. This figure illustrates the spatial relationships that are critical to the workings of TRAFFIC. The figure shows a 2-D drawing of a cup. For ease of exposition two features have been chosen. f1 is the handle of the cup, f2 is the body of the cup. Each feature possesses its own reference frame. The procedure begins by recovering the spatial disposition of these reference frames relative to the origin of the image – the (ifs) in the figure. These relations are expressed in image coordinates. In object coordinates the relationship of each featural reference frame to the canonical object reference frame is specified – the (fo) in the figure. (With this example the f2 reference frame coincides with the object reference frame.) Recovering any featural reference frame allows the system to recover the canonical reference frame as specified in object coordinates. This in turn allows the system to impose the object reference frame back onto the image.

Overall this kind of featural indexing is discussed in passing by Marr (1982). It is particularly useful if parts of the object are missing or occluded. From the visible parts of the object the system can then retrieve a complete description of the whole object.

Here the subscript $_{if}$ signifies how a parameter specified in terms of the image frame of reference relates to the feature frame of reference. In vector notation the point (x_i, y_i), in image co-ordinates, maps onto the corresponding point (x_f, y_f), in feature-based co-ordinates, via the multiplication:

$$\begin{bmatrix} x_f \\ y_f \\ 1 \end{bmatrix} = T_{if} \begin{bmatrix} x_i \\ y_i \\ 1 \end{bmatrix} \tag{3.7}$$

This process fixes the origin of the image co-ordinates relative to each feature in turn. Having computed the first transformation via T_{if}, other relations have to be considered. T_{of} is fixed and is specified at the level of the object description. The problem therefore is to uncover T_{oi}. As it turns out this is reasonably straightforward because it can be computed by multiplying the transformation matrices T_{of} and T_{if} together. The four $_{oi}$ relations can then be computed according to the following four equations:

$$x_{oi} = s_{of} \cos\theta_{of} x_{if} - s_{of} \sin\theta_{of} y_{if} + x_{of} \tag{3.8}$$
$$y_{oi} = s_{of} \sin\theta_{of} x_{if} + s_{of} \cos\theta_{of} y_{if} + y_{of} \tag{3.9}$$
$$\theta_{oi} = \theta_{of} + \theta_{if} \tag{3.10}$$
$$s_{oi} = s_{of} s_{if} \tag{3.11}$$

The network instantiation of this process is shown in Figure 3.14. Here the net operates according to the principle of multiplying the weight on a connection by the state of the afferent unit. The efferent unit then computes sum of these constituent values. As can be seen, the reference frame transformation between feature space and object space is encoded directly in the weights on the connections between the two set of units.

Appraisal of TRAFFIC

Although the model appears quite straightforward as described, real problems remain. For instance, the description has only considered a single feature, yet a central assumption is that for every discernible feature there exist four feature instantiation units, four object-instantiation units and their interconnections as shown in Figure 3.14. An overriding impression is that in spite of the savings in hardware, through doing away with the mapping units, problems in scaling still exist. The model demands a special mini-network for every discernible feature of every object. This indefinitely large demand for hardware appears to threaten the model's neurological plausibility.

An additional problem is that the system must be able to integrate the activity across all object instantiation units for all features across the image in order to arrive at a globally consistent description of the input. Additional and elaborate extra hardware is needed to accomplish this. Zemel (1989) describes this extra

OBJECT–INSTANTIATION UNITS

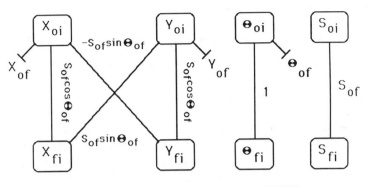

FEATURE–INSTANTIATION UNITS

Figure 3.14. The matrix T_{fo} is a fixed co-ordinate (linear) transformation between the featural and object reference frames. Each discernible feature is encoded by such a network. The figure shows how T_{of} can be built into the weights on the connections between the feature- and object-instantiation units (based on Zemel *et al.*, 1988, Figure 2).

hardware at some length but consideration of these mechanisms would take the present discussion too far away from the issues at hand. Indeed, something of a feel for the complete model can be gauged from the discussion of BLIRNET in Chapter 4. TRAFFIC utilizes many of the features of BLIRNET to build up a globally consistent description of the features of an input object.

In its current form, TRAFFIC seems to require that a reasonably sophisticated amount of preprocessing has to be carried out before the model can be put into operation. Some form of sophisticated segmentation process is seemingly required to divide the image up into its constituent salient features before these features can be mapped onto stored object-based descriptions.

Independently, of all of the above, the major problem with the account, from a psychological point of view, is that there seems to be no psychological data to hand that provides any evidence for the details of the model. Indeed it seems that the model may well be solving a set of problems that have no relevance for the operation of the human visual system. This point is further elaborated on in the next section.

A final worry is that the model describes a device capable of seeing only familiar objects. There is simply no mechanism for seeing novel objects. Indeed, major questions remain about how such a system as TRAFFIC could acquire any of the necessary hardware to do any seeing at all. On these grounds it seems that the real worth of the work lies in the suggestions regarding the representation of multi-valued parameters as distributed across a set of units. Moreover, the novel conception of weights on links between units is clearly ingenious.

Object recognition on the basis of privileged views

Perhaps the greatest weakness of both the Marr and Hinton models is their inability to explain how it is that the human visual system acquires canonical viewpoint-independent representations of objects. Both the catalogue of 3-D models in Marr's account and the object units in Hinton's model are assumed a priori: neither account provides an explanation of how these representations may develop. Indeed, it is not at all clear how, for example, Hinton's system could, in principle, acquire the sorts of 3-D model representations that are central to the operation of the model. In these final sections, two models will now be outlined that address the issue of how representations useful for object recognition may develop.

The Poggio and Edelman model

In a very recent paper, Poggio and Edelman (1990) set out the fundamentals of a theory of object recognition that stands in stark contrast to the framework espoused by Marr and Hinton. The first radical departure is that Poggio and Edelman do away with the notion of canonical viewpoint-independent representations. Instead they describe a model based around the idea of matching an input to one of a number of privileged views.

They begin with the idea that any perspective view of an object can be mapped onto a 'standard view' via a smooth function. Moreover, this function can be approximated, i.e. acquired, from a small number of views. In other words, object recognition here is characterized as being able to map any perspective view onto a stored 'standard view' and the means (the function) that allows this can be acquired by having the system experience only a small number of views. Consequently, Poggio and Edelman set out to build a neural net such that exposure to a few views of an object will allow it to acquire the ability to classify a novel view of the object.

More formally, Poggio and Edelman deal with generalized radial basis functions (GRBFs) defined as:

$$f(\mathbf{x}) = \sum_{\alpha=1}^{K} c_\alpha G(\|\mathbf{x} - \mathbf{t}_\alpha\|)\tag{3.12}$$

This function is most easily understood with reference to the network architecture shown in Figure 3.15.

The input to the net comprises a $2N$ vector in which each paired component specifies the x, y co-ordinates of critical features of an input object. This $2N$ vector is the $\mathbf{x}$ in Equation (3.12). The simulation solely deals with the processing of 2-D images of 3-D bent-wire structures. The critical features of each wire structure are the two end-terminators and the intrinsic points of maximum curvature (i.e. the bends in the wire). It is best to think of the net as possessing a

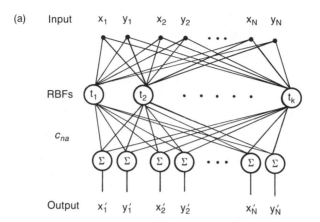

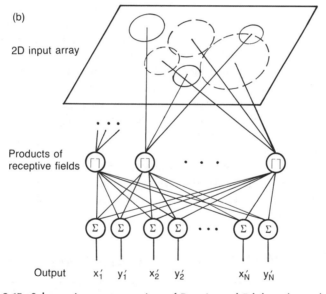

Figure 3.15. Schematic representation of Poggio and Edelman's model of shape recognition. (a) roughly shows how the mathematics of the account are mapped onto the structure of the net. The input comprises pairs of *x, y* coordinates. Each hidden (RBF) unit takes as input a **t** vector of these coordinates, computes the distance of the input view from its centre and then applies to it the radial function. The output of each hidden unit corresponds to G ($\|\mathbf{x} - \mathbf{t}_a\|$) as specified in Equation 3.12. Output units simply sum these values. (b) shows a schematic representation of the net architecture. The solid and dashed circles pick out respectively the receptive fields of units sampling different views of the same object. (From Poggio and Edelman, 1990, adapted with permission, *see* p. xvi.)

2-D input array of units. The input units feed into a next layer of hidden units known as basis units. There are K basis units (hence the subscript α ranges from 1 to K in Equation (3.12)) and each basis unit has an associated $\mathbf{t}$ vector. Again the $\mathbf{t}$ vector is a $2N$ vector where each paired component corresponds to the x, y co-ordinates of a particular salient part of a given prototypical view of an object. (The model is capable of learning these prototypical views during a training phase.)

In detail, each basis unit has N connections with the input array and each connection is actually equivalent to a circular receptive field. Points on the input array within a receptive field are weighted according to a Gaussian function, the G in Equation (3.12). In a sense therefore, points within a given receptive field activate the corresponding basis unit according to its distance from the centre of the receptive field. This allows each basis unit to respond differentially to input patterns that do not quite match with the prototypical view. Overall each basis unit is computing the weighted difference between an input set of co-ordinates and a target set of co-ordinates. In this respect the activity of each basis unit is equivalent to the $G(\|\mathbf{x} - \mathbf{t}_\alpha\|)$ term in Equation (3.12). To complete the function, $f(\mathbf{x})$, the outputs of the basis units, are multiplied with the coefficients (the weights, the C_α's in Equation (3.12)) between the basis units and the output layer. As can be seen, the output layer of the net encodes a new set of x, y co-ordinates. In the ideal situation the output of the net corresponds to the x, y co-ordinates of the 'standard view' of the object. (One of the original training views was simply chosen as the standard view for the purposes of the simulation.)

In the initial simulations Poggio and Edelman presented separate views of a single object were shown in turn and weights (i.e. C_α's) were modified in proportion to a measure of error between the net's output and the desired standard view. Following such a training session the net was tested with novel views of the same object. Success was achieved if it produced x, y values that corresponded to those of the standard view. An impressive aspect of the net was comparatively small number of views (i.e. 80 – 100) that were needed during training in order to get the net to recognize new views of the target object.

The Edelman and Weinshall model

The second model of object recognition based on the storage of privileged views of an object is very much in the spirit of the work of Poggio and Edelman. This second model has been described by Edelman and Weinshall (1989) and is in several respects more impressive than Poggio and Edelman's. For instance, instead of operating with input vectors of x, y co-ordinates, Edelman and Weinshall's model possess a simulated retina and takes real image data directly from the retina. In contrast, the input vector used in Poggio and Edelman's model implicates a degree of preprocessing of images that begs many questions. Another worry with the scheme outlined by Poggio and Edelman is that they assign features to co-ordinates. Consequently they, and not the model, are solving an important correspondence problem that the human visual system must solve. In the context of the real world, deciding about which features are present and locating them, are fundamental problems that the human visual system must overcome.

Another advantage of the Edelman and Weinshall model is that, unlike the Poggio and Edelman model, it operates in the absence of supervision. That is, the model is not trained to recognize a target wire figure relative to a predetermined standard view of that figure. The model simply acquires representations of the figures that prove useful for recognition. In this sense the model does not have to be initialized with a standard view of a target object.

The model comprises two layers of units: a feature, or F-layer and a representation, or R-layer. The F-layer comprises a 64 × 64 array of photo-receptors: the R-layer comprises an array of 16 × 16 units. Between the two layers there exist vertical, or V-connections. As in the Poggio and Edelman model, each R-unit possesses a circular receptive field and within this receptive field Gaussian weight connectivity exists between the R- and F-units. Receptive fields of the R-units are overlapping. In addition to the V-connections there are lateral, or L-connnections between R-units. Each R-unit is connected to all other R-units and at the outset, the strength of each L-connection is initialized at zero.

Overall, the aim of research was to see whether it was possible to train the model with certain views of an object in order for it to be able to recognize novel views of the object. In the simplest case the model was trained with various views of a single wire object. The actual input used was a pointillistic representation of the bends and terminators of the object as projected onto the 2-D F-layer.

Edelman and Weinshall describe the operation of the model in terms of three processes: namely, a winner-take-all process, a process of adjusting coefficients and a process of between-views association. The winner-take-all process refers to activity on the R-layer. Each R-unit possessed a threshold and initially thresholds were set reasonably high. As a consequence, at the outset when an input pattern was presented, no R-units came ON. Over time, though, thresholds were systematically decreased until at least one R-unit came ON. Clearly because of the nature of the V connectivity matrix (i.e. overlapping receptive fields) more than one R-unit could be ON when the thresholds were decreased. A transition could therefore exist between a state of no R-units being ON to a state where more than one R-unit came ON. For simplicity though, it is best to consider the situation where a single R-unit is eventually found to be ON after thresholds have been decreased a certain number of times. This R-unit (the winner) therefore comes to represent the particular view of the object as projected onto the F-layer. However, to establish this, the process of adjusting coefficients, i.e. weights and thresholds, was invoked.

Having ascertained a winning unit, its threshold was raised. This ensured that this unit would be less likely to respond to a different view of the same object when the different view was again projected onto the retina. In concert with raising the unit's threshold, its V-connections were strengthened via a process of Hebbian modification. Here each connection was strengthened by an amount proportional to the activity of the joined F- and R-units.

Perhaps the most ingenious part of the model concerns the process of associating different views. Here it is the modification of the L-connections between the R-units that is being referred to. Different views of the same object became related by a principle of temporal association embodied again in a Hebbian form of weight modification on the L-connections. Across a sequence of inputs the views of the object were systematically ordered. The views followed a natural order that specified an arbitrary 3-D rotation of the object. This was justified on the grounds that this sequence of views was a discretized analogue of what actually happens when the appearance of an object changes whenever there is relative movement between a viewer and an object. Connections were therefore modified between the winner R-unit at time t and the next winner R-unit at time $t + k$. Here k is some time constant. These two R-units represented successive views of the same object. Of particular psychological import is that the modification of L-connections was made in proportion to a variable that signalled the strength of apparent motion between the two successive views. This term was included because of a particular psychological demonstration. It has been shown that human observers tend to perceive two unfamiliar views of a given object as belonging to the same object only if they experience apparent motion when the views are alternated (cf. Foster, 1975).

From exposure to the inputs, a group of R-units becomes dedicated to a particular object. Each R-unit in the group represents a different view of the object and because of modifications to their lateral interconnections these R-units begin to form a mutually supportive group. Such a group is known as the 'footprint' for the object. In this sense the model acquires units that function as a group but whose individual members individually represent a different privileged view of the same object. There are no canonical 3-D model representations in this system.

In summary, during training the net acquires footprint structures through repeated presentation of object images. Having formed these structures, it was then able to generalize to novel views of the previously experienced objects via similar methods to those used in the Poggio and Edelman (1990) model.

A particularly satisfying aspect of the model, apart from its ability to simulate successful object recognition, was its inability to recognize novel views of objects that were very atypical or unfamiliar. This inability to recognize atypical views is also found with human observers and has been experimentally demonstrated by Rock and co-workers (Rock & DiVita, 1987; Rock, Wheeler & Tudor, 1989).

A more speculative claim made by Edelman and Weinshall is that the footprint structures may provide something of an account of mental rotation. Here the neural account of mental rotation is that units that signal different views of an object are successively switched ON when a particular rotation is being imagined. Such a sequence of ON signals is the internal analogue of the perception of the real object undergoing a rotation.

Concluding comments

In conclusion, this chapter contains discussion of only a few examples of new connectionist models of visual information processing. An ever-increasing number of other examples are continually being published. It is clear that much of this research speaks to a number of fundamental issues in human perception. In particular, the promise of the approach is that it will provide a coherent account of how the brain operates as a perceiving machine. Witness, in particular, the work of Linsker (1986a, 1986b, 1986c).

To return to Marr's three levels of explanation, new connectionist accounts of visual processes provide something of a bridge between the hardware level and the level of the representation and the algorithm. Indeed, new connectionism appears so good at showing how higher-level phenomena emerge out of the interactions between neural units, that it is easy to be seduced into believing that it can provide adequate computational accounts as well. Having considered the contrast between the different computational accounts of Marr and Hinton, on the one hand, and of Edelman and co-workers, on the other, it is clear that in practice this is simply not true. Merely building a working connectionist model cannot settle deeper theoretical issues about psychological functioning. As with all other AI implementations, working connectionist models only provide a sufficiency test of a target set of theoretical ideas. Rather counter-intuitively, therefore, simulations are most instructive when they demonstrate that the target theory cannot be made to work in practice. Consequently, and as with other aspects of AI, it is the new connectionist failures that tend to be the most instructive. In this chapter a failure to provide an adequate account has typically been gauged by considerations regarding neural plausibility. In several cases the models cease to be plausible when scaled versions are considered simply because of the huge number of processing units that the models demand.

Chapter 4

Aspects of language

Like Chapter 3, this chapter is loosely structured according to Marr's framework of different levels of information processing. The aim is to examine different levels of language processing and to give examples of the ideas that new connectionism contributes to understanding these levels. A wide range of topics will be considered and simulations of normal and abnormal language behaviour will be discussed. It is important to consider the new connectionist work on abnormal language behaviour because much interest surrounds the recent work on lesioning nets previously trained to exhibit some form of mature linguistic processing. In many ways this work is as revealing about how brains dysfunction as empirical cognitive neuropsychology is.

The discussion starts with a consideration of a recent connectionist model of phoneme recognition: this is taken as being a model of a low-level language process. The intermediate levels of language are considered to be those concerning word recognition. Sentence processing will be considered a high-level language behaviour. A brief consideration of some work on sentence processing will be considered in the next chapter alongside other aspects of higher-order aspects of cognition. The present chapter ends with a discussion of a new connectionist model that primarily deals with mapping the orthographic specification of a letter string on to its phonological specification. Final remarks concern the effects of lesioning this model and the corresponding ramifications for understanding a specific language impairment.

Unlike the previous chapters, much here concerns human experimental psychology. A serious attempt has been made to treat the models in the same way as any other account of human performance and to assess just how well they explain the available data. In this respect, many details are included about the experimental methods that have been used with humans. It remains true that this area of new connectionism is distinctive in being particularly concerned with simulating the details of human performance in certain experimental situations. As a consequence, there tends to be a close fit between experiments and simulations and it is not possible to fully appreciate one without some understanding of the other.

Phoneme recognition

The first account of phoneme recognition to be considered is that described by Waibel and co-workers (Waibel & Hampshire, 1989; Waibel, Hanazawa, Hinton, Shikano & Lang, 1989). To be fair, although Waibel *et al.* make no strong claims about the neural plausibility of their model, a number of points arise from the work that are relevant to psychology. Moreover, the work points to wider issues within the new connectionist framework. For instance, it provides an example of how a parallel distributed model of processing can be used to encode salient sequential characteristics of input.

The model of Waibel and co-workers

Waibel *et al.* set out two related aspects of speech that any model of speech recognition should be able to account for. Both concern temporal characteristics of speech. According to Waibel *et al.*, primarily, any model of speech processing should be able to represent temporal relationships between acoustic events. The model should also be able to recognize salient acoustic events independently of their absolute temporal positions in the speech signal. In addressing these problems Waibel *et al.* devised a rather complex net architecture comprising an input layer, two layers of hidden units and an output layer. The eventual net was labelled a time-delay neural network (TDNN). In describing the TDNN architecture it is appropriate to deal with the input layer first as this reveals the central assumptions about the coding of the speech signal made in the model.

Traditionally, the nature of the speech signal has been analysed by using speech spectrograms. A speech spectrogram is, essentially, a 2-D pictorial representation of the component frequencies of the speech signal. In a graph notation, values on the y axis of the spectrogram represent component frequencies; the x axis represents time. In plotting frequency of the signal against time, the amplitude or loudness of the component frequencies is also marked by the degree of blackening of the plot. A spectrogram therefore allows for the temporal analysis of component frequencies and their amplitude. Very dark bands on the spectrogram signify the presence of bursts of energy, which in turn represent resonant frequencies of the speech signal. All vowels show at least two such dark bands known as formants. The formants reveal vowel quality. Salient shifts in formants known as formant transitions have been shown to be perceptually important in

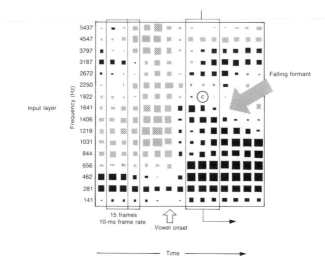

Figure 4.1. Schematic representation of the speech input to the Waibel *et al.* model. (From Waibel and Hampshire, 1989, adapted with permission, *see* p. xvi.)

the discrimination of a certain class of phonemes known as the stopped consonants (i.e. $/p/$, $/b/$, $/t/$, $/d/$, $/k/$, $/g/$) (Stork & Widdowson, 1974).

Waibel *et al.* use a digital analogy of a speech spectrogram as the input to their TDNN. An example of an input is shown in Figure 4.1. This is essentially an input array of 16 × 15 processing units. Columns in the array signify temporal slots, rows represent component frequencies. Each unit therefore represents a different frequency component at a given time point. Input units along the same row represent the energy of a given component over the time-course of the speech signal. States of the units could vary from −1 to +1 and were an average of speech energy in the real speech signal over a 10 msec interval. The total row of 15 units therefore collectively represent 150 msec of speech. Negative states are labelled in grey, positive states are labelled in black. The size of the coloured blocks denote the level of activation of the units. Overall, the amount of colouring signifies the amount of speech energy at each frequency/time point. Negative values were allowed because some preprocessing of the signal was carried out prior to presentation to the net. Essentially, the average energy computed from all 15 frames was subtracted from each component and therefore, 0 energy states of the units in reality corresponded to the average energy state. Further details of the preprocessing are provide by Waibel *et al.* (1989).

Architecture of the model

The first layer of hidden units was organized as an 8 × 13 array and there was

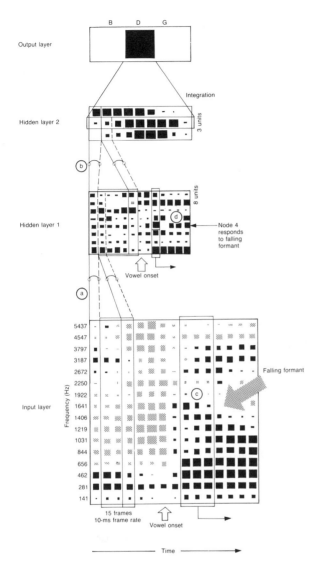

(a) Each unit in hidden layer 1 samples from three adjacent columns of units in the input layer. Each hidden unit samples three 10 millisecond input slices of speech. (b) Each unit in hidden layer 2 samples from five slices of hidden layer 1. (The links at a and b pick out corresponding time-delay connections.) (c) The rectangular section of the input delimits the occurrence of the initial formants. This area is sampled by the similar rectangle shown in the first hidden layer. (d) The weights on the connections to the unit shown in the small square are shown in full in Figure 4.3 (From Waibel and Hampshire, 1989, adapted with permission, *see* p. xvi.)

Figure 4.2. Architecture of the Waibel *et al.* model.

special connectivity between the input units and the hidden units. Figure 4.2 shows the net in schematic form.

Initially, and for ease of exposition just consider the first column of units in hidden layer 1. Every unit in this column is connected to the first three columns in the input layer. So each hidden unit in a given column is connected to the same set of input units: within a given column of hidden units the same hidden unit is essentially duplicated 8 times. Every hidden unit receives inputs from a 3 × 16 array of input units which corresponds to a 30 msec window of activity of each frequency component. As Waibel *et al.* state, some work has suggested that a 30 msec window is sufficient to capture low-level acoustic-phoneme events important for the recognition of stop consonants. Each hidden unit takes into account the state of the 16 frequency components over three time slots; i.e. time t, (current time), time $t + 1$ and time $t + 2$. By letting connections be defined according to temporal delays the hidden units were known as time-delay units.

An additional coarse coding scheme was used by having the hidden units in adjacent columns share overlapping receptive fields. Units in the first column of hidden layer 1 were connected to columns 1, 2 and 3 of the input layer; units in the second column of hidden layer 1 were connected to columns 2, 3 and 4 of the input layer; and so on. In effect, every column of hidden units was a duplicate of the first column in so far as each column of hidden units had the same kind of connectivity with the input layer. In this sense the net was simulating the step-by-step movement of a filter over the speech signal.

A similar form of connectivity was employed between hidden layers 1 and 2. However, at hidden layer 2 the units were arranged into a 3 × 9 array. This is because each of these units received inputs from an 8 × 5 window on hidden layer 1. Units in this layer therefore were sampling over a longer time period than were the units in hidden layer 1. Whereas each hidden layer 1 unit sampled 3 time slices of the input, each hidden layer 2 unit processed seven time slices. In this sense, units in hidden layer 2 were set up to respond to more global patterns in the speech signal than the units in hidden layer 1. They were designed to become sensitive to higher-order temporal characteristics of speech.

Finally there were three output units: one for each of the voiced stops $/p/$, $/d/$ and $/g/$. Each output unit received inputs from a different row of nine hidden layer-2 units. A different row of units in hidden layer 2 was dedicated to encode a distributed representation of a given phoneme. Such a distributed representation formed the input to a localist 'output' phoneme detector. The general idea was to have the phoneme units come ON wherever the corresponding phoneme appeared on the input units. These units therefore were designed to signal the presence of a phoneme regardless of where it occurred in the speech stream. In this way the net met one of the initial aims of the research that 'the model should also be able to recognize salient acoustic events independently of their absolute temporal position in the speech signal'. Indeed, having both distributed and localist representations in the model there is a passing similarity with the neurophysiology of the auditory system. According to Anderson, Silverstein, Ritz and Jones (1977), cells with both sharply tuned and widely tuned responses are found in real brains.

Functional characteristics of the model

The net was trained using a variant of the back-propagation technique. The method in propagating forward and backward signals was to treat each time-slice as being quite separate. However, weight changes across time-slices were highly constrained. Again, for ease of exposition just consider the connectivity between hidden layer 1 and the input layer. Similar principles were employed at the higher levels. Remember the connectivity matrices for the columns of hidden units were isomorphic with each other. Remember also that every hidden unit in the same column shared full connectivity with all input units in three adjacent columns. It is therefore possible to identify the same connection in each connectivity matrix. For example, the connection to the input unit in the top left-hand corner of every receptive field of three input columns is the same connection at different time points. In this sense it is possible to identify corresponding connections in each matrix. Such corresponding connections are known as time-shifted connections (Waibel, Sawai & Shikano, 1989). Over each set of corresponding connections error derivatives were computed. However across the 13 columns of hidden units the averages for corresponding connections were computed. These averages were then used to change weights on corresponding connections across all matrices. Therefore, corresponding connections were updated by the same amount. This type of manoeuvre has been used several times previously (see Rumelhart *et al.*, 1986) and speeds learning and allows learning to be generalized from one part of a net to another. Indeed, in the Waibel *et al.* model, by so constraining weight changes across the different connectivity matrices (i.e. across different time-slices) this allowed the net to recover salient speech events regardless of their absolute position in the speech signal. Even though the same weight changes were made across the different matrices, different weights accrued to the different matrices. Across the different matrices the weights eventually reflected different temporal characteristics of the speech signal. As Waibel *et al.* state, across the different matrices the weights formed 'a moving acoustic-phonetic feature detector' (p. 336) that was sensitive to different speech events across the duration of the speech signal. The general point, though, is that the values of the weights were defined temporally. Different values of weights obtained on the corresponding connections at different points in time. This underlines the dynamic nature of the net.

The net was trained to discriminate the voiced stops /p/, /d/ and /g/. Training comprised presenting the net with 800 speech samples and running between 20,000 and 50,000 iterations of the back-propagation procedure. Clearly the computational demands of this procedure were immense (three days of supercomputer time have been quoted; Waibel, 1989), and a number of steps were taken to try to minimize these demands. Most significantly, a variant of the training regime was used. Here the net was trained initially with just three tokens of each phoneme. When good performance was attained with this sample, the sample size was increased according to the series 6, 9, 24, 99, 249, 780. This training regime allowed the net to initially adjust it weights into a reasonable region of weight space. Increasing the sample size allowed the net to converge slowly onto an appropriate minimum. As a consequence, the latter stages of the learning regime took an immense amount of computer time. With the small sample sizes, convergence was achieved quickly, although the net's ability to generalize was poor. Generalization was good only after the completion of the complete training regime. Importantly though, separate nets were trained with speech samples taken from different speakers. Within this context, ability to generalize therefore refers to a given net being able to correctly classify new utterances from its own particular speaker. This is clearly a profound limitation of the model as a model of human performance. Nevertheless, in more recent papers encouraging results are reported where extensions to the model have been trained and tested with utterances from several speakers (Hampshire & Waibel, in press; Hataoka & Waibel, 1989).

Initial appraisal of the model

This work shows clearly that although the back-propagation learning algorithm is computationally expensive, the eventual performance of the trained net can be very impressive. Indeed, Waibel *et al.* compared recognition performance of the TDNN with that of a more traditional means of doing phoneme recognition. Here comparisons were made with a hidden Markov model trained on the samples of the same three phonemes. (A hidden Markov model is a stochastic method that captures speech regularities according to the probabilities of making certain transitions between the composite salient speech events. The details of the actual model used are provided by Waibel *et al.*)

The results of the comparisons were clear-cut in showing that whereas the hidden Markov model demanded relatively trivial amounts of computing resources during training, its eventual recognitive abilities were poorer than those of the TDNN. Both models were presented with many speech tokens of the same three phonemes, and whereas the TDNN achieved an average 98.5% correct performance, the hidden Markov model achieved on average 93.7% correct performance. This seems to contradict Bridle's (1988) claim that 'stochastic model based methods work best at present' (p. 4): his other point that neither method can begin to match human performance is worth noting, though.

As in other studies (e.g. Gorman & Sejnowski, 1988), an analysis of the internal representations developed by the net was carried out. Particular interest was devoted to the weights on the connections between the input layer and hidden layer 1. An example of one connectivity matrix between one hidden unit and the input layer is shown in Figure 4.3.

Here white blocks signify positive weights, black blocks signify negative weights. Demarcated in the figure are salient weight patterns showing connections that detect rising formants (upward-sloping energy bursts) those that detect falling formants (downward-sloping energy bursts). In this example, the net has been presented with the sound / *do* / and the weight matrix shown picks out the acoustic events related to the start of the vowel sound.

Two general points suffice. Firstly, as Figure 4.3 shows, the net recovered representations (i.e. weights) that encode formant transitions in the absence of

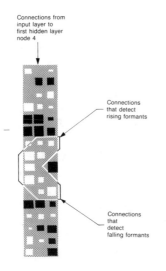

Connections from
input layer to
first hidden layer
node 4

Connections
that detect
rising formants

Connections
that
detect
falling formants

Figure 4.3. An example of the weight matrix between the input and first hidden layer of units acquired by the model. (From Waibel and Hampshire, 1989, adapted with permission, *see* p. xvi.)

any training that picked these out as being of special significance. In other words, the net became sensitive to aspects of the speech signal that have been shown to be of perceptual importance to humans. More importantly, this is an example of a net that starts out with essentially random weights and then acquires structures that are both useful for the task and also have some psychological credibility. This kind of demonstration stands in stark contrast to whole classes of models of pattern recognition (e.g. hierarchical featural models; see Lindsay & Norman, 1972) that start out by positing whole classes of feature detectors and go on to use these to explain performance. As with many new connectionist accounts of pattern recognition, the TDNN system develops structures (i.e. weights) that function as classical feature detectors in non-obvious and non-intuitive ways. This work therefore provides yet another example of how new connectionism provides novel insights about how real brains may operate as perceiving machines.

The second main point concerns the net's coarse coding schemes. These enabled it to correctly classify speech signals when they were shifted by up to 30 msec either side of a standard speech pattern used in training. This was taken as being something of a demonstration that the net could detect significant acoustic events regardless of absolute temporal position.

Waibel and Hampshire (1989), in a brief summary article, sketch how the model has been extended to deal with a larger set of phonemes. The general method has been to train sub-nets on sets of three phonemes at a time and then combine these sub-nets into something called a supernetwork. In this supernetwork the independently trained sub-networks were joined together by having a common input layer. In addition, the original hidden layer 1 units were retained and supplemented with new hidden layer 1 units known as 'glue' units. The glue units provided further links between input and hidden layer 2 units and were said to extract 'interclass discriminatory features' (Waibel *et al.*, 1989). From an example given, a sub-net trained on the /b /, /d /, /g / distinctions was joined together with a sub-net trained on the /p /, /t /, /k / distinctions. This supernet was then given examples of all phonemes in the set and put through additional training. Without glue units the net achieved a recognition rate of 98.1 when presented with speech from a single speaker. With the glue units the net achieved a corresponding recognition rate of 98.6. Waibel and Hampshire add the further rider that these kind of modular supernets perform as least as well as a corresponding monolithic supernet trained from the outset on all phonemes. However, training the modular net was significantly faster than training the monolithic net. Here again, though, several days (i.e. 18) of supercomputer time were needed (Waibel, 1989).

General appraisal of the work on phoneme recognition

There is much to commend in this work. Perhaps the most impressive aspect is the ability of the net to discover speech characteristics that are perceptually important, even though the model was not particularly motivated by psychological considerations. However, what would be particularly encouraging would be to see if the net could simulate more detailed aspects of human performance: a number of phenomena suggest themselves. For instance, it would be of interest to test the net with a more systematic set of stimuli in the manner described by Anderson *et al.* (1977) in their simulations of categorical perception. It is well established that humans show 'categorical' effects in the processing of phonemes (see Eimas & Corbit, 1973; and Studdert-Kennedy, 1975 for a review). When presented with a range of stimuli across which one speech characteristic is varied continuously, humans demonstrate strong boundary effects between distinct phonemes: performance does not vary continuously across the range of stimuli, but discretely according to the phoneme boundaries. Anderson *et al.* (1977) also note that consonants give rise to stronger category effects than do vowels (Fry, Abramson, Eimas, & Liberman, 1962). Some believe that these effects demonstrate that humans do not hear the continuous variation across the set of stimuli, but an abrupt shift from one phoneme to the next (Eimas, 1985). In contrast, Massaro (1989a) is distinctive in arguing that such effects are equally consistent with post-perceptual accounts. The claim here is that the 'categorical' effect does not reveal something about perceptual processing but something about having to make discrete responses. Irrespective of these disputes about interpretation, the effects are robust, and not naturally predicted from the operation of the TDNN model. Indeed, upon reflection, it seems that the model fits equally with the perceptual and post-perceptual accounts. It seems that for stimuli near phoneme boundaries the net would give a graded response on the phoneme units; i.e. more than one phoneme unit would be partially activated, although one might be more active than the others. As the model stands, the output from the output units is a non-linear continuous (sigmoid) function of their inputs. To model categorical perception, however, the output units could be thresholded. Alternatively, some form of categorical decision mechanism could be grafted onto the model if a post-perceptual account were favoured. This seemingly trivial point relates to a major issue in new connectionism regarding mapping overt responses onto distributed patterns of activity over several units. This particular issue occurs repeatedly in the literature on new connectionist models of psycholinguistic abilities and it remains to be adequately resolved. More on this issue is covered later in the chapter.

In its favour, the kind of work undertaken by Waibel *et al.* (1989) compares well with other research that makes many assumptions about the nature of the early stages of encoding carried out by the nervous system. At its worst this latter kind of research is confused in taking a formal linguistic description of speech as being unquestionably psychologically valid. Although detailed discussion of such models is not necessary, it is instructive that in modelling phonology, Dell (1986) makes the following assumptions. In his account, the machinery for dealing with the encoding of phonology is structured according to a loose hierarchy where feature units feed into phoneme units, phoneme units then feed into cluster, rime, and syllable units. The syllable units in turn feed into morpheme units. The feature units encode the point (e.g. bilabial, dental, etc.) and manner (e.g. stop, nasal, etc.) of articulation typically used by phoneticians to categorize speech sounds (see Stork & Widdowson, 1974, Chapter 2). It is not that this method for describing speech is of no use in practice, but merely that in the absence of empirical evidence, the psychological status of the specified features remains in doubt. It remains a central empirical question as to whether the particular linguistically motivated features are the fundamental primitives that underlie perceptual processing. An allied point is that even if it does turn out that theoretical features are shown to be psychologically important, additional evidence is needed to show that the brain possesses feature detectors (Anderson *et al.*, 1977) that directly correspond to the particular units posited in Dell's account. As has been repeatedly demonstrated by new connectionist models, pattern recognition devices exist that develop and subsequently process information in ways that are quite unpredictable from the outset (see also Anderson & Mozer, 1981; and Quinlan, 1987, for more on this point). These nets perform without explicit structures that honour a priori theoretical distinctions.

At a more general level, the work by Waibel *et al.* is even more instructive. It clearly demonstrates that in order to obtain an effective speech-recognition system a reasonable amount of structure has to be pre-wired (a point concurred with by le Cun, 1988b). In the TDNN described, there are rigid wiring constraints at all levels in the net even though initial weight values were allocated on a random basis. Moreover, the whole enterprise of building modular nets and then grafting them onto one another is also instructive. This seems to indicate that an underlying modular organization is most suitable for the task of effective speech recognition. Indeed, although the model has been developed within the framework of parallel distributed processing, the eventual account is both highly modular and relies, fundamentally, on a localist form of representation. These latter points are not criticisms but merely statements of fact.

Before moving the discussion on, it is useful to make a few further points about time-shifted connections. The basic idea with this system is that, independently of the weight changes during learning, different weights accrue on the same links during signal processing. The weight on link x at time t is different to the weight on link x at time $t + 1$. This is what time-shifted connections model. In this respect what is being described is a quite different conception of weights on connections than in other neural net applications. The more general case is where, once learning is complete, weights on connections remain fixed and do not then change during signal processing. If indeed weights in a neural net are conceived as being the synaptic strengths on connections between neurons then there seems now a choice to be made between constant and variable strengths. If variable strengths are accepted then a difficult problem remains over how it is that the system learns the appropriate variations. In the TDNN this problem is solved by having connections duplicated. Such a solution, however, is beyond the realms of neural plausibility. Nevertheless, the general idea of variable weights will, no doubt, be explored in greater depth in future work.

At a more fine-grained level, a worry with the model (as an explanation of psychological processing) is not so much that it fails to emulate human discriminative performance, but that it fails to account for how context affects phoneme recognition. It is therefore important to consider other connectionist models that do.

Context effects and the top-down/bottom-up distinction

The whole issue of top-down versus bottom-up processing continues to be hotly debated in many areas in the literature on perception. The distinction concerns whether the derivation of a percept is determined in a typically passive way driven by the stimulus, or whether processing is directed from 'above' in line with knowledge of and/or expectations about the stimulus. An example of a passive model of speech processing is that of Morton's logogen model (1969). In this model each different type of word in the language is represented by a separate logogen. A logogen is an abstract unit that accrues evidence consistent with its corresponding word. With enough confirmatory evidence the logogen fires: an event which signifies recognition of the corresponding word. In the absence of any clear details as to how logogens accrue evidence, it is easiest to assume that each is an essentially passive recipient of evidence (after Corcoran, 1971). Indeed, Morton and Broadbent (1967) explicitly put forward the logogen model as an example of a 'passive' account of spoken and written language recognition.

In contrast to passive theories of perception there are active accounts such as analysis-by-synthesis (Stevens, 1960). In analysis-by-synthesis, after a very brief and cursory analysis of the incoming stimulus, an internal prediction of subsequent information is projected. The system continuously predicts subsequent stimuli on the basis of stored knowledge about these stimuli. These predictions guide the analysis of the input. Indeed, in the account of analysis-by-synthesis given by Liberman, Cooper, Shankweiler and Studdert-Kennedy (1967) the encoded speech signal is matched against the output of the speech production system. Consequently, as Corcoran (1971) states, the phenomenological experience of the input stream is of the output from the production system.

Clearly there are many issues here and a fundamental one concerns embellishment of the input. Passive theories do not assume that the derivation of a percept involves any kind of embellishment. In contrast, active theories, such as analysis-by-synthesis, assume that the eventual percept comprises aspects given externally and aspects provided by internal knowledge. Indeed, at the level of the percept there is no distinction between those aspects provided by the distal stimulus and those provided by embellishment. By this view, as perception is assumed to be critically dependent on embellishment, it is nothing more than constrained hallucination. Strong objections to this kind of theorizing have been made repeatedly by Gibson (1950, 1966, 1979). For instance as Neisser (1966) notes, it has never been well specified what happens when there is a mismatch between the predicted and the actual input. Indeed, as Miller (1964) has argued, unless the initial guess is almost correct all of the time, the listener will simply be unable to keep up with rapid speech. These appear to be fatal criticisms. Nevertheless, it is interesting to consider Grossberg and Mingolla's BCS/FCS theory, where they happily agree that perception is fundamentally hallucination (see Chapter 3). With the examples of illusory conjunctions and colour spreading, though, the eventual percept is not so much driven by knowledge of particular objects as by local interactions of many low-level processing units. Grossberg and Mingolla do, however, leave open the question of whether knowledge of particular objects can influence directly the derivation of a percept.

The almost philosophical point here regards ecological usefulness. Surely what is needed is a perceptual device that provides veridical information specifying what is actually present in the environment. The problem with a device that embellishes the input is that it is primarily suited for dealing with possible, and not actual, worlds. It is clear that perception is intimately bound up with making predictions to guide actions (cf. Fodor, 1983) so the above is not an argument against processes of inference in general. All that is being argued is that it is possible to have a theory of perceptual inference without positing a role for processes of perceptual embellishment. Moreover, because the consequences of making errors in embellishment are dire, in ecological terms, it is not at all clear that any theory of perception based around principles of embellishment can be psychologically plausible.

In the next model of speech processing to be considered, very clear statements are made about how the involvement of knowledge of particular objects (i.e. words) governs the perception of particular phonemes. In this respect, the TRACE model (McClelland & Elman, 1986) is a top-down (embellishment) model *par excellence*. Indeed, as McClelland and Elman state, the distinction between perception and (working) memory is completely blurred in the model.

TRACE

The TRACE model comprises three layers of units: feature units that feed into phoneme units, the phoneme units in turn feed into word units. Unlike the TDNN just described, McClelland and Elman start out by assuming that some fairly sophisticated preprocessing of the speech signal has been carried out prior to the operation of the net. Consequently, they only deal with the coding of 14 phonemes and a special 'silence' marker. The phonemes were coded up according to values on seven dimensions. Five of the dimensions (consonantal, vocalic, diffuseness, acuteness and voicing) were taken from the description of phonology set out by Jakobson, Fant and Halle (1952). The power dimension was included to increase the discriminability of vowels from consonants. The seventh burst amplitude dimension was included to increase discriminability of stop consonants. Each dimension could take on a range of values such that the corresponding value signified the extent to which a particular sound registers on that dimension. A value of 0 signified that the sound does not possesses the attribute coded by the dimension.

The architecture of TRACE

It is easiest to explain the model in relation to Figure 4.4, which shows a schematic representation of the net.

As can be seen from the figure, it is best to think of each input dimension as being akin to a 2-D plane in which the y axis represents dimensional value and the x axis represents time. As in the TDNN, time is considered to be digitized into small discrete steps known as time slices. Each plane comprises a different 2-D matrix of units where the individual columns represent a different time slice. Within a given column a separate unit was used for each dimensional value. Within a given row units represented a single dimensional value across time. Therefore, the state of a given unit corresponds to the value of a particular feature at a given point in time. The seven dimensional planes, in being representations of

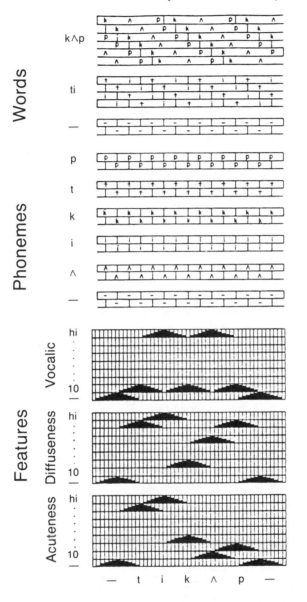

Figure 4.4. Architecture of the TRACE model. (From McClelland and Elman, 1986, adapted with permission, *see* p. xvi.)

different characteristics of concurrent speech, are seen to overlap. Connections from each plane feed directly into the phoneme units. As can be seen from the figure, many phoneme units are used; indeed a separate bank of phoneme units is dedicated to each phoneme. Each bank of phoneme units spans the duration of the speech signal. Across each bank of units, adjacent units sample overlapping receptive fields of the feature planes. There is one phoneme unit centred over every three time-slices and a given unit is connected to (i.e. sampled from) 11 consecutive time slices. This form of connectivity is used to simulate the fact that the physical specification of successive phonemes overlaps in time. Examination of a speech spectrogram shows that the information specifying the constituent phonemes in a word physically overlap in time.

The final level of units, namely, word units, receives connections from the phoneme units. For example, if 'ape' is the input word then the $/p/$ activates not only the word unit for 'ape' at time time t, but also the word unit for 'pea' (and all other words beginning with $/p/$) at time $t + 1$. As with the phoneme layer, a separate bank of units is used for each word. The model could recognize 211 words, hence there were 211 separate banks of word units. Again as with the phoneme units, a bank of word units spans the duration of the speech stream and each word unit is centred over every three time slices defined at the featural level. This overlap of word units was justified on the grounds that in rapid speech there are no pauses between words. Therefore, like phonemes, the information specifying one word overlaps with that specifying the next.

All connections between layers were bi-directional and passed excitation between layers. There were no between-layer inhibitory connections. However, both bottom-up (feature → phoneme, phoneme → word) and top-down (word → phoneme, phoneme → feature) processes occurred in the model. As will be explained shortly, the latter kind of connections were central to the account of top-down effects in phoneme recognition.

Units within each layer were mutually inhibitory. Moreover, inhibition between units was proportional to their temporal overlap: units that sample the same time slices inhibited each other maximally. For example the units for the words 'cat' and 'cap' situated at time t inhibited each other maximally. The unit for 'cat' at time t and that for 'cap' at time $t +1$ inhibited each other less so. Similar inhibitory characteristics were also built into the phoneme layer. At the level of the featural units though, those units switched ON at time t by the input inhibited only those other units in the same time slice.

In summary, within the model there was inhibition between units within a layer, and top-down and bottom-up excitation between layers. In addition, within each layer something known as decay was introduced. Units had resting levels of activation and built in was a tendency for units to decay back to these resting levels after accruing any form of input. Decay was necessary to stop units activated at time t from swamping the units activated subsequently. Overall, ten free parameters concerning resting levels, decay, excitation and inhibition existed. Part of the empirical nature of the study was to vary these parameter values in order to get the model to behave appropriately. Success was achieved in discovering a set of values that allowed the model to simulate various effects found in the human speech-processing literature.

The operation of TRACE

A crude sketch of the operation of the model follows. Initially input is clamped onto the feature units and excitation immediately spreads to the relevant phoneme units. Inhibition also spreads from the currently activated feature units to incompatible others. Phoneme units, in turn, feed back excitation to their compatible feature units, inhibit incompatible phoneme units, and excite compatible word units. Word units in turn inhibit competitors and feed back excitation to their compatible phoneme units. Although inter-level activation is assumed to operate in cascade (McClelland, 1979), the hierarchical arrangement of the net does initially produce a genuine sequential stage account of information flow. Featural information is registered initially. The products of featural analysis are then fed into a stage of processing concerning phonemes. The products of this analysis are then fed into a stage of processing concerning words. After the initial forward flow of activation, though, the simple stages of processing analysis breaks down. Processing now occurs at all levels simultaneously. Overall though, some considerable time needs to elapse before the influence of the word-to-phoneme feedback has any discernible influence on the behaviour of the net (see below).

Aspects of the general mode of operation of TRACE have been examined in many other kinds of neural networks. The general processes are known as interactive activation and competition (henceforth, IAC; see PDP/3, Chapter 2). With such networks, in the ideal cases, the different kinds of interactive processes are seen to drive the constituent units into a set of mutually consistent and stable states. With TRACE, the net is seen to settle into a stable state where a single set of feature units, phoneme units and word units win the competition with other units at their respective levels. A stable state in this net is where relative amounts of activation over the different kinds of units remains constant over time. The winning units remain the most highly activated relative to all other competing units. Recognition in such a net typically corresponds to where just one word unit is highly activated relative to all other units. In special cases, only one word unit is activated above its resting level whilst all other units are either at or below resting level. It is easiest to explain the operation of the net further with the use of a specific example.

Something that McClelland and Elman simulate with TRACE is the finding that lexical knowledge, i.e. knowledge of words, can affect the perception of the input signal. For example, McClelland and Elman give the model an input that specifies an initial feature set that specifies both /p/ and /b/ to an equivalent degree. The remainder of the string specifies the sounds for 'LUG'. The psychological counterpart of this situation shows that when human subjects are presented with such a string, they perceive the word 'plug' rather than the non-word 'blug'. The simulation shows how this might be explained. Initially both the phoneme units for /p/ and /b/ are activated equally by the ambiguous initial feature set. As time elapses though, lexical units consistent with a larger time span of the featural information accrue activation. Eventually, as the net processes the whole speech string, the evidence for the 'plug' word unit becomes maximal relative to all other partially activated lexical units and through the process of word–word competition the corresponding 'plug' unit wins. Not only does the 'plug' unit accrue the most bottom-up activation, i.e., four phonemes-worth, but it also inhibits word unit competitors more than they inhibit it. The 'plug' unit in turn feeds back activation to its corresponding phoneme units, which in turn re-excite it. This demonstrates a characteristic behaviour pattern of IAC nets known as 'the rich get richer' effect. As soon as the 'plug' unit becomes more activated than its competitors it inhibits them to a greater degree and in turn becomes even more activated. So as the 'plug' unit begins to win at the word level, the phoneme unit for $/p/$ accrues the most top-down support and hence wins the competition at the phoneme level. It consequently inhibits the $/b/$ unit and the $/p/$ in $/plug/$ is heard. This shows how the model exhibits a property of human speech recognition whereby the perception of a given speech sound can be radically altered by subsequent speech sounds. In the model, knowledge of particular lexical items critically alters the perception of phonemes. Here is an explicit account of how top-down processes might operate in human perception. Indeed, if the model is to be taken as a literal account of human perceptual processing then there is no distinction between information derived from the senses and that provided from within. The model provides an example of constrained hallucination.

Before leaving the discussion of TRACE a final example of the behaviour of the net is worth noting as this again shows how ideas about top-down influences are implemented in the model. The example concerns the simulation of the categorical perception of phonemes.

To model categorical perception McClelland and Elman devised a range of stimuli by varying constituent featural values to mimic a range of stimuli on the $/g/$ $-/k/$ continuum. Stimuli varied from being more extreme than a canonical $/g/$ to being more extreme than a canonical $/k/$. A vastly pared-down version of the model was used. Firstly, the word units were eliminated and only two phoneme units were included. This version of the model was presented with each stimulus in turn and the behaviour of the net was scrutinized. Firstly, of interest was the amount of initial excitation propagated from the featural planes to the $/g/$ and $/k/$ units. McClelland and Elman plotted the amount of activation spreading from the featural units to the $/p/$ and $/k/$ units for all stimuli and found that across the range of stimuli, activation to both units varied smoothly. The functions were smooth S-shaped. Whereas relatively different amounts of activation to the two units accrued for the extreme stimuli, the same amount of activation accrued to both units for the ambiguous stimuli (see Figure 4.5a). This shows that the model was sensitive to differences across the stimuli. However, the point about categorical perception is that the functions relating human discrimination performance to stimuli were more step-like in nature than S-shaped. A more stepped function was obtained when the activation at the phoneme units was plotted.

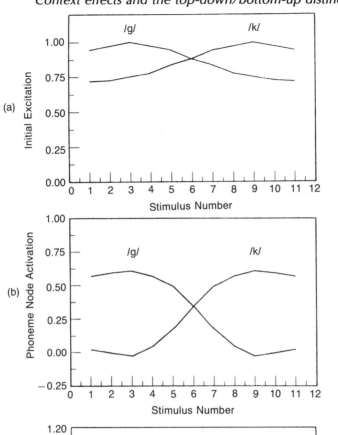

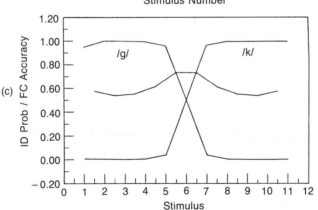

Figure 4.5. Various plots concerning competitive interactions in the TRACE model. (a) Plot of initial excitation of the /g / and /k / phoneme detectors given the various stimuli. (b) Phoneme node activation for the various stimuli after 60 time cycles. (c) Identification functions for /g / and /k / plotted against stimulus number. Such functions as (c) are used to explain categorical perception. (From McClelland & Elman, 1986, adapted with permission, *see* p.xvi.)

The accentuation of the boundary between the $/g/$ and $/k/$ units was due to a 'rich get richer' effect at the level of the phoneme units (see Figure 4.5b). When presented with the canonical stimuli the process of inter-phoneme unit inhibition tended to accentuate the difference in their activity levels. The appropriate phoneme unit produced strong inhibition on its competing unit. However, even more step-like functions were obtained when the net's actual identification performance was plotted against stimulus number (see Figure 4.5c). In order to understand this, further details of the model should be conveyed.

Something of a major issue is developing in the field about how best to map the performance of a given net onto appropriate responses. In many of the new connectionist accounts of pattern recognition, it is normally assumed that some (typically unspecified) kind of response mechanism can be simply grafted onto the output side of the net. Responses can then be made dependent on whenever a unit comes ON. However, problems arise in cases when the net does not possess localist binary units and/or when the net only produces a distributed pattern of activity over a set of units. Later, much will be made of the problems with distributed representations (see the discussion of the Seidenberg and McClelland model, 1989, later in this chapter). The problems McClelland and Elman faced were with dealing with units whose states were continuously varying as a function of their inputs. The units did not have easily discernible ON/OFF states and, moreover, across a given layer, units were in various states of activation. McClelland and Elman therefore devised a mechanism for arriving at a decision for a discrete response on the basis of the activities present over the phoneme units. Remember, results were reported from a version of TRACE in which the word-level units were simply discarded. This kind of manoeuvre was justified on the grounds of bringing the basic mechanisms to the fore.

In modelling categorical perception the problem was to decide which from the two partially activated phoneme units (the unit for $/g/$ and that for $/k/$) was the most appropriate for a given input. In the event McClelland and Elman used a variant of Luce's (1959) choice rule to govern the decision about response selection. The rule gave the probability of choosing a given unit from a given set of partially activated candidate units. Initially a unit's state of activation was converted into a measure of response strength according to the following formula:

$$S_i = e^{ka_i} \tag{4.1}$$

S_i is the response strength of unit i.
k is a constant.
a_i is the actual activation level of unit i.

By the Luce rule, the probability of making a particular response was given by the ratio of the response strength of a given target unit to that of the sum of the corresponding strengths of the other candidate units.

From Equation (4.1) it can be seen that response strength is an exponential function of activation of a target unit. Moreover, as McClelland and Rumelhart (1981) note, the constant k determines how rapidly response strength grows with increases in activation. Indeed, k essentially determined the shape of the identification functions. A judicious choice of a value of k gave rise to the kind of sharpened identification functions depicted in Figure 4.5c. A worrying thought, at this juncture, is the fact that some other value of k would not have produced such sharply changing functions. A rather uncharitable conclusion therefore is that the model has been fixed up to demonstrate categorical perception of phonemes. Categorical perception does not follow from any of the a priori functional characteristics of the net. The choice about how to arrive at a decision about a response is justified purely on the post hoc grounds that it allows the model to simulate categorical perception of phonemes.

With these caveats in mind, it is now possible to consider Figure 4.5c. The figure shows that the model mimics human performance. Stimuli within a particular phoneme category are treated as being equivalent, whereas stimuli either side of the phoneme boundary are treated as being distinct. The model does not produce a graded response to stimuli within a phoneme category. Stimuli that vary from the canonical phoneme are identified with the same conviction as is the canonical phoneme itself. This is because the feedback from the phoneme level to the featural level tends to enhance the featural information towards that which specifies the prototypical phoneme. Indeed, as McClelland and Elman note, a given activated phoneme unit 'tends to impose its canonical pattern of activity on the featural units' (p. 92). This means that sounds that vary from the prototype are altered towards that prototype. Such a process is termed 'canonicalization' of the input. Canonicalization does not occur for stimuli that fall near a phoneme boundary because feedback from one particular phoneme unit tends not to exert more influence than does feedback from another. There is no winner of the competition at the level of the phoneme units so featural information is not altered in any one particular direction.

In allowing the process of canonicalization to take place, McClelland and Elman again provide an example of how top-down processes operate. They argue that canonicalization shows how the model changes the representation of the input from what it is, to some thing quite different: namely, to that of a representation of the prototype. Canonicalization is not so much a process of embellishing the input as of substitution. The representation of the actual input is substituted for a representation of a prototypical instance of the class of things to which the input most likely belongs. Upon reflection and taken literally, this account of perception appears quite wrong. Phenomenologically, the appearance of particular instances is preserved and not changed. The world is not perceived as being populated solely by typical instances. At the very least some form of perceptual record of the actual input is necessary to support successful interactions with the world. A less intuitive appraisal of the model now follows.

General appraisal of TRACE

One of the major points of interest with the TRACE model is that, unlike the TDNN net described previously, it has been motivated primarily by psychological considerations. The model was set out as being a plausible model of the psychological processes underlying speech perception. It is therefore only fitting to try to assess its psychological credibility.

Firstly, some rather general points about research strategy are appropriate. A rather distinctive style of research has been adopted by McClelland and co-workers in attempting to model perceptual/cognitive processes. Typically a reasonably complicated network account is developed in order to simulate a rather selective set of phenomena witnessed with humans. In general, associated with the model are a number of free parameters concerning the dynamic properties of the net, like rate of decay and rate of spread of activation. A substantial part of the research strategy is then to experiment with values of these parameters until a reasonable fit is obtained between the net's performance and the relevant human data. It is true that in many cases the fit between the model's performance and data is very impressive (see, for example, the extensive simulations reported by Rumelhart and McClelland, 1982). In a few cases a fixed set of parameter values has been used to account for many different effects. More typically, though, different simulations demand different sets of parameter values and there is rarely any external justification for changing the parameter values to suit the different cases. Moreover, as Richman and Simon (1989) state, it is not always clear which parameters should be regarded as being necessarily invariant and which should be regarded as being free to vary.

With the TRACE model an instance of changing parameters to suit different cases is with the simulations of categorical perception. With all other simulations, feedback from phoneme units to featural units was set to zero. This was justified on the grounds of speeding up the simulations (McClelland & Elman, 1986, p. 76). However, in order to simulate the categorical perception of phonemes, feedback from the phoneme units to the featural units was critical and was no longer allowed to remain at zero. A feeling of unease here is that this kind of tinkering with the model gives the impression of arbitrariness. Unless such changes can be justified on grounds other than expedience, then the whole enterprise is threatened with charges of being unprincipled. True, the research is more than an exercise in simple curve fitting because explicit statements are made about underlying representations and processes. Yet even in spite of these mechanisms, the eventual parameter adjustment appears to be nothing more than curve fitting.

As well as changing the weights to get the model to simulate categorical perception, McClelland and Elman also discarded the lexical units. This manoeuvre was justified on the grounds of 'bringing the basic mechanisms to the fore', yet no psychological justification was given. This is not to say that a psychological case could not be made for this manoeuvre, but until such a case is made the enterprise cannot withstand charges of arbitrariness.

These points about research strategy may seem trivial but major issues are at stake. If new connectionist research is to be taken seriously as a new means of doing cognitive science then at the very least its methods should be principled. For example, if parameter estimation is to play a major role in the development of the discipline then some form of systematicity needs to be introduced. These points aside, though, other worries remain over the TRACE model.

As with many design features of new connectionist models it is sometimes unclear what their imputed status is. In some cases it is admitted that a given design feature is a temporary measure or a simplifying assumption necessary to get the simulation going (cf. Quinlan, 1987). However, in the absence of another demonstration showing that the feature is truly not necessary, then problems can arise if the feature has questionable psychological status. It is difficult sometimes to be clear about what the exact functional status of a particular implementational detail is. For instance, consider the duplication of the word units in the TRACE model. Unfortunately, it is this design feature that severely questions the model's neurological and computational plausibilities. The whole set of lexical units is duplicated every third time slice in the speech stream. Whereas this is manageable with a lexicon of only 211 words, it is simply unworkable when several thousand words are used. It may well be that the duplication of units over time is claimed to be nothing more than a programming patch used to get the simulation going. This position cannot easily be defended, however, because the duplication of lexical units is fundamental to the whole operation of the model. An entirely different model of spoken word recognition is needed, if the duplication of units over time is not implemented.

In contrast to the duplication of the lexicon over time, the more traditional idea within psycholinguistics is that there is a single internal lexicon (Treisman, 1960) comprising the canonical representation of each word in an individual's vocabulary. In this respect there is an analogy to be drawn with Marr's theory of object recognition in which he posits a catalogue of canonical representation of objects. In both accounts the problem of recognition involves matching a particular input instance to a canonical representation of that instance. In TRACE the whole store of lexical representations is reduplicated over time. This was justified on the grounds that it allowed the model to detect the presence of each word regardless of its onset in the speech signal. Nevertheless, it seems that a far more parsimonious account is that the speech signal is processed so that salient events are time tagged and then recognition of a given word is achieved relative to a canonical representation. Figure 4.6 shows one kind of network instantiation of this kind of system. The actual example is taken from Hinton (1988). In its original version, as a model of visual word recognition, a serial recognizer is passed left-to-right over the constituent letters in the word. In adapting the model for auditory word recognition, and given the time-dependent nature of speech, the signal is in a sense passed over the recogniser. In the model (see Figure 4.6), the first layer of units are value units. One set encode individual phoneme identities; the other set encode individual phoneme positions. This information is then

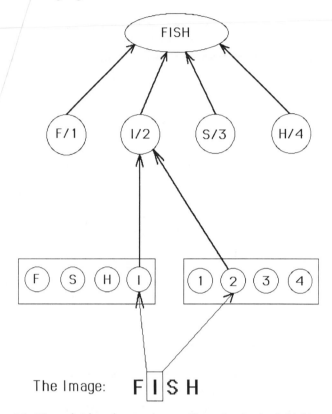

Figure 4.6. Hinton's idea about role-specific units. At the initial layer there are letter detectors and positional markers. Letter identity and position are tied together at the second layer of the system where there are role-specific, letter-position detectors. The general idea that this hardware acts as a sequential, letter detector in which an attentional 'window' is moved over a word in a left-to-right manner. (From Hinton, 1990, adapted with permission, *see* p. xvi.)

combined at the level of role-specific units that capture phoneme/position conjunctions. These role-specific units are in turn mapped onto appropriate canonical lexical units. As canonical lexical units are used in this model, the duplication of units is avoided.

Massaro's critique of TRACE

The whole idea of top-down support operationalized by interactive activation has recently been severely criticized by Massaro (1989b) on empirical grounds. It is important to discuss this topic in some detail as Massaro's attack on the TRACE model is based on empirical test and not just on argument. McClelland and Elman's research is primarily an exercise in model development. They demonstrate how a model based on certain assumptions about interactive activation and competitive processes can simulate well-established psychological phenomena. This model can be made to provide a good fit with several well-documented results in the speech-processing literature. In contrast, Massaro takes the model and uses it to make detailed predictions about what effects should obtain in a particular experimental setting. Massaro justifies this on the grounds that 'demonstrating the adequacy of a model is not as productive as testing its fundamental assumptions within the spirit of falsification' (1988, p. 217). Prior to Massaro's detailed critique it was difficult not to be impressed by the ability of TRACE to simulate various characteristics of human speech processing. Indeed, it appeared that the model was so powerful and elegant that the basic ideas provided a general and simple framework for understanding all aspects of speech processing. Against this backdrop Massaro set out to test some alternative ideas about speech perception and was able to flesh out predictions of TRACE in terms of signal detection theory (henceforth, SDT).

In SDT (Green & Swets, 1966) two measures of performance are central: d', a measure of sensitivity; and, ß, a measure of bias. As Massaro notes, sensitivity primarily concerns the discriminability of two events. Discriminability can in turn index both external strength of the stimulus or how sensitive the perceptual mechanism is for that input. ß, on the other hand, has more traditionally been assumed to reflect processing subsequent to the initial perceptual analysis. For example, response bias is usually taken as being a characteristic of a post-perceptual stage of processing and ß is normally taken as being an indicator of response bias. Massaro uses an SDT analysis to test the efficacy of the TRACE model in accounting for subjects' performance in a syllable discrimination task.

In Massaro's experiment subjects listened to samples of synthetic speech. Each stimulus comprised an initial consonant /p/, /t/, or /s/, a target phoneme and the final vowel /i/. The target phoneme was sampled at random from a set of stimuli taken from the /l/–/r/ continuum (known as the liquid continuum). Five such target phonemes stimuli were constructed by varying the frequency of a constituent formant. In this way five equally spaced target phonemes were constructed from the /l/–/r/ continuum; the middle ambiguous stimulus was labelled /L/. Subjects, on a given trial, simply had to decide whether the target phoneme was an /l/ or an /r/. Subjects' decisions were analysed as a function of the value of the target phoneme and of the initial consonant.

The rationale here was as follows. Remember sensitivity is defined as being a measure of discriminability of a certain phoneme, and the context of the target phoneme is defined as the initial phoneme. Given the experimental set-up, sensitivity effects are revealed by changes in discriminability of adjacent stimuli on the liquid continuum as a function of context. Fundamentally the aim was to see if discriminability across pairs of adjacent stimuli on the /l/–/r/ continuum varied as function of syllabic context. An additional aim was to consider supplementary response bias effects. Here changes in overall response probability (i.e. the overall probability of responding '/r/' vs '/l/') as a function of context reflects a bias effect. Although bias effects were witnessed in the data, subjects were overall more likely to report an / r / in the presence of the initial consonant /t/ than in the presence of a /p / or /s /– the analysis of these bias effects was of little importance. Main interest was with the analysis of the sensitivity data.

At a very general level, Massaro argued that TRACE primarily predicts sensitivity effects because of the top-down feedback from the word units to the phoneme units. Within TRACE, knowledge of words influences the discriminability of phonemes. In addition, TRACE explains categorical perception through the process of canonicalization (see above). Consequently, the model produces categorical-like behaviour as the sensory (featural) level and not just at a later decision stage. Independently, of these rather general statements about the behaviour of the model, it remains true that exact predictions of IAC models are impossible to set out in advance of running the actual simulations (a point well made by Paap, Newsome, McDonald & Schvaneveldt, 1982). Therefore, in order to be clear about the exact predictions of TRACE, Massaro ran various versions of the model with stimuli from his experiment. The major concern was with two versions of the model: one with top-down connections from word units to phoneme units (i.e. the original model) and one without these connections. The rationale was that comparisons between these two models would unambiguously reveal whether or not the presence of top-down connections accounts for sensitivity differences at the level of the phoneme units.

It was indeed true that the relative difference in activation levels of the / l / and / r / phoneme units did differ across the two models. Top-down connections were therefore having some influence. However, to convert these activation levels into measures of sensitivity they had to be transformed firstly, into response probabilities and next into values of d'. The critical comparisons were now between performance for each context across adjacent levels of the / l /–/r/ continuum. Remember that according to Massaro sensitivity effects are revealed by changes in the discriminability of two adjacent levels along the liquid continuum as a function of context. If / L / is designated the ambiguous middle stimulus then the comparisons of interest were between the / l / and the / L / stimuli and the / L / and / r / stimuli. Massaro was able to demonstrate that indeed there were differences in sensitivity according to the presence/absence of top-down connections. His intuitions about top-down effects produced by the word–phoneme unit connections were indeed borne out. Of particular interest though, is that a careful analysis of the behaviour of the version of TRACE with word unit to phoneme unit connections revealed systematic changes in sensitivity as a function of syllabic context. The most important point, however, was that when a similar analysis was carried out on the data from human subjects no corresponding changes in sensitivity were present. In this respect the TRACE model fails to provide an adequate account of human performance. The model predicted a pattern of results that did not obtain with human subjects.

This particular result is quite damning to the TRACE model as an account of human processing. However, Massaro's demonstration elevates the model from

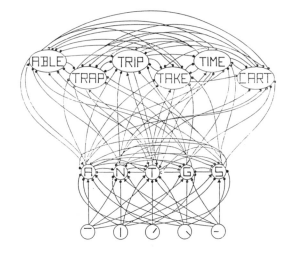

Figure 4.7. The McClelland and Rumelhart IA model. (From McClelland & Rumelhart, 1981, reprinted with permission, *see* p. xvi.)

something more than a mere simulation to that of a falsifiable theory. Prior to Massaro's demonstration there was a nagging doubt that IAC models were flexible enough to simulate any relevant aspect of human performance (Henderson, 1982). This worry is dispelled by Massaro's research. Massaro fleshed out testable predictions from TRACE and showed them not to be supported by the data. Consequently, the model has failed in a critical respect to provide an adequate account of psychophysical data.

New connectionist accounts of visual word recognition

An important precursor to the TRACE model of speech perception is the interactive activation model of visual word recognition (henceforth the IA model) described by McClelland and Rumelhart (1981; see also Rumelhart & McClelland, 1982). The architecture of the model is set out in schematic form in Figure 4.7 and there are many similarities with the TRACE model.

Visual feature units replace the auditory feature units and letter units replace the phoneme units. There are word units in both models. In the IA model, visual feature units that encode line strokes are connected directly to the letter units. Letter units are in turn connected to word units. For each individual letter position in the input string a set of 26 letter units is posited. A complete set of alphabet detectors is duplicated at each letter position in the input array. In being based around processes of interactive activation and competition, the operation of the model is identical in all important respects to TRACE. However, in the 1981 version of the IA model, inter-layer inhibition as well as inter-layer excitation existed. In TRACE only inter-level excitation existed. All word units that specify words beginning with the letter 'b' share excitatory connections with the 'b' letter detector that resides at the first position. The letter detector for the letter 'b' in the first position shares inhibitory connections with those word units that specify words not beginning with 'b'. These inhibitory connections were justified on the grounds that it 'sharpened up' the net bottom-up input to the word units (McClelland, 1986, p. 137). If the input string was SAND, competitors with the SAND unit were the partially activated units for words such as LAND, SANE, SAID, etc. Letter-word inhibition helped to suppress the activation of the competitor word units and so allowed the SAND unit to become highly activated relatively quickly. Without letter-word inhibition, competition at the word level would tend to be unreasonably protracted.

An additional point of difference between the TRACE and the IA model was that in the IA model word units had differential resting levels. This characteristic was not incorporated in TRACE. In the IA model a word unit's resting level of activation was set proportionate to the word's frequency (after, Broadbent, 1967). Differential resting levels are discussed further below.

Some functional characteristics of the IA model

A complete account of the model's truly impressive performance is included in McClelland and Rumelhart's seminal papers (1981; Rumelhart & McClelland, 1982). Only a selected review is included here. The model was essentially derived as an account of the word superiority effect (henceforth, the WSE), although Rumelhart and McClelland went on to describe how a number of other context effects in letter perception could be accounted for by the model. As the WSE was central to the development of the IA model, a brief description is now included.

The experimental task central to the WSE has come to be known as the Reicher–Wheeler paradigm. This is because the WSE was originally described by Reicher (1969) and, independently, by Wheeler (1970). In summary, in his experiments, Reicher presented subjects with three sorts of letter stimuli: real words, unpronounceable non-words and single letters. On a given trial, the target letter string was presented very briefly and then followed immediately by a pattern mask. Following the presentation of the mask, two candidate letters appeared and subjects had to decide which had been present in the target string. This is known as a two alternative forced choice (2AFC) procedure. The results were clear cut in showing that the accuracy of report was best for letters in words, next best for letters in non-words and worst for single letters alone. In developing the IA model, McClelland and Rumelhart took this pattern of results as being evidence for top-down effects in the perception of the constituent letters of orthographically legal strings. Indeed, an index of the success of their model can be gauged by the relative amounts of research carried out on the WSE prior to, (see Henderson, 1982, for a review) and immediately after their papers were published. It is fair to say that the model was so impressive in accounting for many basic effects in the WSE literature that interest in the phenomena quickly waned following the publication of the Rumelhart and McClelland (1982) paper (though see Doyle & Leach, 1988, for a recent study on the WSE). Rather than reiterate the details of the original simulations, a different approach is taken here. The present discussion deals with the testable functional characteristics of the model.

Bearing in mind the criticism of IA models that it is typically impossible to be sure about their behaviour in advance of simulations (Paap *et al.*, 1982), it is nevertheless true that they do exhibit certain replicable behavioural character-istics. Two such examples are the 'rich get richer' effect and the 'gang' effect. Both have empirical consequences and both relate to the set of words activated by a given input letter string. Such a set of words is known as the target string's 'orthographic neighbourhood'. McClelland and Rumelhart discuss the rich-get-richer and the gang effects in relation to the perception of letters in regular non-words. Firstly, consider the rich-get-richer effect. When the net processes the regular non-word MAVE a number of different word units are activated. Most of the corresponding words share three letters with MAVE (such as HAVE and GAVE); others share only two letters (such as MORE and MANY). Units for words that share three letters tend to become relatively highly activated because of the bottom-up support from the activated letter units. These highly activated word units subsequently inhibit the other less activated word units and eventually drive them back to their resting levels. Within the set of the highly activated set of units the rich-get-richer effect is witnessed. As the HAVE unit possesses the highest frequency and consequently, the highest resting level of activity, it soon accrues the most activation relative to the competing neighbourhood units. This is because the HAVE unit is able to inhibit the competing units more than they are able to inhibit it. This is the rich-get-richer effect.

The gang effect arises because of certain partitionings that occur across an input string's orthographic neighbourhood. This is again easiest to explain with reference to the processing of the non-word MAVE. A salient grouping within its orthographic neighbourhood comprises all words that share the position-specific codings of the 'M', 'A' and 'E'; i.e., MAKE, MALE, MADE, etc. It is this set of words that comprise the MA–E gang. In a similar fashion, there is a –AVE gang in the orthographic neighbourhood of MAVE. Interactions in the model allow members of such gangs to support each other mutually. Orthographically distinct words such as MOVE consequently suffer from being inhibited by the collective hostile activity of gangs. So although the MALE and MOVE units start out with equivalent resting levels of activation because they are equally frequent in the language, the unit for MOVE remains relatively inactive because of the rivalrous inhibitory interactions produced by the gang allegiances of other units. The high activation of the MALE unit and the corresponding low activation of the MOVE unit are both characteristics of the gang effect.

Some amount of detail has been covered in discussing orthographic neighbourhood effects exhibited by the model. This is because very detailed empirical predictions have been drawn from the IA model on the basis of these effects. For instance, the WSE effect itself is explained by top-down activation from the word to letter units. When a word is presented it becomes highly activated and in turn feeds back activation to support its constituent letter units. No such systematic feedback occurs when a single letter is presented (see below). The superior performance with pseudo-word presentations over single letter presentations is also accounted for in the model by top-down activation of letter units by activated word units. With a pseudo-word presentation, units in its orthographic neighbourhood are partially activated. These neighbourhood units in turn feed back activation to the letter units. Such feedback enhances the levels of activation of the constituent letter units and does not occur with single letter presentations. There is no systematic feedback from a coherent set of orthographic neighbourhood units.

General appraisal of the IA model

Unlike the TRACE model, which has attracted relatively little interest within the experimental psychology literature, the IA model has been widely discussed, criticized and tested. Some of the more important critiques of the IA model are now considered.

In attempting to test the IA model in the absence of running the simulations, a general index of orthographic neighbourhood size for any target input string, as generated by the IA model, is given by N defined by Coltheart, Davelaar, Jonassen and Besner (1977). N gives the number of other words created from a string of letters by iteratively varying one target letter and by holding all other letters constant. Each letter in the string serves as the target letter in turn and all other letters of the alphabet are considered in place of the target. Superficially, a lack of an N effect in any experiment on the WSE might be construed as being damaging to the IA model (see for example Doyle & Leach, 1988). However, as McClelland and Rumelhart (1981) note, 'the pattern of activation produced by a particular pseudo-word is complex and idiosyncratic' (p. 395) – a point that again emphasizes the fact that the behaviour of the IA model cannot be predicted in advance of the simulations. Nevertheless, irrespective of these caveats, Paap *et al.* (1982) were able to draw meaningful comparisons between the IA model and their own activation-verification (henceforth, AV) model. Specific details of the AV model can be found in the original Paap *et al.* (1982) paper and these will not be repeated here. Nevertheless, a few points suffice. The AV model is a purely feedforward account in that following the detection of letter features, letter detectors activate word detectors. In accounting for phenomena like the WSE, activation of both the letter detectors and the word detectors is taken into consideration when making decisions about response selection. The probability of making a correct response is computed by taking into account a component due to the activation of letter detectors and a separate component due to the activation of word detectors. In contrast to the IA model, there is neither word to letter feedback nor word/word inhibition. The AV model therefore does not operate according to principles of interactive activation and competition. Independently of this point, though, of prime import are the differences in how the IA and AV models define orthographic neighbourhoods. In the AV model an input string's neighbours are primarily determined by measures of letter similarity. It is the degree of visual similarity between the letters of a target string and those of other words that determines the string's orthographic neighbourhood. That is, the neighbours of an input string are defined according to the pairwise position-specific similarities of their constituent letters. The indices of visual similarity were given by values obtained from a letter confusion matrix. In brief, words in the lexicon are activated to a degree proportional to the similarity of each constituent letter with its corresponding letter in the input string. Lexical units accrued activity levels gauged by these letter similarities and all units above a pre-set level of activity formed the input string's orthographic neighbours. For example, when the word PORE is presented, the activity level for the PORE unit is 0.553, it is 0.276 for PORK, 0.275 for GORE, 0.254 for BORE, 0.245 for LORE and 0.242 for POKE. All were activated above the critical pre-set value of 0.24.

It was the differences in defining orthographic neighbours that allowed Paap *et al.* to compare how well the AV and IA models accounted for various sets of data. For expository purposes Paap *et al.* considered the example of using the Reicher–Wheeler paradigm and presenting the word SINK and probing with the target letter 'S'. In the AV model this input invokes three compatible word units and four incompatible word units. The compatible word units (known as 'friends') are those for the words SING, SINE and SINK. The incompatible word units (known as 'enemies') are for the words LINK, WINK, FINK and RINK. In contrast, in the IA model five additional friends are invoked (SICK, SANK, SINS, SILK and SUNK) and two new enemies (PINK and MINK). To compare the performance of the two models, Paap *et al.* derived the proportion of friends in each of the two neighbourhoods and used this as an index of the top-down support for the 'S' in the string. These proportions were then used in correlations with the size of various effects in empirical data. Paap *et al.* found that the AV model gave rise to an overall higher average correlation than did the IA model. It must be noted though, that both models accounted for a surprisingly small amount of variance in the empirical data. Average correlations for the AV and IA models were 0.24 and 0.14, respectively.

In further comparisons the AV model again fared better than did the IA model. However, as Paap *et al.* note, it seems possible that at least one version of the IA model could be generated to fit with the data. They state that in its original form the IA model was basically insensitive to subtle feature-extraction processes that occur early on during letter encoding. However, the model is flexible enough to allow these early processes to be simulated by changing the value of a parameter governing the probability of feature detection. This parameter was fixed in the original IA model simulations. In this respect the IA model might well be salvageable. However, further empirical observations lead to a less comfortable conclusion about the model.

Firstly, an application of the IA model to word pronunciation will be considered. This will be followed by further consideration of two further examples of how the IA model accounts for certain other aspects of visual processing.

Interactive activation and word naming

In discussing word naming, Brown (1987a, 1987b) considers variants of the IA model (e.g. see Seidenberg, Waters, Barnes, & Tanenhaus, 1984) and how they explain certain well-known findings in the literature. One such result is that humans are slower to prepare to pronounce exception words like PINT than they are to prepare to pronounce consistent words like PILL (Glushko, 1979). Within the IA model framework this pattern of results is explained with reference to subtle differences in the two words' orthographic neighbourhoods. PINT is known as an exception word because when considered against the other members of its orthographic neighbourhood (e.g. MINT, HINT, TINT, etc.) it is the only instance where INT is pronounced / *Int* / (iant) and not / *int* / (int). In contrast, PILL is known as a consistent word because together with all other members of its orthographic neighbourhood (e.g., MILL, HILL, TILL etc.), ILL has the same pronunciation in all of these cases.

The general IA account of the basic finding is given by the gang effect. Members of consistent gangs accrue much support, hence they are highly activated relatively quickly. In contrast, exception words suffer as a consequence of the inhibition generated by the members of the consistent gang in the orthographic neighbourhood. Brown offers a quite different explanation, which arises from another empirical finding regarding the pronunciation of unique words such as SOAP. SOAP is the only four-letter word in the language that ends in OAP. As a consequence it cannot be construed as being an exception word like PINT because SOAP has no inconsistent neighbours. Nevertheless, the pronunciation of SOAP is comparably as slow as is the pronunciation of PINT. Brown argues that the slow pronunciation of words like SOAP and PINT arise solely because of the low frequency of occurrence of the spelling-to-sound correspondence of INT → / *Int* /. By this account, the distinction between exception and unique words can be construed as being nothing more than a linguistic description: there is no underlying functional distinction in the manner in which the two sorts of words are pronounced. Both the OAP → /oap/ and INT → /Int/ mappings are rare, therefore the pronunciations of SOAP and PINT are comparatively slow.

A number of observations are worth making. In the absence of Brown's research the IA framework provided a seemingly natural and straightforward account of certain empirical findings regarding word naming, the general point being that according to the IA framework, pronunciation times reflect orthographic neighbourhood effects (i.e. gang effects). Brown cogently demonstrates that the same pronunciation effects are more appropriately explained in terms of the frequency of the contingent spelling-to-sound correspondences (though see later discussion). Brown's explanation works for exception words and unique words alike. Moreover, Brown's own model of the data comprises a hierarchical feedforward net comprising a letter level, a bigram level, a trigram level and a word level. Arguably Brown's account could be construed as being yet another version of the IA model. However, an important difference between Brown's model and the standard IA model is that whereas there is top-down feedback in the IA model there is no such feedback in Brown's model. This again questions the necessity for positing top-down activation. A final clarifying point is worth making. Brown has demonstrated that the theoretical notion of interactions between the units of an input string fails to predict certain empirical phenomena regarding word naming. This is therefore not a demonstration showing that such orthographic neighbourhood effects cannot explain the standard WSE in the Reicher–Wheeler paradigm. Neither is it an argument that word knowledge directly influences the perception of the constituent letters of a target string. The argument is simply that neither is demanded by the data.

Further issues concerning visual word recognition

In closing this section, two further examples of how the IA model deals with other aspects of visual word processing will now be considered. These are firstly, a recent demonstration by Humphreys, Evett and Quinlan (1990) concerning letter positional encoding; and, secondly, other work by Massaro (1979) on the WSE. Whereas the attack launched by Humphreys *et al.* is against the assumption in the model of letter position-specific units, Massaro's attack is against the more general claims in the IA account of top-down processes influencing letter detection.

Perhaps the greatest amount of controversy surrounding the IA model concerns the postulated letter position-specific detectors. At a neuropsychological level these devices seem to make little sense. Although the duplication of units is reasonable with small vocabularies of four-lettered words, larger vocabularies demand an unfeasible number of units and connections. Indeed, a combinatorial explosion in units and connections occurs with a more realistic vocabulary that approximates to an adult's. This sort of consideration appears to be damming to the IA account of human word recognition. Unfortunately, the full force of this criticism seems not to have been taken seriously. The model provides an operational account of an immense amount of data, yet it does so through using devices that seem to have little neuropsychological credibility.

For whatever reasons, it is easy to remain unconvinced by argument alone and for these reasons it is important to examine some results recently reported by Humphreys *et al.* (1990) that do not fit with the idea of letter position-specific detectors. Using a four-field priming technique (Evett & Humphreys, 1981; Humphreys, Evett, Quinlan & Besner, 1987), Humphreys *et al.* assessed the ability of subjects to report whole words from brief and pattern masked displays. In the four-field priming technique, a pattern mask is initially presented for a brief (e.g. 100 msec) period. This is followed by a stimulus field comprising a prime string of lower-case letters. The prime field is then followed by a target field comprising the target string of letters (usually a word) presented in upper case. This is then followed by the re-presentation of the original masking field. Many variations on this theme are possible (see for example, Humphreys, Besner & Quinlan, 1988), but two have been used repeatedly in concert. The relative durations of the four fields can be varied and the orthographic relationship between the prime and target can be manipulated. In the experiments reported by Humphreys *et al.* (1990) the relative character lengths of the prime and target strings were varied. Subjects simply had to write down any letters, in the appropriate case, that they perceived. Durations of the fields were set individually for each subject such that subjects typically never reported seeing any lower-case prime letters. Whole-word target report was set at approximately 40% correct.

One set of results is important for the IA model. In the critical experiment, five different priming conditions were used and across the conditions a four-letter prime preceded a five-letter target. The conditions were:

(i)   the 1245 condition – e.g. 'blck' preceded 'BLACK';
(ii) the 1425 condition – e.g., 'bclk' preceded 'BLACK';
(iii) the 1dd5 condition – e.g., 'botk' preceded 'BLACK';
(iv) the d24d condition – e.g., 'olct' preceded 'BLACK'; and,
(v)   the dddd condition – e.g., 'gote' preceded 'BLACK'.

In the 1245 condition both end letters of the prime and target were the same and the positional order of the internal letters was maintained. In the 1425 condition end letters were again the same in the prime and target strings but the order of the internal letters was reversed across the two strings. In the d24d condition the prime and target had different end letters but the positional order of the internal letters was maintained. Finally, in the dddd condition, the prime and target strings comprised different letters. In this respect the dddd condition is a control condition against which any orthographic priming effects could be assessed.

The results were clear cut in showing evidence for relative position and not position-specific priming. Remember any priming in the experiment must be position relative, given that all prime strings were four letters long and all targets were five letters long. The results in detail showed that priming was greatest in the 1245 condition. Smaller yet significant amounts of priming occurred in the 1425 and 1dd5 conditions. These results provide further evidence for the primacy for end-letter encoding in visual word recognition (Humphreys *et al.*, 1987). More importantly though, these are the first reported data to show relative positional priming as opposed to absolute position-specific priming. Indeed, in a later experiment in the same paper Humphreys *et al.* show that end-letter priming effects were even observed when a three-letter prime preceded a five-letter target.

Independently of these end-letter effects, internal letters did produce some priming given the benefit of the 1245 condition over the 1dd5 condition. Nevertheless, it is the position of the internal letters relative to the end letters which is critical: witness the benefit of the 1245 condition relative to the 1425 condition. It is therefore not just the number of shared letters which is important but the relative ordering of the letters.

Overall this pattern of results is particularly damning to the letter coding scheme incorporated in the IA model set out by McClelland and Rumelhart. Neither the relative position priming effects nor the importance of end-letter codings fit with the simple letter position-specific encoding scheme used in the original IA model. However, having noted this, it is true that the end-letter priming effects could perhaps be accounted for in terms of the later Rumelhart and McClelland (1982) version of the IA model. In this version additional assumptions were made about certain serial position effects Rumelhart and McClelland found in experiments using variations on the standard Reicher–Wheeler paradigm. Rumelhart and McClelland noted that accuracy of letter report varied little over serial position when all letters in the target string were presented simultaneously. However, when the presentation of the context letters was separated in time from the presentation of the target letter, strong serial position effects emerged. In these cases, performance was enhanced for the end letters relative to the internal letters. In simulating such an 'outside-in' form of processing Rumelhart and McClelland embellished the IA model, allowing the rate of uptake of featural information to vary across the four letter positions. In addition, assumptions were made about serial read-out of information from the letter level. To provide adequate fits with the data the rate of uptake of information favoured the first letter position whereas it was assumed that the read-out process gave priority to the end letters followed by the second letter then the third. Overall, it is difficult not to despair at the amount of tinkering needed to get the model to produce good fits with the data. Moreover, it is also easy to see how similar tinkering might allow the model to provide a reasonable account of the end-letter priming effects reported by Humphreys *et al.* (1990). Irrespective of these considerations though, the relative position priming effects appear to demand a quite different processing account that implicates a radically different letter position coding scheme than that utilized in the IA model.

Massaro's critique of the IA model

The second substantial critique of the IA model will now be considered. The critique is based on a re-examination of some earlier results on the WSE reported by Massaro (1979). In Massaro's experiment subjects took part in a 2AFC task. Throughout a block of trials subjects made decisions about one particular target pair of letters. Massaro used pairs of letters such as 'c' and 'e' and treated them as lying at opposite ends of a letter continuum. By systematically altering a critical feature, it was possible to generate a set of characters whose members lay at different points along the continuum. With the c–e pair the length of the underfolded bar of the 'e' was varied. Long bar lengths specified 'e'-like characters, short bar lengths specified 'c'-like characters and intermediate bar lengths specified characters that were neither prototypical 'e's nor 'c's. Six such characters were used in four orthographic contexts. The four contexts were:

(i)   'e' and not 'c'; e.g. 'e' is the only admissible letter in the context '–dit';
(ii) not 'e' and not 'c'; e.g. 'neither 'e' nor 'c' forms a word in the context '–tsa';
(iii) 'e' and 'c'; e.g. both letters form word in the context '–ast'; and
(iv) 'c' and not 'e'; e.g. 'c' is the only admissible letter in the context '–oin'.

Using exactly the same analysis as that used in examining TRACE, Massaro (1988) tested the IA model's predictions of performance in this task. As before, Massaro correctly argued that given the top-down influences inherent in the IA model, it predicts sensitivity effects across the different orthographic contexts. According to this account, orthographic context should produce differences in discriminability between adjacent characters on the letter continuum. In other words, telling characters apart should be critically affected by orthographic context. In the IA model word-to-letter activation alters the input in such a way as to favour the particular letter given by the orthographic context.

In complete contrast to the predictions of the IA model, the results of the experiment showed no such effects on letter discriminability. Orthographic context did, however, produce large effects on the overall probability of classifying the characters as 'c' or 'e'. In other words, response effects did occur due to orthographic context. Moreover, even though orthographic context failed to produce an effect of discriminability, discriminability was significantly affected by the masking interval. In this respect the experiment did show some discriminability effects. The critical point is that it just failed to show those discrim-inability effects predicted by the IA model.

Extensions to the early IA model of visual word recognition: processing more than one word at a time

Independently of the many detailed criticisms of IA models just considered, McClelland (1985) also expressed some dissatisfaction with the TRACE model and the 1981 version of the IA model. For instance, he admitted that the mass duplication of units and connections in the TRACE model seemed unsatisfactory and agreed that access to a central store of lexical knowledge was the more viable option. His other feelings of dissatisfaction concerned the rather limited account of parallel processing provided by the IA model. In the 1981 IA model, parallel processing is achieved by having independent letter detectors at each letter position in the input string. In this way the model carries out spatially parallel processing; the model processes different letters in a string at the same time. The model only achieves this spatially parallel processing through the duplication of a whole alphabet of units at each letter position in the field.

There is a second sense in which the model implements parallel processing. Soon after the presentation of the input string, processing is going on at all levels in the system simultaneously; i.e. units at each of the feature, letter and word levels are activated. Once activation has spread through the levels in series, simultaneous processing operates at all levels. This kind of parallel processing is the essence of IAC models (cf. Richman & Simon, 1989).

Nevertheless, there is one critical sense in which the model is inherently a sequential processing device: it can only sensibly process one word at a time. The ideal case under which the model operates is where an input string remains clamped on the feature units until the net settles into a stable state. If the string is removed or replaced by another stimulus such as a mask (see Rumelhart & McClelland, 1982), there is less of a guarantee that the net will settle into an appropriate stable state. In the masking case, the input string is removed and replaced by masking characters (i.e. hash marks – '#') on the feature units (McClelland & Rumelhart, 1981, p. 390). The net is therefore disrupted in processing the original letter string. There has been some debate on this point in the psychological literature (Holender, 1986; Evett, Humphreys, & Quinlan, 1986) over whether the model provides an interference or an interruption account of masking (Turvey, 1973). As Henderson (1982) notes, masking conceived as a process of integration is where the target and mask 'become treated as a single montage at later processing stages' (p. 308). In contrast, masking conceived as a process of interruption implies that the target and mask compete for processing resources. Effective masking is where the mask wins the competition to the extent that the processing of the target is abandoned in favour of the processing of the mask. Neither branch of the dichotomy between integration and interference ideally captures how the IA model explains masking. Indeed, aspects of both accounts apply. Immediately following the presentation of the mask, the letter units previously activated by the target letter string remain partially activated even though the featural units now represent the features specifying the masking characters. Later on, though, undifferentiated activation from the masking characters wipes out any sensible letter unit activation. The central point is that the model only operates effectively when presented with one input string at a time.

In considering human visual word recognition, McClelland (1985) argued that it was more appropriate to develop accounts where more than one word can be dealt with at once. On this point, the data reported by Mozer (1983) were seen to be critical. Mozer had subjects view briefly presented and pattern-masked two-word arrays. Each word pair horizontally straddled the central fixation point and subjects had to attend to both but report only one. The target word was indicated after the offset of the mask. Given these experimental conditions, subjects made many letter migration errors: if the array 'LINE LACE' was presented, subjects reported LANE or LICE. In detail: consider the example of the array 'SAND LANE' where SAND is the probed target. On 69% of trials subjects were correct. On 13.3% of trials the data revealed single letter migrations such as SANE or LAND. Double migration errors such as reporting LANE rather than the probed SAND occurred on only 0.5% of trials. Other errors occurred on 17.2% of the trials.

At the time these results were reported Mozer was at pains to argue that letter migrations were perceptual in nature rather than being the product of some form of post-perceptual mechanism. (This was even though the task was perceptual report rather than, say, target detection.) The main evidence for this claim was that number of letter migrations tended to vary inversely with the separation distance between the words. Mozer argued that the effect of word separation would not have been predicted by accounts of letter migrations based on post-perceptual mechanisms such as memory confusions. He argued therefore that letter migrations were due to subjects misperceiving the constituent words. Consequently, connectionist research on letter migrations has dealt with perceptual accounts of the phenomenon.

Two accounts attempting to deal with more than one word at once will now be described. CID, the first such account, was set out by McClelland (1985); BLIRNET, the second such account, was set out by Mozer (1987). Only a brief description of CID is included as it is an unfortunately complicated and unsatisfying model. BLIRNET is of more interest as it addresses a number of issues central to connectionism and psychology. For instance, a recent application of BLIRNET has been described in terms of simulating attentional processes in visual word recognition (Mozer, 1988).

CID

Firstly consider CID (McClelland, 1985, 1986). To reiterate, CID was primarily set out as a demonstration of how a connectionist net could process more than one word at once. It was particularly concerned with simulating letter migrations as described by Mozer (1983). Oddly enough though, Mozer's data demonstrate profound limitations humans exhibit in trying to process two words at the same time.

Architecture of CID

A schematic example of CID is given in Figure 4.8. There are essentially three main components to the model, comprising programmable modules, a central module and a connection activation system (henceforth the CAS). The programmable modules comprise programmable letter units interconnected to programmable word units. As in the IA model in each programmable module a set of letter units is duplicated at each letter position. In the example given in the figure, the programmable module can only process two-letter words and it can only recognize four letters in each position. There are two such programmable modules shown; consequently the model can deal with two words simultaneously. By extension, a programmable module is dedicated to each position on the retina where a word can occur. In this respect, and as is the case with the TRACE model, there is mass duplication of hardware. However, whereas the duplication of hardware in TRACE was necessary to account for the pick-up of auditory information over time, here hardware is duplicated to account for the pick-up of visual information over space at the same time. Unlike TRACE though, in CID, there is a central knowledge store or canonical lexicon, known as the central module, to which the programmable modules are connected. The number of units and their interconnectivity in the central module is isomorphic with that used in the programmable modules. Moreover, there is special connectivity between the programmable modules and the central module. Direct excitatory connections between the letter units in the programmable modules (i.e. programmable letter units) and their counterparts (the central letter units) in the central module exist. This means that whenever a particular letter is present in a particular position in either word, it activates its counterpart in the central module directly. There were no inter-level inhibitory connections in this model. Activation from the particular programmable letter unit spreads upwards to its corresponding central letter unit. In addition, activation from the programmable letter unit spreads to all programmable word units to which it is connected. Activation from the corresponding central letter unit then spreads along its connections to its corresponding central word units. These units in turn act to feed back activation downwards to both programmable modules through the CAS. Activation via the CAS, feeds back to 'gate' the connections between the programmable letter units and the programmable word units in both programmable modules.

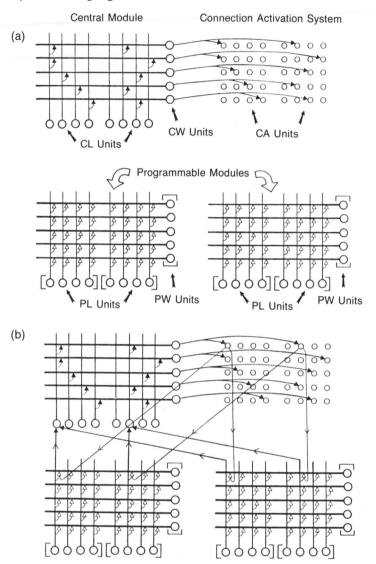

Figure 4.8. Schematic representation of the architecture of CID. (a) shows a schematic representation of the separate module. (b) shows a skeleton of the connections between the modules. (From McClelland, 1985, adapted with permission, *see* p. xvi.)

Functional characteristics of CID

In the case where a word is presented to only the left programmable module the overall effect is that the model attempts to reproduce the pattern of activity found in the left programmable module in the right programmable module. This is perhaps best explained by example. If the word IN is presented to the left programmable module then the 'I' in the first position activates the central representation of the 'I' in the first position in the central module. It subsequently activates the programmable word units for IN and IS to some degree. Connections exist between the 'I' unit in the first position and IS programmable word unit (the I → IS connection) and the 'I' unit in the first position and the IN unit (the I → IN connection). The central letter unit for 'I' in the first position activates the central word units for IS and IN and these in turn begin to produce feedback. Activation spreads from these units via the CAS to the corresponding I → IN and the I → IS connections in both programmable modules. Consequently, the IS and IN programmable word units in both programmable modules become activated. This is despite the fact that no word is actually present in the right programmable module.

In the case where two words are present at once the model succeeds in being able to recover the right pattern of activity across the net such that the appropriate programmable word units become highly active in the separate programmable modules. This is even in the face of the considerable cross-talk that takes place across the two modules. Indeed, it is cross-talk that allows the model to simulate Mozer's data on letter migrations. In demonstrating this via simulations, McClelland plotted out the activation levels of the programmable word units in one programmable module (say the left module) when SAND is presented to it and LANE is presented to the other (right) programmable module. In this example the SAND unit accrues the highest level of activity in the left module. Next highest are the levels for the LAND and SANE units. Both LAND and SANE can be construed as being single letter migrations. The unit for LANE, a word construed as a double letter migration, accrues hardly any activation. Overall, the order of the levels of activation of the word units mirrors the order of the incidence of the different sorts of responses in Mozer's experiments. Consequently, the model is taken as providing a simulation of human performance in the task.

Unfortunately, it seems that some legitimate objections to this claim can be made. It is indeed true that the order of the levels of activation of programmable word units does mirror the incidence of the different kinds of responses in the task. Nevertheless, the relative sizes of difference between the levels of activation for the various kinds of word units does not fit with the relative differences in the order of the various kinds of responses in the task. To reiterate, correct responses occurred on approximately 70% of the trials; single migrations occurred on approximately 13.0% of the trial; and double letter migrations occurred on 0.5% of the trials. The problem here is that when the levels of activation for the corresponding kinds of words is examined, correct types accrued a value of 0.7; single migrations accrued a value of 0.3; and double migrations are driven slightly below the baseline. This seems to suggest that the model would predict that single migrations should occur about half as often as correct responses. This simply did not happen. Indeed, it is still difficult to see how the model could ever make an error given that the correct programmable word unit always accrues the most activation. Independently of the relative level of activation in the different kinds of word units the model always succeeds in arriving at the correct interpretation of the letter strings in the modules.

Irrespective of these considerations, McClelland does attempt to set out the virtues of the model. For instance, a distinctive aspect of the net is that it uses sigma-pi (see Chapter 2) or multiplicative connections in the programmable modules. Activation from the central module essentially modulates excitation flowing from the programmable letter units to the programmable word units. It is in this way that stored knowledge affects perceptual processing. The feedback via the CAS dynamically alters the activity levels on the connections in the programmable modules. It is this idea of dynamically modifiable connections that is of some interest. In CID, the connections in the programmable modules are modified by an external input (in this case, stored knowledge) independently of the stimulus presented to the net. By allowing such external influences it is easy to see how the model could be extended to account for other 'top-down' effects in word recognition, such as those attributed to attention, expectation, prediction, etc.

In closing, there are two senses in which the programmable modules are programmable: firstly, with respect to the modifiable connections, as just described; and secondly, with respect to the constituent letter and word units. The claim is that it is possible to view the programmable modules as being abstract mechanisms that are not tied to any particular alphabet or script. In this sense the whole net could be reprogrammed to operate with a different language whilst maintaining the basic architecture.

BLIRNET

In a quite different account of modelling spatially parallel processing of separate words, Mozer developed a connectionist net known as BLIRNET. BLIRNET is an acronym derived from the fact that the model is said to build location-independent representations of multiple words. The net comprises six independent layers of units. L1, the first layer, comprises a 36 × 6 2-D array of input units that are sensitive to five different primitive letter-stroke features. L1 encodes the retinotopic position of: (1) left-diagonal strokes; (2) right-diagonal strokes; (3) horizontal strokes; (4) vertical strokes; and (5) stroke terminators. Letters in words are therefore presented to the model in terms of the appropriate sets of five primitive features. From this information the model is meant to be able to identify which words are present on the retina independently of their actual retinal position.

The 36 × 6 retina is then mapped onto L2, in which each unit coarse codes activities in L1. Coarse coding is invoked at each layer up to L5 to the extent that progressively fewer units are used in moving through the layers to L5. Unfortunately, the nature of the representations coded by the units at L2–L5 are not specified. However, units in L6 are said to represent letter cluster information and consequently become highly activated whenever and wherever their appropriate letter clusters appear on the retina. The net is described as being able to extract a translation-invariant representation of whichever letter clusters are present on the retina. L6 units encode letter triples in four consecutive letter slots. Consider the word MONEY; the letter cluster units that represent this word are **M, **_O, *MO, *_ON, *M_N, MON, M_NE, MO_E, ONE, O_EY, ON_Y, NEY, NE_*, N_Y*, EY*, E_**, and Y**. (The asterisks specify white spaces and the underscores specify any letter.) What is particularly appealing about this form of representation is that it fits well with the demonstrations by Humphreys *et al.* (1990) that end letters are given some form of priority during recognition, that the ordering of the internal letters is important and that internal letters are specified relative to the end letters. For instance, as Mozer (1987) notes, the first two letters and the last two letters are explicitly coded as such (**M, **_O, E_**, and Y**). So the end letters and the letters adjacent to the end letters are specified as such and the relative ordering of the letters is preserved in this coding scheme. This is not to argue that the scheme is completely adequate, all that is being argued is that it avoids and overcomes the profound problems associated with the letter position-specific detectors used in the earlier IA models.

In addition to representational considerations, the model also embodied some ideas about learning. For whereas the weights on the connections up to L5 were fixed, the weights on the connections between L5 and L6 were modifiable. In an initial training period, one word at a time was chosen at random from a set of 909 and presented at a randomly chosen position on the retina (i.e. on L1). Activation spread through the net and the weights on the connections between L5 and L6 were modified according to the delta rule (see Chapter 2). Although specific details are not included in the paper, Mozer (1987) states that whereas the net factors out explicit location information from the input in affecting the L1–L5 mapping, the eventual L5 representation did change as the string is moved across the retina. However, the L5 representation for a given string was said to include translation-invariant cues. Given this, the learning procedure was used to allow the net to map these L5 cues onto the specific letter clusters represented at L6. In this respect the model is said to learn to be able to recognize letter clusters independently of where on the retina they fell.

Of particular note is the nature of the activation function implemented with the units. Units sum the product of the weight and states on the connections to units in the previous layer and then pass this sum through an S-shaped logistic function. The exact function is given by Mozer (1987, p. 91), but the steepness of the function is given by an exponent constant known as k. Large values of k force the units to behave in a highly non-linear fashion approximating to that of a binary threshold logic units. High k values give rise to an S-shaped function that approximated a step function. Smaller values of k give rise to nearly linear behaviour. In the model, the largest value of k was provided for L2 units, successively smaller k values were provided for units ascending up to L6. The non-linear L2 units consequently behaved so as to signal the presence/absence of local relationships among letter features. The linearities higher up allowed the units to produce a more graded response. Overall, this is a really elegant demonstration of how a uniform set of units can appear to be type-distinct simply because they behave in superficially different ways.

After training, the model did show some success in dealing with single word presentations. That is, it was able to recover the appropriate letter clusters for the input string independently of the string's absolute retinal position. Of particular interest, though, was the model's ability to deal with more than one word at a time. Again some success was achieved in recovering the appropriate letter clusters for two words presented at the same time. However, fundamental problems arose when BLIRNET attempted to process two words at once.

Essentially, the whole model was predicated upon the belief that word identity could be recovered from the appropriate set of active letter cluster units. Consider the example, CAT: here the appropriate letter cluster units are **C, **_A, *CA, *_AT, *C_T, CAT, C_T*, CA_*, AT*, A_**, T**. As Pinker and Prince (1988) state in relation to a similar coding scheme, it is rather misleading to set out these units in the strict left-to-right manner given because no such interdependencies between the letter cluster units exist in the model. Nevertheless, the claim is that the word CAT, and only the word CAT, can be reconstructed from the set of letter cluster units listed. However, all that the net recovers when it processes two words at once is the union of two sets of appropriately activated letter cluster units. It does not mark the letter cluster units according to which input string they are associated with. This is just one of the profound limitations of dealing with a fully distributed system hinted at before. Given this problem, an additional mechanism was developed to put the representations of the letter clusters back together again in appropriate ways. This mechanism was known as the pull-out net.

The pull-out net was a duplicate layer of the letter cluster units in L6. However, in the pull-out net, the units were interconnected in systematic ways. Compatible letter cluster units were connected together with excitatory connections; incompatible letter cluster units were connected together with inhibitory connections. It is through these connections that the pull-out net captured lexical/orthographic knowledge. For example, an excitatory connection existed between the *CA_ unit and the *_AT unit because the string CAT is an orthographically legal string in written English. An example of a pair of units conjoined with an inhibitory connection was **P and **B. This inhibitory connection captures the fact that an English word cannot begin with both 'P' and 'B'. In the reported simulations the pull-out net was set up to extract a consistent set of letter units that specified just one word. The model, although capable of processing more than one word at a time, was only capable of identifying one word at a time. This point will be returned to shortly. Through interactive processes of competition and co-operation the pull-out net was able to settle on a consistent set of letter cluster units that specified a single word. Indeed, some errors the net made in producing single word responses were interesting when BLIRNET was presented with two words at once. Although there are few details given, Mozer stated that the net did produce errors similar in nature to the letter migration errors previously described. For instance, when the words SAND and LANE were presented, the units for S_NE, SA_E, and LA_D became highly activated. It is just these letter cluster units that would be activated by the words reported by subjects and classified as letter migrations; i.e. SANE, and LAND. Mozer simply states that occasionally the pull-out net errs in producing a string constituting a letter migration.

In addition to the pull-out net the model was further embellished with something known as an attention mechanism (Mozer, 1988). The attentional mechanism (or AM) was a layer of units isomorphic with the L1 units. Units in the attentional mechanism (henceforth, AM units) influenced the probability of transmission of activation between L1 and L2. In discussing the AM units Mozer builds in certain assumptions about the nature of visual attention as characterized as a spotlight (Posner, 1980; Treisman & Gelade, 1980). By analogy, it is possible to view visual attention as a spotlight to the extent that attention can be directed and moved around like a real spotlight. The claim is that anything that falls with this spotlight of attention accrues either priority of processing or some other form of enhanced analysis. Moreover, the movement of the spotlight is governed by the attention-capturing aspects of a stimulus as well as by being under the control of some internal executive. Both internal and external forces are therefore accommodated within BLIRNET because the state of a given AM unit is governed in part by components due to inputs from the retina (L1) and inputs from something termed 'higher levels of cognition'. It is therefore easy to see that conflicts can exist between internal and external influences governing the movement of the attentional spotlight. In the model these conflicts were resolved by allowing the AM to use a relaxation procedure to arrive at a solution to this rather specialized example of constraint satisfaction. Detailed examples can be found in Mozer (1988).

Critical appraisal of BLIRNET

BLIRNET is an interesting case of where a distributed system is used to model the lexicon. As was noted above, since Treisman (1960) introduced the idea of an internal lexicon that specifies an individual's vocabulary, many have explored its theoretical implications in terms of localist representationalist schemes. It has typically been the case that theorists have posited a single unit, detector or logogen (Morton, 1969) for each word. Minimalists assume that all such a unit encodes is the orthographic specification of the word in some abstract form. In BLIRNET, however, there are no such single word detectors. In the absence of the pull-out net all that exist are the letter cluster units. Indeed, even with the pull-out net the only nodes are the letter cluster units. Importantly though, it is the connections between the pull-out units that specify orthographic relations. Moreover, the pull-out net is designed to only process one word at a time and because of this, although the net can process more than word at a time, it can only identify one word at a time.

It is nevertheless possible to think of two kinds of capacity limitation in the model. The first is located at the rather late stage in processing, namely at the stage of the pull-out net. The second capacity limitation occurs earlier on in processing and is situated at the level of the AM. Here the spotlight of attention could only be centred over one retinal place at a time. Given these two different kinds of capacity limitation Mozer points out that BLIRNET cannot be sensibly characterized as implementing either a traditional 'early' or 'late' selection account of attention. The model possesses both early and late capacity limitations.

Given these points concerning capacity limitations, it is pertinent to discuss here some more recent data on attentional processes in word recognition that speak to the general issue of parallel processing. In very much the spirit of Mozer's study, Mullin and Egeth (1989) presented subjects with displays of either one string or two strings of letters. However, in this case strings were situated above and below the central fixation cross, were presented for 150 msec and were not masked. Unlike Mozer's original experiments, these were not primarily concerned with perceptual report. Subjects in Experiment 1 had to decide whether the two words referred to an instance of the same natural category (e.g. animals, vehicles): in Experiment 2 subjects had to make decisions about the lexical status of both strings. In both experiments the same stimuli were used on positive trials and with the two-word displays the same word was situated above and below the fixation point. Both experiments used an RT paradigm though subjects only responded on positive trials.

Interest in this paradigm was that any differential effects found across the one- and two-word displays might be construed as evidence for parallel processing. The data were therefore instructive in showing no effect of number of words when subjects did the semantic classification task, yet when subjects made lexical decisions, responses were slower to one-word displays than they were to two-word displays. Remember that with the two-word displays the same word occurred twice. The speeding of responses to the two-word displays here is essentially an effect typically known as a redundancy gain (Biederman & Checkosky, 1970). When subjects had to make lexical decisions, RTs to two-word displays (i.e. the redundant target displays) were significantly slower than were RTs to single-word displays. Mullin and Egeth termed this poor performance with two-word displays a redundancy loss. Redundancy losses were witnessed when, in the two-word displays, the identical word was repeated and when different words were used.

In a final experiment subjects were run again on the semantic categorization task but this time on positive trials different words from the same category were paired. As in the previous case, where the same instance was repeated in two-word displays, there was no difference in RTs to either single-word or two-word displays. Overall very detailed analyses were carried out to establish whether the redundancy gains and losses were really indicative of parallel processing. These analyses eventually allowed Mullin and Egeth to discount an alternative account that the redundancy effects came about by subjects randomly selecting to attend to one target position over another. Mullin and Egeth therefore went on to draw the following conclusions. Firstly, that two separate but identical letter strings can be processed in parallel to the extent that they can be classified as being familiar words. However, the ability to make lexical decisions to displays comprising two words suffers relative to these when a single string is presented. Moreover, in the case where subjects had to assess whether two different words refer to instances of the same natural category there are no indications of an ability to use parallel processing.

In the absence of having access to a running version of BLIRNET, it is difficult to know whether the model does naturally account for the pattern of lexical decisions reported by Mullin and Egeth. Mozer does not describe simulations where the model is presented with repetitions of the same word. Some remarks are made in passing about how the model fares with presentations comprising repetitions of letters but performance with repetitions of words is not described (Mozer, 1989, p. 299). An impression, though, is that the model might well account for the redundancy gains and losses given the various co-operative and competitive processes posited. Nevertheless, the general points about severe capacity limitations at the later stages of processing concerning the handling of different words needs to be explored in further depth. As it is presently described BLIRNET seems not to offer a ready explanation of the capacity limitations with semantic classification of simultaneously presented different words.

The pronunciation of written words

Much current work in experimental cognitive psychology is concerned with attempting to understand reading. Although some work has concerned the reading of passages of connected prose (see Garnham, 1987, for a review), very much more work has concerned the reading of single words in isolation (see Henderson, 1982, for a review). Indeed, this rather narrow aspect of psycholinguistic ability has dominated the empirical and theoretical work on reading. Much has been invested in attempting to specify the underlying representations and processes upon which single word reading is based. To this end, and according to Seidenberg (1988), consensus now exists over the explanation offered by the arrows-and-boxes model shown in Figure 4.9.

Although variants on this general scheme have been occasionally put forward, there is some agreement about the model in general, and, moreover, the overall style of theorizing. Traditional experimental cognitive psychology has it that human processing can be adequately understood in terms of arrows-and-boxes, flow diagrams that specify component processes and representations. It is against this academic atmosphere that the radical nature of Seidenberg and McClelland's (1989) model of reading can be assessed. Figure 4.10 shows the model in schematic form.

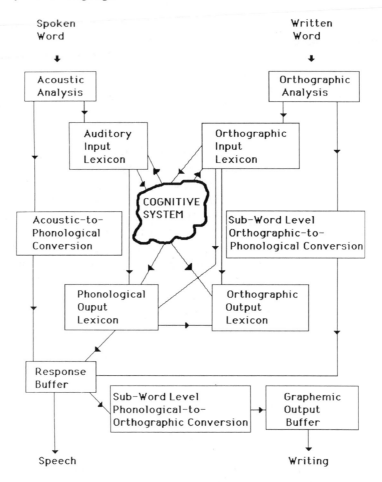

Figure 4.9. A classical arrows-and-boxes diagram of the component processes underlying recognition, comprehension and production of spoken
and written words and non-words. (From Seidenberg, 1988, adapted with
permission, *see* p. xvi.)

Architecture of the Seidenberg and McClelland model

The model comprised three components: a set of 400 orthographic units, a set of
200 hidden units and a set of 460 phonological units. The orthographic
representation of a given string was given by a variant of Wickelgren's (1969)
triples scheme: a scheme not too dissimilar to that used in BLIRNET. Words were
decomposed and coded into triples of adjacent characters. The example given is
that of encoding the word MAKE into **MA, MAK, AKE, KE** (where

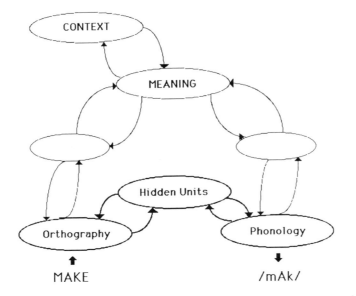

Figure 4.10. Schematic representation of the Seidenberg & McClelland, 1989) model. Each oval stands for a separate module of processing units. Only the bold modules have been implemented. (From Seidenberg and McClelland, 1989, adapted with permission, *see* p.xvi.)

double asterisks signify a white space). However, it was not the case that a single orthographic unit coded a single triple because a distributed coding scheme was used. Each orthographic unit comprised three slots where each slot could take 10 possible characters. The middle slot took 10 possible characters; the beginning and end slot took 10 letters or 9 letters and a white space. The model was initialized by assigning characters to the units on a random basis. Moreover, when a string was presented to the net many orthographic units turned ON simply because any given character triple was encoded by more than one orthographic unit. Each orthographic unit encoded 1000 character triples. So when an orthographic unit turned ON it was impossible to say, in the absence of the actual input, which of the possible 1000 character triples was responsible. For ease of exposition this form of coarse coding will be known as array coding. A similar form of array coding employed with the orthographic units was used with the phonological units. The phonological encoding scheme was adapted from an earlier model of word processing set out by Rumelhart and McClelland (1986b). The example quoted is that of the phonological representation of the word MAKE being rendered into the phonological triples /**mA /, /mAK /, and /AK**/. The actual phonological encoding was slightly different though, because the constituent phonemes were recoded at the level of phonemic features, i.e. features specifying the place and manner of articulation. At the level of the phonological units the phonemic triples were broken into three slots respectively for the preceding context, the central phoneme and the following context. Each character in turn was broken down into its constituent phonemic features and these lists of features were in turn encoded across a range of 16 different phonological units. Sixteen phonological units turned ON for each phonological triple. Again each phonological unit comprised an array form of representation with three slots for 11, 10 and 11 features respectively. An example of the featural representation in one phonological unit is [vowel, fricative, stop]. Between the orthographic and phonological layers of units was a set of hidden units. Full connectivity existed between the orthographic units and the hidden units and between the hidden units and the phonological units. Moreover, weights on all connections were initialized with small random values (i.e. between −0.5 and +0.5). The hidden units were central to the account of learning. The method was to use a variant of the back-propagation algorithm to train the model to produce an appropriate pattern of activation across the phonological units whenever a word was encoded by the orthographic units. Having trained the net, the aim was then to see how the model could account for various results in the psycho-linguistic literature.

Training

The training regime was reasonably straightforward. On a given trial a word chosen from the target set was presented to the net and immediately encoded by the orthographic units. Activation was then propagated forwards to the hidden units, and forward again to the phonological units. Most distinctively though, immediately activation from the orthographic units was received at the hidden units, feedback from the hidden units to the orthographic units occurred. Given this, Seidenberg and McClelland state that the phonological representations do not influence the construction of orthographic representations. It is the pattern of activity across the hidden units combined with the weights on the links between the hidden units and the orthographic units which is critical. The feedback from the hidden units induces a new pattern of activity across the orthographic units and this in turn can be compared to the original input. Any discrepancy (known as the orthographic error) is then used as an index of changes to the weights on the connections between the orthographic and hidden layers. Activation from the hidden units to the phonological units in turn induces a pattern of activity across the phonological units. This is then compared against the desired phonological pattern of activation and any discrepancy (known as phonological error) is used to alter the weights on the connections between the hidden and phonological layers. If this particular training regime is to be taken literally it suggests that learning to read consists of producing an utterance in the presence of a teacher who then provides feedback in the manner of the correct pronunciation. This particular view of learning to read seems to fit well with actual teaching practices. Unfortunately, it remains unclear what the psychological counterpart to the feedback from the hidden units to the orthographic units could possibly be.

Seidenberg and McClelland were clear in stating that the actual training set of words is critical to the eventual behaviour of the net: a fact which has subsequently formed a critical point for debate (see the discussion below regarding Besner, Twilley, McCann & Seergobin, 1990; and Seidenberg & McClelland, 1990). Consequently, in assessing the psychological plausibility of the net it is important to know what sorts of words were used. The main subset of words were uninflected, monosyllables of three or more letters selected from the Kucera and Francis (1967) word-count. Other words not listed in the word-count were also added to the input corpus because they had been used in previous experiments in the literature. An aim was to see whether the model could eventually simulate effects with these words as previously reported in the human reading literature.

The number of words in the training set was 2897; however, not all words were presented equally often. Words in the set were presented to the net a number of times proportionate to the log of their frequency of occurrence in the language. (Real frequency counts range from 0 to several tens per million.) Taking the log of the frequency compressed the range of number of presentations of the words. This was justified on the grounds that it reduced the variation of presentations of the different words and that it in turn allowed a sensible number of iterations of the training regime to be completed. A number of reasons were given in defence of the psychological plausibility of this manoeuvre: a main one being that the large spread of frequency values in the norms is a gross over estimate of the range of frequencies which occur in a child's early language experience. Overall the net was trained on 150,000 learning trials.

Mature performance

Following training, Seidenberg and McClelland then went on to use the net to explain performance in many different word-processing tasks. The manner in which they did this is again instructive. The general method was to present words to the adult net and compute the orthographic and phonological error scores. The orthographic error scores were then used as an index of performance in lexical decision tasks; the phonological error scores were used as indices of performance in naming tasks. Seidenberg and McClelland define a phonological error score as the sum of the squared differences between the actual activation for each phonological unit and its counterpart in the desired pattern of activation. The orthographic error score was defined in a similar manner with respect to the input string and to the orthographic units. To take just one example, Seidenberg and McClelland used the phonological error score as an index of naming performance with the words taken from a study by Taraban and McClelland (1987). Central to this endeavour was the claim that error scores are monotonically related to RTs and to accuracy. The actual naming speeds are graphed in Figure 4.11a: the corresponding phonological error scores are graphed in Figure 4.11b. It is this kind of startling fit between the error scores and performance that is repeated over many other tasks in the literature and reported in detail by Seidenberg and McClelland.

Initial analysis of the Seidenberg and McClelland model

Given the impressive abilities of the model to simulate much real data, controversy rages over how serious an alternative it really is. Perhaps the most controversial aspect of the model is that it utilizes only distributed representations and nothing in the model appears to correspond to the notion of a lexicon. There are no identifiable word units in the model like those employed by the IA and TRACE models. This is particularly important given that the whole idea of accessing lexical entries has played a fundamental role in traditional attempts at understanding lexical decision. In so far as the Seidenberg and McClelland model provides something of an explanation of lexical decision performance, it is clearly a radical departure because it does not possess a lexicon. There are no single word units corresponding to localist representations of lexical entries. An additional reason as to why the lack of a lexicon is radical departure is that the processing account of naming provided by the model does not fit well with either the traditional dual-route or analogy accounts of naming. Dual route theory as put forward by Coltheart (1978) assumes that word naming can arise through the application of either of two procedures. A word's phonological specification can either be addressed or assembled (Patterson & Coltheart, 1987). Addressed phonology is simply accessed from the lexicon. The orthographic specification of the word is used as an index to the lexical entry of the word; the lexical entry specifies amongst other things the phonological specification of the word. In the dual-route theory assembled phonology comes about through the operation of grapheme-to-phoneme rules. A graphemic parser operates on the input string to produce a phonological specification of the string according to rules that specify grapheme-to-phoneme correspondences.

In contrast to the dual-route theory there is analogy theory (Kay & Marcel, 1981). Here the orthographic specification of the input string invokes an orthographic set of neighbours and their corresponding phonological specifications. The pronunciation of the input string is then assembled, in some typically unspecified manner, from the phonological specification of the orthographic neighbours. For more thorough treatments of both dual-route and analogy theories see Patterson and Coltheart (1987). Nevertheless, both dual-route and

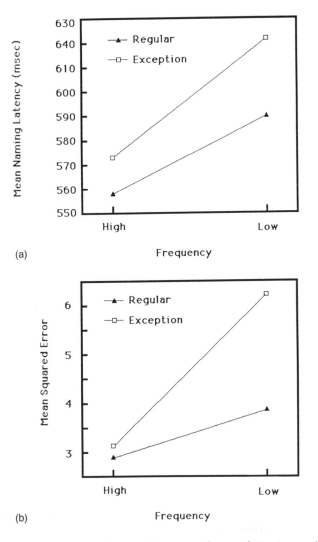

Figure 4.11. (a) Graph of the word frequency by regularity interaction found by Taraban and McClelland (1987), (b) A similar interaction between frequency and mean squared error score. Data produced by the Seidenberg and McClelland model. (From Seidenberg and McClelland 1989, adapted with permission, *see* p. xvi.)

analogy theories posit a role for an internal lexicon. Given this, it is clear therefore that Seidenberg and McClelland's model cannot be adequately classified as being either a dual-route or an analogy theory. In Seidenberg and McClelland's latest writings, though (Seidenberg & McClelland, 1990), there is a sense in which the model is a dual-route model in so far as two routes to phonology are posited. Only one has been implemented, however, and this is the one going from orthography to phonology via the hidden units. The route not yet specified is one assumed to traverse orthography to phonology via a meaning system (see Seidenberg & McClelland, 1990, for more on this point).

Much of the radical nature of the model therefore hinges on this idea of not possessing a lexicon. It is interesting to read in this respect that Besner *et al.* (1990) dispute the claim that the model does not possess a lexicon. Although this point is not fully argued, they state that although there are no lexical entries in the model there are distributed representations that do function as lexical represent-ations. The distributed representations in the model allow systematic interactions to take place between the semantic store, the phonological store and the orthographic store. Such functional roles have traditionally been associated with lexical entries. Regardless of these details, it is important to appreciate how the model simulates the data of Taraban and McClelland given that it does not possess a lexicon.

The overall target pattern of results is that naming RTs to high-frequency words are faster than are naming RTs to low-frequency words. Moreover, whereas there is little or no difference in naming RTs to regular and exception high-frequency words, with low-frequency items exception words are named more slowly than are regular words. As Patterson and Coltheart state, a natural account of this frequency-by-regularity interaction is that provided by dual-route theory. They state that recovering the addressed phonological specification from the lexical orthographic representation is likely to take more time for low-frequency words than for more familiar high-frequency words. Consequently, any exception effects are most likely to be revealed with low-frequency words. In these cases, effects due to assembling phonology will be witnessed because this takes less time than does the retrieval of phonology. Problems with low-frequency exception words are likely to be revealed because the phonology assembled will specify the regular pronunciation of the string and not the exceptional pronunci-ation.

Nevertheless, it is the general dual-route account of the data that is thrown into doubt by the Seidenberg and McClelland simulations. The critical thing to remember is that the implemented model only possesses a single route from orthography to phonology. The argument therefore is that the frequency-by-regularity interaction does not in and of itself license claims about dual routes. In the context of the model the explanation of the frequency-by-regularity interact-ion is explained away ultimately in terms of familiarity effects. As Seidenberg and McClelland state, both effects of frequency and of regularity arise because connections have been more finely tuned for the frequent and regular items than they have been for infrequent irregular items. In general the training procedure alters the weights in such a way as to improve performance on the presented items. However, there is an important caveat to be applied here. As Jared, McRae and Seidenberg (1990) note, words that have a similar orthography and phonology, e.g. the rhyming neighbours FEAT and TREAT, have similar effects on the weights during training. This means that exposure to one of the pair improves performance on the other. In contrast, training with items with similar orthography but dissimilar phonology like TREAT and GREAT benefits neither. Nevertheless, the more often an item is presented, the more often the weights are changed in a direction to facilitate good performance on that item and items orthographically similar to it. The upshot of this is that the model will tend to perform well on high-frequency items because it has simply been exposed to these more often during learning than it has been exposed to low-frequency items. A knock-on effect is that weights that accommodate high-frequency items will also tend to be relevant to regular items; hence regular items benefit from the changes due to high-frequency items. Clearly such beneficial changes do not obtain for either low frequency or irregular items. As Jared *et al.* (1990) boldly state, 'the weights come to encode facts about the consistency of spelling–sound correspondences in the training corpus'. In this respect the model seems to conflict with the data collected by Brown (1987a, 1987b). Remember Brown showed that naming latencies to exception unique words were comparable. According to Taraban and McClelland (1987), this shows that there is no difference between naming times to words with enemies compared with words with no enemies. Brown's interpretation of the result was that the only determiner of naming speed was the frequency of correspondence of a particular orthographic to phonological conversion. In this respect Brown's data and interpretation do not gel with the Seidenberg and McClell and account of word processing. However, certain problems remain with Brown's position and it is to these that the discussion now turns.

The general problem is that on at least two occasions predictions of the Brown model have not panned out. Firstly, Kay and Bishop (1987) report no support for the ideas from a post-hoc analysis of some of their own naming data. They found that there was no difference in naming speeds to consistent words with few neighbours than consistent words with many neighbours. This was even though the former words had a grossly lower combined lexical frequency than the latter words. Brown's model predicts the corresponding directional difference between the two sets of words. Secondly, they found that with low-frequency items regular-consistent words were pronounced faster than regular-inconsistent words. Again there is a conflict here because Brown would not have predicted such a difference given that there was no contingent frequency difference between the two sets of word types.

The second difficulty with Brown's model is that Seidenberg and McClelland also failed to find support for his ideas in some of their own naming data (Seidenberg, McRae & Jared, 1988). Seidenberg *et al.* (1988) reported strong inconsistency effects in a naming task with a set of items equated for frequency, length and initial phoneme. Such inconsistency effects are not compatible with Brown's model of word naming. Furthermore, Taraban and McClelland (1987) also report a post-hoc analysis of some their naming data that fails to support

Brown's original idea. They picked out words balanced for frequency, length, initial phoneme and number of orthographic friends. However, these words were in turn divided into two sets of high- and low-enemy items. On the assumption that the time to pronounce a word can be deleteriously affected by having enemies, Taraban and McClelland predicted a directional difference between times to name the high- and low-enemy items. This prediction was borne out by the results. Overall, therefore, Brown's strong claim that the only determiner of naming speed is the frequency of a given orthographic-to-phonological conversion seems no longer to be tenable. However, it is interesting to note that in all the subsequent work looking at this claim, none has disputed the original result of slow naming to lexically unique words. Relevant to this point is another post-hoc analysis this time of Brown's own stimuli (Jared *et al.*, 1990). Jared *et al.* examined these stimuli and considered the number and frequencies of the enemies of the exception words. Remember it is the comparison between exception words and unique words that is of prime import. What Jared *et al.* discovered was that the summed frequencies of the enemies of the exception words used by Brown were relatively low and hence any possible 'conspiracy effects' of these enemies on the target words may well have been minimal. As they argue, the naming of words may only be slowed if the words have high-frequency inconsistent neighbours.

Following on from this intense debate about the existence of inconsistency effects in word naming, some consensus is emerging. It is now generally agreed that both the absolute frequency of occurrence of orthographic segments and the nature of a word's orthographic neighbourhood can influence naming speeds (Andrews, 1989; Brown, personal communication, 1990; Seidenberg & McClelland, 1989). Both Seidenberg and McClelland (1989) and Jared *et al.* (1990) claim that both frequency and neighbourhood factors can be accounted for in terms of the Seidenberg and McClelland model of word pronunciation. Indeed, Jared *et al.* claim that the Seidenberg and McClelland model simulates the results of Brown's (1987) study 'quite closely'.

Lesioning the Seidenberg and McClelland model

Following the publication of the Seidenberg and McClelland (1989) model, extensions to the work have been reported by Patterson, Seidenberg and McClelland (1989) in the context of attempting to simulate a specific language impairment. Essentially, Patterson *et al.* took the net and lesioned it in a number of different ways and then presented this 'damaged' system with various kinds of letter strings. Error scores for these strings were then computed and comparisons were drawn between these error scores and performance of language impaired human subjects. Patterson *et al.* were particularly interested in seeing how well the model simulated the condition known as surface dyslexia. As with many syndromes there can be disputes over exactly how to characterize a particular condition, so Patterson *et al.* defined surface dyslexia according to a distinctive pattern of reading behaviour. In brief, a person with surface dyslexia is said to exhibit the following pattern of reading. Firstly, regular words, e.g. PINE, are read better than are irregular words, e.g. PINT. Secondly, non-word reading can be relatively normal. Sometimes reading performance also reveals the frequency-by-regularity interaction discussed above. Nevertheless, there is a general tendency to regularize. Typically though, reading speeds can be within the normal range.

Given these target criteria, the research began by looking at the amount and location of lesions made to the net. Lesions to connections were introduced by setting weights on the connections to 0. Lesions to units were made by simply removing them from the computations. Overall, three sorts of lesions were made: (i) lesions to the connections between the orthographic and the hidden layers; (ii) lesions to the connections between the hidden units and the phonological units; and, finally, (iii) lesions to the hidden units themselves. For each kind of lesion, four levels of damage were independently examined; namely, 10%, 20%, 40% and 60%, respectively. In addition, two sets of measures of performance were calculated. The first set of measures comprised the means and standard deviations of the phonological error scores. These statistics were computed from repeated testing with a sample of letter strings. Ten tests were used for each amount of damage and across the tests lesions were introduced on a random basis. For the different tests, a different pattern of units and connections were lesioned. The second kind of performance measure was related to something known as a reversal rate. Patterson *et al.* defined a reversal as those instances where the model produced a lower error score for a mispronunciation than for a correct pronunciation of an orthographic string input. For example, consider the word PINT. Here the correct pronunciation is $/p\mathit{Int}/$; the regular, yet incorrect, pronunciation is $/pint/$. A reversal would be where the model produces a lower error score for PINT relative to $/pint/$ than to $/p\mathit{Int}/$.

Lesioned versions of the model were tested with 16 regular and 16 irregular words equated for frequency. In order to measure reversal rates the following steps were taken. For each regular and irregular word two output strings were considered. For the regular words the two types were the correct pronunciation and another pronunciation. For example, the correct pronunciation of TINT, a regular word, is $/tint/$, the other pronunciation considered was $/t\mathit{Int}/$. For the irregular words the two types were the correct pronunciation and the regular pronunciation. For example, the correct pronunciation of PINT, an irregular word, is $/p\mathit{Int}/$, the regular pronunciation is $/pint/$.

The results in brief were as follows. Firstly, when the mean error scores were examined, the amount of damage produced more pronounced effects than did the location of the lesion. Error scores for correct pronunciations bore an approximate linear relationship to the amount of damage. Large error scores were witnessed for both other and regularized pronunciations in all conditions. Nevertheless, both kinds of errors tended to worsen with amount of damage. In comparing across regular and exception words it was found that there was a generally bigger difference between the error scores for the correct pronunciations and the other pronunciations for regular words than between the correct pronunciations and the regularized pronunciations for the exception words. That is, the model performed generally better with regular rather than exception words. Indeed, for the highest levels of damage the error scores for the correct pronunciations and the regularized pronunciations for the exception words were almost equivalent. When the variability of the error scores was considered, a different pattern emerged, however. Here it was found that error variability was high when the hidden units were damaged but low when the connections between the hidden and phonological units were damaged. In this respect, location of the lesion was important.

In summary, the overall pattern of results was that higher reversal rates occurred with higher levels of damage and with the highest levels of damage there were more reversals to exception words than to regular words. Higher reversal rates obtained when the hidden units were damaged than when the connections between the hidden units and the phonological units were damaged. As Patterson *et al.* state, the notable number of reversals for exception words means that the model produces regularizations and that this aspect of pathology is reminiscent of surface dyslexia.

As something of an aside Patterson *et al.* also discuss the differences in variability of error scores with the location of the lesion. Here high levels of error variability were associated with damage to the hidden units and not with damage to the connections between the hidden units and the phonological units. This is explained in terms of different notions of distributed representation. Simply put, for a given word activation was spread over many connections but comparatively few hidden units. Lesions to the connections tended to affect all words to a certain degree. In contrast, it was generally true that a given word activated only 24 hidden units. Consequently, the likelihood of a subset of a particular units being lesioned over the repeated tests was reasonably small. For one test several units of a given 24 would be lesioned; for the next none would be. This gave rise to the large variability in error scores when the hidden units were lesioned.

A final issue raised by this particular modelling work concerns a phenomenon observed in surface dyslexia where a patient produces an odd pronunciation of a string that is quite different to a regularization. Examples are where SOUL is read as /s Yl /, BALD as /bOld / and ROOK as /rok /. Here it is the vowel graphemes that are being mispronounced: There are no English words in which OO is pronounced /o /. Patterson *et al.* state that such errors have traditionally been classified as being 'visual' or 'orthographic' confusions, the implication being that such errors could only have arisen because of some impairment to the early graphemic/visual analysis stage of the processing. However, the model did produce such errors even in cases where no lesions were introduced to the orthographic units. This result is enlightening because it again demonstrates that radically different explanations of cognitive phenomena can be suggested by new connectionist research. From the behaviour of the Seidenberg and McClelland lesioned model, it can be seen that 'visual' errors in reading need not arise through impairment to an early stage of visual analysis. This kind of theoretical point will be elaborated in the next chapter when another model of a specific reading impairment is discussed.

General appraisal of the Seidenberg and McClelland model

Given both the radical and impressive nature of Seidenberg and McClelland's model in simulating real data it is important to try to provide a proper assessment of the model's psychological status. Therefore, it is useful to consider a recent and thorough critique set out by Besner *et al.* (1990).

Besner *et al.* make a number of substantive points in which they question the success of the model as a plausible candidate psychological explanation. Their first concern was with a claim central to the model that regular words, irregular words and non-words are all read via the same orthographic–hidden unit–phonological route. Besner *et al.* set out, and defend, the alternative view: namely, that non-words and familiar words are read via different routes; respectively, the rule-based route and the direct lexical route. In an attempt to judge the psychological credibility of the Seidenberg and McClelland model, Besner *et al.* assessed how well it dealt with non-words. Here the method was to examine the phonological output of the model when it was presented with non-words and to compare this output with the actual pronunciations humans make when presented with the same strings.

The first result was that when presented with non-words, the model tended to produce a smaller error score with respect to the 'wrong' pronunciation than to the right pronunciation. (Remember the error score is a measure of the discrepancy between an actual pattern of activation and a target pattern of activation. Error scores are then computed with respect to some target pattern of activation.) For example, in reading the non-word KEAD, the model produced an error score lower for the incorrect pronunciation $/ked/$ than for the correct pronunciation $/kEd/$. Here, 'correct pronunciations' were those produced by subjects in Glushko's (1979) study. Overall the model failed to produce the correct pronunciation with over 30 per cent of the non-word instances. Besner *et al.* contrast the model's rather poor performance with non-words, with its rather good performance with those words that it was originally trained with. With these words, the model erred with only approximately 3 per cent of the instances. Besner *et al.* state that this pattern of results shows how poorly the model generalises from the initial training set to novel strings not previously encountered.

Besner *et al.* go further and analyse how the model deals with the stimuli used by McCann and Besner (1987). These stimuli were divided into three subsets:

namely, pseudohomophones (i.e. non-words which when read sound like real words, e.g. BRANE); real word counterparts to the pseudohomophones (e.g. BRAIN) and non-word controls (e.g. FRANE). Whereas subjects performed equally well in pronouncing these strings under speeded conditions, the model performed well with the words, but very badly with both sorts of non-words. Again this reflects the fact that whereas the model performs well with the stimuli that it was trained with (i.e. the real words used), it performs rather poorly on novel stimuli.

A final demonstration regarding naming is that the model also fails to account for some data collected by Campbell and Besner (1981). In their study, subjects had to pronounce non-words beginning in the initial cluster 'TH'. The hypothesis under examination was that context should determine whether the strings be pronounced with the initial unvoiced / TH / or the voiced / TH /. Indeed the hypothesis was supported, for when the strings were presented in isolation, rather than in a sentential context, in the Campbell and Besner study, the overwhelming bias was for subjects to pronounce the / TH / as unvoiced. The model however, showed no such bias when presented with isolated strings. Phonological error scores computed for the unvoiced and voiced versions of the string were equivalent.

Finally, it is important to consider the points Besner *et al.* make about how the model simulates lexical decision. The account of lexical decision provided by the model is based around assessing the orthographic error score for a given input string. A criterion value is set such that any orthographic error score greater than the criterion value is taken to indicate that the presented string is a non-word. Error values smaller than the criterion are taken to signify the presence of a word. However, problems arise with this particular account. It can happen that the distribution of error scores for non-words and for unusually spelt words (i.e. 'strange' words such as 'aisle') overlap to a considerable degree. The model cannot help but reject strange words as non-words. No simple criterion account of responding will therefore suffice. Given this, Seidenberg and McClelland are forced back onto a position of arguing that, in certain cases, lexical decisions may be computed on the basis of the phonological error scores.

Besner *et al.* systematically examined these claims by presenting the model with the word sets originally used by Seidenberg and McClelland to make the argument. They then computed the distribution of phonological error scores for these items. This revealed that the amount of overlap in the distribution of the phonological error scores for words and non-words was of the same magnitude as the amount of overlap witnessed for the orthographic error scores. Besner *et al.* therefore state that the lexical status of an input string cannot be accounted for by any simple criterion account based on orthographic error scores, phonological error scores or some pooling of such measures. All such simple criterion accounts of lexical decisions give rise to unacceptable and unreal error rates not witnessed in the human data.

The final thrust of the critique set out by Besner *et al.* concerns the so-called pseudohomophone effects in lexical decision and naming. Besner *et al.* state that in lexical decision a common finding is that subjects are slower to classify pseudohomophones as non-words than they are to make similar classifications about non-homophonic non-word controls. In naming, though, facilitation is observed with pseudohomophones: pseudohomophones are named faster than are non-homophonic non-word controls. The traditional account of these effects are reasonably straightforward. For pseudohomophones, tradition has it that lexical decision is slowed because although the phonological specification of the string matches that of a word, its orthographic specification does not. This conflicting state of affairs gives rise to an RT penalty. In contrast, facilitation in naming occurs because the phonological specification of a pseudohomophone is already familiar. Consequently, the string can be easily articulated.

According to the Seidenberg and McClelland model both effects can be explained because pseudohomophones yield smaller orthographic and phonological error scores than do non-word control. They state that the model predicts both the slowed lexical decisions and speed naming times of the pseudohomophones because of the comparatively small orthographic and phonological error scores. Before discussing the rebuttal of this claim set out by Besner *et al.*, it seems that other considerations stand in the way of Seidenberg and McClelland's account. A problem remains over Seidenberg and McClelland's claim that a smaller orthographic error for a non-word naturally leads to a slower response. In so far as the orthographic error score for a pseudohomophone indicates (incorrectly) a word, then the model should surely predict more errors for the pseudohomophones than other non-word controls. This impinges on a more general point regarding the whole methodology adopted by Seidenberg and McClelland in attempting to model real data. As Patterson *et al.* (1989) note, there are serious difficulties in attempting to account for speed and accuracy data with just a single measure. If speed and accuracy are monotonically related to each other then correlating performance with a single measure is a reasonable procedure. However, any adequate theory of human performance needs to acknowledge that such a monotonic relationship obtains only some of the time. It is instructive to note therefore (cf. Besner *et al.*, 1990) that Seidenberg and McClelland report only RT data and not accuracy data in follow-up studies on the pseudohomophone effects.

In relation to the pseudohomophone effects, Seidenberg and McClelland argue that they arise because of the orthographic similarity of pseudohomophones to real words: pseudohomophones tend to be more word-like than do the non-word controls (a point examined previously by Martin, 1982). Seidenberg and McClelland argue that it is the orthographic similarity of BRAIN to BRANE that eventuates in the net performing better with BRANE than with its non-word control, FRANE. Training with BRAIN initially sensitizes the net to similar orthography of BRANE. Addressing this account directly, Besner *et al.* re-examined the RTs collected by McCann and Besner (1987) and McCann, Besner and Davelaar (1988), and ran the experimental stimuli through the model to derive the orthographic error scores. Using regression techniques on the (naming and lexical decision) RTs with these error scores, Besner *et al.* were able to partial out the orthographic contribution to performance. The rationale was that if the pseudohomophone effect arises solely because of factors concerning orthography then to partial out the orthographic contribution should eliminate the effect. The results of the analysis showed, however, that removal of the orthographic contribution left a significant and substantial pseudohomophone effect. Besner *et al.* go further and demonstrate a quite different state of affairs for the model. The analysis was straightforward and consisted of calculating the orthographic and phonological error scores for pseudohomophones and controls. Besner *et al.* found that there was a high correlation between orthographic and phonological error scores. Moreover, there were smaller phonological error scores for the pseudohomophones than for the controls and it seemed quite possible that this arose because the model performed better with the pseudohomophones at the orthographic level than it did with the controls. In other words, the suspicion was that for the model the pseudohomophone effect was orthographic in nature. Support for this suspicion was forthcoming, for when the orthographic component was partialed out, equivalent phonological error scores obtained for the pseudohomophones and controls. Consequently, Besner *et al.* argue that whereas there is a clear phonological component to the pseudohomophone effect in the human data, this is not true of the performance of the model.

In conclusion, Seidenberg and McClelland's research is an example of a very impressive piece of modelling work to the extent that their account of single word reading provides a good fit with a considerable amount of data. More important, though, is the fact that the model does this in ways quite distinct from those that have traditionally been put forward. Indeed, for those swayed by arguments concerning theoretical parsimony, the model is also attractive on the grounds that its components and their operation are simple. This again stands in stark contrast to the massively complicated accounts typically found in the psycholinguistic and cognitive neuropsychological literature.

Overall, therefore, there is much to admire in the research strategy adopted by Seidenberg and McClelland. On the other hand, if the criticisms of Besner *et al.* carry any force, then it seems that the model is wrong both generally and in its particulars. The main thrust of the critique set out by Besner *et al.* is that the model possesses neither lexical representations nor some sort of rule system for sounding out letter strings. Besner *et al.* claim that both form the basis of the human word processor. They are also happy with the ancillary claim that a whole host of other 'dissociable, nonsemantically mediated "routines" ' can be used to pronounce letter strings. Such a claim, if not completely incompatible with the Seidenberg and McClelland account, seems not to be too easily reconciled with the model. Indeed Seidenberg and McClelland, in reply to the Besner *et al.* critique, do seem to admit that human subjects may indeed have a number of different strategies at their disposal to pronounce letter strings. However, they argue that modelling these is outside the realm of their theory.

Of the many other points they make, perhaps the most substantial is that their model cannot possibly be expected to simulate every aspect of adult human performance given that it has been trained only on a very small and limited kind of vocabulary. On the face of it this seems a fair point (it is undoubtedly true); however, this leads to a rather awkward state of affairs. Seidenberg and McClelland seem to have adopted a position where if the model fails to simulate data then this can be explained away by arguing the point about its limited experience with language. It is therefore difficult to know how to go about falsifying the theory.

Concluding comments

In as much as most of the work covered in this chapter has been published in the psychological literature and explicit claims have been made about psychological plausibility, the primary objective in writing this chapter has been to assess how valid such claims are. It cannot be denied that much of the work is very impressive in providing working computer models of some aspects of language processing. However, it is also true that when the specifics of these accounts are scrutinized many limitations are revealed. Undeniably though, most of the work described here has spurred others to re-examine their own traditional theoretical views and to further assess the new connectionist alternatives. This cannot be a bad thing.

It is clear that with the advent of new connectionism much of what traditional cognitive psychologists hold dear is under serious threat. Things like the notion of clearly defined stages of processing, highly modular subsystems and lexical representations no longer seem to form the firm foundations for theorizing that they once did. An overall impression gained from reading the new connectionist literature is that regardless of the seeming complexities of human language processing, a few unified and general principles of learning and processing will suffice. Framed thus, it is easy to see why rather caustic comparisons have been drawn between new connectionism and old behaviourism (see, for example, Fodor & Pylyshyn, 1988).

In closing, a rather sober assessment of the new connectionist approach is that regardless of the initial power demonstrated by the models in simulating many aspects of human performance, a careful analysis has revealed subtle yet important discrepancies between data and theory (see for example, the many complaints set out by Besner *et al.*, 1990). It is agreed that the very simplicity of Seidenberg and McClelland's account of word naming is attractive on the grounds of theoretical parsimony, yet serious questions continue to be raised about its theoretical adequacy. If anything, the development of the model has made some even more firmly entrenched in their views about the existence of a set of grapheme-to-phoneme rules that form a fundamental aspect of the human internal word processor (see Besner *et al.*, 1990). Nevertheless, it may well turn out to be true that something very much like the Seidenberg and McClelland network model is correct, in so far as some simple form of associative learning can account for how humans learn the proper pronunciation of exception words. However, it may also turn out that some form of rule-based system also operates to deal with more regular forms. If this is accepted then it appears that no general and uniform account of word processing will suffice because type-distinct subsystems exist.

Now it also may turn out that some form of connectionist net account of rule-processing can be derived and therefore that both a direct route and a rule-based route can be modelled by new connectionist principles. A serious complaint though, is that at present this cannot be a primary goal. The distinction between a direct route to reading and a rule-based route came about through painstaking experimental work with humans. It is classical cognitive psychology that has made the distinction. It was classical cognitive psychology that set out the basic functional characteristics of the human word-processing device. The modelling exercise then reduces to developing operational accounts that honour these basic functional categories. On this view, what connectionism provides are detailed accounts of what is going on inside the boxes in the arrows-and-boxes diagrams so beloved by traditional cognitive psychologists. However, if all that new connectionism can do is provide the details of how a traditional account might be implemented in neural hardware, then this is clearly no alternative at all (cf. Fodor & Pylyshyn, 1988). It is should be clear that this is a rather belittling conclusion because the promise of new connectionism is that it can provide radically different accounts of processing to those previously envisaged. A more thorough discussion of this point is included in the next chapter.

Chapter 5

Higher-order aspects of cognition

To complete the survey of new connectionist models of psychological processes, this chapter covers some higher-order aspects of cognition not previously considered. In discussing higher-order aspects of cognition much relates to the notion of semantics. Processing the input to determine the meaning of a word is typically classified as taking the analysis to a deeper level than, say, scanning the word for a particular letter. Such an idea is central to the 'levels-of-processing approach' in the study of human memory (Hyde & Jenkins, 1973). Indeed, semantic representation plays such a basic role in theories of thought and reasoning that it is clearly appropriate to deal with new connectionist models of semantics in this chapter.

Initially two models concerning semantic representation, developed by Hinton and his co-workers, will be considered in detail. Both models simulate the process of analysing an orthographic representation of a word to yield its meaning and both models have been discussed in relation to the cognitive neuropsychological disorder known as deep dyslexia.

Following this, a discussion of the double-dissociation methodology in cognitive neuropsychology is included. The demonstration of a double dissociation has typically been treated within cognitive neuropsychology as constituting strong evidence for underlying modular processing systems (Shallice, 1979). It is therefore instructive to consider new connectionist accounts that arguably demonstrate double dissociations even though they utilize non-modular distributed processing.

The central sections of the chapter deal with distributed models of conceptual structure. Particular concern is with the kinds of mental representation that new connectionists postulate. The final sections of the chapter include a detailed discussion of how distributed systems yield behaviour that appears, at first sight, to be characteristic of quite different computational devices.

Many of the ideas discussed in this chapter bear on fundamental issues in psychology and connectionism. To some, the whole credibility of new connectionism as framework for thinking about psychology rests upon how it approaches these issues (Fodor & Pylyshyn, 1988). As a consequence, many of the ideas discussed will be re-considered when, in the final chapter, a general appraisal of the new connectionist approach is made.

Accessing meaning from print: new connectionist accounts of deep dyslexia

Aspects of meaning tend to be treated as being fundamental issues in philosophy and psychology, but it is easy to slip into a morass of conjecture without making any points of substance. Within connectionism, though, the issue of semantic representation is approached in a straightforward manner. Take, for example, Hinton's (1986) treatment. He divides the relevant theoretical work into two camps. In one camp are the structuralists, in the other camp are the componentialists. According to structuralist theories of semantic representation, 'concepts are defined by their relationships to other concepts rather than by some internal essence' (Hinton, 1986, p. 1). In contrast, componentialists argue that each concept is defined by a set of semantic features. Examples of both sorts of theories can be found in the cognitive science literature (see Quillian, 1968, for a roughly structuralist account and Smith, Shoben & Rips, 1974, and Katz & Fodor, 1963, for componentialist accounts). Hinton states that connectionism typically provides componentialist accounts of semantic representation. Later, an example of how aspects of componentialist and structuralist theories can be combined in a connectionist model is provided. However, connectionist models of meaning typically invoke semantic primitives (Winograd, 1978) as being the fundamental atoms of semantic representation. For instance, a unit may represent a semantic primitive such as BIG. When the unit is ON it signals that part of the meaning of a given input word is that it signifies something big. This simple explanation summarizes, in crude fashion, the sense in which new connectionism has a theory of meaning. Clearly, many linguists and philosophers would be appalled by its naivety. For example, if the unit signifying BIG remains OFF this does not necessarily mean that the input word refers to something small because there may well be another unit that represents the semantic primitive for SMALL. Moreover, although it is obvious that a binary threshold logic unit, in having discrete states, can signify the presence/absence of a semantic characteristic, it is not at all clear what a variable unit is signifying if it is assumed to represent a semantic primitive. (The possibilities of attempting to model the analogical representation of meaning remain unexplored.) Such issues as these, and many more, remain unresolved within the new connectionist framework. It is only fair, therefore, to note, before continuing, that there is no work in new connectionism that begins to offer a general and principled account of meaning.

Semantics 1: The Hinton and Sejnowski model

One of the reasons why reading possesses an important problem for connectionism is that the mapping between the orthographic form of a word and its semantic representation is arbitrary. The graphemic representation of a word bears only an arbitrary relation to its meaning because there is nothing intrinsic about how a word looks that links it to what it means. Hinton (1984) does note that 'words starting with "sn" usually mean something unpleasant to do with the lips or nose (sneer, snarl, snigger)' (p. 18), but consideration of the words 'snake', 'snag', 'snuggle', 'snail', 'snow', etc., demonstrate that this rule is frequently violated. The mapping between orthography and meaning is clearly arbitrary. It is the acquisition of this arbitrary mapping that poses a central problem for any account of learning to read. In addressing this problem, Hinton *et al.* (1986) discuss two different network systems, both of which are shown in schematic form in Figure 5.1. Each system is idealized, and although Hinton discusses a programmed version of the one shown in Figure 5.1b, the program used neither real words nor identifiable semantic primitives.

In Figure 5.1a an input layer of letter position specific units feed into a hidden layer of lexical units: each hidden unit represents a single word. The hidden units in turn feed into a set of output units known as sememe units. Each output unit represents a particular semantic primitive. This scheme has appealing and unappealing characteristics. A particularly attractive feature of the model is that it can pick out the arbitrary mapping for each word independently of the mappings for other words. This is because the print–meaning association for each word can be picked out via the set of connections to and from its dedicated hidden word unit. The chief disadvantage of this scheme is that it fails to benefit from automatic generalization found with alternative coarse coding schemes. Remember, in other coarse coding schemes each hidden unit codes the presence of many instances. As a consequence, states of a hidden unit associated with one instance automatically generalize to the other instances coded by that hidden unit. Figure 5.1b sets out an alternative coarse coding scheme considered by Hinton. Here again are graphemic (input) and semantic (output) units, but this time the hidden units coarse code sets of words. For this reason they are known as word-set units. Word-sets, captured by the hidden units, cluster according to physical similarity: i.e. the word-sets captured by a given unit share letters, e.g. CAT, CAN, CAR, etc. With this coding scheme the model can produce automatic generalization (i.e. across a given word-set), but it remained unclear whether it was possible to implement arbitrary mappings between graphemic and semantic

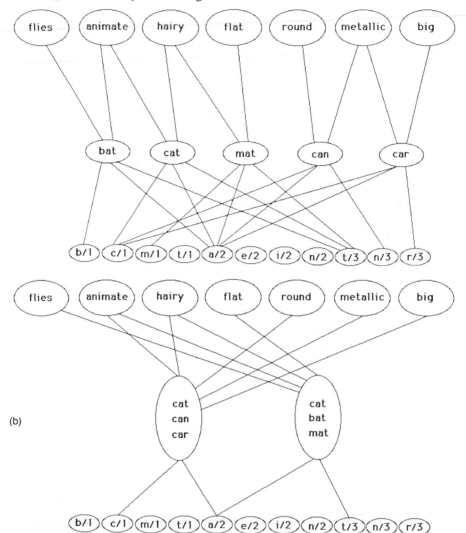

Figure 5.1. Two nets that map the constituent letters of words onto semantic features that represent their meaning (based on Hinton *et al.* 1986, Figure 5). (a) utilizes a set of hidden units that operate as localist representations. (b) utilizes fewer hidden units than used in (a). In this case the hidden units coarse code the input letter information. In the text these are referred to as word-set units. (From Hinton *et al.*, 1986, adapted with permission, *see* p.xvii).

units using this architecture. Indeed to test the model properly, it was important to ensure that, in the generation of the word-set units, no particular word-set corresponded to a discernible semantic category. For instance, as Hinton (1984) states, a word-set unit for all words meaning 'nice' is not allowed. Clearly had such a word-set unit existed then it would have violated the aim of trying to get automatic generalization from a distributed system of representation. Generalizations from one word in the set to others should arise naturally because they are represented via the one word-set unit. The ideal is to have automatic generalization for different words represented as a distributed pattern of activity over the hidden word-set units.

Given the uncertainty of the behaviour of the second network, a version was programmed and details of its behaviour are now discussed. In fact it seems that many versions of the model were tried and tested and the account given by Hinton *et al.* (1986) seems to have been distilled from many runs with the different versions.

Architecture of the model

The particular model studied comprised 30 grapheme units, 20 word-set units and 30 sememe units. There was full connectivity between grapheme units and word-set units and between the word-set units and the sememe units. To allow the model to learn appropriate mappings between graphemic and semantic levels, several additional steps were taken.

Firstly, the graphemic units were divided into three sets of ten such that each three-lettered input word activated one graphemic unit in each of the three sets. There was one set of ten graphemic units for each letter position.

Secondly, a given word-set unit provided positive activation to each sememe unit appropriate for any word in its set. For instance, when the word-set unit for CAT, CAN, CAR, etc. was turned ON, it activated all the sememe units for CAT, CAN, CAR, etc., regardless of which of these words was presented. Indeed, as can be seen from Figure 5.1b, each word is represented by more than one word-set unit. For example, CAT occurs in the 'CA_' unit and the '_AT' unit. In this respect, generalizations from CAT occurred because of its relations to 'CA_' words as well as its relations to '_AT' word. In this respect the model provides an account of automatic generalizations from distributed representations. Whenever a word was presented to the net, a collection of word-set units were activated. These in turn activated many sememe units.

A third step in developing the system concerned the actual choice of the input and output representations. For input, three-lettered strings were chosen at random from a set of letters. Typically the strings were not legal English words. For the output, the semantic representations assigned to the input strings were chosen at random. Although no convincing justification for these manoeuvres is given, it appears that randomizing the input and output patterns and their mappings was an attempt to set up the system so that completely arbitrary associations had to be learnt. Again this particular strategy seems to follow in the spirit of seeing whether a fully randomized system can acquire structures that support systematic behaviour. Some reasons to question the usefulness of this approach have already been put forward in Chapter 1.

Finally, interconnections between sememe units were introduced and fine-tuning (i.e. hand-tuning) of individual weights also took place. Connections between all pairs of sememe units were introduced to allow the net to do something known as 'clean-up' (described below).

Operation of the model

When an input string was presented to the net, the pattern of activity across the input units activated a collection of word-set units, which in turn activated many sememe units. In the ideal case, the set of sememe units would correspond to those explicitly chosen to be correct for the input string. However, it turned out that during the development phase, the net tended to switch ON inappropriate sememe units. Sememe units only turned ON if they received activation from all currently activated word-set units. Occasionally, however, an inappropriate sememe unit received activation from the collection of word-set units associated with a target input word. In this respect, the net was prone to produce incorrect output patterns and much initial effort was expended in trying to get the net to minimize the generation of these spurious outputs. To overcome these errors, fine-tuning of weights took place and interconnections between the sememe units were introduced. The interconnections between the sememe units now allowed these units to influence one another directly. It was the co-operative interactions between the sememe units that formed the basis of the process known as 'clean-up'. The additional inputs propagated along the interconnections between the sememe units allowed the system to clean up semantic representations that were only partially correct. Unfortunately the process of clean-up was not described in detail in the original papers, yet it seems that the weights on the interconnections between the sememe units forced these units to produce a pattern of activity that conformed to a familiar semantic representation. For example, if the net produced a pattern of semantic activity that closely resembled a target pattern then the process of clean-up ensured that the weighted connections between the units forced the units to adopt that target pattern.

It is best to think of the weights on the interconnections as specifying relationships between semantic features (an idea originally discussed by Hinton & Sejnowski, 1984). For instance, it can be envisaged that a negative weight would develop on the interconnection between the 'HAS WINGS' and 'BARKS' sememe units. There is nothing that has wings and barks. So the sememe unit for 'HAS WINGS', when turned ON, should inhibit the 'BARKS' unit from coming ON. It was through the interconnections between the sememe units that the net was able to learn familiar pair-wise combinations of semantic characteristics.

In developing the net, Hinton and Sejnowski (1986) report that the best system was one in which the chosen patterns of sememe unit activity were clamped onto the sememe units, and then these units alone went through an initial training period. Initially the target set of semantic representations were learnt through the acquisition of a set of weights on the interconnections between the sememe units.

The secondary stage of learning involved learning the mapping between the already experienced semantic representations and the input orthographic representations.

Although later interest focused upon the behaviour of the lesioned model, it seems true that much initial effort was expended in forcing the model to work. The net learnt by means of the Boltzmann procedures described in Chapter 2 and an extremely convoluted annealing procedure was needed for the net to learn a reasonable set of weights. Although it might be tempting to classify such work as an experimental exercise, it suffers from being little more than constrained trial and error. Success seems to have been achieved almost solely as a result of serendipity. Such remarks suggest that, at best, much important work still needs to be done in deriving principles and guidelines for the future development of learning procedures and net architectures. The introduction of arbitrary learning regimes adds nothing to the scientific credibility of the approach.

Lesioning the model

Eventually the net achieved a 99.9% rate of success in being able to produce 20 appropriate semantic patterns to 20 input orthographic patterns. This was taken as being an existence proof that a system with coarse coding can acquire a set of arbitrary input–output mappings and that it can also exhibit automatic generalization.

In lesioning the net it was found that removal of any one word-set unit tended to produce erroneous outputs to several words instead of just one. This is just as is expected from the distributed nature of the encoding used. Indeed, on extensive testing with the net when only one word-set unit was removed, interesting behaviour was witnessed. The majority of errors produced now corresponded to the semantic representation appropriate to another word. This kind of behaviour was attributed to the process of clean-up. Remember clean-up ensured that the net tended to produce outputs it already 'knew'. With meagre levels of damage the tendency was to produce an output only slightly different from the correct output. For larger levels of damage the net produced a pattern for a different yet familiar pattern. The net tended not to produce novel outputs.

The overwhelming biases to err by producing a familiar semantic pattern after lesioning was taken by Hinton and Sejnowski (1986) to be essentially akin to deep dyslexia. For, as they state, a deep dyslexic subject tends to produce a semantically related word to a target word even though the two words have radically different sounds and spelling. For example, in reading the word 'PEACH' a patient might say 'APRICOT'. Like the net, the patient is producing an output that is semantically but not visually similar to the correct output. As with many such demonstrations in new connectionism, this again questions a widely held belief in the utility of traditional arrows-and-boxes theorizing. Figure 5.2 shows in schematic form a traditional arrows-and-boxes model of deep dyslexia, that of the 'two-route' model of reading put forward originally by Marshall and Newcombe (1973).

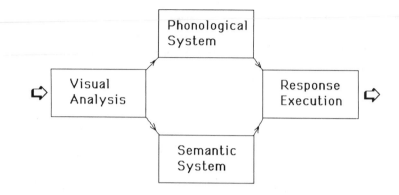

Figure 5.2. Schematic representation of the dual route model of reading put forward by Marshall and Newcombe (1973).

The account of deep dyslexia that this model affords is that there is local damage to the phonological route, so patients have only the semantic route at their disposal. In so far as phonological analysis is lost or damaged, the patient will tend to produce words that reflect reading by the semantic route. Although the details of this model have been disputed and elaborated on at length (see Shallice, 1988), this form of arrows-and-boxes theorizing continues with vigour. Indeed, in many respects recent work in cognitive neuropsychology is almost totally reliant upon explanations where arrows are severed, and boxes are either removed or their contents damaged. It is against this theoretical backdrop that the radical nature of the demonstrations with lesioned artificial neural networks can readily be seen. In the net just described there are not two separate routes but just one. Consequently, the contingent account of deep dyslexia is radically different to that provided by the two-route model. In the net, mechanisms concerning orthographic aspects of the words remain intact and there is no phonological route in the model. If the model is to be construed as being a specification of the semantic route then it is damage to this semantic route that is causing all the difficulties in deep dyslexia.

Two additional points are worthy of note; both concern simulations with a damaged version of the net. Hinton *et al.* re-ran the model by damaging it in a way other than by lesioning. Random noise was added to the connections to and from the hidden units. Performance now fell from 99.9 per cent correct to 64.3 per cent correct; yet during retraining, the net exhibited very rapid relearning. As Hinton and Shallice (1989) note, a rapid recovery of function has also been observed with many neurologically damaged patients (Geschwind, 1985). Moreover, such rapid relearning remains unexplained within the framework of traditional cognitive neuropsychology.

In the simulations retraining removed the noise from the connections in the net. The spontaneous recovery of unrehearsed items came about because retraining

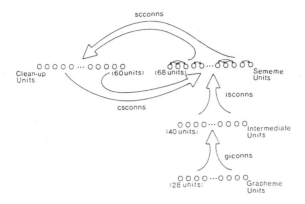

Figure 5.3. Schematic representation of Hinton and Shallice (1989) model (see text for full explanation). (From Hinton and Shallice, 1989, adapted with permission, *see* p. xvii.)

caused noise to be removed from every weight in the net. As all connections carried information about all associations, removal of noise from the connections benefited all associations. Moreover, in cases where some of the original words were omitted from the retraining, performance on these words improved as a function of experiencing the other members of the set. This was even though the words and their semantic representations were only arbitrarily associated. Hinton *et al.* even went so far as to claim that the spontaneous recovery of unrehearsed items is the 'signature of distributed representations' (p. 104) because a system with localist representations would not behave accordingly. A less contentious conclusion, perhaps, is that it is not obvious, in the absence of a working model, how spontaneous recovery of unrehearsed items could arise in a system with localist representations.

Semantics 2: The Hinton and Shallice model

In extending the Hinton and Sejnowski model, Hinton and Shallice (1989) went on to provide a more thorough analysis of the sorts of reading errors produced by deep dyslexics.

Architecture of the model

The architecture of the model is shown in schematic form in Figure 5.3.

As can be seen, it is essentially the Hinton and Sejnowski model in another guise. As before, there are input/graphemic units and output/sememe units. The grapheme units were identical to the letter position-specific units used in the

McClelland and Rumelhart (1981) IA model. So now the model was presented with real three- and four-lettered English words and a decision was made to use the 'more efficient' back-propagation learning algorithm instead of the previous Boltzmann procedures. Given this, the units in the net were real-valued and not binary stochastic units (see Chapter 2). The real values of the sememe units were treated as being probabilities of the semantic primitive being true. In total 68 sememe units were used and these were divided into 19 groups. Some of these groups comprised a single unit; however, the interesting groups comprised more than one unit. Such groups were interconnected into something known as a 'winner-take-all' net (after Feldman & Ballard, 1982). Each unit shared inhibitory connections with all others in the group and each also possessed a strong self-excitatory connection. In this way, sets of sememe units within a group were taken by analogy to be mutually exclusive values along a real-word dimension such as size or shape. In each winner-take-all net, one unit was ensured to come ON and this unit then signified the appropriate dimensional value. The single active unit tended to suppress the other units in the set from coming ON.

As before, there were hidden units between the graphemic and sememe units. These were now known as intermediate units so as to distinguish them from another set of hidden units known as clean-up units. The clean-up units were a quite separate bank of units interconnected with the sememe units. In the previous Hinton and Sejnowski model only pairwise connections between sememe units were used. This allowed pairwise contingencies between semantic primitives to be acquired. In order to acquire other higher-order contingencies between the semantic primitives, the 'hidden' clean-up units were used. As in the earlier Hinton and Sejnowski model, the clean-up units allowed the net to alter an output vector in a direction commensurate with a familiar pattern of semantic activation.

Semantic representation in the model

The net was trained on 40 words taken from five categories of eight instances. Each word was paired with a semantic pattern generated from the available 68 semantic primitives. In order to understand the behaviour of the model it is important to understand what sorts of representations the net acquired. Some initial points are therefore included on the nature of (semantic) vector space. Given that the model possessed 68 sememe units, the associated vector space was defined relative to 68 dimensions. A given semantic vector corresponded to a fixed point in this 68-dimensional space. Such points were rather frighteningly referred to as vertices of a 68-dimensional hypercube. The shifting terminology, however, also refers to them as 'point attractors' lying at the bottom of 'basins of attraction'. In the language of vector landscapes, familiar meanings not only corresponded to fixed points but each of these fixed points was associated with a separate basin of attraction. It is perhaps best to imagine a real 3-D landscape with valleys. These valleys correspond to basins of attraction: a point at the very bottom of a valley corresponds to one of the 68 points of attraction. The implication here is that vectors that only partially map onto a familiar vector will correspond to a point within a particular basin of attraction. The process of clean-up can then be readily understood as moving that point towards the bottom of the basin of attraction.

To appreciate fully this kind of account of information processing, it is essential to understand the notion of multidimensional spaces, and of points within such spaces. Some degree of success can be achieved by thinking in terms of naturally occurring landscapes and then attempting to reason by analogy. The result is that such a conception of semantic memory is quite unlike the traditional accounts based upon semantic networks (Quillian, 1968) and frame theory (Minsky, 1975). Nevertheless, points of contact can be made between the connectionist and traditional accounts. For as Shallice (1988) puts it, '[semantic] access can be conceived of as the attainment of a series of increasingly close approximations to the "correct" state of the elements [units]' (p. 289; text in brackets added). Accessing a semantic representation is a notion central to the traditional semantic network accounts of understanding. So although by analogy it is possible to compare new connectionist and traditional cognitive psychology accounts of semantic memory, very different notions are being described within the two frameworks. Yet to be fair this is not the first time that researchers have used multidimensional scaling techniques to model semantic memory (see Rumelhart & Abrahamson, 1973, after Henley, 1969), so in this sense the work of Hinton and Shallice is not totally new. What is new is their operationalization of the ideas within a neural net architecture. Indeed, their work is innovative in many respects and main interest was with the behaviour of the net when damaged.

Lesioning the model

Three kinds of damage were inflicted on the net: (i) weights on connections were set to 0, (ii) noise was added to connections (this was achieved by adding small random numbers to the weights), and (iii) hidden units were ablated. In each case, a number of different levels of damage were considered and results were averaged over 10 different runs with each kind of damage. As with a deep dyslexic patient, the errors made by the damaged net were classified using four categories. The categories were: (i) semantic errors – where the output resembled a vector belonging to another instance of the same category (e.g. 'cat' for 'dog'); (ii) visual errors – the output corresponded to an instance from another category whose label was visually similar to the input (e.g. 'bun' for 'bug'); (iii) mixed errors – the output corresponded to an instance that was semantically and visually similar to the input (e.g. 'ram' for 'rat'); and (iv) other errors (e.g. 'hawk' for 'log'). As Hinton and Shallice note, deep dyslexics produce all four types of errors. Moreover, explanations of their performance have typically been couched in terms of damage to isolable processing subsystems – the occurrence of visual errors being due to damage to an orthographic lexicon and, the occurrence of semantic errors being due to damage to the semantic stage of processing (Patterson, 1978). Why mixed errors occur remains to be fully explained within the traditional cognitive neuropsychological framework.

A quite different account of the errors arises from consideration of the performance of the damaged net. The results of the extensive simulations carried out can be summarized briefly. All four kinds of errors occurred with all kinds of lesions although the distribution of the proportion of errors did vary across the lesion types. Lesions to connections to the intermediate units from the graphemic units tended to give rise to visual errors: few semantic errors occurred. In explaining visual errors, Hinton and Shallice described the visual inputs being used by the net as pointers to positions in semantic space. Disruption to the visual input meant that the pointer now addressed a different position in semantic space: namely, a position that fell within a basin of attraction corresponding to a member of another category.

With lesions to the connections between the intermediate and sememe units a majority of semantic errors arose and some visual errors also occurred. Although mixed errors occurred with lesions to connections to and from the intermediate units, of particular interest is the fact that visual and mixed errors did occur with damage to the later parts of the system. According to traditional accounts, the occurrence of visual errors has been attributed to some form of breakdown at an early stage of visual analysis. In contrast, the model shows that both visual and mixed errors can occur with damage to later parts of the system. In the model damage to the later semantic parts of system constituted a reshaping of the vector landscape to the extent that the positions of the basins of attraction underwent change. So although the vsual inputs into the semantic system had not in themselves changed, the semantic space had. Hence the visual pointers now addressed quite different semantic patterns of activity than in the intact model. Consequently, the model did produce visual and mixed errors with damage to the later parts of the net.

The overall claim is that the model provides a general account of the range of different errors produced by deep dyslexics. The complete range of errors arose with all of the variants of the damaged model tested. Hinton and Shallice state therefore that the varied pattern of errors reflects a breakdown characteristic of a lesioned distributed net. Indeed, they go further in claiming that the prevalence of the various error types seems to accord better with arguments for damage to layered connectionist systems than with arguments for damage to systems comprising isolable modules.

Further points about semantic classification

Two further results will be now considered: both concern the categorization performance of the damaged net and both again offer provocative support for adopting new connectionism as a framework for thinking about neuropsychological functioning. The first concerns category-specific deficits and the second concerns the performance of the model in those cases where the outputs failed to resemble closely any familiar stored semantic vector.

Category-specificity

One of the more surprising aspects of the performance of the damaged net was that it exhibited a strong category-specific effect. This is again a counter-intuitive finding given that the net uses fully distributed representations. Within the traditional framework category-specific deficits fit most comfortably with ideas about well-demarcated category-based knowledge systems. Nevertheless, for one level of severity of damage to the connections between the clean-up and sememe units, the net continued to respond well to the FOOD instances but performed dismally with instances from all other categories. Similar patterns of performance have been well documented in the cognitive neuropsychological literature and a number of quite different accounts of the phenomenon have been set out (see Shallice, 1988, Chapter 12). The model, however, provides quite an idiosyncratic account of the phenomenon, although it can be roughly described as an account where damage to the semantic store has taken place. Unfortunately the category-specific effect reported with the model is not thoroughly examined in the paper and it would unwise to speculate as to why it occurred. Moreover, the effect arose with one version of the net but not another. The two versions of the net differed only in the initial starting weights. Given this, Hinton and Shallice noted that category-specificity cannot arise purely because of the input–output contingencies; the initial starting state of the net is crucial. Category-specificity therefore seems not to be an inevitable consequence of damaging a distributed network.

Semantic classification without conscious identification

The final set of observations concerning the damaged net rest on a more complete understanding of converting actual output vectors into discernible responses. Remember in the language of vector landscapes, any output vector can be located as a point on the vector landscape. Given this, inter-vector similarity can be assessed in terms of distances between points across the vector landscape. An output vector was taken to resemble most the already familiar vector closest to it on the vector landscape. To flesh these ideas out in terms of measuring inter-vector similarities two indices were used. These were respectively known as proximity and gap. Proximity was essentially a measure of the nearest neighbour to a given output vector (a full description of the measure is given by Hinton and Shallice, though it is more generally explained by Jordan, 1986). A proximity value of 1 corresponded to where an output vector fell at the same position as another. To discover the nearest neighbour to a given output vector the proximity of that vector to all stored vectors was computed and the smallest value indexed the nearest neighbour. In the ideal case, with the intact model, every output vector should yield a proximity value of 1 because the output vector should fall at the same position as its corresponding stored vector. However, when the net was damaged a range of proximity values occurred. The problem now was to decide upon a criterion value of proximity. Values above the criterion would therefore signify a reasonable fit between an actual and stored vector; values below the criterion would not. Consequently, with the large proximity values it was assumed that the model would be able to make some form of identification response. It would be unable to make any such response on the basis of a small proximity value. The criterion proximity value was set at 0.8 as this approximated to the median value across the set of input words used.

In addition the second gap-criterion was defined for those cases where the output vector resembled several stored vectors. The gap criterion ensured that the model could only produce a response when the actual output vector fell closer to a stored vector than to the next closest vector by a specified amount: the amount being the gap value. Having set both criteria, Hinton and Shallice assessed performance of the model in those cases where it failed to produce a response. In order to do this systematically, the following steps were taken.

For each of five categories the associated vectors were considered and their positions were noted. From these positions a central position, or centroid, was computed. This centroid can be considered as being the representation of the prototypical category instance. Five such centroids were computed and it was with respect to these five centroids that the net's classificatory performance was assessed. A given output vector was then assigned to that category whose centroid it was closest to. (Remember, though, performance was only assessed for those cases where the outputs failed to match the pre-specified proximity and gap criteria.) This first assessment of the net's classificatory performance will be known as between-category assignment, and, as Hinton and Shallice note, this is akin to a five alternative forced choice (5AFC) procedure. Having assigned the output to a category, within-category assignment took place. Here the nearest of the eight category members was computed. In this case the analogy is with an eight alternative forced choice (8AFC) procedure. So having made a choice about which category the instance belonged to, a choice was then made about which category instance the output most resembled. Overall, between-category assignment gave an index of how likely it was that the output signified a member of that category; within-category assignment gave an index of how likely it was that the output was a particular familiar instance.

The rather striking and surprising result was that in all cases examined, within-category assignment performed as well as between-category assignment. Unfortunately, from the very sparse details given, it is difficult to be clear about how and why this particular pattern of results occurred. Indeed, to try to explicate the behaviour of the model further would tend towards speculation, given that few details are provided. Indeed, the results would be more understandable if more details about the actual clustering of the different categories has been included. It would be particularly useful to know whether the categories formed overlapping or separable sets. It is difficult to get a feel for whether the model did form categories in sense of demarcating one part of semantic space for all the indoor objects and a different part of space for all the foods. (From a recent personal communication from Plaut, however, it turns out that the instances did tend to cluster in their categories in different parts of semantic space. However, there was quite a degree of overlap between the indoor objects and foods categories. Unfortunately, in the absence of further details, this particular fact makes the earlier category-specific deficit even more difficult to interpret.)

In summary, the central result was that in the cases where the model was unable to provide an identification response, it was able to perform within-category assignment at a level comparable to that on between-category assignment. Both tests were performed at levels greater than chance, hence the model did demonstrate the retention of some knowledge even though it was unable to produce an identification response. Hinton and Shallice note that, in this respect, the model makes the counter-intuitive prediction that a similar pattern of performance should be observed in the patient population. Intuitively, it seems that between-category assignment should be easier than within-category assignment. For instance, it is usually trivial to say that something is an animal rather than a plant. It is sometimes not as easy to say which particular animal or plant that thing is. Hinton and Shallice note, however, that the counter-intuitive pattern of performance has been observed in the patient population. They cite the work of Coslett and Saffran (1989) with patients classified as pure alexics. In an experiment with the rapid presentation of single words, patients were unable to report the identity of the words, yet they did demonstrate some knowledge of what had been presented. This knowledge was demonstrated by having the patients point to which of two pictures depicted the referent of the word.

Two forms of the test were administered. In the between-category case the two pictures were of instances taken from different categories. A stricture was that the names of the two instances started with the same initial cluster of letters e.g. house–horse. In the within-category case, the pictures showed instances of the same category e.g. giraffe–goat. Again some attempt was made to control for the initial letters of the names. Of the three patients run on both versions of the test, performance was marginally better in the within-category case than in the between-category case. Both tests were performed better than chance.

In considering the analogy between the model and the patient it is perhaps best to consider first exactly what it is that the model is doing. For between-category assignment the model is comparing its output to the prototypical instances of all five categories. Having made a category decision, the model then makes a within-category assignment by comparing its output to each of the eight category instances. Given the description of the patient testing situation, it can be seen that this scenario is quite different to that of the model. A more direct analogy would be where the patient had first to make a category decision about the word (by using forced choice procedures) and then had to make a within-category decision (again by using forced choice procedures). In actual fact, for both the within- and between-category tests the patients had to select a picture of the named instance from two possibilities. Stated in these terms, it is clear that the patient and model scenarios bear little resemblance to one another. Given this, therefore, it seems inappropriate to state that the damaged model behaves in a similar manner to certain brain-damaged patients. Nevertheless, this conclusion should not detract from the fact Hinton and Shallice's work does provide intriguing insights into how various category effects can arise through damage to a massively parallel and distributed system.

Concluding remarks about the psycholinguistics of lesioned nets

In closing this discussion of the simulations of deep dyslexia, it is fitting to make some general points about the psycholinguistics of new connectionism. According to Patterson *et al.* (1989), a central dogma of the dual-route model of written word pronunciation (Coltheart, 1985) is that quite different mechanisms subserve the pronunciation of exception words and non-words. The lexical route subserves the pronunciation of exception words and the grapheme-to-phoneme route subserves the pronunciation of non-words. From Chapter 4 it will be remembered that Patterson *et al.* claimed that they had instead described a single mechanism that 'supports the pronunciation of all types of letter strings' (p. 176). This is clearly at odds with Coltheart's dual-route theory. However, at a more global level, new connectionism *does* offer a dual-route account of reading. On the one hand, there is the orthography-to-phonology model set out Patterson *et al.* (1989). When lesioned, this model is said to account for surface dyslexia. On the other hand, there is the orthography-to-semantics model of Hinton and Shallice (1989). When lesioned, this model is said to account for deep dyslexia. Stated in these terms it seems that researchers who have adopted the new connectionist stance have perhaps unwittingly provided operational accounts of reading that fit surprisingly well with the simple dual-route model set out by Marshall and Newcombe (1973).

A brief digression concerning double dissociations is now included. The digression is important and relevant in discussing higher levels of cognition. The demonstrations of double dissociations in distributed processing systems question a central tenet of the classical approach to cognition; namely, that the brain can be decomposed into isolable subsystems at a functional level.

Double dissociations

Of the many important aspects of new connectionism, one of the more striking is that it affords a variety of novel and counter-intuitive interpretations of several cognitive deficits observed in human patients. Some of these have already been discussed; others arise in considering how parallel distributed systems can exhibit double dissociations.

Although the methodology of the double dissociation is generally accepted as a powerful tool in clinical neuropsychology, there remains disagreement about how best to characterize it. The disagreement has recently been described by Shallice (1988), who states that the double dissociation has been characterized in two ways, only one of which is valid. According to Shallice (1988), the *invalid* characterization has been set out by Coltheart (1985) – a double dissociation occurs when patient A performs significantly better at Task 1 than at Task 2, and the reverse pattern of performance obtains with patient B. By contrast, Shallice (1988), claims that the *valid* characterization of the double dissociation is where patient A performs Task 1 significantly better than patient B, this situation being reversed for performance on Task 2. The latter characterization is claimed to be valid because it rules out any explanation of the pattern of results set out in terms of artefacts due to the availability of cognitive processing resources in the different patients. The argument is given in full by Shallice (1988, Section 10.5) and need not be reiterated. The important point is that, barring caveats due to processing resources, a double dissociation is typically taken as constituting strong evidence for isolable processing subsystems both at the psychological and neuropsychological levels (Shallice, 1979). From Shallice's description, Task 1 is accomplished because of the operation of one subsystem; a quite different subsystem is responsible for performance on Task 2. Separate lesions to the different subsystems give rise to the highly specific performance deficits witnessed across patients A and B. The argument goes that, if the two tasks were subserved by the same system, then any damage to that system would affect both tasks.

From a distance, therefore, any evidence about the modularity of the mind could be taken as conflicting with new connectionism on the grounds that new connectionism is generally assumed to provide non-modular accounts of processing. It might therefore seem natural to believe that the approach is wedded to the idea that the brain is a non-modular processing device given the adherence to principles of parallel distributed processing. Such a caricature of new connectionism stands in opposition to accounts of human information processing based on assumptions concerning modular subsystems. Researchers who adopt the modular approach espouse the view that the brain comprises many special-purpose devices that are autonomous and operate according to quite different principles of operation (see Fodor, 1983). Consequently, there is a contrast between non-modular connectionism and modular traditional cognitive neuropsychology.

Given this exaggerated dichotomy between modular and non-modular accounts of processing, it should be clear that any demonstration of a double dissociation using distributed processing within a simulated neural network does have important consequences. At the very least it would falsify the argument that the demonstration of a double dissociation necessarily supports the modular approach. In so far as such important issues are at stake, it is only reasonable to discuss in some detail the work of Wood (1978).

Wood's account of double dissociations

Wood (1978) argued that he was able to show how a double dissociation could arise within an information processing system embodied in a non-modular neural net. The work in question comprised a simple application of the linear associative memory developed by Anderson and co-workers (Anderson, 1977; Anderson *et al.*, 1977). The model comprised two sets of eight neurons: the α set comprised input neurons; the β set comprised output neurons. There was total connectivity between the input and output sets and real-valued vectors represented the pattern of activity across the units. A given real number signified the activity level of neuron in the net. Initially Wood trained the model to associate paired sets of **f** input patterns (vectors) with corresponding **g** output patterns. Performance was assessed by re-presenting each original **f** vector and by noting the corresponding **ĝ** output vectors. To assess how well the model had learnt the input–output mappings, the **ĝ** vectors were correlated with the corresponding original **g** output vectors. As has been already noted (see Chapter 2), when the **f** vectors are orthogonal, the **ĝ** output vectors correlated perfectly with the original **g** vectors. However, a more detailed analysis of the performance of the model was afforded by computing the correlation matrix for all **g**/**ĝ** pairings. This correlation matrix was treated as being akin to a confusion matrix where the diagonal elements indexed how well the model recognized the original vectors and the off-diagonal elements revealed how well the model discriminated between the various vectors. The diagonal elements revealed how well the new output **ĝ** vectors resembled their original **g** counterparts. The off-diagonal elements indexed by how much each **ĝ** output vector resembled every other **g** output vector. In this respect, the off-diagonal elements revealed the degree to which the model produced an inappropriate output vector to an input vector.

Wood's important extension to the work with the linear associative memory was to train the net on many input–output vectors and then to introduce lesions. A particular lesion was carried out by setting the value of a vector component to 0. On the assumption that each component represented the activity of a given neuron, this kind of lesioning was taken to be akin to ablating a neuron. Wood's main demonstrations concerned systematically lesioning different numbers of input and output neurons. In the case of lesioning each individual input and output neuron separately, the results showed that although performance suffered relative to the intact model, performance decrements were equivalent across the cases. This was taken as being evidence for equipotentiality: in quantitative terms, the results of lesioning any particular neuron were the same as lesioning any other neuron.

In addition to the single neuron lesions, Wood also separately assessed all possible combinations of up to seven input neurons and up to seven output neurons. Here the results were interpreted in terms of mass action. The size of a lesion, and not its location, was important. Decrements in performance increased as a function of the number of neurons lesioned: there were no systematic effects attributable to the location of the lesions.

It is, however, Wood's final demonstration that is potentially the most damaging for modular accounts of neuropsychological functioning. This can only be appreciated with respect to the actual results reported. Table 5.1a shows the original **f** and **g** vectors used in the simulation. Table 5.1b shows the correlation matrix for the case where neuron 1 is lesioned. Table 5.1c shows the correlation matrix for the case where neuron 2 was lesioned.

As can be seen from Table 5.1, vectors $\mathbf{f}_3$ and $\mathbf{f}_4$ are distinctive. $\mathbf{f}_3$ and $\mathbf{f}_4$ are identical on all components apart from the first two. Remember the component numbers signify the activity levels of the corresponding neurons in the net. Hence the activity levels of neurons 1 and 2 are critical in distinguishing the vectors $\mathbf{f}_3$ and $\mathbf{f}_4$. The activity levels of neuron 1 and neuron 2 in $\mathbf{f}_3$ are swopped over in $\mathbf{f}_4$. As can be seen, the activity level of neuron 1 is less than that of neuron 2 in $\mathbf{f}_3$: the reverse is true in $\mathbf{f}_4$. Indeed, the consequence of lesioning either neuron 1 or 2 was that the net retained the ability to respond appropriately to $\mathbf{f}_1$ and $\mathbf{f}_2$, but it performed less well with vectors $\mathbf{f}_3$ and $\mathbf{f}_4$. Indeed, the detailed behaviour of the lesioned model is revealed by consideration of the confusion matrices shown in Table 5.1.

For Wood, the critical comparisons regard the recognition performance with $\mathbf{f}_3$ and $\mathbf{f}_4$. Remember it is the diagonal elements in the confusion matrices that index recognitive ability, the off-diagonal elements index the degree to which the vectors are now confusable. When neuron 1 was lesioned the recognition scores were .914 and .522 respectively for $\mathbf{f}_3$ and $\mathbf{f}_4$. When neuron 2 was lesioned the recognition scores for $\mathbf{f}_3$ and $\mathbf{f}_4$ were .526 and .956 respectively. Comparing across these two situations, Wood claimed that this is analogous to the state of affairs that occurs with a double dissociation. With one lesion performance is better with Task 1 (i.e. responding to $\mathbf{f}_3$) than with Task 2 (i.e. responding to $\mathbf{f}_4$), with a separate lesion performance is better with Task 2 (i.e. responding to $\mathbf{f}_4$) than with A (i.e. responding to $\mathbf{f}_3$). Characterized in this way, Wood appears to draw the analogy between the two versions of the net (version 1: neuron 1 lesioned vs. version 2: neuron 2 lesioned) and patients studied in a clinical neuropsychological setting.

Wood is clear in arguing that such a demonstration as this is difficult to reconcile with traditional modular accounts of information processing simply because it arises from a mechanism that behaves according to principles of equipotentiality and mass action. The model is one that embodies parallel distributed processing.

Table 5.1

(a) Corresponding input and output vectors used in Wood's simulation of a double dissociation.

	Input vectors				Output vectors		
f_1	f_2	f_3	f_4	g_1	g_2	g_3	g_4
-.196	-.229	.114	.912	1.000	-1.000	1.000	-1.000
.000	-.459	.912	.114	1.000	-1.000	-1.000	-1.000
-.196	.459	-.114	-.114	1.000	1.000	1.000	1.000
.392	.229	.228	.228	1.000	1.000	-1.000	1.000
.558	-.459	.114	.114	-1.000	-1.000	1.000	1.000
.558	.000	-.114	-.114	-1.000	-1.000	-1.000	1.000
-.196	-.229	-.114	-.114	-1.000	1.000	1.000	-1.000
-.196	.459	.228	.228	-1.000	1.000	-1.000	-1.000

(b) Confusion matrix when neuron 1 is lesioned.

	$\hat{g}_1$	$\hat{g}_2$	$\hat{g}_3$	$\hat{g}_4$
g_1	.943	-.299	.083	.276
g_2	-.309	.898	-.315	.081
g_3	.088	-.322	.914	.803
g_4	.088	.025	.241	.522

(c) Confusion matrix when neuron 2 is lesioned.

	$\hat{g}_1$	$\hat{g}_2$	$\hat{g}_3$	$\hat{g}_4$
g_1	.960	-.319	.209	-.087
g_2	-.259	.933	.163	-.127
g_3	.064	.062	.526	.251
g_4	-.086	-.154	.809	-.956

Appraisal of Wood's model

Shallice (1988) takes exception to Wood's central claims regarding the double dissociation. Firstly, he argues that what is lost in Wood's lesioned net is the ability to retain individual associations. It is the ability to associate certain **f–g** parings that is lost. On the contrary, Shallice argues that 'A dissociation in neuropsychology is the loss not of an association, but of the ability to perform a certain type of operation.' (p. 255). However, this a very rigid interpretation of the results. It seems quite reasonable to think of the operation of the model in more liberal terms. For example, the inputs to the model could stand for names for category instances and the outputs could stand for the operation of pointing to a relevant picture of those category instances.

Shallice continues his critique by stating that in the simulation it is the loss of inputs to the system that results in the double dissociation. Yet this demonstration is not surprising given that the model's discrimination responses are based on the inputs and it is these that are impoverished. Shallice seems to imply that the double dissociation arises solely because of some form of input deficit and not because of damage to mechanisms that intervene between input and output stages. Some might well observe that any demonstration of a double dissociation in a parallel distributed system is nevertheless a revealing and counter-intuitive result. Moreover, as will become clear, Shallice's criticism cannot be levelled against all simulated accounts of double dissociations.

Shallice also takes exception with the fact that the model's discrimination responses are critically dependent on the behaviour of individual neurons. Shallice objects that a double dissociation in clinical neuropsychology typically occurs 'as a consequence of the principle of organisation of the system lesioned' (p. 255). However, yet again this criticism rests on a literal and rigid interpretation of the results. There seems no reason why the units in Wood's model have to be taken as standing for individual neurons. As McClelland and Rumelhart (1985, p. 161) argue, units in the models could signify the operation of a whole complex of cells depending what level of analysis is assumed.

A far more wounding attack has been launched by Coltheart (personal communication), who points out that the double dissociation produced by Wood's model is quite consistent with the traditional ideas about localization of function. According to the traditional view, somewhere in the system there is a module, or some kind of functional unit, that is specialized for processing f_3 but not f_4, and somewhere else in the system is a different module that is specialized for processing f_4 but not f_3. Upon closer inspection it does seem that the behaviour of the model can be explained in just these terms. Neuron 2 is vital for processing f_3 but not for f_4 and neuron 1 is vital for the processing of f_4 but not f_3. To bolster these claims Coltheart points out that when neuron 2 is lesioned the correlation between the actual output vector and the true output vector increases for f_4: for the intact model the correlation is .92, and this increases to .96 when neuron 2 is lesioned. A similar but smaller increase occurs when neuron 1 is lesioned and the correlation is computed for f_3. This time the correlation increases from .89 to .91.

Further support for Coltheart's argument is provided by presenting the model with just the component for neuron 2 in f_3 and then separately with just the component for neuron 1 in f_4. In the first case, the correlation between the actual and target vectors falls from .89 to .88, in the second case the correlation actually rises from .92 to .94. What all of this really means is that even though the model has been developed in accordance with principles of parallel distributed processing, there are units in the net that have developed specific functional roles (cf. Anderson & Mozer, 1981). The moral is clear: parallel distributed processing models need not be incompatible with ideas about functional specialization nor ideas about physical localization of function (see Quinlan, 1987, for more on this point).

Coltheart's critique establishes that Wood's demonstration of a double

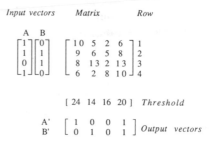

Input vectors   *Matrix*   *Row*

Figure 5.4. Schematic representation of Sartori's model of a double dissociation. Two input patterns A and B are shown. The numbers in the central matrix correspond to the weights on the links between pairs of input and output units. Output units possess thresholds as shown. A' and B' are the corresponding output patterns for A and B.

dissociation is not as theoretically significant as it would at first appear. However, more recently another attempt at simulating a double dissociation using distributed processing methods has been reported by Sartori (1988). Figure 5.4 shows the model in schematic form. Here again is a simple pattern associator but this time the net possesses four input units and four output units. Each output unit has a threshold and for a unit to come ON, the sum of the products of the inputs and the weights should be greater than or equal to its threshold value. From the example shown, this reduces to adding up only those numbers on a given column of the weight matrix that are matched with a 1 in the input vector. Each column corresponds to the input lines for a given output unit.

Sartori now describes two different hypothetical lesions to the weighted connections. One lesion affects the weighted connection in row 1 column 1. Its effect is to reduce this weight from 10 to 1. Importantly, with this lesion, performance on pattern A is affected whereas performance on B is left intact. When B is presented the net produces the same output; when A is presented the net produces [0,0,0,1] and not the correct vector [1,0,0,1]. Quite the reverse deficit is observed when the weighted connection in row 2 column 4 and that in row 3 column 4 are damaged. Here the weight on the first connection is reduced from 8 to 4; the weight on the second connection is reduced from 13 to 6. Now performance on A is preserved but the net fails to produce the correct vector for B. Given this particular model it seems safe to conclude that a double dissociation can arise when the information-processing system is embodied in a parallel distributed architecture. In particular, as Sartori states, the demonstration shows that a double dissociation does not necessitate positing two independent processing components. More specifically, the demonstration does not suffer at the hands of Shallice's criticism regarding damage to inputs (see above). In Sartori's example it is the intervening mechanisms (i.e. the connections) that are damaged and not the inputs to the system.

Semantics 3: Distributed representations as lists of properties

A basic assumption within the new connectionist framework is that a concept is represented as a pattern of activity distributed over many units. A distributed representation is defined as being the simultaneous pattern of activity over a number of different units. Consequently, different patterns of activity of the same set of units represent different concepts. This is quite unlike traditional localist schemes where a different unit, or node in a semantic net, represents each different concept. Whereas the localist accounts hold that some given information is stored in and retrieved from some particular 'place', in distributed models it is assumed that it is the concurrent activation of many different units which is critical and that the mere presence of this activity constitutes a given memory trace. In so far as different patterns of activation in the same units constitute different memories, location alone cannot be used to distinguish different memories.

Overall, the contrast between traditional and connectionist views on the storage and retrieval of information rests upon very different conceptions of how best to characterize mental representation. To understand the claims about distributed representations better, it is easiest to consider actual examples described in the literature.

McClelland and Rumelhart's model of prototype abstraction

Initially, consider three examples of distributed patterns that are said to represent three real-world concepts. The examples, taken from McClelland and Rumelhart (1985), show patterns of activity said to correspond to a prototypical DOG, CAT and BAGEL:

```
DOG      + - + - + - + -   + - + + - - - - + + + + + - - -
CAT      + + - - + + - -   + - + + - - - - + - + - + + - + 
BAGEL    + - - + + - - +   + + - + - + + - + - - + + + + -
```

In this representational scheme each '+' and '−' stands for the activity level of a particular unit. A '+' signifies a positive level of activity and a '−' signifies a negative level. A positive level signals that the unit is above its baseline of activation; a negative level signals that the unit is below its baseline of activation. Each pattern of '+'s and '−'s is known as a state vector. Each component of the vector represents the state of a given unit and the whole vector represents the simultaneous states of all of the units. In the examples shown, the first 8 units code the name of the concept; the remaining 16 units code visual features.

Interestingly, though, the distinction between units that code name information and units that code visual information was of little importance to the operation of the model. Strictures were introduced though, because McClelland and Rumelhart devised the prototype vectors such that the three name patterns were very different from one another. However, the patterns for DOG and CAT were more similar to each other than they were to the pattern for BAGEL.

The actual patterns shown were acquired by an associative net following training with a number of other patterns corresponding to DOGS, CATS, and BAGELS. This was shown by presenting the model with instances of the three classes and then probing the model with incomplete state vectors. Performance was assessed by examining the output patterns that the model produced in response to an incomplete input pattern. For instance, when presented with activity levels for the name input units for a given prototype, the model was able to produce the correct pattern of activity over the visual units. This was true even though the model never experienced the prototype pattern during training. Hence the net was said to have been able to form representations of the appropriate prototypes of the three classes merely from experiencing individual instances. Similar claims have been made about humans in the traditional experimental cognitive psychology literature (Posner & Keele, 1968, 1970). However, the distinctive claim is that knowledge of these three classes of objects is stored in the same set of weights on the interconnections between the units in a neural net. As a consequence, different patterns of activity over the same output units correspond to different instances of these classes. In turn, the implication seems to be that this simple model, when scaled up considerably, corresponds directly to how the brain stores and retrieves all conceptual knowledge. There are, however, good reasons to doubt this conclusion.

Appraisal of the model

One problem with the model is that it is difficult to be clear about what the psychological significance is of the output units taking real values between +1 and −1. Just what is it that these units are signalling? The only nearly plausible account is one in which the activity level of a given unit is taken to be a probability. Here the value would signal the probability that a given concept has an associated visual feature (cf. Hinton & Sejnowski, 1986). The outputs could then be somehow transformed into values between 0 and +1 rather than between −1 and +1 such that 0 would signal that the feature is irrelevant to the concept and +1 would signal that the feature is a defining characteristic. Overall, this is a rather charitable interpretation and is really rather forced. It cannot hope to capture the many well-documented nuances of the psychology of conceptual knowledge relevant to the nature and representation of category prototypes. Irrespective of these feelings of unease, other difficulties remain.

An additional problem is that all instances are coded on all primitives: this seems hopelessly clumsy. In the limit this seems to point to a system where every instance is represented in terms of all possible primitives, e.g. a BAGEL would score on all conceivable visual primitives. Indeed, BAGEL is encoded on exactly the same set of primitives as DOGs and CATs are. Moreover, BAGEL shares many values with DOGs and CATs on these primitives yet this is clearly ludicrous. On these grounds alone, the model cannot be taken as a serious account of human conceptual memory. Nevertheless, the idea that conceptual knowledge can be fully captured by a system of state vectors is taken by some to be a fundamental tenet of new connectionism (Smolensky, 1987, 1988). The discussion will turn to these ideas shortly.

Finally, it is difficult to take this model seriously as a psychological account, because of the failure to specify the nature of the primitives used. Perhaps the defence is that it is quite legitimate to leave the primitives undefined on the grounds that it is the formal nature of the system that is being explored. A more jaundiced view, though, is that there are insurmountable difficulties in attempting to specify what the primitives could actually represent. This particular issue has been vigorously discussed in other parts of the literature (Miller & Johnson-Laird, 1976; Schank, 1976; Wilks, 1976, 1977; Winograd, 1978), with no consensus on what constitutes an adequate set of primitives. Indeed, the possibility that human conceptual knowledge cannot be reduced to values on sets of primitives is not even contemplated by McClelland and Rumelhart (1985). This point might be construed as mere sniping, but there are profound philosophical problems with any account that proposes that human conceptual representation entails decomposition into a set of semantic primitives (Fodor, 1981; Fodor, Garrett, Walker & Parkes, 1980; Shannon, 1988).

Having considered the particulars of the McClelland and Rumelhart model, it is fitting now to turn to Smolensky's (1987) ideas about mental representation. Here again is another view of distributed representations as being lists of properties.

Smolensky's views on distributed representations

Following Kolers and Smythe (1984), it is useful to offer the following definition of what 'symbol' means in classical computational theories of cognition (see Fodor & Pylyshyn, 1981). Kolers and Smythe define a symbol to mean 'anything that refers, denotes, or stands for something else' (p. 293). More specifically, within the classical computational theories of cognition, symbols are defined as being differentiable, articulated and identifiable. In quoting Goodman (1976), Kolers and Smythe state that the principal feature is that the symbols must not be mistaken for one another.

This working definition of symbols can now be used to discuss Smolensky's (1988) distinction between symbolic and subsymbolic levels. From the classical perspective, it is the idea of a differentiable and identifiable symbol that plays a central role. For example, in thinking about COFFEE it is quite legitimate for a classical theorist to posit a differentiable and identifiable symbol for COFFEE. For Smolensky, however, this is not at all appropriate. Thinking about COFFEE entails having a state vector that comprises 'entities that correspond to constituents of the symbols used in symbol [classical] paradigm' (1988, p. 3; text in brackets added). Smolensky continues that these entities can be referred to as subsymbols where a given subsymbol corresponds to the activity of a particular unit in a connectionist net. This terminology is all rather awkward because Smolensky not only argues that the most adequate level of psychological explanation is that couched at the level of subsymbols, he also argues that this level can and should replace theorizing at the symbolic level. The upshot of this is a claim that classical distinctions drawn at the level of symbols may not be honoured at the subsymbolic level. So by this view there could well be a new connectionist account of sentence processing in which it is not possible to draw a one-to-one correspondence between functional units in the model and the traditional word classes of subject, verb and object. Given Smolensky's argument, it is more appropriate to substitute the term 'micro-feature' (Hinton, 1981) for 'subsymbol', for now there is no implication that the micro-featural representation of a concept implies a higher symbolic level.

By way of example, reconsider the prototypical representations of DOG, CAT and BAGEL set out above. Although McClelland and Rumelhart draw the distinction between name units and visual units, this distinction is of little functional significance in the operation of the model. Here each name unit signifies a micro-feature of the name of the concept and each visual unit signifies a micro-feature of a visual attribute of the concept. McClelland and Rumelhart went on to test the model with either (a) the activity over the name units, or, separately, (b) the activity over the visual units as partial cues for recall. Nevertheless the activity over any subset of units might well as acted as an effective cue. Indeed, they found that when the net was trained without the name patterns included, the cued recall performance of the model was appreciably better than chance. When cued with any subpart of a visual pattern the net produced the correct complete pattern on the output units. The classical distinction between the name of a concept and its visual attributes plays no significant role in the operation of the model.

Smolensky's central point is that distinctions made at a micro-featural level of description need not honour distinctions drawn at the classical symbolic level. Micro-features are said to specify a finer level of representation than do symbols. However, very few further details are given by way of definition. Smolensky (1987) has stipulated that units are constrained to express only sensory properties of stimuli and has offered the following intuitive account of what the state vector for CUP WITH COFFEE might be:

ON – UPRIGHT CONTAINER
ON – HOT LIQUID
OFF – GLASS CONTACTING WOOD
ON – PORCELAIN CURVED SURFACE
ON – BURNT ODOUR
ON – BROWN LIQUID CONTACTING PORCELAIN
ON – PORCELAIN CURVED SURFACE
OFF – OBLONG SILVER OBJECT
ON – FINGER-SIZED HANDLE
ON – BROWN LIQUID WITH CURVED SIDES AND BOTTOM

In turn CUP WITHOUT COFFEE is represented as:

ON – UPRIGHT CONTAINER
OFF – HOT LIQUID
OFF – GLASS CONTACTING WOOD
ON – PORCELAIN CURVED SURFACE
OFF – BURNT ODOUR
OFF – BROWN LIQUID CONTACTING PORCELAIN
ON – PORCELAIN CURVED SURFACE
OFF – OBLONG SILVER OBJECT
ON – FINGER-SIZED HANDLE
OFF – BROWN LIQUID WITH CURVED SIDES AND BOTTOM

By comparing these two sets of micro-features and their constituent values it can be seen that the representation of COFFEE is:

OFF – UPRIGHT CONTAINER
ON – HOT LIQUID
OFF – GLASS CONTACTING WOOD
ON – PORCELAIN CURVED SURFACE
ON – BURNT ODOUR
ON – BROWN LIQUID CONTACTING PORCELAIN
OFF – PORCELAIN CURVED SURFACE
OFF – OBLONG SILVER OBJECT
OFF – FINGER-SIZED HANDLE
ON – BROWN LIQUID WITH CURVED SIDES AND BOTTOM

In other words, COFFEE is represented as a burnt odour and a hot brown liquid with curved sides and bottom surfaces contacting porcelain.

This scheme is advanced as a real alternative to classical symbol processing accounts not least because the representation of COFFEE is said to be a context-dependent representation. There is no generic context-independent representation of individuals in this framework. There is only a set of context-dependent representations. Given this, it is simply inappropriate to discuss *the* representation of COFFEE. There is no canonical (context-independent) representation of COFFEE. The representation of COFFEE changes depending on its context. As Fodor and McLaughlin (1990) state, 'there is no single vector that counts as *the* COFFEE representation, hence no single vector that is a component of all the representations which, in a Classical system, would have COFFEE as a Classical constituent' (p. 193). In other words, in Smolensky's scheme, there is nothing that acts as the symbol for COFFEE. It is this kind of statement that is used to bolster the claim that a subsymbolic implementation of mental representation need not honour classical symbolic distinctions. However, this leaves something of a dilemma because there is an important sense in which there has to be something that allows the system to recognize the various instances of COFFEE as being instances of COFFEE. The system must be able to recognize COFFEE (i.e. act appropriately) when confronted with coffee. The upshot of this is that Smolensky is forced back on stating that the system must be able to deal with family resemblances. It is a family of distributed activity patterns that makes up the extension of the concept of COFFEE. (The extension of a concept is the set of all instances of that concept.) Consequently, the system operates by honouring these family resemblances. Unfortunately, as Fodor and McLaughlin (1990) unmercifully point out, just how the system could do this is left unspecified.

A full and detailed critique of Smolensky's ideas can be pieced together from the writings of Fodor and Pylyshyn (1988) and Fodor and McLaughlin (1990). Apart from the claim that Smolensky gives no details about how such a system could work, there are other problems that remain in trying to equate state vectors with mental representations. For instance, Smolensky's system fails to honour the distinction between the intension and extension of a concept. The intension of a concept is essentially the means for fixing the extension of the concept. It is with reference to the intension that all the instances of the concept can be identified. Of course, there has been much debate over how best to characterize the intension of a concept, but this issue is independent of the shortcomings of Smolensky's framework. Even though Smolensky admits that, in simulating the human conceptual system, the model must must have a means of assigning members of an extension, there is no way in which his system can do this.

A second point is that the system of representation seems to be overly constricting. In order to recover the representation for COFFEE, the state vector for CUP WITHOUT COFFEE had to be subtracted from the state vector for CUP WITH COFFEE – subtracted in the formal sense of the actual vector operation. However, vector subtraction is only allowed between vectors that have the same number of components. Consequently, CUP WITHOUT COFFEE and CUP WITH COFFEE must comprise the same units, otherwise the subtraction cannot be enacted. As Fodor and McLaughlin (1990, p. 190, fn. 7) point out, this leads to a ridiculously constrained system. In an allied point, Fodor and McLaughlin go on to state that the GLASS CONTACTING WOOD unit remains OFF in all cases discussed by Smolensky. They therefore speculate that this unit is required when

COFFEE has to be represented in other contexts. Here again they claim that this leads to ludicrous consequences. For as they state, 'if GRANNY combines with COFFEE to yield GRANNY'S COFFEE, GRANNY must contain activation levels for all the units in COFFEE and vice versa' (p. 190).

A third and final point concerns the fact that a state vector, as construed by Smolensky, essentially consists of an unordered property list. Dependencies between values of the units are not represented and it is this lack of relational information that severely limits the applicability of this form of representation. There exists a vast body of data and research which shows that it is both parts and the relations between those parts that are important at the psychological level (see e.g. Hinton, 1979; Hinton & Parsons, 1981). Indeed, there is a near consensus of opinion in perceptual psychology that, fundamentally, perception is a process of description (see Rock, 1983). The perceptual system appears to deal with descriptions of stimuli to the extent that the underlying perceptual representation codes the salient parts of a stimulus and their relations (see Quinlan, 1991, for a more thorough review of these ideas). In only coding parts and not their relations, a state vector cannot ever achieve psychological credibility.

In conclusion, Smolensky claims that new connectionism offers a radically different alternative to classical ideas about mental representation. It is unfortunately true, though, that the alternative he describes seems both unworkable and untenable. Of course this is not an argument that all connectionist formalisms are in principle inadequate. The discussion therefore continues with a seemingly more powerful set of ideas put forward by Hinton.

The implementation of classical symbols?

A general point that Anderson and Hinton (1981) make in discussing alternatives to the classical approach to human information processing is that any critique of this tradition must also take into account why the approach is as successful as it is in explaining human intellectual abilities. This admission reflects a real tension in the new connectionist literature: whereas Smolensky is firm in trying to offer a real alternative to the classical approach, Hinton has attempted to show how traditionally defined cognitive structures can be instantiated in neural net architectures. This is even though new connectionism is otherwise heralded as being a significant paradigm shift (in the Kuhnian sense) for psychology (Schneider, 1987).

Hinton (1984) has claimed that it is quite incorrect to view distributed representational systems as alternatives to other classical representational schemes: they should be viewed as one way of implementing these schemes. In addition to implementing those schemes, connectionist systems have other impressive characteristics that are not shared with the other classical schemes. Here reference is to the powerful and sometimes unexpected emergent properties of certain net architectures. It is these that can provoke novel insights about psychological functioning. However, it is difficult to be sure, sometimes, what the intended meaning of the term 'emergent properties' is in the new connectionist literature. The most neutral interpretation is that nets exhibit properties that are either, in some sense, counter-intuitive or that they behave in ways that could not have been predicted at the outset. This is not to argue that the nets are unpredictable, although in many cases this seems a valid characterization, but merely that their eventual behaviour was not explicitly predicted. The phrase 'emergent properties' can also be interpreted relative to nets exhibiting graceful degradation, and automatic generalization. Both properties may be observed in nets after they have been trained on some particular set of inputs. They are said to emerge out of the intricate dynamics of a massively parallel and distributed processing system.

Much discussion has already been directed to graceful degradation. This property has been fully examined in the work on the lesioned nets. Automatic generalization, however, has only been described in passing – for instance as a property of pattern associators. Automatic generalization is a natural consequence of how these nets learn. Having experienced n examples of a given category, pattern associators can then respond appropriately to m other examples on the basis of the similarity relations that exist between their corresponding input patterns (see Chapter 2 for a thorough discussion of this point). When a net learns to respond appropriately to a given instance it does so by modifying the weights on many interconnections. These weight changes affect similar inputs in similar ways. If during training an instance is presented that differs greatly from all other previous instances, then the contingent weight modifications will, to a small extent, adversely affect the subsequent processing of the other instances. In other words, the weight changes for distinctive instances will be in a direction that is maladaptive relative to the changes made for the other instances.

Automatic generalization refers to the ability of the net to respond appropriately to one instance on the basis of how similar it is to all previously experienced instances. For Hinton, automatic generalization is a fundamentally important property of PDP systems. In particular, automatic generalization underlies a net's ability to learn to respond systematically to a whole class of instances. Moreover, it does this without acquiring an explicit representation of a rule that determines the classification. In this respect the net's behaviour can be said to be conforming to the rule, but there is no sense in which the rule is 'encoded' or 'used' by the net (cf. Stabler, 1983). It is in this sense therefore that rule-following behaviour (i.e. automatic generalization) is said to be an emergent property of the net.

Hinton's account of conceptual structure

Figure 5.5 shows an example of a net discussed by Hinton (1984). Here there are three distinct sets of units: (i) units that constitute the AGENT set; (ii) units that

RELATIONSHIP

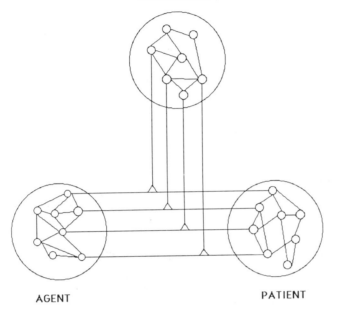

AGENT   PATIENT

Figure 5.5. Schematic representation of Hinton's model of representing constituent structure. Each set of units specify a different semantic role. However the RELATIONSHIP units modulate the activity between the AGENT and PATIENT units. (From Hinton *et al.*, 1986, adapted with permission, *see* p. xvii.)

constitute the RELATIONSHIP set; and (iii) units that constitute the PATIENT set. Each unit is said to represent a micro-feature. Across a given set of units the current pattern of activity is the distributed representation of a given instance. The representation specifies the instance as comprising a particular set of values on the particular set of micro-features. Within each set of units the units share connections that are said to stand for micro-inferences. The best analogy here is with the sememe units discussed before and their interconnections. These connections specified the real-world contingencies between different semantic primitives. Recall the BARKS and FLIES example above. An additional point is that stable patterns of activity over the units are said to violate the minimal number of the micro-inferences.

It remains true that the micro-features and micro-inferences are left unspecified. Hence, the framework falls foul of the criticisms of the McClelland and Rumelhart model set out above; namely, that it is difficult to assess the psychological plausibility of the scheme in the absence of this information. However, the critical point is that the distributed representations described by

Hinton are not the same as the simple property lists or state vectors of the kind espoused by Smolensky. Firstly, the representations discussed by Hinton do honour classical constituent structures. From Figure 5.5, it can be seen that the representation clearly honours the classical divisions between AGENT, RELA-TIONSHIP and PATIENT. A second point concerns the distinction between micro-features and micro-inferences. The micro-features specify (abstract) pro-perties and the micro-inferences capture relationships between these properties. So the distributed representations described by Hinton do possess constituent components and the components are structured. Therefore these representations cannot be construed as being simple unordered lists of properties.

The role/filler distinction

There is, however, an additional way in which these distributed representations honour a classical distinction. Each set of units is said to stand for a role and the current state of the units in each role is said to stand for a filler. This role/filler distinction is how the net is said to capture the classical distinction between a variable and its value. Variables are identified with roles and the values of these variables are said to be fillers. In this context Hinton (1988) draws an analogy of symbols being like variables as used in programming languages. The paradigm case of a working symbol system is a computer programming language. In computing, a variable is defined as pointer to a certain type of data structure. The data structure could itself specify an integer (i.e. a whole number) a real (or fractional number), some form of character, some form of string of characters, etc. Operationally the variable 'points' to that part of memory where the full description of the data structure resides. As Hinton states, the variable operates as a reduced description of the data structure. Moreover, this is exactly what a symbol is: 'It is a small representation of an object that provides a 'remote access' path to a fuller representation of the same object.' (p. 1). For example, the variable X could be made to point to the complete character set of the machine. This means that somewhere the variable X points to some address in memory where the complete character set is stored. However, the central point is that at different times a variable in a computer language can point to different addresses, i.e. it can take on different values. With new connectionist schemes Hinton claims that distributed representations act just like pointers in allowing the different states of a set of units to stand for different role-specific representations. An important constraint, though, is that only one role-specific representation can be processed at a time. Therefore here again is an example of where a PDP system is fundamentally constrained to operate in a sequential manner. So although much is made about the advantages of parallel distributed systems over their serial counterparts, in many respects connectionist systems turn out to be fundamentally sequential in nature. To fully appreciate these ideas it is best to consider an actual example discussed in the literature.

The particular hardware configuration shown in Figure 5.5 can in principle

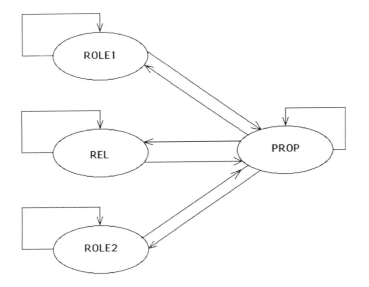

Figure 5.6. Hinton's extended model of constituent structure. Each oval signifies a complete set of units. There are now two general ROLE capturing sets of units, a general REL set of units and a final PROP set of units. Each set of units is self-activating. Otherwise the different sets interact via the interconnections shown. (From Hinton, 1981b, adapted with permission, *see* p. xvii).

represent any combination of a valid AGENT, RELATIONSHIP and PATIENT such as JOHN LOVES MARY. Here the variables are AGENT, RELATION-SHIP and PATIENT and the respective values of these variables are JOHN, LOVES and MARY. Different patterns in the three set of units can then signify PETER LIKES JANE, i.e. another set of values of the three variables. The reason why this scheme is an implementation of a classical formalism is that it honours the classical semantic distinctions between AGENT, RELATIONSHIP and PATIENT. However, the net operates according to principles of parallel distributed processing. Indeed, the scheme was partially developed in a bid to show how a PDP system can appear to produce rule-like generalizations without an explicit representation of those rules. Figure 5.6 is pertinent here and is taken from Hinton's (1981b) earlier work on semantic nets.

Neural nets and reasoning

The configuration is slightly different from that shown in Figure 5.5; in couched at a higher level of abstraction because there are now tw' dedicated to abstract ROLEs and a third set of units dedicat

RELATIONSHIP. All three set of units are interconnected to a fourth set of units: an abstract PROPOSITION set of units. In classical terms a (two-place) proposition comprises a predicate and two arguments. This PROPOSITION set of units is the mechanism that allows the net to process two-place propositions. In new connectionist terms the PROP units are hidden units and are said to capture higher-order contingencies between the constituent patterns of activity over the three input sets of units. The input to the net comprises a pattern of the activity over ROLE1, REL and ROLE2 units. This is construed as being an ordered triple. In being presented with many such triples, the PROP set of units are essentially abstracting higher-order contingencies across the subpatterns that constitute the triples. The net was eventually tested with incomplete patterns. A test input comprised only two constituents of a triple and the net was assessed on how well it reinstated the appropriate third member of the triple. The subpatterns that constituted the two members of the triple produced activation in the PROP units. These in turn produced activity in the units that constituted the third member of the triple. This is explained via the following example, simplified from Hinton (1981b).

The net shown in Figure 5.6 is presented with the following inputs:

	ROLE1	REL	ROLE2
	ERNIE	COLOUR	GREY
(1)	ERNIE	COLOUR	GREY
(2)	ELEPH	COLOUR	GREY
(3)	PERSON	COLOUR	PINK

Three separate patterns of activity in the PROP units would be learnt for each of these inputs. These were respectively ERNIECOLOURGREY, ELEPH-COLOURGREY and PERSONCOLOURPINK. The net is then tested with novel and incomplete patterns such as:

	ROLE1	REL	ROLE2
(4)	CLYDE	COLOUR	0

and then separately with

	ROLE1	REL	ROLE2
(5)	BILL	COLOUR	0

The net was able to respond correctly with

ROLE1	REL	ROLE2
CLYDE	COLOUR	GREY

and then

ROLE1	REL	ROLE2
BILL	COLOUR	PINK

The reason for this is that for (4) the net recovers the state that corresponds to ELEPHCOLOURGREY and for (5) the state that corresponds to PERSON-COLOURPINK. The traditional account for (4) would be that the net has 'reasoned' (syllogistically) that as CLYDE is an elephant and that as elephants are coloured grey then CLYDE must be coloured grey. The critical point, however, is that the net cannot be construed as providing an implementation of this line of reasoning because there is nothing in the operation of the net that corresponds to the steps in the argument. True, the net has arrived at the valid conclusion but it has done so purely on the basis of the similarity relationships between the underlying representations of the constituents involved. That this is so can be seen from the actually distributed representations used for the instances of ROLE1 used in the simulation. These are shown below:

111000 000000	ELEPH
000111 000000	PERSON
111000 111000	CLYDE
111000 000111	ERNIE
000111 101010	SCOTT
000111 010101	BILL

As can be seen, each instance is portrayed as a pattern of activity over 12 input units. ROLE1 comprised 12 units. The critical point is that the representations for the various instances are systematically related. For as can be seen from the examples, each vector is divided into two sets of six components. The first six components in a sense signal the generic class of the instance, the next six components specify the instance itself. In traditional terms the first six components specify the type of instance, the second six specify the token of that type (Hinton, 1984). The net was taught with propositions concerning ELEPH, PERSON and ERNIE but it was able to deal appropriately with an incomplete proposition regarding CLYDE and one regarding BILL solely on the grounds of the similarities of the underlying representations. As can be seen, CLYDE is defined as an ELEPHANT pattern and BILL is defined as a HUMAN pattern. Given this, it should be clear that the net is not reasoning syllogistically. It is not following the argument:

Premise 1	CLYDE is an ELEPHANT
Premise 2	ELEPHANTS are GREY

Conclusion	CLYDE is GREY

The net is, in a sense, being presented with Premise 1 – CLYDE is an

ELEPHANT, because this fact is explicitly coded in the representation of CLYDE. The net is then able to arrive at the correct conclusion solely on the bases of the similarity of the CLYDE vector to all other ELEPHANT vectors that the net has experienced. Therefore the example is not so much an example of a neural net reasoning, but more an example of how a net can exhibit 'property inheritance' (Fahlman, 1979). The net shows how instances of a given class inherit class properties purely on the basis of the similarity relations that exist between the respective underlying representations. The work is nevertheless instructive because it provides a clear example of how property inheritance can come about through automatic generalization in a connectionist net.

Context-independent representations

A limitation of this scheme is that all the representations discussed are role-specific (context-dependent) representations. This Hinton (1989a) has freely admitted is a limitation, primarily because it provides no means of generalizing from one role-specific representation to another. Things known about JOHN being the agent of LOVES should apply and be accessible in cases where JOHN is the patient of LOVES. With the role-specific representations of JOHN as AGENT and JOHN as PATIENT there is no means of making the necessary generalizations. One way out of this is to allow for a context-independent representation of JOHN and a scheme for operationalizing context-independent representations is given in Figure 5.7.

Here the context-independent representation of JOHN is captured by a pattern of activity over the units in the IDENTITY set. As before, there are other sets of units that allow for various other variables; in this example there are AGENT, PATIENT and LOCATION units. The central distinction though is between the representation of JOHN over the AGENT units and the representation of JOHN over the IDENTITY units. The connections between these two sets of units are gated by connections from the ROLE units. These gated connections essentially establish that the JOHN acting as AGENT is the particular JOHN represented in the IDENTITY units.

A scheme such as this appears to offer a way forward on the issue of how to implement context-independent representations in a connectionist net. Unfortunately, however, the true nature of the ideas has yet to be examined in the context of a working model. It would therefore be unreasonable to attempt to assess them critically.

Limitations of the framework

Apart from the obvious implementational problems with the scheme set out by Hinton, it is interesting to speculate whether this kind of theorizing can hope to deal with nuances of language use that bear on the issue of words acting as variables. For example, Woods (1975) discusses subtle differences that humans

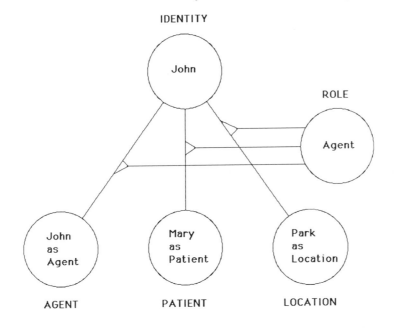

Figure 5.7. An example of a context-independent representation implemented in a distributed system. (From Hinton *et al.* 1986, adapted with permission, *see* p. xvii.)

must be able to deal with in order to understand superficially simple sentences. Two examples are given below -

(i)   Every boy loves his dog.
and
(ii)   Every boy needs a dog.

Here the issues hinge on the uses of the term 'dog'. In these sentences 'dog' behaves like a variable, yet it is being used in quite different ways across the two sentences. In (i) 'dog' is marked, linguistically, as a definite noun. It operates like a variable because it can take on different values depending on which 'boy' is being referred to. Each boy has a different dog, hence the variable 'dog' takes on a different value with each boy. Woods calls 'dog' in this case a definite variable: its value changes because a different dog is being referred to in every instance. In Hinton's scheme the whole of the apparatus shown in Figure 5.5 does take account of just this phenomenon. In (ii), however, 'dog' is being used as an indefinite variable. On one reading the sentence is prescriptive: each boy needs a dog but no particular dog, in any one case, is implied. It is this kind of situation which is not handled by the machinery shown in Figure 5.7. The net account of variables and their use does not cover the case of an indefinite variable just described.

Although it may seem unfair to criticize Hinton's scheme because it fails to address the distinction between a definite and an indefinite variable, this does seem to be justified if the account is to be taken seriously as a psychological theory. It stresses that the notions of a role and a filler and role-specific representations are not wholly adequate. The machinery fails to capture a subtle yet important distinction in natural language between a definite and an indefinite variable. It remains true also that Hinton's scheme fails to deal with many aspects of natural language. This is simply because it does not constitute, nor was intended to be, a general theory of symbolic thought. The research does address the issue of variables in natural language but it fails to capture a subtle and important difference in the way in which words act as variables.

Connectionist nets and rule-governed behaviour

Having considered in some detail the ways in which connectionists have approached the issue of having structured representations, a whole number of other important issues concern information processing rules. How is it that a connectionist net can be said to behave in a rule-governed fashion without having the rules explicitly represented in the system? As with much of the discussion, the paradigm case of a rule-following device used for expository purposes is a digital computer. The operation of the computer is said to be rule-governed not only because its behaviour accords with a set of rules, but also because the rules that govern the operation of the system are explicitly represented in the system. Connectionists have it that, although their neural nets are rule-governed, there is 'no explicit representation or application of rules within the system' (Anderson & Hinton, 1981, p. 21). This is a radical claim and begs further scrutiny.

Firstly, nets can be said to be rule-governed because the operation of individual units is fully understood and described by rules of activation and propagation of activity, i.e. rules of mathematics. Smolensky makes this point in a slightly different way. He again invokes the distinction between symbolic and subsymbolic levels. For him 'Subsymbols are not operated upon by symbol manipulation: They participate in numerical – not symbolic – computation.' (1988, p. 3) Here Smolensky is arguing that a full understanding of human information processing can be attained by examining state vectors and the branch of vector arithmetic known as tensor product theory (details of which need not be discussed here). As a consequence, the claim is that new connectionism offers a quite different account of mental processes than those offered by the symbolic approach. In part this claim rests on a quite different interpretation of the term 'rules' to that in the symbol processing framework. For Smolensky, the rules of operation are those of mathematics. It is mathematics which specifies the operating characteristics of units and links. In contrast, within the classical framework, a rule specifies a transformation of a symbol or set of symbols. A good example of this kind of rule is a re-write rule found in the syntactic theory of Chomsky (1975, p. 26). For example:

NP→T + N

where NP stands for noun phrase, T stands for the word 'the', N stands for noun, → stands for 're-write as', and + stands for simple concatenation. The rule stipulates that a noun phrase should be re-written as (i.e. transformed into) 'the' plus a noun. In providing theoretical accounts of language processing, several claims about the psychological status of such re-write rules have been put forward within cognitive science: namely, that (i) the symbols map directly onto psychological entities; (ii) there is something akin to a syntactic parser that instantiates such rules; (iii) the parser sequentially applies the rules; and (iv) states of such a parser correspond to psychological states. Major debates rage over the exact nature of the parser and the rules but the general theoretical framework is well established within cognitive science (see the later papers in Marslen-Wilson, 1989). Nevertheless, this general view has been roundly attacked within new connectionism.

Waltz and Pollack (1985) have questioned the validity of studying syntactic parsing independently of the other kinds of information that are clearly brought to bear during the normal process of understanding language. They prefer to see sentence understanding as a massively parallel constraint satisfaction process where syntactic, lexical and contextual information is used interdependently. Consequently, they argue against the claims regarding the strictly serial account of parsing put forward. However, they happily endorse the traditional constituent linguistic structures such as noun phrase, adjective, determiner, etc. The more tendentious claims of new connectionism question the validity of the traditional theories of syntactic structures, especially when syntax refers not only to the grammar of sentences but to compositional structure in general. Some of the issues have already been discussed when considering Smolensky's ideas about state vectors. A more thorough treatment is offered here in terms of Rumelhart and McClelland's (1986b) model of learning the past tense. This model has been taken apart (the pejorative sense is also intended) in the literature (see Pinker & Mehler, 1988) and little would be achieved here by reciting the critiques here. Only a limited number of points about the model need be made.

McClelland and Rumelhart's model of past tense learning

In English, regular verbs honour the rule of adding the affix 'ed' to the end of the verb stem. Examples are walk/walked, laugh/laughed, cough/coughed, etc. In classical notation, to generate the past tense of the regular verb x apply the rule:

Past(x) → x + 'ed'

(i.e. the rule states 're-write "x" as "x" plus "ed" '.) With regular verbs, as Pinker and Prince (1988) argue, the past form is 100% predictable from its present form. This does not hold for irregular verbs, however. Irregular verbs come in, essentially, three different varieties: (i) hit → hit, the present and past forms are identical; (ii) come → came, there exists a vowel change across the present and past forms; and (iii) go → went, the mapping across the present and past forms is essentially arbitrary. Given this variety of different verb endings, the mapping of present to past tense forms poses an interesting developmental problem. McClelland and Rumelhart address this problem by constructing a neural net around a two-layered pattern associator. Their implication was that all kinds of the present–past tense mapping can then be accounted for by the operation of a single mechanism.

The inputs to the model were distributed representations of the phonological characteristics of the stem of a verb and the outputs from the model were distributed representations of the phonological characteristics of the past tense form of the verb. For both input and output representations a Wickelfeatural coding scheme was used. Some discussion of this kind of encoding has been included in the discussion of the Seidenberg and McClelland model in Chapter 4. However, some further points can be usefully made here. For example, an important distinction exists between Wickelphones and Wickelfeatures. The Wickelphone representation of the word 'strip' comprises the set of triples {ip#, rip, str, tri, #st}: each triple is one Wickelphone. The '#' stands for a white space and the letters pick out individual phonemes. However, reasons against using such a coding scheme with the model were advanced. Firstly, the possible number of legal triples for English is immense and would have placed great demands on the hardware of the net architecture. On the assumption that one node would be needed to code each triple, Pinker and Prince note that over 43,000 nodes would be needed for each of the input and output layers. Moreover, with full connectivity between the input and output layers, such a net would need over two billion interconnections. A second psycholinguistic concern related to the fact that phonological generalizations from stems to past forms are carried, not at the phonetic level, but at the level of sub-phonetic features like the place and manner of articulation. Given these considerations a Wickelfeature coding system was introduced. This meant that each element in every Wickelphone triple was decomposed into a Wickelfeature representation. Each Wickelfeature in turn comprised three features such as 'VowelUnvoicedInterrupted'.

In the model one node in each of the input and output layers was dedicated to a single Wickelfeature. As a consequence there were 460 nodes in each layer and 211,600 interconnections between the layers. Each verb presented to the model was represented as a pattern of activation over the full 460 input nodes, though, of course, only a subset of these nodes were be activated by the component Wickelfeatures in the word.

The model was trained on 420 stem–past tense pairs and then tested with 86 new pairs. A total of 80,000 training trials were used in all. The net was trained with a variant of the delta rule and weights on the interconnections were changed according to the guidelines set out by the perceptron convergence theorem (see Chapter 1).

Of the 86 test verbs there were 72 regular instances and 14 irregular. The model erred on 24 (i.e. 33%) of the 72. Merely in terms of quantifying good performance, it seems that the model performed poorly, and on these grounds alone it is difficult to take the model seriously as an adequate candidate psychological account of human performance. However, in qualitative terms, the model's performance was reasonably impressive with respect to the variety of pairs it was able to deal with. As Pinker and Prince note, the model was successful in mapping 'hit' to 'hit', 'make' to 'made', 'sing' to 'sang' and 'go' to 'went'. Moreover, the model reproduced the stages that children pass through as they develop language skills. It is well documented that with irregular verbs such as 'eat' children initially tend to use the correct past form 'ate'. They then tend to regularize the verbs, saying 'eated' or 'ated'. Finally they stabilize on the correct form 'ate'. McClelland and Rumelhart demonstrated a similar pattern of development with their model during the training phase of their study. However, such mimicking of human performance only came about because McClelland and Rumelhart introduced systematic changes in the training examples prior to the first two stages in the developmental sequence.

McClelland and Rumelhart reasoned that children are most likely to learn high-frequency verbs first. So they initially presented the model with two regular and eight irregular high-frequency verb instances 10 times each. This difference in the proportion of regular and irregular verbs was motivated because high-frequency verbs tend to be irregular and low-frequency verbs tend to be regular. During this initial phase the model learnt to produce the correct irregular forms for the irregular verbs. Following this initial phase, 420 high-frequency and medium-frequency pairs were presented 190 times each. Now though, 80% of these pairs were instances of regular verbs. As expected, during the initial period of this second training stage the model tended to produce regularizations of irregular forms (e.g. 'eated'). With the passage of time, however, the model began to correct these errors and perform well with both regular and irregular forms. Like McClelland and Rumelhart, Pinker and Prince took the model as a literal account of human linguistic development but they systematically examined its empirical consequences. For instance, they scrutinized the hypothesis that the developmental changes witnessed in children come about purely as a function of a changing language environment. In stark contrast to this hypothesis Pinker and Prince found that the proportion of regular verbs in a child's immediate language environment remains constant throughout the developmental sequence. As a consequence there never is a period when the child primarily experiences regular verbs. It is this kind of disparity between data and theory that has seriously undermined the credibility of McClelland and Rumelhart's past-tense model.

There is no need to dwell on the other serious deficiencies in the model as it is now generally acknowledged as being inadequate in many respects (McClelland, 1988). Detailed criticisms can be found in a variety of sources (see, for example, Lachter & Bever, 1988; Marchman & Plunkett, 1989; Pinker & Prince, 1988, 1989; and Plunkett & Marchman, 1989). It is more appropriate to consider the implications if the model had worked perfectly. Consider the hypothetical case where the model had learnt to map correctly between the present and past forms the regular verbs and all kinds of irregular verbs. Such a hypothetical case would truly be a radical alternative to traditional rule-following accounts of linguistic processing. Tradition has it that language use is predicated upon the application of internally represented rules. With the model there are no explicitly represented rules and there are no functional units that map onto the classical linguistic divisions between 'word', 'root', 'stem', 'irregular verb', 'regular verb' and so on (cf. Plunkett & Marchman, 1989). The model would appear to be honouring these distinctions yet nothing in the system would correspond to symbolic counterparts or rules that operate on these symbols. It is exactly this kind of radical alternative account of syntactic processing that new connectionism promises to offer. The promise is that, whatever linguistic descriptions of language behaviour are used, these would not necessarily aid in understanding language behaviour. An even more radical proposition is that such linguistic descriptions actually hinder understanding because they arise from nothing more than observing the emergent properties of a PDP system. In this sense the symbols attributed to the device play no causal role in the workings of the device. For instance, the formal distinction between 'root' and 'affix' is merely a description of the output from a PDP system that arises purely because of the myriad interactions that take place in the system.

Concluding comments

Many different aspects of new connectionist research have been covered in this chapter. A unifying theme, though, has been that all of the research addresses higher-order issues in cognition. Initially much discussion was directed towards a variety of models of how semantic information can be represented in connectionist systems. Some concern was with lesioning these systems and comparing impaired performance of these systems with performance of brain-damaged humans. These considerations lead naturally on to a discussion of some research directed to the question of whether it is possible to simulate double dissociations with PDP systems. Two main examples were considered and both provide non-obvious accounts of how double dissociations may obtain.

The final sections of this chapter have dealt with more abstract notions of mental representation and various connectionist attempts at modelling these have been considered. One of the most important problems facing neural net researchers at present is that of trying to model structured representations. Some preliminary attempts have been considered here, but these have been shown to be of only limited interest. At best the examples are interesting implementations of traditional constructs; at worst they fail to provide anything that could constitute a radical alternative to what tradition has dictated. A more thorough analysis of these remarks is included in the final chapter.

Chapter 6

New connectionism: a critical appraisal

In offering a critical appraisal of new connectionism, issues at several levels of explanation will be addressed. The very notion of different levels of explanation has itself featured in several critiques of the new connectionist framework (Broadbent, 1985; Fodor & Pylyshyn, 1988), but rather than become embroiled in these debates, a more modest aim is to use the notion of levels of explanation as an aid to structuring the following discussion. Initially consideration will be given to issues relevant to the neurological or hardware level (Marr, 1982). In so far as new connectionism has been heralded as being neurally inspired and that it constitutes a form of 'brain-style' theorizing (Fodor & Pylyshyn, 1988), it is only sensible to consider how exact the mapping between actual neurology and the 'neurology' of artificial neural networks actually is. There are those who argue that it is not fruitful to think that current knowledge of neurology should constrain theorizing at the psychological level (Fodor & McLaughlin, 1990; Mehler, Morton, & Jusczyk, 1984). According to this view neurology is best kept as being a completely separate discipline from psychology. Such an opinion, however, is out of step with much work in present-day cognitive science. A consensus does seem to be emerging that much can be learned about mental life by adopting a multi-disciplinary approach: one in which neuroscience plays a central role.

In the middle sections of this chapter points about the algorithmic level are addressed. Much discussion deals with examples where multi-layered nets have been used to simulate aspects of human cognition. The use of hidden units will be covered and other aspects concerning the limitations of the back-propagation algorithm will be described. Predictably enough, the final sections concern the computational level of explanation. Some of this implicates the Fodor and

Pylyshyn critique (1988). Other points relate to the issue of just how like associationism new connectionism is.

A cautionary note is worth mentioning before continuing. Most of this book has been written with a view to portraying the psychological import of new connectionism. A guiding principle has been to try to tease out those aspects of new connectionist theorizing that are relevant to understanding human cognition. A subsidiary aim has been to try to make the field more accessible to those not fully acquainted with such formal disciplines as computer science, neuroscience and advanced mathematics. Given this, much of the material has been expository in nature. However, some critical comment has also been included. In assessing the psychological worth of the approach, it has been necessary to use the same criteria as would be used with any other form of psychological theory. Much of the research has failed to meet these criteria of theoretical adequacy. This does not mean, however, that all of the research reviewed must be swept aside. There are enough examples in this book of truly innovative research that it would be wrong to castigate the whole of the new connectionist approach as being of little worth. Nevertheless, a worry remains, and this is that new connectionism is beginning to degenerate into a discipline in which a whole range of small-scale models are being developed, in isolation, to account for this and that aspect of cognition. There are now enough examples of working models in cognitive science that the development of yet another should only form the basis of some research enterprise: it should not be viewed as an end in and of itself. A primary question therefore is to ask what sorts of principles can be abstracted from the workings of some such device. For it is crucial to divorce the assessment of the implementation of the ideas from concerns about the ideas themselves. Surely what are needed are some well-worked-out statements about general principles. For instance, it is of fundamental importance to know, if possible, what class of problems a particular type of network architecture can hope to solve.

At this juncture it is only fair to mention one aspect of new connectionism that will probably endure as being a distinctive. This is the notion of mutual constraint satisfaction. Although this idea was originally discussed in the context of early work in computer vision (see the blocks worlds programs reviewed by Mackworth, 1976), new connectionists have adopted this idea as their own. Moreover, the ways in which connectionist systems have been used to operation-alize mutual constraint satisfaction are clearly innovative and ingenious. Indeed, there are enough supportive examples, especially in the field of visual perception, to clinch the argument that mutual constraint satisfaction is a fundamental property of how the brain operates.

New connectionism is now so well established that it might be seen as being negligent in not teaching it as a core component of cognitive science. Neverthe-less, as a counterpoint to the almost evangelical rhetoric that surrounds neural network research it is fitting to discuss the very real problems that exist. In the interests of obtaining a balanced view, it is necessary to consider carefully just what the critics of the approach are saying. A rather sober conclusion is that unless these problems are addressed, the approach cannot hope to make further substantive contributions to psychological thinking.

Neurological considerations

In his 1988 paper Smolensky set out a table that itemized the ways in which new connectionism honours and fails to honour known facts about neurology. He shows that new connectionism is consistent with current neurological knowledge in a number of ways. A typical artificial neural network possess the following characteristics; all are properties of the cerebral cortex:

(i)   The states of the units are defined by continuous numerical variables.
(ii)   These states change continuously.
(iii) Changeable parameters model inter-neuron interactions.
(iv)   Large numbers of state variables are used.
(v)   Highly complex interactions exist.

However, having set out the commonalities, Smolensky goes on to discuss the salient differences between real and simulated neural networks. For instance, it is typically the case in artificial neural networks that units have no spatial location and are connected by uniformly dense connections: neither fact is true of real brains. In the cerebral cortex the location of a neuron is critical and the connectivity between neurons is far from being uniform. Neurons are densely connected with their nearest neighbours and share only a few connections with neurons further away. In oversimplifying such hardware considerations, new connectionism clearly fails to take seriously the complex topology of the cerebral cortex (see Szentagothai, 1978).

Apart from points relating to neurological structure, Smolensky also under-lines other differences between simulated and real brains that relate to signal processing. Whereas the integration of signals in artificial nets is linear, in real brains intricate signal integration takes place at individual neurons. Artificial neural nets also operate with a single signal type. In contrast real brains operate with numerous signal types. Smolensky therefore establishes firm structural and processing differences between artificial and real neural nets. In addition, and as was discussed in Chapter 5, he also argues that new connectionism should be construed as offering radically different accounts of cognition to those offered by the classical human information processing approach. According to Smolensky, new connectionism provides working models that do not honour neurological constraints and such models do not honour the classical distinctions set out by traditional psychological theory. In setting new connectionist theories apart from traditional classical psychological and neuropsychological accounts, Smolensky goes on to state that, 'The fundamental level of the subsymbolic paradigm, the subsymbolic level, lies between the neural and conceptual level.' (p. 9) This allows him to argue that subsymbolic models should not be viewed as neural models, yet neither should they be treated as conceptual models. This argument establishes that new connectionist models should be construed as being radically different to any other form of theorizing in cognitive science. Unfortunately the desire to be radical is not without its problems. A rather dim view of Smolensky's position is that it allows for a theory of some aspect of mental life to fail to take account of neurological facts and to fail to honour classical psychological distinctions. All of this clearly establishes the radical nature of the framework but it also invites anarchy. It seems to give license to any sort of modelling that produces an operational account with little regard for the relevant data. From the current survey of new connectionism a major conclusion is that the selective disregard of data has lead researchers to generate working models that are of little relevance to understanding mental life.

Crick and Asanuma's assessment of neurophysiological evidence

Another view of the relevance of neurology to connectionism has been provided by Crick and Asanuma (1986). The impression they create is that the weight of evidence does point to certain neurological properties that should act as constraints on brain-style theorizing. Crick and Asanuma describe a series of neurological facts, only a handful of which will be discussed here. They discuss at length the structural and functional properties of neurons. For example, they state that in the cerebral cortex the initial segment of axons may receive synapses, and also that dendrites can form synapses onto other dendrites. Such structures as these may be allowing signal gating to be carried out in the cortex in the same way that signal gating is carried out by sigma pi units in artificial neural nets. In this respect some new connectionist devices do seem to have neurological counter-parts. However, there are other problems. For instance, some retinal neurons operate with respect to graded, not action, potentials. This seems to emphasize a limitation of connectionist work that it only deals with discrete signals (cf. Smolensky, 1988). Discretizing the updates of neuronal units may be forced upon researchers by the limitations of serial computers. It may also be necessary in order to maintain parity with the relevant mathematical proof. Nevertheless, some real neural systems operate continuously and not in a digital fashion.

Crick and Asanuma also point out that there are only two kinds of synapses found in the cerebral cortex; namely, excitatory and inhibitory. Most importantly though, it seems that no axon makes excitatory synapses at one site and inhibitory synapses at another. In the language of new connectionism this means that no unit should have excitatory and inhibitory connections with other units. Despite this, units with excitatory and inhibitory interconnections are germane to

Hopfield and Boltzmann nets. As a consequence both kinds of artificial nets violate known neurophysiological facts. Hence, neither can provide an adequate model of cognitive neuropsychology.

In something of a digression Crick and Asanuma go on to reiterate some ideas about inhibition being a consequence of excitation. It seems that inhibition is caused by the excitation of inhibitory neurons and therefore acts as a brake, or dampener, on the build up of excitation. As was noted in Chapter 1, a similar idea was originally discussed in the psychological literature by Milner (1957).

A final general point they make is that it is much easier to implement addition, subtraction and division than it is to implement multiplication in a single neuron. Although they do not argue that it is impossible to envisage a single neuron doing multiplication, the implication is that real neurons appear not to. If this is indeed true, and that such facts are to constrain theorizing, then the consequences for all models that compute the weighted sum of inputs appear to be dire.

So although new connectionism does provide a forum for brain-style theorizing, the contact with neurophysiology is more apparent than real. As Crick (1989) has recently argued, if connectionists were to take the brain seriously then their models would end up being radically different to anything that has been developed to date. In this respect it is interesting to conclude with a brief comment on the work of Shepherd (1978). As pointed out by Brown (personal communication), Shepherd is more concerned with looking at the functional significance of the microcircuits defined relative to the dendritic structures of cells, rather than dealing at the more global level of the neuron. According to Shepherd, it is not the neuron that is the fundamental processing element in the brain, but the synapse. By this view the neuron comprises many functional units, namely, its dendritic synaptic circuits. Clearly this is a radically different view of neural architecture to that typically found in the new connectionist literature.

Additional hardware constraints

To round off this section on neurological considerations it is important to consider some other criticisms of the claims new connectionists make about the biological plausibility of their models (this is independent of the arguments set out by Smolensky). Fodor and Pylyshyn (1988) describe such claims as these as being the 'lures' of connectionism.

Fodor and Pylyshyn initially discuss the 100-step constraint described by Feldman and Ballard (1982). The 100-step constraint is based on the fact that real neurons take tens of milliseconds to fire, i.e. they can only fire once every few tens of milliseconds. Taken literally, and were the brain a rigidly serial device, this means that any cognitive task executed in less than second (such as recognizing a word or a picture) must operate within the constraint of 100 or less instructions. Here comparisons are made relative to the operation of a standard serial digital computer. Fodor and Pylyshyn object that such comparisons are absurd and hence that all the 100-step constraint rules out is the claim that computers and brains implement cognitive architectures in the same manner. They also point out that it is far from certain that the firing of a neuron is the critical functional characteristic: many other electrochemical interactions take place, are not fully understood, and remain to be explored.

Chater and Oaksford (1990) have recently replied by arguing that the 100-step constraint does severely limit the class of cognitively plausible algorithms. However, it appears that they confuse the issue. Fodor and Pylyshyn address a possible neurological constraint on psychological processing. Chater and Oaksford discuss the 100-step rule in terms of it constraining a class of cognitive algorithms, hence their argument addresses a different level of explanation. They go on to state that 'Only by *doing PDP* will we discover what neural properties are computationally relevant.' (p. 96) Yet surely this is mistaken too: work on real brains is essential if neural properties are to be discovered. These neural properties may then constrain theorizing at the computational level. However, Chater and Oaksford's other claims about some classical cognitive processes being implausible are well taken. For instance, models of word recognition based on a serial search of the lexicon (e.g. see Forster, 1976) are simply untenable in principle.

Fodor and Pylyshyn go on to discuss the claim that conventional AI architectures are acutely sensitive to damage and noise whereas connectionist systems are not. This claim is associated with another property of connectionist systems, namely, that they display graceful degradation when damaged. Resistance to damage and graceful degradation are witnessed in some lesioned new connectionist models (see Chapters 4 and 5 for examples) and some neurologically impaired humans. Given this commonality, new connectionists can claim a degree of biological plausibility. In contrast, Fodor and Pylyshyn argue that these points address the implementational and not the cognitive level. On the understanding that classical representations and processes may be implemented in a connectionist net, this system would also exhibit resistance to damage and graceful degradation. For this reason Fodor and Pylyshyn insist that these issues concern implementation and hence cannot settle debates about cognitive representations and processes. Indeed it is interesting to speculate about how some new connectionist models exhibit certain 'brittle' characteristics. There are many models in which the values of whole sets of processing parameters are fixed and are critical to the successful operation of the model. The simple point is that if these parameter values are changed, even slightly, then the model will no longer provide a good fit with the human data. Indeed, in many cases a major effort is expended on the fitting procedure, i.e. hitting on the exact parameter values to do the job. It is the difficulty of hitting on the right set of values that underlines just how fragile some of the new connectionists models really are. Indeed, there is another way in which new connectionist systems are fragile and this relates to learning. In many cases, the initial weight settings are critical to how successfully the model develops. This is most clearly demonstrated by the example of the net of Hinton and Shallice (1989) discussed in Chapter 5. Remember that whereas one version of the model demonstrated interesting category-specific deficits when lesioned, another did not. However, the only difference between the two versions concerned their initial weight values. Different random weights were assigned in the two cases.

Problems with hidden units and the back-propagation algorithm

Massaro's critique

One of the most thorough and challenging critiques of the new connectionist framework has been provided by Massaro (1988). Main sections of his paper address the IA models of spoken and written word recognition (McClelland & Elman, 1986; McClelland & Rumelhart, 1981), and the relevant substantive points have already been discussed in Chapter 4. Of central import here are the points Massaro makes about models with hidden units. A few words are worth setting down before continuing.

The reason why such emphasis is placed on Massaro's critique is that it is distinctive in being more than a reasoned argument. Massaro uses actual connectionist techniques to demonstrate their own limitations. Moreover, from the psychological point of view, he treats network models as being just another set of candidate accounts. On these grounds they should be able to withstand the sort of scrutiny brought to bear on any other kind of psychological theory. Connectionism has matured very rapidly into a discipline in its own right and, as Ratcliff (1990) has recently argued, it is no longer enough just to build a net and use it as a demonstration proof that such and such psychological phenomenon can be simulated. Massaro concurs and went on to test the functional character-istics of several different kinds of net architectures. In addition, Massaro's critique is much more useful than the kind of pessimistic dismissal of computer simulation set out by Dreyfus (1972). Much of that critique reduced to statements about what computers did not do rather than setting out in principle statements about what computers cannot do. Massaro's is a careful and incisive review that seriously challenges central principles of new connectionist methodology.

In summary, the critique rests on three general claims: (i) that models with hidden units are too powerful; i.e. they are 'superpowerful'; (ii) that this superpower 'camouflages' the psychophysics; and (iii) that hidden units camouflage intervening stages of processing. To establish these points, Massaro shows (a) that a single connectionist system simulates results that imply mutually exclusive psychological processes; and (b) that superpowerful models perform adequately with inappropriate assumptions about the information that is used and is available to the human observer.

Evaluation   Integration   Classification

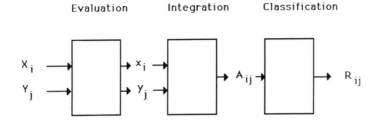

Figure 6.1. Schematic representation of Massaro's model of perceptual
recognition. (From Massaro, 1988, adapted with permission, *see* p. xvii.)

Massaro starts by restating that hidden units were essentially introduced by the
new connectionists to overcome the linear separability limitation of the simple
perceptron (cf. Minsky & Papert, 1969). He rightly points out that the limitation
of linear separability for psychological models is an empirical one and needs to be
settled by empirical means. However, the critique starts properly with an attempt
to see if the same net with hidden units can simulate data produced by three
models composed of different sets of mutually inconsistent processes. The topic of
interest was perceptual categorization and Massaro describes three variants of the
general model set out in Figure 6.1. The model comprises three stages: (i) an
evaluation stage; (ii) an integration stage; and (iii) a classification stage. The
evaluation stage is essentially an input stage where information arriving at the
senses is transformed into corresponding internal psychological values (i.e.
features). Assume that the X and Y correspond to real-world perceptible
dimensions such as frequency and amplitude. Let X_j and Y_j correspond
respectively to a given frequency and given amplitude. x_i and y_i now signify the
internal representation of these values. The evaluation stage produces independent featural values that operate as independent cues to the identity of the stimulus.
A given value such as x_i is said to be the support for stimulus alternative A on the
dimension X. To obtain the total support for stimulus A all values on all
dimensions must be considered. It is at the second stage of integration where the
computation of the total support for a stimulus is carried out.

The general scenario now is to consider models where the evaluation and
classification stages are uniform. It is the processes of integration that differ
across the three models considered. At the integration stage, the separate feature
components are combined to give rise to a composite percept that is summarized
by the total support for the stimulus. The classification of the stimulus is then
carried out on the basis of the total support computed. Massaro contrasts three
forms of integration – multiplicative, additive and minimization. The featural
values are integrated respectively by: (i) multiplying them together (this forms the
basis of Massaro's FLMP model of perception; Massaro, 1988); (ii) adding them
together; or (iii) taking the minimal value of the features. This forms the basis of
traditional fuzzy logic (Zadeh, 1965).

The performance of these models was then tested on the same set of inputs. Each input comprised a unique combination of one of seven values on each of three dimensions. Crudely put, the results showed that each model produced a distinctive pattern of performance in classifying the input patterns. Moreover, the three models were incompatible in so far as they were unable to account for each other's pattern of performance. This established that the three models were both functionally and practically different.

Following on from this, Massaro built a connectionist net comprising 21 input units (one for each featural value used with the other models), 6 hidden units and 2 output units (one for each classificatory response). Three versions of the net were run, each being trained with the same inputs as used before, and the outputs were the responses taken from each of the three previous models. There were three different sets of simulations therefore. The striking result was that each version of the net acquired weights that allowed that version to approximate closely to the performance of its respective other model. This shows that same net architecture can be used to model three quite different functionally distinct models of perceptual integration. This Massaro takes as being the first demonstration of the superpower of nets with hidden units.

The second such demonstration relates to the claim that nets with hidden units 'camouflage' the psychophysics. Central to this demonstration is Massaro's distinction between appropriate and inappropriate featural representations. An appropriate featural representation of a stimulus is one that is primarily motivated by psychological considerations. It is a representation of a stimulus that is assumed to accord with that used by a subject in a given psychophysical task. An inappropriate featural representation is a form of representation that does not conform to the definition of an appropriate representation. It should not accord with anything that the subject might use in the task. The lynch pin of Massaro's argument is that for a model to be a viable psychological account, it should operate naturally with appropriate stimulus representations and fail to operate properly with inappropriate representations. Figure 6.2 shows the examples of appropriate and inappropriate representations used by Massaro.

Seven of each are shown. Each stimulus was defined relative to one value on each of three variables. The stimuli are ordered in the figure according to closeness on each of these three variables. Given that the stimuli can be so ordered, Massaro argues that the input coding to a neural net should also honour this ordering. The claim is that psychological codings preserve the similarity relations that exist across the inputs. Massaro uses this to guide the codings for the neural net simulations. Similar inputs were coded up by overlapping sets of input units. For appropriate codings each stimulus is represented by the activity over three, of a possible nine, input units. Stimuli that are adjacent on the stimulus dimensions share two input units. Stimuli that are one apart on the stimulus dimensions share one input unit. Stimuli that are further apart share no input units. These relationships between stimulus similarity and input codings did not hold for the inappropriate representations. Here the ordering of the stimuli on

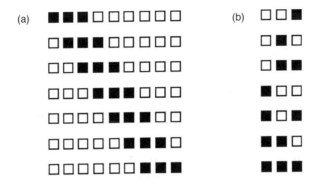

Figure 6.2. Schematic representation of Massaro's (a) appropriate, and (b) inappropriate input patterns. Solid squares represent input units being ON. Empty squares represent input units being OFF. (From Massaro, 1988, adapted with permission, *see* p. xvii.)

the dimension was simply not reflected in any way in the input codings. For some unspecified reasons, whereas the appropriate representations were coded up over a layer of nine input units, the inappropriate representations were coded over an input layer of three units. The 'appropriate' net had six hidden units; the 'inappropriate' net had 15 hidden units. By allowing the nets to have different numbers of hidden units the number of weights across the two was equivalent (i.e. 182).

As before, the three model variants of the integration process were presented with the stimuli coded for the nets and the net's performance was compared with each of the three in turn. The striking result was that a good fit was achieved between the net's and the models' classificatory performance regardless of whether or not appropriate or inappropriate input representations were used. This is again a clear demonstration of the superpower of nets with hidden units. Nets with hidden units are so accommodating that as long as the stimulus–response contingencies are well specified they are essentially insensitive to whether or not the input codings preserve psychologically important relationships. However, there are important strictures on this conclusion. Importantly, the procedure did provide a means for testing the adequacy of the different net architectures. When the number of hidden units was reduced from 6 to 2 for the appropriate net and from 15 to 5 for the inappropriate net, differences in classificatory performance did occur. Under these circumstances the appropriate net gave a better description of the results than did the inappropriate net. All of this merely goes to show that unless net architectures can be constrained in principled ways, then the wisdom of the new connectionist approach appears wanting.

Massaro's final demonstration concerns his claim that hidden units may camouflage intervening stages of processing. Unfortunately, the actual example chosen to make this point is predicated on a number of assumptions that are far from compelling. The argument has a certain coherence, however, and it would not be difficult to generate a less tendentious example to make the same points.

Massaro considers the different tasks of letter identification as compared to letter pronunciation. According to Massaro, identification involves mapping a visual input onto a stored visual description. Pronunciation, however, involves mapping a visual input onto a phonological description. This line of reasoning is consistent with Posner's (1978) ideas about the dual code hypothesis underlying letter recognition. The argument continues that whereas the visual processes underlying identification would preserve the similarity relations between the different letters, this is not true for the mapping underlying pronunciation. For identification the input representations for 'c' and 'o' are more similar than are those for 'c' and 'z'. Moreover, these similarity relations should hold for the stored descriptions of these letters (i.e. the output representations). In contrast, different similarity relations are present with (output) phonological representations of letters than are present between the input (visual) representations. For example (in American English) 'c' (cee) and 'z' (zee) are more similar than are 'c' (cee) and 'o' (oh). The general claim is that in order to do letter pronunciation as compared to letter identification there must be an intermediate stage of processing where the visual representation of a letter is mapped onto its phonological counterpart (cf. Miller, 1982).

To examine this issue with neural net techniques Massaro generated two sets of input–output mappings: respectively a 'good' and a 'bad' mapping. The good mappings defined a linearly separable set and the bad mappings did not. The mappings used are shown in Figure 6.3. Each input pattern was coded over three units and each output pattern was coded over four units. Only one of the four output units was allowed to be turned ON in each mapping, however. For both good and bad mappings, pairs of input patterns received the same output codings. Although it is not immediately obvious from the examples shown, with the good mappings, input pairs that have the same states over two of the three input units map onto the same output pattern. This does not occur across the bad mappings. Here arbitrary input patterns are paired and given the same output pattern. Massaro took these input–output mappings and presented them to five different nets. The nets differed in the absolute number of hidden units and the number of layers of hidden units. The five different nets possessed (i) no hidden units, (ii) two hidden units, (iii) five hidden units, (iv) two layers of five hidden units, or (v) one layer of ten hidden units.

It turned out that both of the nets with ten hidden units were able to learn both good and bad mappings to perfection: hence the third demonstration of the superpower of nets with hidden units. Massaro claims that solving the bad mapping problem is simply attained by having enough hidden units. Moreover, these nets circumvent the need for an internal categorization stage that Massaro claims intervenes between stimulus and response in the letter pronunciation task. In this sense therefore, the argument that some neural nets compromise stages of

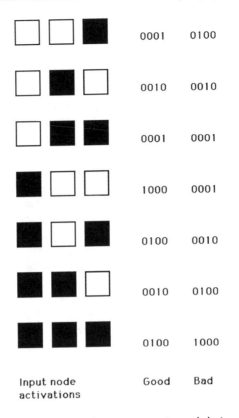

Input node activations	Good	Bad
	0001	0100
	0010	0010
	0001	0001
	1000	0001
	0100	0010
	0010	0100
	0100	1000

Figure 6.3. Input patterns over three input units and their corresponding good and bad outputs. For the input units solid square signify the ON state and empty the OFF state. Over the four output units a 1 signifies the ON states and a 0 signifies the OFF state. (From Massaro, 1988, adapted with permission, *see* p. xvii.)

processing, goes through. Massaro argues that the psychological data vindicate theories predicated on ideas about stages of processing and he goes so far as to argue that if connectionism is to become plausible as a branch of psychology then the models must become more stage-like in nature (Massaro, 1990). This point has recently been most forcefully emphasized by Norris (1990) in his neural net simulations of idiot savant date calculation. It is to these simulations that the discussion now turns.

Norris's simulations

Idiot savants, who are otherwise of limited intellectual abilities, can display amazing mental agility in calculating dates. For example, certain individuals respond correctly to a question such as 'Tell me the date on which 19th October next falls on a Sunday' (Norris, 1990, p. 277) within 5 to 30 seconds. To examine simulations of this performance Norris started from the conjecture that idiot savants acquire this ability on the basis of exposure to a limited set of dates on which particular days fall. From this he went on to examine the behaviour of a simple net comprising one layer of input, one layer of hidden units and one layer of output units. The input units were divided into 31 day units, 12 month units and 15 year units. The year units were further subdivided into 5 for the decade and 10 for the year within the decade. So there were 58 inputs in all, 50 hidden units and 7 output units (one for each named day of the week). The net was therefore designed around the minimal architecture to associate numerical dates (between 1-1-1950 and 31-12-1990) with their named days of the week. Training took place with 50 date pairs from the specified range and the net performed 1000 iterations of the back-propagation algorithm with this training set. The results showed that the net performed well with examples of the original training set, but performance with new pairs was little better than chance. In essence, the net had learnt the training set well but was unable to generalize to new pairs.

Having failed to arrive at a satisfactory model with this net, Norris then carried out a task analysis of date calculation and came up with an algorithm that essentially involves a three-step table look-up procedure. Each step returns an integer value and by adding these values it is then possible to determine the day of the week specified by the date. The procedure rests on having a complete calender representation of a particular month (the base month) in a particular year (the base year). In addition, it is also vital to know two series of offsets. The first specifies the number of days between a base day in the base month and a target day in a target month. For instance, there is a three-day difference between named days in January and the respective days in February. The second series specifies the number of days between respective named days in different years. The simple rule here is that, barring leap years, there is a one-day difference between respective named days in successive years. Importantly, this rule is violated by days falling in January and February in leap years.

Norris takes the example of a target date of 10 March 1975. With a base month of January 1951, the first step is to look up which day fell on the 10th of that month. Step 2 comprises determining the offset in days between the base and target months. This offset is then added to the named day found in step 1. In the present example this gives the day of the month in 1951. The final step involves computing the offset in days between the base year and the target year and combining this with the total offset found from steps 1 and 2.

Norris makes no claims about this necessarily being the way idiot savants calculate dates nor that this three-step procedure could not be reduced to a more complex algorithm involving fewer steps. He is clear, however, that to model the particular algorithm a more complicated architecture than a three-layered net is necessary. The chosen architecture is shown in Figure 6.4.

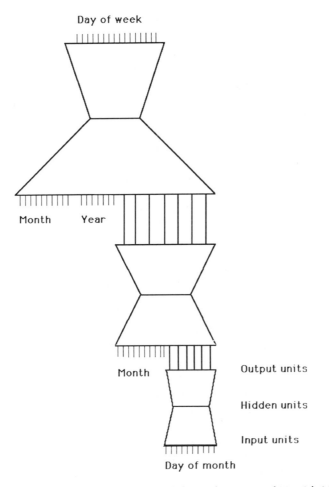

Day of week

Month   Year

Month

Output units

Hidden units

Input units

Day of month

Figure 6.4. Schematic representation of the architecture of Norris's idiot savant date-calculator net. The net comprise three subnets each with its own input, hidden and output layers of units. (From Norris, 1990, adapted with permission, *see* p. xvii.)

It comprises three subnets, each comprising three layers of units (most easily referred to as input, hidden and output layers respectively). However, as can be seen, the outputs for the first two subnets form part of the inputs to the next adjoining subnet. Most importantly though is that this net was trained in a highly structured manner. The first subnet was trained in isolation with the days of the base month. Next the second subnet was harnessed to the training and the whole set of dates for the base year were used. Here the day of the month was input to the first subnet and the month was input to the second. Following this training the second subnet was trained in isolation to output the correct day of the week.

Finally, the third subnet was trained with a random 20% of the dates between 1950 and 1999.

Norris claims that, following this training regime, the net's performance was comparable to the best documented date calculators. In detail, the net performed almost perfectly with dates previously experienced and at over 90% correct with new examples. The majority of the errors arose when the net was presented with dates in leap years and, in particular, dates in January and February in leap years. Remember that it is the calculation of these dates that does not conform to the algorithm sketched above. Indeed, when the net's errors were examined in detail, the impression was that the net treated the critical leap year dates as conforming to the general pattern. The net had failed to learn any way of dealing correctly with these exceptions.

General morals

Norris draws a number of interesting conclusions from this exercise and several of these have been repeatedly stressed throughout this book. Firstly, Norris is clear that work with nets comprising one layer of hidden units may be fatally flawed if the problem being addressed is simply unsolvable with this kind of architecture. The overriding issue is that, at present, there are almost no guidelines for when such an architecture is appropriate and when it is not. It is generally accepted that to solve certain problems that are not linearly separable, it is necessary to use a net with one layer of hidden units. However, Rumelhart and McClelland (1986b) report an example of a simple pattern associator that does solve such a problem with no hidden units. In addition, there are examples where nets with no hidden units fare as well as nets with one layer of hidden units (see the later discussion of the work of Bounds, Lloyd, Mathew, & Waddell, 1988). More startling perhaps are those examples where nets with no hidden units perform better (in terms of psychological validity) than nets with hidden units (Massaro, 1988; Schanks, 1990a).

The real failing is that there are no principles or guidelines that set out the conditions under which one architecture is more appropriate than another. If Ratcliff's (1990) appraisal of the state of connectionist art is correct, then the field has now matured to a point where principles of network construction are necessary. If connectionism is going to offer something more than a set of handy tools for implementing certain ideas, then it must take such issues seriously. It is not the ability to do empirical research that is central to science but the principles upon which that research is based. A rather unfortunate impression is that the proliferation of connectionist software packages has fostered the belief that serendipity should replace a more reasoned approach.

Stage-like models

Norris makes some useful points on the notion of stages of processing. At one point he points out that 'steps in the algorithm (as described above) should not be equated directly with layers in a network' (p. 282, fn. 1). This point is well taken but the alternative he puts forward is that idea that separate stages of processing may be directly equated with subnets of units. There is a loose equivalence between stages of his three-step algorithm and the three subnets used in the simulation. Roughly speaking, therefore, the simulation could be described as simply a connectionist implementation of a classical serial sequential stage model of human information processing. It is as if the boxes of a traditional flow diagram have been broken open to reveal a plethora of simple processing units and connections. This rather crude description points to a serious criticism of new connectionism, set out by Fodor and Pylyshyn (1988), that at one level the endeavour reduces to a set of tools for implementing classical cognitive constructs. This point will be returned to later. Here it suffices to note that Norris has substantiated this claim because his connectionist net honours the three-step algorithm. Of course the model operates in ways quite unlike anything that has been envisaged within the classical framework but it does decompose according to three steps in the algorithm.

Structured learning

In developing the supernet used for date calculation, Norris also had to introduce a highly structured learning regime. This involved training the separate subnets individually. Firstly, each subnet was introduced to training in a serial sequential fashion. When subnet x had been trained successfully subnet $x + 1$ was then trained; moreover, the training of subnet x ceased whilst the training of subnet $x + 1$ was carried out. The rationale here was to allow the different subnets to become specialized for different operations underlying date calculation. This poses difficulties for the back-propagation algorithm because it suffers from something known as the problem of code stabilization (Grossberg, 1988; Ratcliff, 1990): if a trained net is presented with new inputs it can show unlearning of old inputs if the weights are changed in ways that are incompatible with the previously trained instances. Norris (1990) explains this point with reference to his net. Suppose that subnet x is trained to perfection and then that subnet $x + 1$ is introduced. When subnet $x + 1$ is introduced the overall net begins to perform poorly. At this stage the weights in subnet $x + 1$ need to be trained up and those in subnet x ought to be left alone. However, given the nature of back-propagation all weights in both nets will be changed. Hence unlearning will be witnessed in subnet x.

Even more problems with the back-propagation account of human learning: Ratcliff's simulations

The very severe nature of this unlearning process has recently been documented by Ratcliff (1990) in his simulations of recognition memory. Ratcliff trained a three-layered net (one input layer, one hidden layer and one output layer) using something called remote rehearsal and the back-propagation algorithm. Remote rehearsal refers to the step of presenting a list of input instances in a serial and sequential fashion and maintaining the ordering of the instances throughout training (i.e. ABCDABCDABCD, etc.). To examine the unlearning process Ratcliff presented three inputs (i.e. 1, 2 and 3) in serial fashion and trained them to criterion using an identity mapping across the input and output nodes. This will be known as stage 1 training. He then took input 4 and trained the net to criterion with this input alone (henceforth stage 2 training).

Ratcliff examined four different kinds of training regimes. In the first all weights on all connections were used in both stages of training. The results showed that following training with the fourth input, the net was basically unable to reproduce any of the first three inputs correctly. Training with the fourth input produced strong interference that disrupted memories of the original three. Typically, outputs constituted a blend of old and new items; however, a startling result was that, on the occasion when one of the original inputs was re-presented, the net produced the pattern associated with the last studied item as its output. Ratcliff (1990) states that the net in a sense 'tracks' the item last presented to the extent that any item will tend to produce it (p. 306). Although it is true that such perseveration errors have been documented in the cognitive neuropsychological literature (Shallice, 1988) this particular effect is not a signature of normal human short-term memory.

The second attempt at training was slightly more sophisticated. Following criterion training at stage 1 the connections were divided up according to whether they possessed large or small weights; the assumption being that small weights were unimportant to the processing of the initial three inputs. Clearly in the limit a weight of 0 adds nothing to the computations (see Mozer and Smolensky, 1989, for a similar point). The results showed some slight improvements over the case where all weights were changed, yet performance was far from perfect.

Finally Ratcliff examined two cases where an extra hidden unit was added before stage 2 training. In the first instance, during stage 2 training the weights on all connections were modified; in the second, only the weights on the connections to and from the extra hidden unit were changed. When all weights were changed performance was now overall better than previously but still far from perfect. When only the extra connections were changed a distinctive pattern of performance arose. The net performed reasonably with the first three inputs but badly with the fourth. This time learning with the original inputs markedly interfered with learning of the fourth. From this general pattern of results Ratcliff observed that there is a trade-off between two sorts of interference. Later items can interfere with the memory of earlier items but when extra hardware is added the interference can go in the opposite direction.

Ratcliff replicated this general pattern of results from simulations with a much more elaborate three-layered net. He also observed one further effect. If following stage 2 training another item was selected and trained to criterion in isolation, this produced huge interference with the items trained during stage 2. The fact is that this kind of interference simply is not witnessed in human learning and memory. In particular, the models revealed forgetting of well-learned material at much faster rates than is observed with humans. Ratcliff concludes that multi-layered nets exhibit severe problems when considered as models of human memory. More importantly though, they fail to meet the explanatory adequacy shown by other established models of memory.

There can be no doubt now that the back-propagation algorithm simply does not provide an adequate account of the psychology of human learning. If this is accepted then a possible fall-back position is to assume that back-propagation provides just one means of acquiring a useful set of weights on the connections in some form of multi-layered net. Now, it is not the acquisition of the weights that is critical but the performance of the mature net. The net may act as some form of demonstration proof that this kind of mechanism can simulate some psychological phenomena. If this fall-back position is accepted then a preferred course of action may be to do away with the back-propagation algorithm altogether and to use a more effective form of gradient descent instead. One such alternative is Shawe-Taylor and Cohen's (1990) linear programming algorithm. This is many times faster than standard back-propagation.

However, even the fall-back position might be resisted because of worries with the general account of learning provided by all gradient descent techniques. The central question is whether it is proper to characterize human learning as being akin to a process of gradient descent. By the Chomskian view, at least, language learning is more appropriately characterized as being a process of hypothesis generation and testing. This is a quite different conception of learning to that of gradient descent. Systematic study is needed to distinguish which, if either, of these accounts of learning is the correct explanation of human performance. Whatever else obtains, the issue is clearly an empirical one where the subjects of study must be humans and not neural nets.

Empirical research that addresses the best way to characterize human learning has recently become the topic of much heated debate in the recent psychological literature. It is to this research that the discussion now turns.

Error correction and human learning

Gluck and Bower (1988) examined cases of medical diagnosis where lists of symptoms were used as inputs to and the diagnoses acted as outputs from a connectionist net. A schematic representation of the net architecture used is shown in Figure 6.5.

The net comprises one layer of input units, no hidden units and two output units. Gluck and Bower used a case of the LMS rule to train the net. Moreover, both the net and human subjects went through the same training regime. Consider

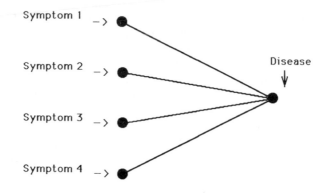

Figure 6.5. Schematic representation of the architecture of Gluck and Bower's net used to do medical diagnosis. Symptom patterns were coded over the input units and each state of the output unit was used to represent a corresponding diagnosis. (From Gluck & Bower, 1988, adapted with permission, *see* p. xvii.)

the subject situation: each subject was presented with sets of four symptoms and was told the actual diagnosis of the associated patient. There were two possible outcomes: a common disease and a rare disease. 75 per cent of the presented cases were classified as suffering from the common disease the remaining 25 per cent of the cases were classified as suffering from the rare disease. Importantly, of the four symptoms, one occurred equally often with the common and rare diseases. For ease of reference this will be referred to as the target symptom. Having undergone the training stage, subjects were then asked to estimate conditional probabilities that a patient with symptom s_i had one or other of the diseases. Although estimates were obtained for all four symptoms and various models were compared against the data, performance with the target symptom was of main interest. The reason for this was that the network model made a prediction that contrasted sharply with a normative (Bayesian) probability account. Had subjects been operating according to the Bayesian model then they should rate P(common disease/target symptom) (i.e. the probability of the common disease given the target symptom) as being equivalent to P(rare disease/target symptom). According to the network model though, subjects should tend to rate P(common disease/ target symptom) as being less than P(rare disease/target symptom). This prediction falls out of the way the LMS rule works. It tends to weight highly input features that occur frequently with particular outputs; it attributes less importance to features that are not good predictors of outputs. Remember, however, that although the absolute number of occurrences of the target symptoms was equated for both common and rare diseases, the target symptom was a more valid predictor of the rare disease than it was of the common disease. Gluck and

Bower found that subjects' performance matched the predictions and the behaviour of the network model. Subjects did not conform to the detailed predictions of the Bayesian model. Gluck and Bower report many other patterns of results with the model and their research has led to a heated debate in the literature (Schanks, 1990a, 1990b; Gluck & Bower, 1990; Markman, 1989). Main interest though here is with simulations reported by Schanks (1990a).

According to Schanks (1990a), Gluck and Bower state that there is a degree of formal equivalence between the version of the LMS rule they used in their simulations and error correcting carried out by back-propagation. Consequently, they claim that a model with one layer of hidden units using the back-propagation algorithm should be as successful in accounting for the data as the LMS rule. However, simulations run with a three-layered net failed to conform to this expectation (Schanks, 1990a). In fact the net appeared to be very good at Bayesian inference; quite unlike human subjects. A general conclusion of the research is that simple two-layered nets without hidden units do provide good operational accounts of a body of human experimental data. This is not to claim they provide a full account of all effects in the literature (Gluck & Bower, 1989, discuss some findings that the simple model cannot hope to account for), but merely that it provides a good account of their data. Moreover, Schanks (1990a) has shown that a net with hidden units performs in ways that are quite different to humans.

Minsky and Papert's critique

Of all of the critiques of new connectionist accounts of learning, perhaps the most devastating is that set out by Minsky and Papert in the Epilogue to the expanded edition to the perceptrons book (Minsky & Papert, 1988). Much of this critique is directed to the details of the chapter by Rumelhart *et al.* (1986) in PDP/1. However, Minsky and Papert also address more general issues about the nature of the back-propagation algorithm and nets with hidden units.

Initially they consider the symmetry predicate and how two different nets can recognize patterns that possess a reflectional symmetry. Both nets are shown in Figure 6.6. Figure 6.6a shows a schematic representation of a net of order 2 that recognizes such a reflectional symmetry. Each of the six 'hidden' unit receives inputs from only two retinal points and all of the coefficients in the net are between +1 and −1. Figure 6.6b shows the alternative net architecture examined by Rumelhart *et al.* With this net each of the two hidden units receives inputs from all retinal points, i.e. the net is of order R, where R is the number of retinal points. The striking thing about this net, though, is that the weights on the connections between the input and hidden units appear to grow exponentially. The actual coefficients shown in the figure are those reported by Rumelhart *et al.* as being those acquired by an actual back-propagation simulation. In discussing

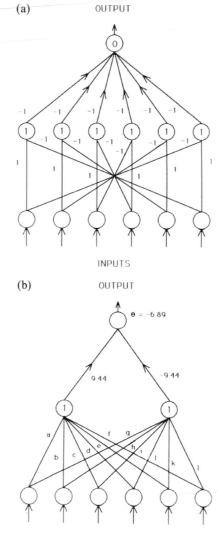

Figure 6.6. Two nets capable of recognizing symmetry. Numbers by links signify the weights; number on units represent thresholds.
(a) is an order-2 net discussed by Minsky and Papert (1988).
(b) is an order-R net where R is the number of retinal units. However, whereas the net shown in (a) has R hidden units, only two hidden units are used here. The coefficients shown were derived from an actual simulation. Of particular imports are the weights on the links to the hidden units. These are labelled a–f and g–l. There values are, in order, −3.18, −.633, −12.56, −12.56, 2.32, 3.17 and 3.16, 6.32, 12.52, −12.51, −6.34, −3.17. (From Minsky & Papert, 1988 adapted with permission, *see* p. xvii.)

this particular example Minsky and Papert repeat their concerns about scaling. It is true that the net solves the problem of learning to recognize symmetry in an interesting manner. Critically though, the solution fails to scale in a reasonable fashion. In other words, increases in the size of the retina are accompanied by exponential increases in the size of the weights. With the network shown in Figure 6.6a, whereas the number of hidden units must grow with the size of the retina, the size of the weights on all connections remains small (i.e. still within the range +1 to −1). In addition, further connections would be needed to link up the larger retina to the hidden units.

Overall, Minsky and Papert note that the whole idea of storing information in the weights on connections does have a biologically plausible 'ring' to it (1988, p. 263); however, they argue that any such biological plausibility tends to fade when the weights have to be calculated to within an accuracy of over 10 orders of significance.

Minsky and Papert also observe that in order to acquire the particular set of weights shown in Figure 6.6b the net had to experience 1,208 cycles through 64 possible inputs. (Later on in the discussion they also state that with many of the small applications described in the PDP books, an exhaustive search of the possible weight assignments would have hit on a solution in about as much time as the training regimes used.) Again they pose the question about how many learning trials would be necessary to train a net with 100 retinal points. The central issue here, as it was in the original perceptrons book, is that although many interesting phenomena can be observed with small nets on small problems, very real problems occur when larger-scale examples are addressed. An implication is that Rumelhart *et al.* have really only provided evidence in support of one of the early and profound misgivings Minsky and Papert had about perceptron research (1969).

On the topic of learning Minsky and Papert are particularly dismissive of the back-propagation algorithm and its use of the generalized delta rule. In particular they stress that the algorithm is nothing more than a straightforward gradient-descent algorithm. Given this, it faces the same kind of local minima problem that all such algorithms face. Moreover, they argue that in at least one sense back-propagation is less powerful than the perceptron convergence procedure. This is because whereas the perceptron convergence procedure will discover a solution if one exists, this is not true of back propagation.

To conclude, it is important to note the following few points. None of these are stressed in Minsky and Papert's critique yet they seem to reveal fundamental limitations of multi-layered nets. Minsky and Papert state that all of their conclusions about order-limited predicates (see Chapter 1) apply to multi-layered nets because 'the order of any unit in a given layer is bounded by the product of the orders of the units in earlier layers' (1988, pp. 251–2). As a consequence this means that multi-layered nets will fail to recognize connectedness for the same reasons that simple perceptrons fail. This does not mean, however, that all connectionist nets are doomed to so fail. Nets that have units arranged in loops are not order-limited, therefore they should be able to succeed where order-limited nets fail. For instance, they should be able to recognize connectedness through the operation of these loops. Importantly, though, nets with loops operate in a highly sequential manner: by definition a loop is an iterative process. This essentially means that such a net will be able to recognize connectedness but only because of its inherently cyclical (i.e. serial) processing. The general point is that artificial neural networks will be able to recognize certain geometric properties because of serial and not parallel processing. This is yet again a vindication of models based on serial, sequential stages of processing.

Minsky and Papert end by outlining their views about the brain being a highly modular mechanism composed of many special-purpose devices. Each device is in turn composed of simple processing units yet each develops according to 'somewhat different principles' (p. 273); hence the view that the search for a general theory of learning is flawed. Aligned with this view is that the claim that genetic principles dictate, to a large degree, the development of such special-purpose processing devices. Indeed, if it is not already obvious, many of the criticisms of new connectionist theories of learning are veiled arguments for innate predispositions of one kind or another. At the very least it has been concluded that nets with random connectivity are of little interest. Once this has been accepted, any assumptions made about structuring a net are arguments for the innate predisposition of these structures.

In conclusion, this is not the place to describe in detail the framework that Minsky and Papert put forward as an alternative to new connectionism. The arguments cover issues not of primary import here. It suffices to note that Minsky and Papert do sketch an alternative view: a view that will undoubtedly be unappealing to those gripped with the fervour generated by running PDP simulations.

Connectionism and thought: higher levels of cognition revisited

It is perhaps easy to be seduced into believing that because human reasoning is clearly a complex topic, it demands complex explanations. The appeal of new connectionism is that it promises simple explanations. This is because, typically, all that is posited is a set of well-understood processing units and their connections. Massively parallel processing then provides an operational account of the phenomena under consideration. To illustrate this kind of argument it is fitting to consider a neural net that operates in fashion resembling an expert system: i.e. a computer program that aids diagnosis of a given problem area (see Gallant, 1988, for a more thorough discussion of expert systems). Although no claims have been made about the psychological status of the nets to be discussed, the work clearly demonstrates how such 'high-level' aspects of cognition as reasoning and decision making can be carried out by nets of stark simplicity. One implication is that this again emphasizes just how forcefully neural net research demands a serious reappraisal of the traditional 'classical' approach to cognition. The work to be considered was that carried out by Bounds *et al.* (1988). It concerned a simple but innovative application of back-propagation to the diagnosis of back pain.

Back pain can be classified into four kinds: (i) simple low back pain (SLBP), i.e. simple backache; (ii) root pain (ROOTP), i.e. nerve root compression; (iii) spinal pathology (SPATH), i.e. serious back pain due to tumour, inflammation or infection; and (iv) abnormal illness behaviour (AIB), typically, psychosomatic symptoms.

The diagnosis of back pain poses an interesting problem because symptoms present with simple low back pain also arise with the most serious category of spinal pathology. In other words, it is quite possible to confuse a trivial ailment with a serious illness. In applying network techniques to the problem of back-pain diagnosis, the idea was to have a set of input units represent a given patient's symptoms and have a set of output units code the diagnosis. Inputs to the net comprised responses that patients made to a questionnaire of 50 questions, with some regarding their symptoms and others regarding other relevant aspects of their medical history. Answers to the questions were coded as 0s or 1s. Where there was no response, a value of 0.5 was recorded. One input unit was dedicated to each question on the questionnaire. Responses to 200 questionnaires were collected and a random 100 were used as training examples; the remaining 100 were used as test materials.

Two kinds of output codings were tried: one with an output unit for each category of back pain; for the other, two output units were used. In this case each pair of output states corresponded to a different category. The output codings for the four categories were (0,0) for SLBP, (0,1) for AIB, (1,0) for ROOTP and (1,1) for SPATH. This ensured that the coding for the least serious cases (SLBP) was maximally dissimilar to that for the most serious case (SPATH).

In addition to the two output coding schemes tried, various numbers of hidden units (between 0 and 50) were used. The rather intriguing finding was that the results of the simulations were insensitive to the number of hidden units. On average, and across the various nets examined, approximately 78 per cent of the test cases were correctly diagnosed. However, two versions of the net were scrutinized in detail. Both had two output units: one had 30 hidden units, the other had no hidden units. Even though the two nets tended to perform at equivalent levels, the version with hidden units did show slightly better performance.

Of perhaps more importance, though, are the striking comparisons drawn between this net and various other diagnoses. Here direct comparisons were drawn between the the net's diagnoses, diagnoses by Bristol neuro-surgeons, Glasgow Orthopaedic surgeons, Bristol General Practitioners and diagnoses performed by a system based around fuzzy logic. The results were clear cut in showing that the best systems were the net and the fuzzy logic system. The net correctly diagnosed all AIB cases and correctly diagnosed more cases of SPATH (the most serious category) than all others. The net scored poorly on the SLBP cases. Bounds *et al.*, however, suggest that performance with this category might well improve if the net's training had been more extensive.

From a radical point of view it is tempting to conclude that the work shows that something that otherwise might be classified as a high-level process, i.e. the diagnosis of back pain, can be carried out most successfully by a very simple neural net. In turn, a rather provocative speculation is that this kind of research should force psychologists to abandon theories of thought and reasoning predicated on complex AI systems and begin to work with principles more directly relevant to brain functioning. There are, however, good grounds to hesitate in accepting this radical view. It is easy to be seduced by the startling pattern of results produced by the nets examined by Bounds *et al.* However, the simulations actually worked too well to be taken as an adequate account of human reasoning. Given that the nets worked better than the physicians at diagnosing back pain, they clearly are not behaving like the physicians. In this respect it seems premature to argue that new connectionism can provide an adequate account of human reasoning. To further emphasize this point, more details of Fodor and Pylyshyn's (1988) critique will now be considered.

New connectionism and human reasoning

Fodor and Pylyshyn cover many detailed points in their extensive, and almost philosophical, critique of new connectionism. Their major points address what are essentially computational level issues because they attempt to establish the fundamental nature of cognitive representations and processes.

A major point they make is that new connectionism only provides theories couched at the implementational level. They claim that new connectionists either (i) develop models that operationalize classical theories, or (ii) provide alternative accounts that prove to be totally inadequate (see the discussion of the criticisms of Smolensky's research in Chapter 5).

Rather than repeat the points relevant to (ii) here, it is more appropriate to dwell initially on (i). In Chapter 5 it was argued that even when a connectionist claims to have offered a network account that 'implements' a classical mechanism, as is the case with Hinton and his simulations of semantic networks, this turns out to be mistaken. Hinton's model of syllogistic reasoning does indeed provide the correct conclusions when queried with certain inputs. Nevertheless, it is quite incorrect to argue that the device simulates the line of reasoning assumed to be followed by humans. On these grounds, the model is therefore not an implementation of the classical account. It is simply an operational account of how a device could produce a particular kind of output given a particular kind of input.

If it is agreed that the net does not implement the classical account of reasoning, it may still be argued that it provides a better framework for understanding human reasoning than does the classical account. On these grounds, it would be true to assert that new connectionism has provided an alternative account of reasoning to the classical one. Perhaps it is the excitement of this kind of possibility that attracts those with a radical bent. The new connectionist framework promises to offer accounts of human information processing that are quite different to those previously envisaged within the classical framework (see Seidenberg, 1988, for just this kind of argument). An implication is that connectionist theorizing should therefore replace classical theorizing (cf. Smolensky, 1988). Fodor and Pylyshyn, however, set out what they consider to be basic problems with this line of argument.

They base their arguments around a number of claims concerning what they consider to be the fundamental nature of human thought. The general framework they describe is termed the representation theory of mind. This framework rests on assumptions about symbols and symbol processing. Some of these ideas have already been discussed in Chapter 5, but it is fitting, nonetheless, to extend the discussion here. For example, a central notion is that the elements of the system (i.e. the representational system) are a set of differentiated, articulated and identifiable symbols. Fodor and Pylyshyn develop their argument by considering the nature of language. They are, however, wedded to the idea that there is a language of thought and so all of the points they make about language apply directly to thought (cf. Fodor, 1975).

For example, consider the sentence JOHN BITES (see Fodor, 1987). The constituents of this sentence are the words JOHN and BITES and in the representational system there are corresponding symbolic tokens for these words. Fodor and Pylyshyn go further and argue that the mental representation of the sentence is composed of the symbolic constituents for and JOHN and BITES. Moreover, the claim is that the mental representation also possesses a constituent structure. The mental representation of the sentence specifies its syntactic structure to the extent that JOHN being a noun and BITES being a verb are both marked according to these syntactic categories. The rules of syntax specify legal combinations of the symbolic constituents that go to make up sentences. There is nothing novel about any of this, it is simply a reworking of Chomsky's (1975) arguments about syntactic structure.

Given this framework, Fodor and Pylyshyn argue that a number of distinctive characteristics now follow. Firstly, they restate another Chomskian notion: that of productivity. Given that mental representations have constituent structure, and that there is a combinatorial syntax, then this allows for the expression and interpretation of an infinite number of legal sentences. Such an infinite capacity is given by the system having a finite number of syntactic rules. Hence the term generative grammar. The grammar or set of rules has the power to generate the infinite number of legal sentences of the natural language under discussion.

They continue by introducing the notion of systematicity. Systematicity refers to the fact that 'the ability to produce/understand some sentences is intrinsically connected to the ability to produce/understand certain others' (p. 37). They state that understanding the sentence 'JOHN LOVES THE GIRL' necessarily implies an ability to also understand 'THE GIRL LOVES JOHN'. Such sentences are systematically related because (i) they are composed of the same constituents, and (ii) the very same combinatorial mechanisms that determine the meaning of one of the sentences determines the meaning of the other (cf. Fodor, 1987). (Fodor and Pylyshyn label (ii) compositionality.)

Unfortunately, and as with much of Fodor's writing, the arguments about systematicity and compositionality are obfuscatory. It is therefore best to try to flesh out the ideas in terms of particular examples. Fortunately, Mackintosh (1988) has written a very clear review of some of the animal-learning literature which centres on the notion of systematicity. Here the concern is with the differences between the abilities of pigeons and corvids to learn classificatory rules. Typically, the scenario is where the birds are given initial training on a given classification problem. They are then tested on their generalization abilities with another problem of the same kind as the original training problem. Consider the example of matching and oddity discriminations. During training the birds respond to one of two coloured lights. In the matching task the rewarded light is signalled by a third light of the same colour as the designated target. In the oddity task the rewarded light is the odd one out.

Pigeons and corvids can learn to solve both tasks yet marked differences across the bird types are witnessed on transfer trials. At transfer the birds are presented with a new example of the same type of discrimination that they had been trained on. The central result is that whereas the corvids show rapid transfer to the new problem, the pigeons show no such transfer effect. It was as if the corvids had learnt to respond according to some general rule as exemplified by the training problem. In contrast, the pigeons had simply learnt to respond appropriately on the basis of the particulars of that classificatory problem used during training. Indeed, Mackintosh pieces together a picture of pigeons only ever being capable of learning on the basis of individual associations. As he has it, 'they learn a long list of conditional discriminations: if the sample is blue, choose blue; if green, choose green; if triangle, choose triangle; etc.' (p. 518). Given that this is indeed how the pigeon learns, then these birds are not operating according to the principle of systematicity set out by Fodor and Pylyshyn. Systematicity dictates that an abstract rule of classification is applied and, moreover, that the organism can operate appropriately when confronted by instances that conform to the rule. Systematicity implies generalization on the basis of a rule; in this respect it implies that behaviour is governed by something more than the simple formation of individual associations.

Mackintosh (1988) is firm in his conclusion that there is a real difference between associative learning (evidenced by the behaviour of pigeons) and rule learning (evidenced by the behaviour of corvids). As such it is simply mistaken to deny that there is no such difference or to argue that rule-learning 'can . . . be explained within a general associative or connectionist framework' (p. 523). This is, in essence, Fodor and Pylyshyn's main point. Connectionist nets do not exhibit systematicity, therefore they simply cannot explain it. In addition, connectionist nets exhibit a form of learning identical in kind to the associative learning witnessed in pigeons. According to Mackintosh (1988), however, no theory of pigeon learning will ever add up to a theory of human learning. As Mackintosh concludes, 'associations alone do not generate rules'.

Having consider systematicity it is useful to now consider a few brief comments about compositionality. Again it is best to carry the discussion forward in terms of a particular example. Fodor and Pylyshyn (p. 46) consider the following inference:

(i)   Turtles are slower than rabbits.
(ii) Rabbits are slower than Ferraris.

(iii) Turtles are slower than Ferraris.

Fodor and Pylyshyn argue that drawing this inference is predicated on (a) comprehending the fact that the same relation (slower than) holds in (i) and (ii) and that it can be applied in (iii); and (b) that the relation is transitive. It is this kind of argument that is used to establish the assertion that the human representational system utilizes context-independent representations. In this case, the argument is that there must be some form of context-independent representation of the relation 'slower than' for the inference to go through. For, as Fodor and Pylyshyn argue, were it true that 'slower than' means different things in the three cases (i.e. in (i), (ii) and (iii)), then there is no obvious reason why the inference is valid. This kind of example reveals serious inadequacies in those connectionist theories that try to get by without context-independent representations (see Smolensky, 1987). The claim is that such models simply cannot begin to address fundamental issues about human thought and reasoning.

To conclude this section, Fodor and Pylyshyn describe productivity, systematicity and compositionality as being fundamental characteristics of the human mind. Any system that purports to simulate the mind must therefore show how these characteristics come about. Fodor and Pylyshyn are adamant that no form of connectionist theory can, at present, meet this challenge.

Concluding comments

The main aim of this chapter has been to set out serious limitations of the connectionist approach to modelling neurological and cognitive structures and processes. There can be no question that some of the points covered reveal fundamental weaknesses in the approach. Nonetheless, citing such evidence does not give licence to the claim that the whole approach is worthless. Merely because problems exist at present, does not imply that future research cannot overcome these problems. Connectionism has galvanized psychologists, computer scientists and neuroscientists alike and it would be overly pessimistic to argue that no serious advances will come of such a concerted research effort.

To avoid any unnecessary misapprehensions, it is important to reiterate that the primary aim in writing this book has been to present both the strengths and the weaknesses of new connectionism in order to provide a balanced view. Enough examples of truly innovative research have been described in the preceding chapters, that the case for doing connectionist research should have been clearly established. If anything, many serious suggestions have been made about how to avoid pitfalls in future research. Indeed, a primary concern is that psychological data should be taken more seriously by modellers if they are to do work of substance. Research that ignores the last fifty years of experimental psychology fails to be credible.

One of the main themes in the book has been to show the ways in which connectionism provides important insights into how mental processes may arise through the myriad interactions of many simple processing units. Prior to the rebirth of neural network research, very little serious thought was given to such a proposition. This is even though the proposition appears eminently sensible. Many believe today that it is right to construe the brain as being a mass of simple processing units and interconnections. Moreover, they feel that it is only appropriate to view mental processes as arising from neurological processes. Given these basic assumptions, it seems only sensible to argue that some form of neural network theory of the mind must be ultimately desirable. The hope is that such a theory can be developed by carrying out connectionist research.

In closing, though, it is best to end with Hinton's (1989a) cautious appraisal of the prospects of future research. He believes that real advances will be made on a number of fronts in the near future. Firstly, according to Hinton, progress will be made in developing more efficient learning procedures. In particular, Hinton predicts that larger-scale learning problems will prove tractable with future developments. Secondly, he predicts that connectionist solutions to 'difficult' tasks will be found. The example he cites is that of speech recognition. He believes that network models will be developed to process speech successfully. Thirdly, he is sure that technological advances will allow the behaviour of very large networks to be examined. Finally, he is certain that the new connectionist approach will provide further important insights into how real neural nets operate. Obviously, the degree to which psychological theory will be affected by these projected advances remains to be seen.

References

Ackley, D. H., Hinton, G. E., & Sejnowski, T. J. (1985). A learning algorithm for Boltzmann machines. *Cognitive Science*, **9**, 147–69.

Aleksander, I., & Morton, H. (1990). *An introduction to neural computing*. London: Chapman and Hall.

Alkon, D. L. (1989). Memory storage and neural systems. *Scientific American*, July, 26–34.

Anderson, J. A. (1977). Neural models with cognitive implications. In D. La Berge & S. J. Samuels (Eds.), *Basic processes in reading: Perception and comprehension* (pp. 27–90). Hillsdale, NJ: Lawrence Erlbaum Associates.

Anderson, J. A., & Hinton, G. E. (1981). Models of information processing in the brain. In G. E. Hinton & J. A. Anderson (Eds.), *Parallel models of associative memory* (pp. 9–48). Hillsdale, NJ: Lawrence Erlbaum Associates.

Anderson, J. A., & Mozer, M. C. (1981). Categorization and selective neurons. In G. E. Hinton & J. A. Anderson (Eds.), *Parallel models of associative memory* (pp. 213–36). Hillsdale, NJ: Lawrence Erlbaum Associates.

Anderson, J. A., & Silverstein, J. W. (1978). Reply to Grossberg. *Psychological Review*, **85**, 597–603.

Anderson, J. A., Silverstein J. W., Ritz, S. A., & Jones, R. S. (1977). Distinctive features, categorical perception, and probability learning: Some applications of a neural model. *Psychological Review*, **84**, 413–51.

Anderson, J. R. (1976). *Language, memory and thought*. Hillsdale, NJ: Lawrence Erlbaum Associates.

Anderson, J. R. (1979). Further arguments concerning representations for mental imagery. A response to Hayes-Roth and Pylyshyn. *Psychological Review*, **86**, 395–406.

Anderson, J. R., & Bower, G. H. (1973). *Human associative memory*. Washington, D.C.: V. H. Winston.

Andreae, J. H. (1977). *Thinking with the teachable machine*. London: Academic Press.

Andrews, S. (1989). Frequency and neighborhood effects on lexical access: Activation or search? *Journal of Experimental Psychology: Human Memory and Cognition*, **15**, 802–14.

Arbib, M. A. (1987). *Brains, machines and mathematics* (2nd edn). New York: Springer-Verlag.

Arbib, M. A. (1989). A review of 'Perceptrons: An introduction to computational geometry' by Marvin Minsky and Seymour Papert. Cambridge, Mass: The MIT Press, 1969. *IEEE Transactions on Information Theory*, **IT-15**, No. 6, Nov., 738–9.

Ballard, D. H. (1986). Cortical connections and parallel processing: Structure and function. *Behavioral and Brain Sciences*, **9**, 67–90.

Barlow, H. B. (1972). Single units and sensation: A neuron doctrine for perceptual psychology? *Perception*, **1**, 371–94.

Barlow, H. B., & Reeves, B. C. (1979). The versatility and absolute efficiency of detecting mirror symmetry in random dot patterns. *Vision Research*, **19**, 783–93.

Barrow, H. G. (1989). AI, neural networks and early vision. *AISB Quarterly Newsletter*, **69**, 6–25.

Becker, S., & le Cun, Y. (1988). *Improving the convergence of back-propagation learning with second order methods*. (Tech. Report. CRG-TR-88-5). Toronto: University of Toronto, Department of Computer Science.

Besner, D., Twilley, L., McCann, R. S., & Seergobin, K. (1990). On the connection between connectionism and data: Are a few words necessary? *Psychological Review*, **97**, 432–46.

Biederman, I., & Checkosky, S. F. (1970). Processing redundant information. *Journal of Experimental Psychology*, **83**, 486–90.

Blasdel, G. G., & Salama, G. (1986). Voltage-sensitive dyes reveal a modular organization in the monkey striate cortex. *Nature*, **321**, 579–85.

Bliss, T. V. P., Errington, M. L., Feasey, K. J., & Lynch, M. A. (1986). Presynpatic mechanisms in hippocampal long-term potentiation. In H. Matthies (Ed.), *Learning and memory: Mechanisms of information storage in the nervous system* (pp. 5–11). New York: Pergamon Press.

Block, H. D. (1962). The perceptron: A model for brain functioning, 1. *Reviews of Modern Physics*, **34**, 123–35.

Block, H. D. (1970). A review of 'Perceptrons: An introduction to computational geometry' by Marvin Minsky and Seymour Papert. *Information and Control*, **17**, 501–22.

Bounds, D. G., Lloyd, P. J., Mathew, B., & Waddell, G. (1988). *A multi-layer perceptron network for the diagnosis of low back pain*. London: HMSO.

Bridle, J. S. (1988). *Connectionist approaches to artificial perception and temporal processing: A speech pattern processing perspective*. Technical Program for the SGAICO Science Project International Conference 'Connectionism in perspective', Zurich, October.

Broadbent, D. E. (1967). Word frequency effect and response bias. *Psychological Review*, **74**, 1–15.

Broadbent, D. E. (1985). A question of levels: comment on McClelland and Rumelhart. *Journal of Experimental Psychology: General*, **114**, 189–92.

Brown, G. D. A. (1987a). Resolving inconsistency: A computational model of word naming. *Journal of Memory and Language*, **26**, 1–23.

Brown, G. D. A. (1987b). Constraining interactivity: Evidence from acquired dyslexia.

Proceedings of the 9th Annual Conference of the Cognitive Science Society (pp. 779–93), Seattle, July. Hillsdale, NJ: Lawrence Erlbaum Associates.

Campbell, C., Sherrington, D., & Wong, K. Y. M. (1989). Statistical mechanics and neural networks. In I. Aleksander (Ed.), *Neural Computing Architectures* (pp. 239–57). London: North Oxford Academic.

Campbell, R., & Besner, D. (1981). This and thap: Constraints on the pronunciation of new, written words. *Quarterly Journal of Experimental Psychology*, **33A**, 375–96.

Chan, L.-W., & Fallside, F. (1987). An adaptive training algorithm for back-propagation networks. *Computers, Speech and Language*, **2**, 205–18.

Changeaux, J.-P., & Dehaene, S. (1989). Neuronal models of cognitive functions. *Cognition*, **33**, 63–109.

Chater, N., & Oaksford, M. (1990). Autonomy, implementation and cognitive architecture. *Cognition*, **34**, 93–107.

Chomsky, N. (1975). *Syntactic structures*. The Hague: Mouton.

Coltheart, M. (1978). Lexical access in simple reading tasks. In G. Underwood (Ed.), *Strategies of information processing* (pp. 151–216). Amsterdam: North Holland.

Coltheart, M. (1985). Cognitive neuropsychology and the study of reading. In M. I. Posner & O. S. M. Marin (Eds.), *Attention and performance*, vol. XI (pp. 3–37). Hillsdale, NJ: Lawrence Erlbaum Associates.

Coltheart, M., Davelaar, E., Jonasson, J. T., & Besner, D. (1977). Access to the internal lexicon. In S. Dornic (Ed.), *Attention and performance*, vol. VI (pp. 535–55). Hillsdale, NJ: Lawrence Erlbaum Associates.

Corcoran, D. W. J. (1971). *Pattern recognition*. Harmondsworth: Penguin Books.

Coslett, H. B., & Saffran, E. M. (1989). Evidence for preserved reading in 'pure alexia'. *Brain*, **112**, 327–59.

Crick, F. H. C. (1989). The recent excitement about neural networks. *Nature*, **337**, 129–32.

Crick, F. H. C., & Asanuma, C. (1986). Certain aspects of the anatomy and physiology of the cerebral cortex. In J. L. McClelland, D. E. Rumelhart and the PDP Research Group, *Parallel distributed processing: Explorations in the microstructure of cognition*. vol. 2: *Psychological and biological models* (pp. 333–71). Cambridge, MA: The MIT Press.

Crick, F. H. C., & Mitchison, G. (1983). The function of dream sleep. *Nature*, **304**, 111–14.

le Cun, Y. (1988a). *A theoretical framework for back-propagation*. (Tech. Report. CRG-TR-88-6). Toronto: University of Toronto, Department of Computer Science.

le Cun, Y. (1988b). *Multi-layer neural networks*. Tutorial Program for the SGAICO Science Project International Conference 'Connectionism in perspective', Zurich, October.

Davis, S. N., Lester, R. A. J., Reymann, K. G., & Collingridge, G. L. (1989). Temporally distinct pre- and post-synaptic mechanisms maintain long-term potentiation. *Nature*, **338**, 500–3

Dell, G. S. (1986). A spreading-activation theory of retrieval in sentence production. *Psychological Review*, **93**, 283–321.

Doyle, J. R., & Leach, C. (1988). Word superiority in signal detection: Barely a glimpse, yet reading nonetheless. *Cognitive Psychology*, **20**, 283–318.

Dreyfus, H. L. (1972). *What computers can't do: A critique of artificial reason*. New York: Harper & Row.

Durbin, R., & Mitchison, G. (1990). A dimension reduction framework for understanding cortical maps. *Nature*, **343**, 644–7.

Edelman, S., & Weinshall, D. (1989). *A self-organizing multiple-view representation of 3D objects* (Tech. Rep. AI Memo 1146. CBIP Memo 41). Cambridge, MA: MIT AI Laboratory and Center for Biological Information Processing.

Eimas, P. D. (1985). The perception of speech in early infancy. *Scientific American*, **252**, 46–52.

Eimas, P. D., & Corbit, J. D. (1973). Selective adaptation of linguistic feature detectors. *Cognitive Psychology*, **4**, 99–109.

Evett, L. J., & Humphreys, G. W. (1981). The use of abstract graphemic information in lexical access. *Quarterly Journal of Experimental Psychology*, **33A**, 325–50.

Evett, L. J., Humphreys, G. W., & Quinlan, P. T. (1986). Identification, masking and priming: Clarifying the issues. *Behavioral and Brain Sciences*, **9**, 31–2.

Fahlman, S. E. (1979). *NETL: A system for representing and using real-world knowledge.* Cambridge, MA: The MIT Press.

Fahlman, S. E. (1981). Representing implicit knowledge. In G. E. Hinton & J. A. Anderson (Eds.), *Parallel models of associative memory* (pp. 145–59). Hillsdale, NJ: Lawrence Erlbaum Associates.

Feldman, J. A., & Ballard, D. H. (1982). Connectionist models and their properties. *Cognitive Science*, **6**, 205–54.

Fodor, J. A. (1975). *The language of thought.* New York: Crowell.

Fodor, J. A. (1981). *Representations.* Cambridge, MA: The MIT Press.

Fodor, J. A. (1983). *The modularity of mind.* Cambridge, MA: The MIT Press.

Fodor, J. A. (1987). *Psychosemantics: The problem of meaning in the philosophy of mind.* Cambridge, MA: The MIT Press.

Fodor, J. A., Garrett, M. F., Walker, E. C. T., & Parkes, C. H. (1980). Against definitions. *Cognition*, **8**, 263–7.

Fodor, J. A., & McLaughlin, B. P. (1990). Connectionism and the problem of systematicity: Why Smolensky's solution doesn't work. *Cognition*, **35**, 183–204.

Fodor, J. A., & Pylyshyn, Z. W. (1981). How direct is visual perception? Some reflections on Gibson's 'Ecological Approach'. *Cognition*, **9**, 139–96.

Fodor, J. A., & Pylyshyn, Z. W. (1988). Connectionism and cognitive architecture: A critical analysis. *Cognition*, **28**, 3–71.

Fogelman Soulie, F. (1988). *Introduction to neural nets: A tutorial.* Tutorial Program for the SGAICO Science Project International Conference 'Connectionism in perspective', Zurich, October.

Forster, K. I. (1976). Accessing the mental lexicon. In E. C. T. Walker & R. J. Wales (Eds.), *New approaches to language mechanisms* (pp. 257–87). Amsterdam: North Holland.

Foster, D. H. (1975). Visual apparent motion and some preferred paths in the rotation group SO(3). *Biological Cybernetics*, **18**, 81–9.

Fry, D. B., Abramson, A. S., Eimas, P. D., & Liberman, A. M. (1962). The identification and discrimination of synthetic vowels. *Language and Speech*, **5**, 171–89.

Gallant, S. I. (1988). Connectionist expert systems. *Communications of the ACM*, **31**, 152–69.

Garner, W. R. (1974). *The processing of information and structure.* Hillsdale, NJ: Lawrence Erlbaum Associates.

Garnham, A. (1987). *Mental models as representations of discourse and text.* Chichester: Ellis Horwood.

Geman, S., & Geman, D. (1987). Stochastic relaxation, Gibbs distributions, and the

Bayesian restoration of images. In M. A. Fischler & O. Firschein (Eds.), *Readings in computer vision: Issues, problems, principles, and paradigms* (pp. 564–84). (Reprinted from *IEEE Transactions on Pattern Analysis and Machine Intelligence*, 1965, 6, 721–41)

Geschwind, N. (1985). Mechanisms of change after brain lesions. *Annals of the New York Academy of Sciences*, **457**, 1–11.

Gibson, J. J. (1950). *The perception of the visual world*. Boston: Houghton Mifflin.

Gibson, J. J. (1966). *The senses as considered as perceptual systems*. Boston: Houghton Mifflin.

Gibson, J. J. (1979). *The ecological approach to visual perception*. Boston: Houghton Mifflin.

Gluck, M. A., & Bower, G. H. (1988). Evaluating an adaptive network model of human learning. *Journal of Memory and Language*, **27**, 166–95.

Gluck, M. A., & Bower, G. H. (1990). Component and pattern information in adaptive networks. *Journal of Experimental Psychology: General*, **119**, 105–9.

Glushko, R. J. (1979). The organization and activation of orthographic knowledge in reading words aloud. *Journal of Experimental Psychology: Human Perception and Performance*, **6**, 674–91.

Goodman, N. (1976). *Languages of art: An approach to a theory of symbols* (2nd edn). Brighton, Sussex: The Harvester Press.

Gordan, I. E. (1989). *Theories of visual perception*. Chichester: John Wiley & Sons.

Gorman, R. P., & Sejnowski, T. J. (1988). Analysis of hidden units in a layered network trained to classify sonar targets. *Neural Networks*, **1**, 75–89.

Green, D. M., & Swets, J. (1966). *Signal detection theory and psychophysics*. New York: John Wiley & Sons.

Gregory, R. L. (1973). *Eye and brain: The psychology of seeing* (2nd edn). London: Weidenfeld & Nicolson.

Gregory, R. L. (1974). Brain function in terms of probability and induction. In R. L. Gregory (Ed.), *Concepts and mechanisms of perception* (pp. 521–36). London: Duckworth.

Grossberg, S. (1978). Do all neural models really look alike? A comment on Anderson, Silverstein, Ritz and Jones. *Psychological Review*, **85**, 592–6.

Grossberg, S. (1987). Competitive learning: from interactive activation to adaptive resonance. *Cognitive Science*, **11**, 23–63.

Grossberg, S. (1988). Nonlinear neural networks: principles, mechanisms, and architectures. *Neural Networks*, **1**, 17–61.

Grossberg, S., & Marshall, J. A. (1989). Stereo boundary fusion by cortical complex cells: A system of maps, filters, and feedback networks for multiplexing distributed data. *Neural Networks*, **2**, 29–51.

Grossberg, S., & Mingolla, E. (1985). Neural dynamics of form perception: Boundary completion, illusory figures and neon color spreading. *Psychological Review*, **92**, 173–211.

Guiver, J. P., & Klimasauskas, C. C. (1988). *Hopfield Networks*. In Neuralworks professional II (revision 2.00) (pp. 411–34). Sewickley, PA.: Neural Ware Inc.

Hampshire, J. & Waibel, A. (in press). Connectionist architectures for multi-speaker phoneme recognition. In D. Touretzky (Ed.), *Advances in neural information processing*. San Deigo: Morgan Kaufmann.

Hanson, S. J., & Burr, D. J. (1990). What connectionist models learn: Learning and representation in connectionist networks. *Behavioral and Brain Sciences*, **13**, 471–89.

Hataoka, N., & Waibel, A. (1989). *Speaker-independent phoneme recognition on TIMIT database using integrated time-delay neural networks (TDNNs)*. (Tech. Rep. CMU-CMT-89-115). Pittsburgh: Carnegie-Mellon University, School of Computer Science.

Hayes-Roth, F. (1979). Distinguishing theories of representation: A critique of Anderson's 'Arguments concerning mental imagery'. *Psychological Review*, **86**, 376–82.

Hebb, D. O. (1949). *The organisation of behavior: A neuropsychological approach*. New York: John Wiley & Sons.

Henderson, L. (1982). *Orthography and word recognition in reading*. London: Academic.

Hendricks, I. M., Holliday, I. E., & Ruddock, K. H. (1981). A new class of visual deficit: Spreading inhibition elicited by chromatic light stimuli. *Brain*, **104**, 813–40.

Henley, N. M. (1969). A psychological study of the semantics of animal terms. *Journal of Verbal Learning and Verbal Behavior*, **8**, 176–84.

Hilgard, E. R., & Bower, G. H. (1966). *Theories of learning* (3rd edn). New York: Appleton-Century-Crofts.

Hinton, G. E. (1979). Some demonstrations of the effects of structural descriptions in mental imagery. *Cognitive Science*, **3**, 231–50.

Hinton, G. E. (1981a). A parallel computation that assigns canonical object-based frames of reference. *Proceedings of the 7th International Joint Conference on Artificial Intelligence* (pp. 683–5). Vancouver, BC, Canada.

Hinton, G. E. (1981b). Implementing semantic networks in parallel hardware. In G. E. Hinton & J. A. Anderson (Eds.), *Parallel models of associative memory* (pp. 161–87). Hillsdale, NJ: Lawrence Erlbaum Associates.

Hinton, G. E. (1981c). Shape representation in parallel systems. *Proceedings of the 7th International Joint Conference on Artificial Intelligence* (pp. 1088–96). Vancouver, BC, Canada.

Hinton, G. E. (1981d). The role of spatial working memory in shape perception. In *Proceedings of the 3rd Annual Conference of the Cognitive Science Society* (pp. 56–60). Berkeley, CA.

Hinton, G. E. (1984). *Distributed representations* (Tech. Rep. CMU-CS-84-157). Pittsburgh: Carnegie-Mellon University, Department of Computer Science.

Hinton, G. E. (1986). Learning distributed representations of concepts. *Proceedings of the 8th Annual Conference of the Cognitive Science Society* (pp. 1–12). Amherst, MA.

Hinton, G.E. (1987). *Connectionist learning procedures* (Tech. Rep. CMU-CS-87-115). Pittsburgh: Carnegie-Mellon University, Department of Computer Science.

Hinton, G.E. (1988). *Representing part-whole hierarchies in connectionist networks* (Tech. Rep. CRG-TR-88-2). Toronto: University of Toronto, Department of Computer Science.

Hinton, G. E. (1989a). Connectionist learning procedures. *Artificial Intelligence*, **40**, 185–234.

Hinton, G. E. (1989b). *Neural networks*. The First Sun Annual Lectures in Computer Science at the University of Manchester, July.

Hinton, G. E., & Anderson, J. A. (Eds.). (1981). *Parallel models of associative memory*. Hillsdale, NJ: Lawrence Erlbaum Associates.

Hinton G. E., & Anderson, J. A. (1989). Introduction to the updated edition. In G. E. Hinton & J. A. Anderson (Eds.), *Parallel models of associative memory* (pp. 1–13). Hillsdale, NJ: Lawrence Erlbaum Associates.

Hinton, G. E., & Lang, K. J. (1985). Shape recognition and illusory conjunctions. In *Proceedings of 9th International Joint Conference on Artificial Intelligence* (pp. 251–9). Los Angeles.

Hinton, G. E., McClelland, J. L., & Rumelhart, D. E. (1986). Distributed representations. In J. L. McClelland, D. E. Rumelhart and the PDP Research Group, *Parallel distributed processing: Explorations in the microstructure of cognition.* vol. 1: *Foundations* (pp. 77–109). Cambridge, MA: The MIT Press.

Hinton, G. E., & Parsons, L. M. (1981). Frames of reference and mental imagery. In A. D. Baddeley & J. Long (Eds.), *Attention and performance*, vol. IX (pp. 261–77). Hillsdale, NJ: Lawrence Erlbaum Associates.

Hinton, G. E., & Sejnowski, T. J. (1983a). *Analysing co-operative computation.* Paper presented to the 5th Annual Conference of the Cognitive Science Society, Rochester NY, May 1983.

Hinton, G. E., & Sejnowski, T. J. (1983b). Optimal perceptual inference. *Proceedings of the IEEE Conference on Computer Vision and Pattern Recognition*, 448–53.

Hinton, G. E., & Sejnowski, T. J. (1984). Learning semantic features. *Proceedings of the 6th Annual Conference of the Cognitive Science Society* (pp. 28–30). Boulder, CO, June.

Hinton, G. E., & Sejnowski, T. J. (1986). Learning and relearning in Boltzmann machines. In J. L. McClelland, D. E. Rumelhart and the PDP Research Group, *Parallel distributed processing: Explorations in the microstructure of cognition.* vol. 1: *Foundations* (pp. 282–317). Cambridge, MA: The MIT Press.

Hinton, G. E., Sejnowski, T. J. & Ackley, D. H. (1984). *Boltzmann machines constraint satisfaction networks that learn* (Tech. Rep. CMU-CS-84-119). Pittsburgh: Carnegie-Mellon University, Department of Computer Science.

Hinton, G. E., & Shallice, T. (1989). *Lesioning a connectionist network: Investigations of acquired dyslexia* (Tech. Rep. CRG-TR-89-3). Toronto: University of Toronto, Department of Computer Science.

Holender, D. (1986). Semantic activation without conscious identification in dichotic listening, parafoveal vision, and visual masking: A survey and appraisal. *Behavioral and Brain Sciences*, **9**, 1–66.

Hopfield, J. J. (1982). Neural networks and physical systems with emergent collective computational abilities. *Proceedings of the National Academy of Science USA*, **79**, 2554–8.

Hopfield, J. J. (1984). Neurons with graded response have collective computational properties like those of two-state neurons. *Proceedings of the National Academy of Science USA*, **81**, 3088–92.

Hopfield, J. J., Feinstein, D. I., & Palmer, R. G. (1983). 'Unlearning' has a stabilising effect in collective memories. *Nature*, **304**, 158–9.

Hopfield, J. J., & Tank, D. W. (1985). Neural computation of decisions in optimization problems. *Biological Cybernetics*, **52**, 141–52.

Hopfield, J. J., & Tank, D. W. (1986). Computing with neural circuits: a model. *Science*, **233**, 625–33.

Hubel, D. H., & Wiesel, T. N. (1962). Receptive fields, binocular interaction, and functional architecture in the cat's visual cortex. *Journal of Physiology*, **160**, 106–54.

Hubel, D. H., & Wiesel, T. N. (1965). Receptive fields and functional architecture of two nonstriate visual areas (18 and 19) of the cat. *Journal of Neurophysiology*, **28**, 229–89.

Hubel, D. H., & Wiesel, T. N. (1977). Functional architecture of macaque monkey visual cortex (Ferrier lecture). *Proceedings of the Royal Society of London*, B, **198**, 1–59.

Humphreys, G. W. (1983). Reference frames and shape perception. *Cognitive Psychology*, **15**, 151–96.

Humphreys, G. W. (1984). Shape constancy: The effects of changing shape orientation and the effects of changing the position of focal features. *Perception and Psychophysics*, **36**, 50–64.

Humphreys, G. W., Besner, D., & Quinlan, P. T. (1988). Event perception and the word repetition effect. *Journal of Experimental Psychology: General*, **117**, 51–67.

Humphreys, G. W., Evett, L. J., & Quinlan, P. T. (1990). Orthographic processing in visual word identification. *Cognitive Psychology*, **22**, 517–60.

Humphreys, G. W., Evett, L. J., Quinlan, P. T., & Besner, D. (1987). Orthographic priming: Qualitative differences between priming from identified and unidentified primes. In M. Coltheart (Ed.), *Attention and performance*, vol. XII: *The psychology of reading* (pp. 105–25). Hillsdale, NJ: Lawrence Erlbaum Associates.

Humphreys, G. W., & Quinlan, P. T. (1986). Comments on 'Explanation in computational psychology' by C. Peacocke. *Mind and Language*, **1**, 355–7.

Humphreys, G. W., & Quinlan, P. T. (1987). Normal and pathological processes in visual object constancy. In G. W. Humphreys & M. J. Riddoch (Eds.), *Visual object processing: A cognitive neuropsychological approach* (pp. 43–105). Hove and London: Lawrence Erlbaum Associates.

Humphreys, G. W., & Quinlan, P. T. (1988). Priming effects between two-dimensional shapes. *Journal of Experimental Psychology: Human Perception and Performance*, **14**, 203–20.

Hush, D. R., & Salas, J. M. (1988). Improving the learning rate of back-propagation with the gradient reuse algorithm. *Proceedings of the 2nd IEEE International Joint Conference on Neural Networks*, **1**, 441–7). San Diego.

Hyde, T. S., & Jenkins, J. J. (1973). Recall for words as a function of semantic, graphic and syntactic orienting tasks. *Journal of Verbal Learning and Verbal Behavior*, **12**, 471–80.

Jacobs, R. A. (1988). Increased rates of convergence through learning rate adaptation. *Neural Networks*, **1**, 295–307.

Jakobson, R., Fant, G. G. M., & Halle, M. (1952). *Preliminaries to speech analysis: The distinctive features and their correlates*. Cambridge, MA: The MIT Press.

James, W. (1983). *The principles of psychology*. London: Harvard University Press. (Original work published in 1890.)

Jared, D., McRae, K., & Seidenberg, M. S. (1990). The basis of consistency effects in word naming. *Journal of Memory and Language*, **29**, 687–715.

Johnson-Laird, P. N. (1987). Minsky's mentality. *Nature*, **328**, 387–8.

Jolicoeur, P. (1985). The time to name disoriented natural objects. *Memory and Cognition*, **13**, 289–303.

Jolicoeur, P., & Kosslyn, S. M. (1983). Coordinate systems in the long term representation of three-dimensional shapes. *Cognitive Psychology*, **16**, 243–275.

Jordan, M. I. (1986). An introduction to linear algebra in parallel distributed processing. In J. L. McClelland, D. E. Rumelhart and the PDP Research Group, *Parallel distributed processing: Explorations in the microstructure of cognition*. vol. 1: *Foundations* (pp. 365–422). Cambridge, MA: The MIT Press.

Julesz, B. (1971). *Foundations of cyclopean perception*. Chicago: University of Chicago Press.

Kanizsa, G. (1974). Contours without gradients or cognitive contours. *Italian Journal of Psychology*, **1**, 93–113.

Kanizsa, G. (1979). *Organization in vision: Essays on Gestalt perception*. New York: Praeger.

Katz, J. J., & Fodor, J. A. (1963). The structure of a semantic theory. *Language*, **39**, 170–210.

Kay, J., & Bishop, D. (1987). Anatomical differences between nose, palm, and foot, or, the body in question: Further dissection of the processes of sub-lexical spelling-sound translation. In M. Coltheart (Ed.), *Attention and performance*, vol. XII (pp. 449–69). Hove: Lawrence Erlbaum Associates.

Kay, J., & Marcel, A. J. (1981). One process, not two, in reading aloud: Lexical analogies do the work of nonlexical rules. *Quarterly Journal of Experimental Psychology*, **33A**, 397–414.

Kehoe, E. J. (1988). A layered network model of associative learning: Learning to learn and configuration. *Psychological Review*, **95**, 411–33.

Keppel, G. (1973). *Design and analysis: A researcher's handbook*. Engelwood Cliffs, NJ: Prentice Hall.

Kienker, P. K., Sejnowski, T. J., Hinton, G. E., & Schumacher, L. E. (1986). Separating figure from ground with a parallel network. *Perception*, **15**, 197–216.

Kindermann, J., & Linden, A. (1988). *Pattern completion and classification with back-propagation*. Arbeitpapiere der Gesellschaft für Mathematik und Datenverrarbeittung MBH (Technical Report 329 of the Society for Mathematics and Information Processing Ltd). August, 95–121.

Kirkpatrick, S., Gelatt, C. D. Jr., & Vecchi, M. P. (1983). Optimisation by simulated annealing. *Science*, **220**, 671–80.

Klimasauskas, C. C. (1988). *An introduction to neural computing*. In Neuralworks professional II (revision 2.00) (pp. 3–55). Sewickley, PA.: Neural Ware Inc.

Kolers, P. A., & Smythe, W. E. (1984). Symbol manipulation: Alternatives to the computational theory of mind. *Journal of Verbal Learning and Verbal Behavior*, **23**, 289–314.

Kucera, H., & Francis, W. N. (1967). *Computational analysis of present-day American English*. Providence, RI: Brown University Press.

Lachter, J., & Bever, T. G. (1988). 'There's no safety in numbers . . . or anything else'. *Cognition*, **28**, 195–274.

Land, E. H. (1977). The retinex theory of color vision. *Scientific American*, **237**, 108–28.

Lehky, S. R., & Sejnowski, T. J. (1988). Network model of shape-from-shading: neural function arises from both receptive and projective fields. *Nature*, **333**, 452–4.

Liberman, A. M., Cooper, F. S., Shankweiler, D. P., & Studdert-Kennedy, M. (1967). Perception of the speech code. *Psychological Review*, **74**, 431–61.

Lindsay, P. H., & Norman, D. A. (1972). *Human information processing: An introduction to psychology*. New York: Academic Press.

Linsker, R. (1986a). From basic network principles to neural architecture: Emergence of spatial-opponent cells. *Proceedings of the National Academy of Science USA*, **83**, 7508–12.

Linsker, R. (1986b). From basic network principles to neural architecture: Emergence of orientation-selective cells. *Proceedings of the National Academy of Science USA*, **83**, 8390–4.

Linsker, R. (1986c). From basic network principles to neural architecture: Emergence of orientation columns. *Proceedings of the National Academy of Science USA*, **83**, 8779–83.

Lorente de Nó, R. (1938). Synaptic stimulation of motorneurons as a local process. *Journal of Physiology*, **1**, 195–206.

Luce, R. D. (1959). *Individual choice behavior*. New York: John Wiley & Sons.

Lynch, G., Granger, R., Larson, J., & Baudry, M. (1989). Cortical encoding of memory: Hypotheses derived from analysis and simulation of physiological learning rules in anatomical structures. In L. Nadel, L. A. Cooper, P. Culicover & R. M. Harnish (Eds.), *Neural connections: Mental computations* (pp. 180–224). Cambridge, MA: The MIT Press.

McCann, R. S., & Besner, D. (1987). Reading pseudohomophones: Implications for models of pronunciation and the locus of word-frequency effects in word naming. *Journal of Experimental Psychology: Human perception and performance*, **14**, 693–706.

McCann, R. S., Besner, D., & Davelaar, E. (1988). Word recognition and identification: Do word-frequency effects reflect lexical access. *Journal of Experimental Psychology: Human Perception and Performance*, **14**, 693–706.

McClelland, J. L. (1979). On the time-relations of mental processes: An examination of systems of processes in cascade. *Psychological Review*, **86**, 287–330.

McClelland, J. L. (1985). Putting knowledge in its place: A scheme for programming parallel processing structures on the fly. *Cognitive Science*, **9**, 113–46.

McClelland, J. L. (1986). The programmable blackboard model of reading. In J. L. McClelland, D. E. Rumelhart and the PDP Research Group, *Parallel distributed processing: Explorations in the microstructure of cognition*, vol. 2: *Psychological and biological* models (pp. 122–69). Cambridge, MA: The MIT Press.

McClelland, J. L. (1988). Connectionist models and psychological evidence. *Journal of Memory and Language*, **27**, 107–23.

McClelland, J. L., & Elman, J. L. (1986). Interactive processes in speech perception: The TRACE model. In J. L. McClelland, D. E. Rumelhart and the PDP Research Group, *Parallel distributed processing: Explorations in the microstructure of cognition*. vol. 2: *Psychological and biological models* (pp. 58–121). Cambridge, MA: The MIT Press.

McClelland, J. L., & Rumelhart, D. E. (1981). An interactive activation model of context effects in letter perception: part 1. An account of basic findings. *Psychological Review*, **88**, 375–407.

McClelland, J. L., & Rumelhart, D. E. (1986). Distributed memory and the representation of general and specific information. *Journal of Experimental Psychology: General*, **114**, 159–88.

McClelland, J. L., Rumelhart, D. E. and the PDP Research Group (1986). *Parallel distributed processing: Explorations in the microstructure of cognition*. vol. 1: *Foundations*. Cambridge, MA: The MIT Press.

McClelland, J. L., & Rumelhart, D. E. (1988). *Explorations in parallel distributed processing: A handbook of models, programs and exercises*. Cambridge, MA: The MIT Press.

McCulloch, W. S. (1965). Machines that think and want. In W. S. McCulloch (Ed.), *Embodiments of Mind* (pp. 307–18). Cambridge, MA: The MIT Press. (Originally entitled 'Brain and behavior'. In W. Halstead (Ed.), *Comparative Psychology Monograph 20*, 1950, *Series 103* (pp. 39–50). Berkeley, CA: University of California Press.)

McCulloch, W. S. (1965). What is a number that a man may know it, and a man, that he may know a number? In W. S. McCulloch (Ed.), *Embodiments of mind* (pp. 1–18). Cambridge, MA: The MIT Press. (Reprinted from *General Semantics Bulletin*, 1961, Nos. 26 and 27, Lakeville, CT: Institute of General Semantics, 7–18.)

McCulloch, W. S. (1965). *Embodiments of mind*. Cambridge, MA: The MIT Press.

McCulloch, W. S., & Pitts, W. H. (1965). A logical calculus of the ideas immanent in nervous activity. In W. S. McCulloch (Ed.), *Embodiments of mind* (pp. 19–39). Cambridge, MA: The MIT Press. (Reprinted from *Bulletin of Mathematical Biophysics*, 1943, **5**, 115–33.)

Mackintosh, N. J. (1988). Approaches to the study of animal intelligence. *British Journal of Psychology*, **79**, 509–25.

Mackworth, A. K. (1976). Model driven interpretation in intelligent vision systems. *Perception*, **5**, 349–70.

McNaughton, B. L., & Nadel, L. (1990). Hebb–Marr networks and the neurobiological representation of action in space. In M. A. Gluck & D. E. Rumelhart (Eds.), *Neuroscience and connectionist theory* (pp. 1–63). Hillsdale, NJ: Lawrence Erlbaum Associates.

Marchman, V., & Plunkett, K. (1989). Token frequency and phonological predictability in a pattern association network: Implications for child language acquisition. *Proceedings of the 11th Annual Conference of the Cognitive Science Society* (pp. 179–87). Hillsdale, NJ: Lawrence Erlbaum Associates.

Markman, A. (1989). LMS rules and the inverse base-rate effect: Comment on Gluck and Bower (1988). *Journal of Experimental Psychology: General*, **118**, 417–21.

Marr, D. (1977). The analysis of occluding contour. *Proceedings of the Royal Society of London*, B, **197**, 441–75.

Marr, D. (1982). *Vision: A computational investigation in to the human representation and processing of visual information*. San Francisco: W. H. Freeman.

Marr, D. & Nishihara, H. K. (1978). Representation and recognition of the spatial organization of three-dimensional shapes. *Proceedings of the Royal Society of London*, B, **200**, 269–94.

Marr, D., & Poggio, T. (1976). Cooperative computation of stereo disparity. *Science*, **194**, 283–7.

Marr, D., & Poggio, T. (1979). A computational theory of human stereo vision. *Proceedings of the Royal Society of London*, B, **204**, 301–28.

Marrocco, R. T. (1986). The neurobiology of perception. In J. E. LeDoux & W. Hirst (Eds.), *Mind and brain: Dialogues in cognitive neuroscience* (pp. 33–88). Cambridge: Cambridge University Press.

Marshall, J. C., & Newcombe, F. (1973). Patterns of paralexia: A psycholinguistic approach. *Journal of Psycholinguistic Research*, **2**, 175–99.

Marslen-Wilson, W. (1989). *Lexical representation and process*. Cambridge, MA: The MIT Press.

Martin, R. C. (1982). The pseudohomophone effect: The role of visual similarity in non-word decisions. *Quarterly Journal of Experimental Psychology*, **34A**, 395–409.

Massaro, D. W. (1979). Letter information and orthographic context in word perception. *Journal of Experimental Psychology: Human Perception and Performance*, **5**, 595–609.

Massaro, D. W. (1988). Some criticisms of connectionist models of human performance. *Journal of Memory and Language*, **27**, 213–34.

Massaro, D. W. (1989a). Multiple book review of 'Speech perception by ear and eye: A paradigm for psychological inquiry'. *Behavioral and Brain Sciences*, **12**, 741–94.

Massaro, D. W. (1989b). Testing between the TRACE model and the fuzzy logical model of speech perception. *Cognitive Psychology*, **21**, 398–421.

Massaro, D. W. (1990). The psychology of connectionism. *Behavioral and Brain Sciences*, **13**, 403–6.

Mayhew, J. E. W., & Frisby, J. (1976). Rivalrous texture stereograms. *Nature*, **264**, 53–6.

Mayhew, J. E. W., & Frisby, J. (1980). The computation of binocular edges. *Perception*, **9**, 69–86.

Mehler, J., Morton, J., & Jusczyk, P. W. (1984). On reducing language to biology. *Cognitive Neuropsychology*, **1**, 83–116.

Metzler, J., & Shepard, R. N. (1974). Transformational studies of the internal representation of three-dimensional objects. In R. L. Solso (Ed.), *Theories of cognitive psychology: The Loyola symposium* (pp. 147–201). Potomac, MD: Lawrence Erlbaum Associates.

Miller, G. A. (1964). The psychologists. *Encounter*, **23**, 29–37.

Miller, G. A., & Johnson-Laird, P. N. (1976). *Language and perception*. Cambridge: Cambridge University Press.

Miller, J. (1982). Discrete versus continuous stage models of human information processing: In search of partial output. *Journal of Experimental Psychology: Human Perception and Performance*, **8**, 273–96.

Milner, P. M. (1957). The cell assembly: Mark II. *Psychological Review*, **64**, 242–52.

Milner, P. M. (1974). A model for visual shape recognition. *Psychological Review*, **81**, 521–35.

Minsky, M. L. (1975). A framework for representing knowledge. In P. H. Winston (Ed.), *The psychology of computer vision* (pp. 211–77). New York: McGraw-Hill.

Minsky, M. L. (1987). *The society of mind*. London: Heinemann.

Minsky, M. L. & Papert, S. A. (1969). *Perceptrons: An introduction to computational geometry*. Cambridge, MA: The MIT Press.

Minsky, M.L., & Papert, S. A. (1988). *Perceptrons: An introduction to computational geometry* (expanded edn). Cambridge, MA: The MIT Press.

Minsky, M., & Selfridge, O. G. (1961). Learning in random nets. In C. Cherry (Ed.), *Information theory. Papers read in a symposium on information theory held at the Royal Institution, London, August, 1960*, (pp. 335–47). London: Butterworths.

Moorhead, I. R., Haig, N. D., & Clement, R. A. (1989). An investigation of trained neural networks from a neurophysiological perspective. *Perception*, **18**, 793–803.

Morton, J. (1969). The interaction of information in word recognition. *Psychological Review*, **76**, 165–80.

Morton, J., & Broadbent, D. E. (1967). Passive versus active recognition models or is your homunculus really necessary? In W. Wathen-Dunn (Ed.), *Models for the perception of speech and visual form* (pp. 103–10). Cambridge, MA: The MIT Press.

Mozer, M. C. (1983). Letter migration in word perception. *Journal of Experimental Psychology: Human Perception and Performance*, **9**, 531–46.

Mozer, M. C. (1987). Early parallel processing in reading: a connectionist approach. In M. Coltheart (Ed.), *Attention and performance*, vol. XII: *The psychology of reading* (pp. 83–104). Hove: Lawrence Erlbaum Associates.

Mozer, M. C. (1988). *A connectionist model of selective attention in visual perception* (Tech. Rep. CRG-TR-88-4). Toronto: University of Toronto, Department of Computer Science.

Mozer, M. C. (1989). Types and tokens in visual letter perception. *Journal of Experimental Psychology: Human Perception and Performance*, **15**, 287–303.

Mozer, M. C., & Smolensky, P. (1989). Using relevance to reduce network size automatically. *Connection Science*, **1**, 3–16.

Mullin, P. A., & Egeth, H. E. (1989). Capacity limitations in visual word processing. *Journal of Experimental Psychology: Human Perception and Performance*, **15**, 111–23.

Neisser, U. (1966). *Cognitive psychology*. New York: Appleton-Century-Crofts.

Neisser, U. (1976). *Cognition and reality*. San Francisco: W. H. Freeman.

Newell, A. (1973). You can't play 20 questions with nature and win: Projective comments on the papers of this symposium. In W. G. Chase (Ed.), *Visual information processing* (pp. 283–308). New York: Academic Press.

Norris, D. (1990). How to build a connectionist idiot (savant). *Cognition*, **35**, 277–91.

Paap, K. R., Newsome, S. L., McDonald, J. E., & Schvaneveldt, R. W. (1982). An activation-verification model for letter and word recognition: The word superiority effect. *Psychological Review*, **89**, 573–94.

Palmer, S. E., Rosch, E., & Chase, P. (1981). Canonical perspective and the perception of objects. In J. Long & A. Baddeley (Eds.), *Attention and performance*, vol. IX (pp. 135–51). Hillsdale, NJ: Lawrence Erlbaum Associates.

Papert, S. (1988). One AI or many? *Daedalus*, March, 1–14.

Parker, D.B. (1987). Optimal algorithms for adaptive networks: Second order back-propagation, second order direct propagation, and second order Hebbian learning. *Proceedings of the 1st IEEE International Conference on Neural Networks*, **2**, 593–600. June.

Patterson, K. E. (1978). Phonemic dyslexia: Errors of meaning and meaning of errors. *Quarterly Journal of Experimental Psychology*, **30**, 587–601.

Patterson, K. E., & Coltheart, V. (1987). Phonological processes in reading: A tutorial review. In M. Coltheart (Ed.), *Attention and performance*, vol. XII (pp. 421–47). Hove: Lawrence Erlbaum Associates.

Patterson, K. E., Seidenberg, M. S., & McClelland, J. L. (1989). Connections and disconnections: Acquired dyslexia in a computational model of reading processes. In R. G. M. Morris (Ed.), *Parallel distributed processing: Implications for psychology and neurobiology* (pp. 131–81). Oxford: Clarendon Press.

Peacocke, C. (1986). Explanation in computational psychology: Language, perception and the Level 1.5. *Mind and Language*, **1**, 101–23.

Pearce, J. M., & Hall, G. (1980). A model of Pavlovian learning: Variations in the effectiveness of conditioned and unconditioned stimuli. *Psychological Review*, **87**, 532–52.

Pelton, G. (1988). *The travelling salesman problem*. In Neuralworks professional II (revision 2.00) (pp. 423-32). Sewickley, PA: Neural Ware Inc.

Pentland, A. P. (1986). Perceptual organization and the representation of natural form. *Artificial Intelligence*, **28**, 293–331.

Perret, D. I., & Harries, M. H. (1988). Characteristic views and the visual inspection of simple faceted and smooth objects: 'tetrahedra and potatoes'. *Perception*, **17**, 703–20.

Pinker, S. (1984). Visual cognition: An introduction. *Cognition*, **18**, 1–63.

Pinker, S., & Mehler, J. (Eds.) (1988). *Connections and symbols*. Cambridge, MA: The MIT Press.

Pinker, S., & Prince, A. (1988). *On language and connectionism: Analysis of a parallel distributed processing model of language acquisition*. Occasional paper No. 33. Center for Cognitive Science, MIT.

Pinker, S., & Prince, A. (1989). Rules and connections in human language. In R. G. Morris (Ed.), *Parallel distributed processing: Implications for psychology and neuroscience* (pp. 182–99). Oxford: Oxford University Press.

Plaut, D. C., & Hinton, G. E. (1987). Learning sets of filters using back-propagation. *Computers Speech and Language*, **2**, 35–61.

Plaut, D. C., Nowlan, S. J., & Hinton, G. E. (1986). *Experiments on learning by back-propagation* (Tech. Rep. CMU-CS-86-126). Pittsburgh: Carnegie-Mellon University, Department of Computer Science.

Plunkett, K., & Marchman, V. (1989). *Pattern association in a back propagation network: Implications for child language acquisition.* (Tech. Rep. 8902). La Jolla: University of California, San Diego, Center for Research in Language.

Poggio, T., & Edelman, S. (1990). A network that learns to recognise three-dimensional objects. *Nature*, **343**, 263–6.

Pollard, S. B., Mayhew, J. E. W., & Frisby, J. (1985). PMF: A stereo correspondence algorithm using a disparity gradient limit. *Perception*, **14**, 449–70.

Posner, M. I. (1978). *Chronometric explorations of mind.* Hillsdale, NJ: Lawrence Erlbaum Associates.

Posner, M. I. (1980). Orienting attention. *Quarterly Journal of Experimental Psychology*, **32**, 3–25.

Posner, M. I., & Keele, S. W. (1968). On the genesis of abstract ideas. *Journal of Experimental Psychology*, **77**, 353–63.

Posner, M. I., & Keele, S. W. (1970). Retention of abstract ideas. *Journal of Experimental Psychology*, **83**, 304–8.

Quillian, R. M. (1968). Semantic memory. In M. Minsky (Ed.), *Semantic information processing* (pp. 216–70). Cambridge, MA: The MIT Press.

Quinlan, P. T. (1987). Theoretical notes on 'Parallel models of associative memory'. A commentary on 'Parallel models of associative memory', edited by G. E. Hinton and J. A. Anderson. Hillsdale, NJ: Lawrence Erlbaum Associates. 1981. *Cognitive Neuropsychology*, **4**, 333–64.

Quinlan, P. T. (1988). *Evidence for the use of perceptual reference frames in two-dimensional shape recognition.* Unpublished doctoral dissertation, Birkbeck College, London.

Quinlan, P. T. (1991). Differing approaches to two-dimensional shape recognition. *Psychological Bulletin*, **109**, 224–41.

Ratcliff, R. (1990). Connectionist models of recognition memory: Constraints imposed by learning and forgetting functions. *Psychological Review*, **97**, 285–308.

Reicher, G. M. (1969). Perceptual recognition as a function of meaningfulness of stimulus materials. *Journal of Experimental Psychology*, **81**, 274–80.

Rescorla, R. A., & Wagner, A. R. (1972). A theory of Pavlovian conditioning: Variations in the effectiveness of reinforcement and non-reinforcement. In A. H. Black & W. F. Prokasy (Eds.), *Classical conditioning: II. Current research and theory* (pp. 64–99). New York: Appleton-Century-Croft.

Richman, H. B., & Simon, H. A. (1989). Context effects in letter perception: Comparison of two theories. *Psychological Review*, **96**, 417–32.

Rochester, N., Holland, J. H., Haibt, L. H. & Duda, W. L. (1988). Tests on a cell assembly theory of the action of the brain, using a large digital computer. In J. A. Anderson & E. Rosenfeld (Eds.), *Neurocomputing: Foundations of research* (pp. 68–79). Cambridge, MA: The MIT Press. (Reprinted from *IRE Transactions on Information Theory*, **IT-2**, 1956, 80–90.)

Rock, I. (1983). *The logic of perception.* Cambridge, MA: The MIT Press.

Rock, I., & DiVita, J. (1987). A case of viewer-centered object perception. *Cognitive Psychology*, **19**, 280–93.

Rock, I., Wheeler, D., & Tudor, L. (1989). Can we imagine how objects look from other viewpoints? *Cognitive Psychology*, **21**, 185–210.

Rosenblatt, F. (1958). The perceptron: A probabilistic model for information storage and organization in the brain. *Psychological Review*, **65**, 386–408.

Rosenblatt, F. (1962). *Principles of neurodynamics: Perceptrons and the theory of brain mechanisms*. Washington, D.C.: Spartan Books.

Rumelhart, D. E., & Abrahamson, A. A. (1973). A model of analogical reasoning. *Cognitive Psychology*, **5**, 1–28.

Rumelhart, D. E., Hinton, G. E., & McClelland, J. L. (1986). A general framework for parallel distributed processing. In J. L. McClelland, D. E. Rumelhart and the PDP Research Group, *Parallel distributed processing: Explorations in the microstructure of cognition*, vol. 1: *Foundations* (pp. 45–76). Cambridge, MA: The MIT Press.

Rumelhart, D. E., & McClelland, D. E. (1982). An interactive activation model of context effects in letter perception: part 2. The contextual enhancement effect and some tests and extensions of the model. *Psychological Review*, **89**, 60–94.

Rumelhart, D. E., & McClelland, J. L. (1985). Levels indeed! A response to Broadbent. *Journal of Experimental Psychology: General*, **114**, 193–7.

Rumelhart, D. E., & McClelland, J. L. (1986a). PDP models and general issues in cognitive science. In J. L. McClelland, D. E. Rumelhart and the PDP Research Group, *Parallel distributed processing: Explorations in the microstructure of cognition*. vol. 1: *Foundations* (pp. 110–46). Cambridge, MA: The MIT Press.

Rumelhart, D. E., & McClelland, J. L. (1986b). On learning the past tense of English verbs. In J. L. McClelland, D. E. Rumelhart and the PDP Research Group, *Parallel distributed processing: Explorations in the microstructure of cognition*. vol. 2: *Psychological and biological models* (pp. 216–71). Cambridge, MA: The MIT Press.

Sartori, G. (1988). From models to neuropsychological data and vice versa. In G. Denes, C. Semenza, & P. Bisiacchi (Eds.), *Perspectives on cognitive neuropsychology* (pp. 59–73). Hove and London: Lawrence Erlbaum Associates.

Schacter, D. L. (1988). The psychology of memory. In J. E. LeDoux & W. Hirst (Eds.), *Mind and brain: Dialogues in cognitive neuroscience* (pp. 189–214). Cambridge: Cambridge University Press.

Schank, R. C. (1976). The primitive ACTs of conceptual dependency. In *Theoretical issues in natural language processing* (pp. 38–41). Cambridge, MA: B. B. N.

Schanks, D. (1990a). Connectionism and the learning of probabilistic concepts. *Quarterly Journal of Experimental Psychology*, **42A**, 209–37.

Schanks, D. (1990b). Connectionism and human learning: Critique of Gluck and Bower (1988). *Journal of Experimental Psychology: General*, **119**, 101–4.

Schneider, W. (1987). Connectionism: Is it a paradigm shift for psychology? *Behavior Research Methods, Instruments and Computers*, **19**, 73–83.

Seidenberg, M. S. (1988). Cognitive neuropsychology and language: The state of the art. *Cognitive Neuropsychology*, **5**, 403–26.

Seidenberg, M. S., & McClelland, J. L. (1989). A distributed, developmental model of word recognition and naming. *Psychological Review*, **96**, 523–68.

Seidenberg, M. S., & McClelland, J. L. (1990). More words but still no lexicon. Reply to Besner et al. (1990). *Psychological Review*, **97**, 447–52.

Seidenberg, M. S., McRae, K., & Jared, D. (1988). Frequency and consistency of spelling-sound correspondences. Paper presented at the 29th meeting of the Psychonomics Society, Chicago.

Seidenberg, M. S., Waters, G. S., Barnes, M. A., & Tanenhaus, M. K. (1984). When does irregular spelling or pronunciation influence word recognition. *Journal of Verbal Learning and Verbal Behavior*, **23**, 383–404.

Sejnowski, T. J. (1981). Skeleton filters in the brain. In G. E. Hinton & J. A. Anderson (Eds.), *Parallel models of associative memory* (pp. 189–212). Hillsdale, NJ: Lawrence Erlbaum Associates.

Shallice, T. (1979). Case study approach in neuropsychological research. *Journal of Clinical Neuropsychology*, **37**, 187–92.

Shallice, T. (1988). *From neuropsychology to mental structure*. Cambridge: Cambridge University Press.

Shannon, B. (1988). Semantic representation of meaning: A critique. *Psychological Bulletin*, **104**, 70–83.

Sharkey, N. E. (1989). A PDP learning approach to natural language understanding. In I. Aleksander (Ed.), *Neural Computing Architectures* (pp. 92–116). London: North Oxford Academic.

Shawe-Taylor, J. S., & Cohen, D. A. (1990). The linear programming algorithm for neural networks. *Neural Networks*, **3**, 575–82.

Shepard, R. N., & Cooper, L. A. (1982). *Mental images and their transformations*. Cambridge, MA: The MIT Press.

Shepard, R. N., & Metzler, J. (1971). Mental rotation of three-dimensional objects. *Science*, **171**, 701–3.

Sheperd, G. M. (1978). Microcircuits in the nervous system. *Scientific American*, **238**, 92–103.

Smith, E. E., Shoben, E. J., & Rips, L. J. (1974). Structure and process in semantic memory: A featural model for semantic decisions. *Psychological Review*, **81**, 214–41.

Smolensky, P. (1987). The constituent structure of mental states: A reply to Fodor and Pylyshyn. *Southern Journal of Philosophy*, **26**, 137–60.

Smolensky, P. (1988). On the proper treatment of connectionism. *Behavioral and Brain Sciences*, **11**, 1–74.

Solla, S. A., Levin, E., & Fleisher, M. (1988). Accelerated learning in layered neural networks. *Complex Systems*, **2**, 625–40.

Stabler, E. P. (1983). How are grammars represented? *Behavioral and Brain Sciences*, **6**, 391–421.

Stanton, P. K., & Sejnowski, T. J. (1989). Associative long-term depression in the hippocampus induced by hebbian covariance. *Nature*, **339**, 215–18.

Stevens, C. F. (1989). Strengthening the synapse. *Nature*, **338**, 460–1.

Stevens, K. N. (1960). Toward a model for speech recognition. *Journal of the Acoustic Society of America*, **32**, 47–55.

Stork, D. G. (1989). Is backpropagation biologically plausible? *Proceedings of the 3rd IEEE International Joint Conference on Neural Networks, II*, (pp. 241–6). Washington, D.C.

Stork, F. C., & Widdowson, J. D. A. (1974). *Learning about linguistics: An introductory workbook*. London: Hutchinson Educational.

Studdert-Kennedy, M. (1975). The nature and function of phonetic categories. In F. Restle, R. M. Shiffrin, N. J. Castellan, H. R. Lindman, & D. B. Pisoni (Eds.), *Cognitive theory*, vol. 1 (pp. 5–22). Hillsdale, NJ: Lawrence Erlbaum Associates.

Sutton, R. S., & Barto, A. G. (1981). Toward a modern theory of adaptive networks: Expectation and prediction. *Psychological Review*, **38**, 135–71.

Szentagothai, J. (1978). The neuron network of the cerebral cortex: a functional interpretation (The Ferrier lecture). *Proceedings of the Royal Society of London*, B, **201**, 219–48.

Taraban, R., & McClelland, J. L. (1987). Conspiracy effects in word pronunciation. *Journal of Memory and Language*, **26**, 608–31.

Touretzky, D. S., & Hinton, G. E. (1988). A distributed connectionist production system. *Cognitive Science*, **12**, 423–66.

Touretzky D. S., & Pomerleau, D. A. (1989). What's hidden in the hidden layers. *BYTE*, August, 227–33.

Townsend, J. T. (1972). Some results concerning the identifiability of parallel and serial processes. *British Journal of Mathematical and Statistical Psychology*, **25**, 168–99.

Treisman, A. M. (1960). Contextual cues in selective listening. *Quarterly Journal of Experimental Psychology*, **12**, 242–8.

Treisman, A. M., & Gelade, G. (1980). A feature integration theory of attention. *Cognitive Psychology*, **12**, 97–136.

Treisman, A. M., & Schmidt, H. (1982). Illusory conjunctions in the perception of objects. *Cognitive Psychology*, **14**, 107–41.

Turvey, M. T. (1973). On peripheral and central processes in vision: Inferences from an information-processing analysis of masking with patterned stimuli. *Psychological Review*, **80**, 1–52.

Valentine, E. R. (1989). Neural nets: From Hartley and Hebb to Hinton. *Journal of Mathematical Psychology*, **33**, 348–57.

Virzi, R. A., & Egeth, H. E. (1984). Is meaning implicated in illusory conjunctions? *Journal of Experimental Psychology: Human perception and performance*, **10**, 573–80.

Waibel, A. (1989). Modular construction of time-delay neural networks for speech recognition. *Neural Computation*, **1**, 39–46.

Waibel, A., & Hampshire, J. (1989). Building blocks for speech. *BYTE*, August, 235–42.

Waibel, A., Hanazawa, T., Hinton, G. E., Shikano, K., & Lang, K. J. (1989). Phoneme recognition using time-delay neural networks. *IEEE Transactions on Acoustics, Speech, and Signal Processing*, **37**, 328–339.

Waibel, A., Sawai, H., & Shikano, K. (1989). Modularity and scaling in large phonemic neural networks. *IEEE Transactions on Acoustics, Speech, and Signal Processing*, **37**, 1888–99.

Walker, S. F. (1990). A brief history of connectionism and its psychological implications. *AI and Society*, **4**, 17–38.

Walsh, G. R. (1975). *Methods of optimization*. London: John Wiley & Sons–Interscience.

Waltz, D. L., & Pollack, J. B. (1985). Massively parallel parsing: A strongly interactive model of natural language interpretation. *Cognitive Science*, **9**, 51–74.

Watrous, R. L. (1987). Learning algorithms for connectionist networks: Applied gradient methods for nonlinear optimization. *Proceedings of the 1st IEEE International Conference on Neural Networks*, **2**, (pp. 619–28). June.

Werbos, P. J. (1988). Generalization of backpropagation with application to a recurrent gas market model. *Neural Networks*, **1**, 339–56.

Wheeler, D. (1970). Processes in word recognition. *Cognitive Psychology*, **1**, 59–85.

Wickelgren, W. A. (1969). Context-sensitive coding, associative memory, and serial order in (speech) behavior. *Psychological Review*, **76**, 1–15.

Widrow, G., & Hoff, M. E. (1960). Adaptive switching circuits. *Institute of Radio*

Engineers, Western Electronic Show and Convention, Convention Record, Part 4, 96–104.

Wilks, Y. (1976). Primitives and words. In *Theoretical issues in natural language processing* (pp. 42–5). Cambridge, MA: B. B. N.

Wilks, Y. (1977). Natural understanding systems within the AI paradigm: A survey and some comparisons. In A. Zampolli (Ed.), *Linguistic structures processing. Fundamental studies in computer science*, vol. 5 (pp. 341–98). Amsterdam: North Holland.

Winograd, S., & Cowan, J. D. (1963). *Reliable computation in the presence of noise*. Cambridge, MA: The MIT Press.

Winograd, T. (1978). On primitives, prototypes, and other semantic anomalies. In D. L. Waltz (Ed.), *Theoretical issues in natural language processing-2* (pp. 25-32). University of Illinois at Urbana-Champaign.

Wiser, M. (1981). The role of intrinsic axes in shape recognition. In *Proceedings of the Third Cognitive Science Conference* (pp. 184–6). San Mateo, CA: Morgan Kaufmann.

Wood, C. C. (1978). Variations on a theme by Lashley: Lesion experiments on the neural model of Anderson, Silverstein, Ritz and Jones. *Psychological Review*, **85**, 582–91.

Woods, W. A. (1975). What's in a link: Foundations for semantic networks. In D. Bobrow & A. Collins (Eds.), *Representations and understanding: Studies in cognitive science* (pp. 35–82). New York: Academic Press.

Yarbus, A. L. (1967). *Eye movements and vision*. New York: Plenum Press.

Zadeh, L. A. (1965). Fuzzy sets. *Information and Control*, **8**, 338–53.

Zemel, R. S. (1988). *TRAFFIC: A model of object recognition* (Tech. Rep. CRG-TR-89-2). Toronto: University of Toronto, Department of Computer Science.

Zemel, R. S., Mozer, M. C., & Hinton, G. E. (1988). *TRAFFIC: A model of object recognition based on transformations of feature instances* (Tech. Rep. CRG-TR-88-7). Toronto: University of Toronto, Department of Computer Science.

Zipser, D., & Anderson, R. A. (1988). A back-propagation programmed network that simulates response properties of a subset of posterior parietal neurons. *Nature*, **331**, 679–84.

Subject Index

activation-verification (AV) model, 160–1
active theory of perception, 107
  analysis by synthesis, 143
associationism, 1–3
associative learning, 194, 264–5
attentional, 119–20
  attention mechanism in BLIRNET, 175
  attentional spotlight, 101–2, 175
  and figure-ground segmentation, 101–2
  and visual word recognition, 168
attractors
  basins of attraction, 204
  in a Hopfield net, 72
  point attractors, 204
automatic generalisation, 197, 199, 201,
  224
  and property inheritance, 230

back-propagation, 56–71
  biological implausibility of, 95–7
  limitations of, 244–55
  in phoneme recognition, 136–8
  and shape-from-shading, 94
behaviourism, 3, 193
bias
  definition of, 46–7
binary
  arithmetic, 35–6
  logic, 9–19
  threshold logic unit, 9–19

BLIRNET, 172–7
Boltzmann machines, 76–81, 100–2, 200–1,
  242

canonicalisation, 151
categorical perception, 148–51
category-specific deficits, 261
cell assemblies, 4–5, 7–8
CID, 169–72
clean-up, 200, 204
  units, 203–4
coarse coding, 41–3, 68, 119, 136, 172,
  179, 197, 201
competitive/cooperative processes, 84,
  107–8
  in BLIRNET, 174
  and illusory conjunctions, 118–19
  as interactive-activation and
    competition, 146–7, 157–60
  in the Marr/Poggio algorithm, 86–7
compositionality, 264–5
concepts
  as distributed representations, 217–23
  and prototypes 217–18
connectivity
  the predicate, 26, 29–31, 259
constituent structure, 224–33, 263–5
content addressable memory
  in a pattern associator, 50–1, 54
  and Hopfield nets, 72

Name Index